CU00822427

A SENSE OF THE DIVINE

OF THE

DIVINE

A FRANCISCAN READER

for the

CHRISTIAN YEAR

CANTERBURY
PRESS
Norwich

A Sense of the Divine
is published by **The Canterbury Press Norwich**
a publishing imprint of Hymns Ancient & Modern Ltd
a registered charity,
St Mary's Works, St Mary's Plain, Norwich, Norfolk, NR3 3BH

Edited by
Brother Austin SSF, Brother Nicholas Alan SSF & Brother Tristam SSF

© The European Province of the Society of Saint Francis, 2001

Cover lettering by Stephen Raw and cover design by Leigh Hurlock

Published 2001

The Editors are grateful to all those who gave permission to reproduce copyright material and a full list of the quoted sources is on page 393.

All rights reserved.
No part of this publication may be reproduced in any form or by any means,
electronic or mechanical, including photocopying, recording,
or any information storage and retrieval system,
without permission,
which should be sought in writing from:
The Canterbury Press
St Mary's Works, St Mary's Plain, Norwich, Norfolk, NR3 3BH
enclosing a stamped, addressed envelope.

Such permission does not obviate the need to seek permission
to use any material the copyright of which is held by others.

A catalogue record for this book is available
from the British Library.

ISBN 1-85311-381-6

Computer typeset by the Society of Saint Francis, Hilfield, Dorchester
Printed and bound in Great Britain by Biddles Ltd, *www.biddles.co.uk*

Most High and glorious God,
enlighten the darkness of our hearts
and give us a true faith, a certain hope
and a perfect love.
Give us a sense of the divine
and a knowledge of yourself,
so that we may do everything
in fulfilment of your holy will;
through Jesus Christ our Lord.
Amen.

The prayer of Saint Francis before the San Damiano crucifix

This book is dedicated to
Brother Francis SSF
who has looked forward to its publication
through the generations

Contents

Prayer of Saint Francis   *iii*
Dedication   *iv*
Contents & Calendar   *v*
Introduction   *ix*

Temporale

Advent   1
1ˢᵗ Sunday of Advent *(Sunday between 27 Nov & 3 Dec inclusive)*   1
2ⁿᵈ Sunday of Advent *(Sunday between 4 & 10 Dec inclusive)*   6
3ʳᵈ Sunday of Advent *(Sunday between 11 & 17 Dec inclusive)*   11
Days before Christmas (which supersede all days in Advent 3 & Advent 4)   15
('4ᵗʰ Sunday of Advent' is included in 'The Days before Christmas')
Christmas Eve   21

Christmas   23
Twelve Days of Christmas   23

Epiphany   35
Epiphany   35
Weekdays after Feast of the Epiphany   36
1ˢᵗ Sunday of Epiphany *(Sunday between 7 & 13 Jan – DEL Week 1)*   41
2ⁿᵈ Sunday of Epiphany *(Sunday between 14 & 20 Jan – DEL Week 2)*   46
3ʳᵈ Sunday of Epiphany *(Sunday between 21 & 27 Jan – DEL Week 3)*   50
4ᵗʰ Sunday of Epiphany *(Sunday between 28 Jan & 2 Feb – DEL Week 4)*   55
Presentation of Christ in the Temple – Candlemass   59

On the day after the celebration of Candlemass, Ordinary Time begins
Sundays after Candlemass, *see dated weeks in Ordinary Time, below*

*There is a discrepancy between the Church of England and the Roman Catholic Church dating of
Sundays in Ordinary Time from after Candlemass until Lent; the difference is only one day and
so will usually not overly complicate matters. However, users of this book are advised of this and
it is suggested that adjustments be made locally, using common sense as the criterion.*

Pre-Lent:
5ᵗʰ – 2ⁿᵈ Sundays before Lent, *see dated weeks in Ordinary Time, below*
Sunday Next Before Lent   60

Lent   63
Ash Wednesday   63
1ˢᵗ Sunday of Lent   66
2ⁿᵈ Sunday of Lent   71
3ʳᵈ Sunday of Lent   76
4ᵗʰ Sunday of Lent   81
5ᵗʰ Sunday of Lent   86
Holy Week   91
Maundy Thursday   95
Good Friday   95
Easter Eve   96

Easter *97*

Easter Day *97*

2nd Sunday of Easter *102*

3rd Sunday of Easter *108*

4th Sunday of Easter *113*

5th Sunday of Easter *118*

6th Sunday of Easter *124*

Ascension Day *127*

7th Sunday of Easter *130*

Day of Pentecost *136*

On the Monday after the Day of Pentecost, Ordinary Time resumes, until the eve of Advent

Ordinary Time *137*

Trinity Sunday *137*

Corpus Christi *138*

Divine Compassion – Sacred Heart *138*

Dedication Festival *139*

Sunday between 3 & 9 Feb inclusive *(DEL Week 5)* *141*

Sunday between 10 & 16 Feb inclusive *if before Lent,* *147*

 or Sunday between 8 & 14 May inclusive *if after Pentecost (DEL Week 6)* *147*

Sunday between 17 & 23 Feb inclusive *if before Lent,* *152*

 or Sunday between 15 & 21 May inclusive *if after Pentecost (DEL Week 7)* *152*

Sunday between 25 Feb to 3 Mar inclusive *if before Lent,* *157*

 or Sunday between 22 & 28 May inclusive *if after Pentecost (DEL Week 8)* *157*

Sunday between 29 May & 4 Jun inclusive *(RCL Proper 4 / DEL Week 9)* *162*

Sunday between 5 & 11 Jun inclusive *(RCL Proper 5 / DEL Week 10)* *167*

Sunday between 12 & 18 Jun inclusive *(RCL Proper 6 / DEL Week 11)* *172*

Sunday between 19 & 25 Jun inclusive *(RCL Proper 7 / DEL Week 12)* *179*

Sunday between 26 Jun & 2 Jul inclusive *(RCL Proper 8 / DEL Week 13)* *185*

Sunday between 3 & 9 Jul inclusive *(RCL Proper 9 / DEL Week 14)* *190*

Sunday between 10 & 16 Jul inclusive *(RCL Proper 10 / DEL Week 15)* *195*

Sunday between 17 & 23 Jul inclusive *(RCL Proper 11 / DEL Week 16)* *201*

Sunday between 24 & 30 Jul inclusive *(RCL Proper 12 / DEL Week 17)* *205*

Sunday between 31 Jul & 6 Aug inclusive *(RCL Proper 13 / DEL Week 18)* *211*

Sunday between 7 & 13 Aug inclusive *(RCL Proper 14 / DEL Week 19)* *217*

Sunday between 14 & 20 Aug inclusive *(RCL Proper 15 / DEL Week 20)* *223*

Sunday between 21 & 27 Aug inclusive *(RCL Proper 16 / DEL Week 21)* *228*

Sunday between 28 Aug & 3 Sep inclusive *(RCL Proper 16 / DEL Week 21)* *234*

Sunday between 4 & 10 Sep inclusive *(RCL Proper 18 / DEL Week 23)* *238*

Sunday between 11 & 17 Sep inclusive *(RCL Proper 19 / DEL Week 24)* *243*

Sunday between 18 & 24 Sep inclusive *(RCL Proper 20 / DEL Week 25)* *248*

Sunday between 25 Sep & 1 Oct inclusive *(RCL Proper 18 / DEL Week 23)* *254*

Sunday between 2 & 8 Oct inclusive *(RCL Proper 22 / DEL Week 27)* *258*

Sunday between 9 & 15 Oct inclusive *(RCL Proper 23 / DEL Week 28)* *265*

Sunday between 16 & 22 Oct inclusive *(RCL Proper 24 / DEL Week 29)* *271*

Sunday between 23 & 29 Oct inclusive *(RCL Proper 25 / DEL Week 30)* *275*

Sunday between 30 Oct & 5 Nov inclusive *(RCL Proper 26 / DEL Week 31)* *280*

Sunday between 6 & 12 Nov inclusive *(RCL Proper 27 / DEL Week 32)* *286*

Sunday between 13 & 19 Nov inclusive *(RCL Proper 28 / DEL Week 33)* *290*

Sunday between 20 & 26 Nov inclusive *(RCL Proper 29 / DEL Week 34)* *296*

Sanctorale

305

1	Jan	Naming & Circumcision of Jesus	29
7	Jan	Angela of Foligno, Tertiary, 1309	305
16	Jan	Berard & Companions, First Franciscan Martyrs, 1220	306
20	Jan	Thanksgiving for the Society of the Divine Compassion	306
2	Feb	Presentation of Christ in the Temple (Candlemass)	59
6	Feb	Martyrs of Japan, 1597	308
6	Feb	Founding of the Community of St Clare, Freeland, 1950	309
7	Feb	Colette, Poor Clare, Founder of the Colettine Reform, 1447	310
15	Feb	George Potter, Friar, 1960	311
24	Feb	Vocation of Francis, 1208	312
25	Feb	Rosina Mary Rice & the Founding of CSF, 1905	313
2	Mar	Agnes of Prague, Poor Clare, 1282	314
7	Mar	Helen Elizabeth Christmas, a Founder of CSF, 1950	316
7	Mar	Joseph Crookston, Friar, Founder of the Order of St Francis, 1979	317
25	Mar	Annunciation of our Lord to the Blessèd Virgin Mary	318
28	Mar	William Sirr, Friar, Monk, Solitary, 1937	319
31	Mar	Andrew Ernest Hardy, Friar, 1946	320
3	Apr	Benedict the Black, Friar, 1589	321
10	Apr	William of Ockham, Friar, Philosopher, Teacher of the Faith, 1347	321
16	Apr	Commemoration of the taking of vows by Francis, 1208	322
16	Apr	Founding of the Poor Clares of Reparation & Adoration, 1924	323
21	Apr	Conrad of Parzham, Friar, 1894	324
23	Apr	Giles of Assisi, Friar, 1262	325
24	Apr	Fidelis of Sigmaringen, Friar, Martyr, 1622	326
28	Apr	Luchesio & Buonadonna, First Tertiaries, 1260	327
9	May	Catherine of Bologna, Poor Clare, Artist, 1463	328
12	May	Leopold Mandich of Herceg Novi, Friar, 1942	329
15	May	Pachomius, Founder of Christian Community Monasticism, 346	330
16	May	Margaret of Cortona, Penitent, Tertiary, 1297	331
17	May	Paschal Baylon, Friar, 1592	332
18	May	Felix Porri of Cantalice, Friar, 1587	333
20	May	Bernardine of Siena, Friar, 1444	333
24	May	Dedication of the Basilica of St Francis, 1230	334
31	May	Visit of the Blessèd Virgin Mary to Elizabeth	336
13	Jun	Antony of Padua, Friar, Teacher of the Faith, 1231	337
24	Jun	Birth of John the Baptist	337
30	Jun	Ramon Llull, Tertiary, Mystic, 1315	339
1	Jul	Junipero Serra, Friar, 1784	340
10	Jul	Veronica Giuliani, Poor Clare, 1727	341
11	Jul	Benedict of Nursia, Father of Western Monasticism, c.550	342
15	Jul	Bonaventure, Friar, Bishop, Teacher of the Faith, 1274	342
21	Jul	Lawrence Russo of Brindisi, Friar, Teacher of the Faith, 1619	343
27	Jul	Mary Magdalene of Martinengo, Poor Clare, 1737	344
2	Aug	Mary of the Angels	345
2	Aug	Dedication of All Franciscan Churches (Alternate date: 30 Oct)	139
2	Aug	Portiuncula Indulgence	346
4	Aug	Jean-Baptiste Vianney, Curé d'Ars, Spiritual Guide, Tertiary, 1859	347
6	Aug	Transfiguration of our Lord	348

8	Aug	Dominic, Friar, Founder of the Order of Preachers, 1221	*349*
11	Aug	Clare of Assisi, Founder of the Minoresses (Poor Clares), 1253	*350ff*
14	Aug	Maximilian Kolbe, Friar, Martyr, 1941	*355*
15	Aug	Blessèd Virgin Mary	*356*
25	Aug	Louis Capet, Christian Monarch, Patron of the Third Order, 1270	*357*
7	Sep	Douglas Downes, Friar, Co-Founder of SSF, 1957	*358*
8	Sep	Birth of the Blessèd Virgin Mary	*359*
10	Sep	Agnellus of Pisa, & the Coming of the Friars to Canterbury, 1224	*360*
14	Sep	Holy Cross Day	*361*
15	Sep	Mary at the Cross	*361*
17	Sep	Stigmata of Francis, 1224	*363ff*
18	Sep	Joseph of Cupertino, Friar, 1663	*366*
23	Sep	Pio Forgione, Friar, Mystic, 1968	*367*
29	Sep	Michael & All Angels	*368*
4	Oct	Francis of Assisi, Friar, Deacon, Founder of the Friars Minor, 1226	*369ff*
22	Oct	Peter of Alcantara, Friar, Reformer, 1562	*376*
23	Oct	John of Capistrano, Friar, 1456	*377*
30	Oct	Dedication of Consecrated Churches of the Order *(Alternate date: 2 Aug)*	*139*
1	Nov	All Saints' Day	*378*
2	Nov	All Souls' Day	*379*
8	Nov	John Duns Scotus, Friar, Teacher of the Faith, 1308	*380*
15	Nov	Mary of the Passion, Founder of FMM, 1904	*381*
18	Nov	Elizabeth of Hungary, Philanthropist, Patron of the Third Order, 1231	*382*
		(or 17 Nov or 19 Nov)	
19	Nov	Agnes of Assisi, Poor Clare, 1253	*382*
23	Nov	Algy Robertson, Friar, Co-Founder of the Society of St Francis, 1955	*384*
24	Nov	Commemoration of all Departed Franciscans	*385*
26	Nov	Leonard of Port Maurice, Friar, 1751	*386*
28	Nov	James of the March, Friar, 1476	*387*
29	Nov	All Franciscan Saints	*388*
8	Dec	Conception of the Blessèd Virgin Mary	*389*
15	Dec	Mary Frances Schervier, Tertiary, 1876	*390*
24	Dec	Jacopone da Todi, Friar, Spiritual, Poet, 1306	*390*

Bibliography *393*
Index *398*

Introduction

'The Christian Year, with its cycle of seasons, provides the Church with its most compelling way into the mystery of faith. The scriptures that tell the story of salvation, and the prayers proper to each week and festival, provide an annual framework for all our liturgical celebrations.'[1]

This book journeys through the Christian Year with Francis and Clare and their early followers, using the words of their contemporaries and their immediate successors. The book uses *temporale* (From Advent) and *sanctorale* as a shape, rather than 'chapters'.

TEMPORALE

Advent, being the beginning of the Christian Year, starts with the youth of Francis. As Advent is a season moving towards a climax, this is mirrored in the life of Francis by his gradual conversion moving towards the climax of his vocation. Then, from 20 December onwards, stories of the early years of Francis blend into thoughts on the Incarnation of Christ, taking us up to Greccio on Christmas Eve. The Christmas season concentrates on the Incarnation. Epiphany to the Baptism of Christ focuses on Jesus and the themes of light, using readings from Bonaventure. On the Monday after Epiphany 1, the story of the early brothers resumes, continuing through the visit to Rome, the return to Rivo Torto and the establishing of the community at the Portiuncula. This completes the main historical narrative.

From here on, each week follows a theme. Lent covers penance, prayer, fasting, and almsgiving, the traditional Lenten disciplines, with Passiontide focusing on the cross.

After a week of readings about the power and splendour of God during Easter Week, the readings begin to focus more on Francis and his relationships with those around him. Easter 2 looks at Francis as a spiritual guide to his brothers, and then the weeks of Easter 3 - 6 look at his closest friends in the early days: Bernard, Leo and Clare, and what it means to be Community. In much the same way, the wider church is also reading the Acts of the Apostles during Eastertide, concentrating on the life of the post-resurrection Christian community as a model of what it means to be Church.

The novena from the Friday after Ascension Day to the Day of Pentecost concentrates on life in the Spirit.

[1] From the Preface of *The Christian Year: Calendar, Lectionary & Collects*, CHP, 1997.

Ordinary Time readings begin with selections from *Sacrum Commercium*, an early text in the form of an allegory which depicts the community in its beginnings, full of the love of Lady Poverty. This is followed by some of the first reactions of leaders in the church to this new movement of penitents. The week on chapters at Portiuncula picks up from the establishment of the community there at the end of the readings in Epiphany and shows Francis in his leadership role. As the brothers then went out from the chapters to preach penitence to the world, so the following week shows the power and simplicity of Francis' way of preaching.

Proper 4 in Ordinary Time goes more deeply into the relationship of Francis with the church authorities, particularly in his relationship with Cardinal Hugolino, Bishop of Ostia, who became the Bishop Protector of the Order and later Pope, taking the name Gregory IX. This relationship with the church was acted out on a day-to-day basis for Francis in his devotion to Christ in the Eucharist. This marked him out as a loyal member of the church when heterodox groups of the time were highly critical of the clergy and questioned the importance of the Mass.

The relationship between Francis and Clare is highlighted in Proper 6, following on from the story of Clare as related in the Easter season. His consultation with Clare, as to his vocation to preach or retreat to the mountain hermitages to pray, leads into a week of readings on mission, particularly with Masseo, an early companion on the road. This in turn culminates in his trip to Egypt to talk with the Sultan.

The next three weeks cover the themes of the vows of poverty, chastity and obedience. Together with later triads on prayer, study and work and humility, love and joy, these cover the main themes of Franciscan principles. Proper 12 comes around the time of the Portiuncula indulgence and looks at Francis' attitude to the Portiuncula itself, and houses and hermitages in general.

The weeks of Propers 13 and 14 cover the last days of Saint Clare. During this time the dated readings covering the sequence of events around the death of Clare will supersede some of this provision. The readings provided here give a prelude and postlude to the dated sequence, with the number of readings used before and after varying from year to year.

After the death of Clare, we have a brief interlude of animal stories before returning to the weightier matters of prayer, study and work. This takes us to the Stigmata of Francis on 17 September. Here we have three dated readings to give the actual events of the receiving of the Stigmata, with the readings of this week (Proper 19) filling in the background and describing in more general terms the hermitage on Mount La Verna and the devotion of Francis to the cross of Christ.

The Stigmata occurred two years before the death of Francis and this was a time of much illness and pain. This is reflected in the following week's readings, which describe the composition of the *Canticle of the Creatures* (over progressive days) and the cauterisation of Francis in an attempt to cure the disease of his eyes. Propers 21 and 22 are again likely to be superseded by the dated readings around the death of Francis. The readings in Ordinary Time provision for these two weeks give a general background to the more important readings in the dated sequence.

The last three weeks of this part of Ordinary Time are given to three cardinal values of Franciscan spirituality - humility, love and joy.

All Saints' Day begins a month of reflection on the promise of glory and this is echoed in a series of stories of some of the 'saints' of the Franciscan Order. The reading for All Saints' Sunday gives a composite picture of the virtues of the early Franciscan brothers, and this is followed by readings for six of those mentioned in this passage. The Third Week before Advent concentrates on Brother Giles, who became famous for his pithy sayings and wise counsel to those who travelled to his hermitage. Brother Juniper follows with his inspired foolishness. The final week of Ordinary Time, beginning with the feast of Christ the King, brings the year to a close with stories of later saintly friars and the words of Christ to Francis about the future of the Order.

(DEL in the text refers to the Daily Eucharistic Lectionary Week of the Roman Catholic Church)

SANCTORALE

More than eighty readings are provided for particular dates in the year. These are mainly the feasts of Franciscan patrons, special events in the life of Francis and Clare, and commemorating the lives of some of their followers. In addition, readings will be found for feasts of our Lord, our Lady, Holy Cross Day, Michael & All Angels, John the Baptist, Remigius, Benedict, Dominic, All Saints' Day and All Souls' Day.

The definitive text to use is found in *temporale*. Texts in *sanctorale* should be used sparingly, so as not to interrupt the natural flow of the text in *temporale*. The exceptions to this are the days before and after the feast of Clare, the Stigmata of Francis, and the feast of Francis, when the provision in *sanctorale* should always be used. Otherwise, when deciding whether to use the readings in *sanctorale* or not should be a matter of common sense.

THE SOURCES

Reading the medieval source documents on Francis, Clare and their companions is like travelling to a strange, vibrant and sometimes startling world. In our modern self-consciousness we may find it difficult to understand the fervour of these lives: the depths of self-abasement and desperate consciousness of sin, and the heights of abandonment to God and ecstatic raptures in prayer. These are not cautious lives, but fully lived without reserve.

In order to enter this world of the early Franciscans, a modern reader will need to come to the texts with a humility and willingness to hear, a kind of obedience to the word in which we encounter the Lord. It needs to be recognised that these texts were written not as historical documentary, but as testimonies to inspire faith. To read the stories in the spirit of a sceptical inquiry, wondering 'Did that really happen in exactly that way?' or 'Did he or she really use those words?' is to miss the point of the narrative. These stories are designed to lead to conversion, to encourage a life of penance and complete trust in God here and now. The invitation is for us to follow these examples and live the sanctity of God in our day.

Reading these documents also brings us into a relationship with their different authors, as we begin to recognise the distinctive voice of each one. The earliest texts presented here are the writings of Francis himself. In his letters we hear his heart-felt call to conversion, to penance, and his personal concern for those trying to follow in his way; in his Rules we hear the sometimes despairing call to a disciplined renunciation; but in his prayers we reach to the heart of his faith, full of the exuberance of his love for God.

Francis died in 1226 and the earliest narrative of his life is *The Life of Saint Francis*, sometimes called *The First Life*, by Thomas of Celano. This work was commissioned by Pope Gregory IX in 1228, as an official biography, to popularise the life of the saint whom he had canonised that year. It was an official document, and was approved by the pope in 1229.

Some years later, the Franciscan Minister General commissioned a second work by Thomas, which he completed in 1247 giving it the title *The Remembrance of the Desire of a Soul*. Although sometimes known as *The Second Life of Saint Francis*, it is not strictly speaking a Life, but a *florilegium*, a collection of stories organised around themes such as humility, poverty and prayer, like a bouquet of flowers. Only at the beginning and end of this book does Thomas add to the chronological material of his earlier *Life*.

Sources used by Thomas for this later work include some of the col-
lections of testimonies that had appeared during the 1240s. Probably the
earliest of these was *The Beginning or Founding of the Order*, by John of
Perugia, also known as the *Anonymous of Perugia*. This is a brief, unelab-
orated narrative of the conversion of Francis, the establishment of the
first group of brothers in and around Assisi, and Francis' death. If John
of Perugia was the author, then these stories may go back to Brother
Giles, the third to join Francis, as John was a companion of Giles in later
years.

Most of the material from *The Beginning or Founding of the Order* is
included in the more developed text known as *The Legend of the Three
Companions*. Attached to this latter work is a letter dated 11 August 1246
which describes the contents as the record of events remembered by
Francis' companions Leo, Rufino and Angelo. Scholars have debated
whether the letter really does apply to this *Legend*, but the *Legend* is, in any
case, a warm, personal account of the early days of the community, with
the definite flavour of an eye-witness account, but without the polemic
characteristics of some of the later accounts of Francis.

A more complicated work is *The Assisi Compilation*, also known as *The
Legend of Perugia*. Parts of this work may well be the reminiscences of
those closest to Francis, 'we who were with him' as they identify themselves in the text, written down in the 1240s. Other parts of the document seem to be later material, reflecting the struggles within the
Franciscan movement over poverty and the observance of the Rule. The
Spirituals, represented by this compilation, favoured strict adherence to
the letter of the Rule of Saint Francis, particularly regarding poverty.
They rejected the growing emphasis on study and clerical pastoral ministry among the mainstream community. The final version of *The Assisi
Compilation* may not have been completed until 1311, the date when it is
first mentioned by a contemporary writer. Brother Leo, the close companion of Francis, has traditionally been seen as the source of many of
the stories in *The Assisi Compilation*.

A later work reuses much of the material of *The Assisi Compilation*,
reordering it into a thematic collection called *A Mirror of the Perfection of
the Standing of a Lesser Brother*. It follows in the Leonine tradition, with
a strong emphasis on the observance of the Rule 'to the letter, and without a gloss'. It has been dated to the year 1318.

Back in 1260 the Minister General at the time, Bonaventure of

Bagnoregio, was commissioned by the Franciscan general chapter to write a definitive Life of Francis. This became *The Major Legend of Saint Francis*, and was approved in 1263. Its purpose was to unite the disparate Franciscan community around one common story of its founder, and all other Legends of Francis were suppressed. Bonaventure was a highly educated man, a theologian from the University of Paris, but also a deeply spiritual man of prayer. His devotional works were widely used in the later medieval period. It was his interpretation of Francis that formed much of the subsequent Franciscan theology and spirituality up to this day.

The tradition of the Spirituals continued, however, particularly in the remote mountain hermitages. Their vision of Francis resurfaces in the Latin work *The Deeds of Blessed Francis and His Companions* by Ugolino Boniscambi of Montegiorgio, written sometime in the 1340s, and in its Italian translation and reworking by a Tuscan friar as *The Little Flowers of Saint Francis*. It was the publication of this latter document that led to the 'rediscovery' and popularisation of Saint Francis in the early part of the twentieth century.

Another text concerning Francis and his brothers not mentioned so far is *The Sacred Exchange between Saint Francis & Lady Poverty*. This is a beautiful allegory of the love of Francis for Lady Poverty, his search for her and the banquet that they share. Until recently scholars have dated this work to 1227 making it perhaps the earliest document of the Franciscan movement. The editors of **Francis of Assisi: Early Documents** suggest that its composition is more likely to have been between 1237 and 1239.

For Clare, as for Francis, the most reliable witness to her character and life can be found in her writings. The letters, Testament, and Blessing of her sisters are eloquent testimonies of a woman determined to live to the end the life she felt God through Saint Francis had given her. Her *Form of Life*, or Rule, while influenced by the expectations of the church authorities of her day, is in itself remarkable for being the first religious rule written for women by a woman.

Beyond her writings, some of the earliest descriptions of her life come in the *Acts of the Process of Canonisation* of 1253. These testimonies, recorded in the year of Clare's death, show the inspiration she was to the sisters who had lived with her in the monastery at San Damiano. Their accounts of her life were put into verse form probably in the following year in the *Versified Legend of the Virgin Clare*. Then, after Clare's canonisation in 1255 the *Legend of Saint Clare* was written, probably in that same year, and possibly by Thomas of Celano.

Also included in this book of readings are extracts from the writings of Jacopone of Todi (c.1230-1306) and Angela of Foligno (c.1248-1309). Both these authors take us to the heart of the early Franciscan movement. Jacopone was a successful lawyer trained at the University of Bologna, accustomed to the high life of fine clothing and food, poetry and music. His sudden conversion to a life of penance followed the tragic death of his young wife at a banquet when the balcony on which she and others were dancing collapsed. According to his *Life*, she was found to be wearing a hair shirt, the sign of a penitential life of which Jacopone had no idea. The next ten years he spent as a Third Order penitent as a kind of holy fool, before becoming a Lesser Brother at Todi. His sympathies were with the Spiritual movement, which earned him excommunication by Pope Boniface VIII and imprisonment in an underground dungeon for 5 years. His poems or *Lauds* reveal the despair and joy of his turbulent life.

Angela of Foligno was a visionary and mystic who, after the death of her husband and sons, sold her property and joined the Third Order of Saint Francis. Around her gathered a group of friars who became her spiritual sons and disciples. Among them was Ubertino of Casale, one of the leaders of the Spiritual movement among the Franciscans. Another of her disciples recorded her experiences and teachings and this record became *The Book of Blessed Angela of Foligno*. Angela was typically Franciscan in her devotion to the suffering and crucified Jesus, to Christ present in the Eucharist, and to the Blessed Virgin Mary. But her teaching on Christ as spouse, and particularly on the nothingness experienced in God and the divine abyss connect her with the Beguine spirituality of women in northern Europe and the Rhineland mystics Eckhart and Ruysboeck.

It is with these companions, then, that the reader is invited to enter the world of the early Franciscans. It is a world in which we can encounter the same God who meets us today, who challenges us to return to him in penance and poverty, in sacrificial service to the outcasts of our society, and in the hiddenness of prayer. It is still a message the world needs to hear, and is the message of Jesus, in whose footsteps Francis calls us to follow, who says to us even today:

'The time is fulfilled, and the kingdom of God has come near; repent, and believe the good news.' *(Mark 1.15)*

HOW TO USE THIS BOOK

It cannot be emphasised enough that this is a book for devotional reading, taking extracts from original source documents; this book is not itself a work of scholarly reference. The three-volume *Early Documents* is the definitive text, together with the translations of the other authors from early Franciscanism.[2]

This is a book to be used particularly during the context of prayer and *lectio divina.*

---

[2] See Bibliography, *pp 393.*

Advent

The First Sunday of Advent

(Week beginning on Sunday between 27 November & 3 December inclusive)

Advent 1 — Sunday

A reading from 'The Legend of the Three Companions' of Saint Francis.

Francis was raised in the city of Assisi, which is located in the boundaries of the valley of Spoleto. His mother at first called him John; but when his father, who had been away when he was born, returned from France, he later named him Francis.

When he grew up, endowed with clever natural abilities, he pursued his father's profession: that of a merchant. He was, however, vastly different from his father. He was more good-natured and generous, given over to revelry and song with his friends, roaming day and night throughout the city of Assisi. He was most lavish in spending, so much so that all he could possess and earn was squandered on feasting and other pursuits.

Because of this, his parents often reprimanded him, telling him that he spent so much money on himself and others that he seemed to be the son of some great prince rather than their son. But since his parents were wealthy and loved him very much, they tolerated all these things to avoid upsetting him. When neighbours commented on his extravagance, his mother replied, 'What do you think of my son? He will still be a son of God through grace.'

He was lavish, indeed prodigal, not only in these things, but also in spending more money on expensive clothes than his social position warranted. He was so vain in seeking to stand out that sometimes he had the most expensive material sewed together with the cheapest cloth onto the same garment.   *II,68f*

Advent 1 — Monday

A reading from 'The Legend of the Three Companions' of Saint Francis.

Francis was naturally courteous in manner and speech and, following his heart's intent, never uttered a rude or offensive word to anyone. Moreover, since he was such a light-hearted and undisciplined youth, he proposed to answer back those speaking to him rarely in a brusque manner. His reputation, because of this, became so widespread throughout almost the entire region that many who knew him said that, in the future, he would be something great.

From those stepping stones of natural strengths, he was brought to that grace that prompted him to look within himself, 'You are generous and courteous to those from whom you receive nothing except passing and worthless approval. Is it not right that, on account of God who repays most generously, you should be courteous and generous to the poor?' From that day, he looked on poor people generously and provided them affluently with alms. Although a merchant, he was a very flamboyant squanderer of wealth.

One day when he was in the shop where he was selling cloth, totally absorbed in business of this sort, a poor man came in, begging alms for the love of God. Preoccupied with thoughts of wealth and the care of business, he did not give him alms. Touched by divine grace, he accused himself of great rudeness, saying, 'If that poor man had asked something from you for a great count or baron, you would certainly have granted him his request. How much more should you have done this for the King of kings and the Lord of all!'

Because of this incident, he resolved in his heart, from then on, not to deny a request to anyone asking in the name of so great a Lord.   *II,69*

Advent 1 — Tuesday

A reading from 'The Legend of the Three Companions' of Saint Francis.

At that time [in the year 1202], war broke out between Perugia and Assisi. Together with many of his fellow citizens, Francis was captured and confined in Perugia, yet, because of his noble manners, he was imprisoned with the knights.

Once, when his fellow prisoners were depressed, he, who was naturally cheerful and jovial, not only was not dejected but actually seemed to be happy. One of the prisoners rebuked him as insane for being cheerful in prison. Francis replied vigorously, 'What do you think will become of me? Rest assured, I will be worshipped throughout the whole world.'

One of the knights who was imprisoned with him had injured a fellow prisoner, causing all the others to ostracize him. Francis alone not only acted in a friendly way towards him, but also urged the other prisoners to do the same.

After a year, when peace was restored between those cities, Francis and his fellow prisoners returned to Assisi.   *II,69ff*

Advent 1 — Wednesday

A reading from 'The Legend of the Three Companions' of Saint Francis.

A few years after Francis had returned to Assisi from prison in Perugia, a nobleman from the city of Assisi was preparing himself with knightly arms to go to Apulia in order to increase his wealth and fame. When Francis learned of this, he yearned to go with him to that same place, and to be knighted by that count, Gentile by name. He prepared clothing as expensive as possible, since even though he was poorer in riches than his fellow citizen, he was far more extravagant.

He was completely preoccupied in carrying this out, and was burning with desire to set out when, one night, the Lord visited him in a dream. Knowing his desire for honours, he enticed and lifted him to the pinnacle of glory by a vision. That night, while he was sleeping, someone appeared to him, a man calling him by name. He led him into a beautiful bride's elegant palace filled with knightly arms and on its walls hung glittering shields and other armour of knightly splendour. Overjoyed, he wondered what all this meant and asked to whom these brightly shining arms and this beautiful palace belonged. He was told that all these, including the palace, belonged to him and his knights.

Awakening in the morning, he got up with great joy. Since he had not yet fully tasted the Spirit of God, he thought in a worldly way that he must be singled out magnificently, and he considered the vision a portent of future good fortune. He resolved then to undertake the journey to Apulia to be knighted by the count. He was even more cheerful than usual, prompting many people to wonder. When they asked him the reason why he was beaming with joy, he answered, 'I know that I will become a great prince.'   *II,70*

Advent 1 — Thursday

A reading from 'The Legend of the Three Companions' of Saint Francis.

The day before the vision [of the elegant palace] had occurred, the promise of great chivalry and nobility was so strong in Francis that it may be believed that the vision itself may have provided the motive. On that day, in fact, he donated all the refined and expensive clothes he had recently acquired to a poor knight.

When he set out for Apulia, he reached as far as Spoleto, where he began to feel a little ill. No less anxious about the trip, as he was falling to sleep, yet half awake, he heard someone asking him where he wanted to go. When Francis revealed to him his entire plan, the other said, 'Who can do more good for you: the lord or the servant?' When Francis answered him, 'The lord,' he again said to him, 'Then why are you abandoning the lord for the servant, the patron for the client?' And Francis said, 'Lord, what do you want me to do?' 'Go back to your land,' he said, 'and what you are to do will be told to you.' You must understand in another way the vision which you saw.'

When he woke up, he began to think very carefully about this vision. Just as the first vision had caused him to be almost completely carried away with great joy in a desire for worldly prosperity, the second made him completely introspective, causing him to marvel at and consider its strength, so that he was unable to sleep any more that night.

Therefore when it was morning, buoyant and happy, he quickly returned to Assisi, expecting that the Lord, who had revealed these things to him, would show him his will and give him counsel about salvation. Changed in mind, he now refused to go to Apulia and desired to conform completely to the divine will.   *II,71*

Advent 1 — Friday

A reading from 'The Legend of the Three Companions' of Saint Francis.

A few days after Francis returned to Assisi, one evening his friends chose him to be in charge; so that, according to his whim, he would pay their expenses. He made arrangements for a sumptuous banquet, as he had done so often in the past.

When they left the house, bloated, his friends walked ahead of him, singing throughout the city. Holding in his hand the sceptre of his office as their leader, he fell slightly behind them. He was not singing, but was deeply preoccupied. Suddenly he was visited by the Lord, who filled his heart with so much tenderness that he was unable to speak or move. He could only feel and hear this marvellous tenderness; it left him so estranged from any sensation that, as he himself said later, even if he had been completely cut to pieces, he would not have been able to move.

When his companions glanced back and saw him so removed from them, they went back surprised at seeing him already changed into another man. They asked him, 'What were you thinking about that you did not follow us? Were you perhaps thinking about taking a wife?'

He answered in an unequivocal voice, 'You are right! I was thinking

about taking a wife: more noble, wealthier, and more beautiful than you
have ever seen.' They laughed at him. For he said this not of his own
accord but because he was inspired by God. In fact, the bride was the
true religion that he later embraced, a bride more noble, richer and more
beautiful because of her poverty.   *II,71f*

Advent 1 — Saturday

A reading from 'The Legend of the Three Companions' of Saint Francis.

Francis happened to go to Rome on pilgrimage. As he was entering the
church of Saint Peter, he noticed the meagre offerings made by some
and said to himself, 'Since the Prince of the Apostles should be greatly
honoured, why do they make such meagre offerings in the church where
his body rests?' With great enthusiasm, he took a handful of coins from
his money pouch and threw them through a grating of the altar, making
such a loud noise that all the bystanders were astonished at his
generosity.

As he was leaving and passed the doors of the church, where there
were many poor people begging alms, he secretly exchanged clothes with
one of those poor people and put them on. Standing on the steps of the
church with the other poor, he begged for alms in French, because he
would speak French spontaneously, although he did not do so correctly.

After taking off the beggar's clothes and putting on his own, he
returned to Assisi and began to pray that the Lord would direct his way.
He did not share his secret with anyone; nor did he seek counsel from
anyone, except from God alone and, periodically, from the Bishop of
Assisi. For at that time, no one possessed the real poverty that he desired
more than anything else in this world, in which he yearned to live and die.

II,73f

The Second Sunday of Advent

(Week beginning on Sunday between 4 & 10 December inclusive)

Advent 2 — Sunday

A reading from 'The Legend of the Three Companions' of Saint Francis.

One day, while he was praying enthusiastically to the Lord, Francis received this response, 'Francis, everything you loved carnally and desired to have, you must despise and hate, if you wish to know my will. Because once you begin doing this, what before seemed delightful and sweet will be unbearable and bitter; and what before made you shudder will offer you great sweetness and enormous delight.'

He was overjoyed at this and was comforted by the Lord. One day, he was riding his horse near Assisi, when he met a man suffering from leprosy. And, even though he usually shuddered at the sight, he made himself dismount and gave him a coin, kissing his hand as he did so. After he accepted a kiss of peace from him, Francis remounted and continued on his way. He then began to consider himself less and less until, by God's grace, he came to complete victory over himself.

After a few days, he moved to a hospice for leprosy sufferers, taking with him a large sum of money. Calling them all together, as he kissed the hand of each, he gave them alms. When he left there, what before had been bitter, that is, to see and touch those with leprosy, was turned into sweetness. For, as he said, the sight of lepers was so bitter to him that he refused not only to look at them but even to approach their dwellings. If he happened to come near their houses or to see them, even though he was moved by piety to give them alms through an inter-mediary, he always turned away his face and held his nose. With the help of God's grace, he became such a servant and friend of the leprosy sufferers that, as he testified in his Testament, he stayed among them and served them with humility.   *II,74*

Advent 2 — Monday

A reading from 'The Legend of the Three Companions' of Saint Francis.

Changed into good after his visit to the leprosy sufferers, Francis would take a companion, whom he loved very much, to secluded places, telling him that he had found a great and precious treasure. The man was not a little overjoyed and gladly went with him whenever he was summoned.

Francis often led him to a cave near Assisi and, while he went alone inside, he left his companion outside, eager for the treasure. Inspired by a new and extraordinary spirit, he would pray to his Father in secret, wanting no one to know what was happening within except God alone, whom he consulted about acquiring heavenly treasure.

The enemy of the human race, observing him, strove to lure him from the good he had begun by striking fear and dread in him. There was in Assisi a deformed, hunchback woman, whom the devil, appearing to the man of God, recalled to him. He threatened to inflict him with her deformity unless he reneged on the plan he had conceived. But the very brave knight of Christ, shunning the devil's threats, prayed all the more fervently within the cave that God would direct his path.

He endured great suffering and mental anxiety, unable to rest until he accomplished in action what he had conceived in mind. Different thoughts followed one after the other, and their relentlessness disturbed him even more severely. For he was burning inwardly with a divine fire, unable to conceal outwardly the flame kindled in his soul. He repented that he had sinned so grievously. While his past and present transgressions no longer delighted him, he was not yet fully confident of refraining from future ones. This is why, when he emerged from the cave, he seemed to his companion to have changed into a different man.

II,74f

Advent 2 — Tuesday

A reading from 'The Legend of the Three Companions' of Saint Francis.

A few days had passed when, while Francis was walking by the church of San Damiano, he was told in the Spirit to go inside for a prayer. Once he had entered, he began to pray intensely before an image of the Crucified, which spoke to him in a tender and kind voice, 'Francis, do you not see that my house is being destroyed? Go, then, and rebuild it for me.' Stunned and trembling, he said, 'I will do so gladly, Lord.' For he understood that the voice was speaking about that church, which was near collapse because of its age. He was filled with such joy and became so radiant with light over that message that he knew in his soul that it was truly Christ crucified who spoke to him.

Upon leaving the church, he found a priest sitting nearby and, putting his hands into the pouch, he offered him a handful of coins. 'My Lord,' he said, 'I beg you, buy some oil and keep the light before the Crucified burning continually. When this money runs out, I will again give you as much as you need.'

From that hour, therefore, his heart was wounded and it melted when remembering the Lord's passion. While he lived, he always carried the wounds of the Lord Jesus in his heart. This was brilliantly shown afterwards in the renewal of those wounds that were miraculously impressed on and most clearly revealed in his body. *II,76*

Advent 2 — Wednesday

A reading from 'The Legend of the Three Companions' of Saint Francis.

Overjoyed by the vision and hearing the words of the Crucified Christ, Francis arose, fortifying himself with the sign of the cross. And mounting his horse and taking cloth of different colours, he arrived at a city named Foligno; and, after selling there the horse and everything he was carrying, he returned immediately to the church of San Damiano.

After he found a poor priest there, he kissed his hands with great faith and devotion; he offered him the money he was carrying, and explained his purpose in great detail. The priest, astounded and surprised at his sudden conversion, refused to believe this and, thinking he was being mocked, refused to keep the money. But stubbornly persisting, he endeavoured to create confidence in his words, and he begged the priest more emphatically to allow him to stay with him.

Finally, the priest agreed to let him stay but, out of fear of his parents, did not accept the money. And so the true scorner of money, throwing it on a windowsill, cared for it as much as he cared for dust.

While he was staying there, his father, like a diligent spy, went around seeking to learn what might have happened to his son. And when he heard that he was so changed and was living in that place in such a way, he was touched inwardly with sorrow of heart and deeply disturbed by the sudden turn of events. Calling together his friends and neighbours, he ran to him. *II,77f*

Advent 2 — Thursday

A reading from 'The Legend of the Three Companions' of Saint Francis.

Because he was a new knight of Christ, as Francis heard the threats of his pursuers and knew beforehand of their coming, he left room for his father's anger; and, going to a secret cave which he had prepared for this, he hid there for a whole month. That cave was known to only one person in his father's house. He would eat the food that, from time to time, was secretly brought to him there, praying all the while with flowing tears that the Lord would free him from destructive persecution and that he could favourably fulfill his fervent wishes.

And so he begged the Lord relentlessly in fasting and weeping. Lacking confidence in his own effort and strength, he cast his hope completely on the Lord, who filled him with an inexpressible happiness and enlightened him with a marvellous light, even though he still remained in darkness.

Glowing with this inner radiance, after he left the pit, he made his way to Assisi, lighthearted and happy. Strengthened with Christ's armour of confidence, and burning with divine fervour, he blatantly exposed himself to the threats and blows of his persucutors, accusing himself of laziness and groundless fear.

Those who knew him earlier, seeing him now, reproached him harshly. Shouting that he was insane and out of his mind, they threw mud from the streets and stones at him. For they saw him so changed from his earlier ways and so weakened by starving his body that they blamed everything he did on starvation and madness. But, as he passed through their midst deaf to all these things, neither broken nor changed by any wrong, the knight of Christ gave thanks to God. *II,78*

Advent 2 — Friday

A reading from 'The Legend of the Three Companions' of Saint Francis.

When rumour of Francis' return from hiding spread through the streets and quarters of the city of Assisi, it finally reached his father. After he heard that the townspeople had done such things to him, he instantly arose to look for him: not to free him but rather to destroy him. With no restraint, he ran like a wolf after a lamb and, glaring at him, wild eyed and savagely, he mercilessly took him in tow. Confining him to home and locking him up in a dark prison for several days he strove, by words and blows, to turn his spirit to the vanities of this world.

But since he was neither moved by words nor exhausted by chains and blows, Francis endured all these things patiently, more fit and eager to carry out his holy plan.

When his father had to leave home on a pressing need, his mother remained at home alone with him. Since she did not approve of her husband's action, she spoke to her son in gentle words. When she realized she could not dissuade him from his holy intention, moved by deep feeling for him, she removed the chains and let him go free.

Thanking Almighty God, he returned to the place where he had been before, now enjoying greater freedom, since he passed the devil's temptations and had been taught by the lessons of temptation. More self-confident because of the injuries he had received, he made his way more freely and with an even greater heart. II,79

Advent 2 — Saturday

A reading from 'The Legend of the Three Companions' of Saint Francis.

Francis came before the Bishop of Assisi and was received by him with great joy. 'Your father,' the Bishop said to him, 'is infuriated and extremely scandalized. If you wish to serve God, return to him the money you have, because God does not want you to spend money unjustly acquired on the work of the church. Your father's anger will abate when he receives the money back. My son, have confidence in the Lord and act courageously. Do not be afraid, for he will be your help and will abundantly provide you with whatever is necessary for the work of his church.'

Then the man of God got up, joyful and comforted by the Bishop's words and, as he brought the money to him, he said, 'My lord, I will gladly give back not only the money acquired from his things but even all my clothes.' And going into one of the Bishop's rooms, he took off all his clothes and, putting the money on top of them, came out naked before the Bishop, his father and all the bystanders, and said, 'Listen to me, all of you, and understand. Until now, I have called Pietro di Bernardone my father. But, because I have proposed to serve God, I return to him the money on account of which he was so upset, and also all the clothing which is his, wanting to say from now on, "Our Father, who art in heaven," and not "My father, Pietro di Bernardone." ' At that moment, the man of God was found to be wearing under his coloured clothes a hair shirt next to his skin.

Then his father, overcome with unbearable pain and anger, took the money and all the clothing. While he was carrying these home, those who were present at this spectacle were indignant at him, for he left nothing for his son to wear. Moved by piety, they began to weep over him.

The Bishop, focussing his attention on the man of God's frame of mind, and enthusiastically admiring his fervour and determination, gathered him into his arms, covering him with his mantle. II,80

The Third Sunday of Advent

(Week beginning on Sunday between 11 & 17 December inclusive)

Advent 3 — Sunday

A reading from 'The Life of Saint Francis', by Thomas of Celano.

Francis who once enjoyed wearing scarlet robes now travelled about half-clothed. Once, while he was singing praises to the Lord in French in a certain forest, thieves suddenly attacked him. When they savagely demanded who he was, the man of God answered confidently and force-fully, 'I am the herald of the great King! What is it to you?' They beat him and threw him into a ditch filled with deep snow, saying, 'Lie there, you stupid herald of God!' After they left him, he rolled about to and fro, shook the snow off himself and jumped out of the ditch. Exhilarated with great joy, he began in a loud voice to make the woods resound with praises to the Creator of all.

Eventually, he arrived at a cloister of monks, where he spent several days covered with only a cheap shirt, serving as a scullery boy in the kitchen. He wanted to be fed at least some soup. No mercy was shown him and he was not even able to get some old clothes. Not moved by anger but forced by necessity, he moved on to the city of Gubbio, where he obtained a cheap tunic from an old friend. Shortly afterwards, when the fame of the man of God had grown far and wide and his name was spread among the people, the prior of that monastery, when he recalled the event and understood what had been done to the man of God, came to him and, out of reverence for the Saviour, begged forgiveness for himself and his monks.   *I,194f*

Advent 3 — Monday

A reading from 'The Legend of the Three Companions' of Saint Francis.

Returning to the church of San Damiano, joyful and eager, Francis made a hermit's habit for himself, and comforted the priest of that church with the same words with which the Bishop had comforted him.

Then, getting up and going back to the city, he began to praise the Lord throughout the piazzas and neighbourhoods, like one inebriated with the Spirit. When he finished praising the Lord in this way, he turned to obtaining stones for the repair of the church. 'Whoever gives me one stone,' he would say, 'will have one reward. Whoever give me two will have two rewards. Whoever give me three will have that many rewards.'

Thus, burning with enthusiasm, he also made many other simple statements. Because he was unlettered and simple, the man chosen by God did not speak in the learnèd words of human wisdom, but in everything was quite simple. Many ridiculed him, thinking he was mad, while others, prompted by piety, were moved to tears seeing how quickly he had come from such pleasure and worldly vanity to such an intoxication of divine love. Disregarding their scorn, he thanked God with burning enthusiasm.

It would be long and difficult to relate how he worked on the project, for he, who had been very refined in his father's house, hauled stones on his own shoulders, afflicting himself greatly in the service of God. *II,81*

Advent 3 — Tuesday

A reading from 'The Legend of the Three Companions' of Saint Francis.

The priest of San Damiano church in Assisi judged that the work of re-building his church was beyond the strength of Francis, even though he was offering himself so enthusiastically to divine service. Although poor himself, he obtained special food for Francis, for he knew that, while he was in the world, he had lived rather delicately. Of course, as the man of God later admitted, he would frequently enjoy delicacies and sweets, and refrain from disagreeable foods.

One day, when he noticed what the priest was preparing for him, he said to himself, 'Will you find a priest like this wherever you go who will offer you such human kindness? This is not the life of the poor that you have chosen. As a beggar, going from door to door, you should carry a bowl in your hand and, driven by necessity, you should collect the scraps they give you. This is how you must live willingly, out of love for him who was born poor, lived very poorly in this world, remained naked and poor on the cross, and was buried in a tomb belonging to another.'

As a result, one day he took a bowl and, entering the city, he went door-to-door begging alms. Whenever he put various scraps in his bowl, many who knew what a pampered life he had lived were astonished at how marvellously changed he was, seeing that he held himself in such contempt. But when he wanted to eat the mixed food offered to him, he felt revulsion because he was not accustomed, not only to eating such things, but to even looking at them. At last overcoming himself, he began to eat, and it seemed to him that no delicacy had ever tasted so delicious. *II,81f*

Advent 3 — Wednesday

A reading from 'The Legend of the Three Companions' of Saint Francis.

When his father saw Francis in such disgrace, he was filled with unusual pain. Because he loved him dearly, he was ashamed and felt great sorrow for him. Seeing his flesh half-dead from excessive affliction and cold, he would curse him whenever he came upon him.

Aware of his father's curses, the man of God chose a poor and looked-down-upon man to take the place of his father, and told him, 'Come with me, and I will give you some of the alms that were given to me. When you see my father cursing me, I will also say to you, "Bless me, father." You will then make the sign of the cross over me, and bless me in his place.'

The next time this happened and the beggar was blessing him, the man of God said to his father, 'Do you not believe that God can give me a father to bless me against your curses?'

Afterwards, many of those who mocked him and saw how patiently he endured every abuse marvelled with great astonishment. One winter's morning, while he was at prayer, dressed in poor clothes, [Angelo,] his blood brother was passing by, and remarked sarcastically to his companion, 'You might tell Francis to sell you a penny's worth of his sweat.' When the man of God heard this, filled with a wholesome joy, he answered enthusiastically in French, 'I will sell that sweat to my Lord at a high price.'   *II,82f*

Advent 3 — Thursday

A reading from 'The Legend of the Three Companions' of Saint Francis.

While Francis was working steadily at restoring the church of San Damiano in Assisi, he wanted to have a lamp burning continually in the church, so he went through the city begging for oil. But when he was approaching a certain house, he saw a group of men gathered there for a game. Ashamed to beg in front of them, he backed away. Mulling it over, he accused himself of having sinned. Hurrying back to the place where they were playing, he told everyone standing around his fault, that he was ashamed to beg because of them. And, in fervour of spirit, he entered that house and, for the love of God, begged in French for oil for the lamps of that church.

While labouring with others at that work he used to cry to passers-by in a loud voice, filled with joy, saying in French, 'Come and help me in the work of the church of San Damiano which, in the future, will be a monastery of ladies through whose fame and life our heavenly Father will be glorified throughout the church.'

See how, filled with the spirit of prophecy, he truly foretold the future! For this is that sacred place where the glorious religion and most excellent Order of Poor Ladies and sacred virgins had its happy beginning about six years after the conversion of blessèd Francis, and through the same blessèd Francis.   *II,83*

Advent 3 — Friday

A reading from 'The Life of Saint Francis', by Thomas of Celano.

Francis, the holy man of God, having changed his habit and rebuilt the church of San Damiano in Assisi, moved to another place near the city of Assisi, where he began to rebuild a certain church that had fallen into ruin and was almost destroyed. After a good beginning he did not stop until he had brought all to completion.

From there, he moved to another place, which is called the Portiuncula, where there stood a church of the Blessèd Virgin Mother of God built in ancient times. At that time, it was deserted and no one was taking care of it. When the holy man of God saw it so ruined, he was moved by piety because he had a warm devotion to the Mother of all good and he began to stay there continually. The restoration of that church took place in the third year of his conversion. At this time, he wore a sort of hermit's habit with a leather belt. He carried a staff in his hand and wore shoes.   *I,201*

The Days before Christmas

17 December

A reading from 'The Legend of the Three Companions' of Saint Francis.

While he was completing the church of San Damiano, blessèd Francis wore the habit of a hermit: a staff in his hand, shoes on his feet and a leather belt around his waist.

Then, one day at Mass, he heard those things which Christ tells the disciples who were sent out to preach, instructing them to carry no gold or silver, no wallet or purse, bread, walking stick, or shoes, or two tunics. After understanding this more clearly because of the priest, he was filled with indescribable joy. 'This,' he said, 'is what I want to do with all my strength.'

And so, after committing to memory everything he had heard, he joyfully fulfilled them, removed his second garment without delay, and from then on never used a walking stick, shoes, purse or wallet. He made for himself a very cheap and plain tunic and, throwing the belt away, he girded himself with a cord.

Applying all the care of his heart to observe the words of new grace as much as possible, he began, inspired by God, to be a messenger of evangelical perfection and, in simple words, to preach penance in public. His words were neither hollow nor ridiculous, but filled with the power of the Holy Spirit, penetrating the marrow of the heart, so that listeners were turned to great amazement.

As he later testified, he learned a greeting of this sort by the Lord's revelation, 'May the Lord give you peace!' Therefore, in all his preaching, he greeted the people at the beginning of his sermon with a proclamation of peace.   *II,84*

18 December

A reading from 'The Legend of the Three Companions' of Saint Francis.

As both the truth of blessèd Francis' simple teaching as well as that of his life became known to many, two years after his conversion, some men began to be moved to do penance by his example and, leaving all things, they joined him in life and habit. The first of these was Brother Bernard of holy memory.

He knew well how luxuriously blessèd Francis had lived in the world;

now he observed his constancy and zeal in the divine service, how, in particular, he was restoring dilapidated churches with a great deal of work, and what an austere life he was leading. He planned wholeheartedly to give everything he possessed to the poor and, with determination, to join him in life and garb.

Therefore one day, approaching the man of God in secret, he disclosed his plan to him, and arranged to have him come that evening to his home. Thanking God, for he did not then have a companion, blessèd Francis was overjoyed, especially since Lord Bernard was a person of great stature.

On the appointed evening, blessèd Francis came to his house, his heart filled with great joy, and spent that whole night there. Among many things, Lord Bernard said to him, 'If, for many years, someone holds on to the possessions – many or few – he has acquired from his lord, and no longer wishes to keep them, what is the better thing for him to do with them?' Blessèd Francis answered that he must give back to that lord what was received from him. And Lord Bernard said, 'Then, brother, I want to give away all my worldly goods for the love of my Lord who gave them to me, as it seems best to you.' The saint told him, 'We will go to the church early in the morning and, through the book of the gospels, we will learn how the Lord instructed his disciples.' *II,85*

19 December

A reading from 'The Legend of the Three Companions' of Saint Francis.

Rising at daybreak, Francis and Bernard, together with another man named Peter, who also wanted to become a brother, went to the church of San Nicolò next to the piazza of the city of Assisi. They entered for prayer but, because they were simple, they did not know how to find the passage in the gospel about renunciation. They prayed devoutly that the Lord would show them his will on opening the book the first time.

Once they had finished prayer, blessèd Francis took the closed book and, kneeling before the altar, opened it. At its first opening, the Lord's counsel confronted them: 'If you wish to be perfect, go, sell everything you possess and give to the poor, and you will have treasure in heaven.'

Blessèd Francis was overjoyed when he read this passage and thanked God. But since he was a true worshipper of the Trinity, he desired it to be confirmed by a threefold affirmation. He opened the book a second and a third time. When he opened it up the second time, he saw: 'Take nothing for your journey'; and at the third opening: 'If any one wishes to come after me, he must deny himself.'

Each time he opened the book, blessèd Francis thanked God for confirming his plan and the desire he had earlier conceived. After the third divine confirmation was pointed out and explained, he said to those men, Bernard and Peter, 'Brothers, this is our life and rule and that of all who will want to join our company. Go, therefore, and fulfil what you have heard.'

Then Lord Bernard, who was very rich, after selling all he had and acquiring a large sum of money, went and distributed it all to the city's poor. Peter, likewise, followed the divine counsel according to his means.

After ridding themselves of everything, they both received the habit which the saint had adopted after he had put aside the habit of a hermit; and, from that hour, they lived with him according to the form of the holy gospel, as the Lord had shown them. This is why blessèd Francis said in his Testament: 'The Lord himself revealed to me that I should live according to the form of the holy gospel.'   *II,85f*

20 December

A reading from 'The Assisi Compilation'.

From the beginning of his conversion, blessèd Francis, with God's help, like a wise man, established himself and his house, that is, the religion, upon a firm rock, the greatest humility and poverty of the Son of God, calling it the religion of 'Lesser Brothers'.

On the greatest humility: thus at the beginning of the religion, after the brothers grew in number, he wanted the brothers to stay in hospitals of lepers to serve them. At that time, whenever nobles and commoners came to the religion, they were told, among other things, that they had to serve the lepers and stay in their houses.

On the greatest poverty: as stated in the Rule, let the brothers remain as strangers and pilgrims in the houses in which they stay. Let them not seek to have anything under heaven, except holy poverty, by which, in this world, they are nourished by the Lord with bodily food and virtue, and, in the next, will attain a heavenly inheritance.

He established himself on the greatest poverty and humility, because, although he was a great prelate in the church of God, he wanted and chose to be lowly not only in the church of God, but also among his brothers.   *II,123f*

21 December

A reading from 'The Life of Saint Francis', by Thomas of Celano.

Fields and vineyards,
rocks and woods,
and all the beauties of the field,
flowing springs and blooming gardens,
earth and fire, air and wind:
all these Francis urged to love of God and to willing service.
Finally, he used to call all creatures
by the name of 'brother' and 'sister'
and in a wonderful way, unknown to others,
he could discern the secrets of the heart of creatures
like someone who has already passed
into the freedom of the glory of the children of God.

O good Jesus,
with the angels in heaven
he now praises you as wonderful,
who, when placed on earth,
preached you as lovable to all creatures.

His highest aim, foremost desire, and greatest intention
was to pay heed to the holy gospel in all things and through all things,
to follow the teaching of our Lord Jesus Christ
and to retrace his footsteps completely
with all vigilance and all zeal,
all the desire of his soul
and all the fervour of his heart.

Francis used to recall with regular meditation the words of Christ
and recollect his deeds with most attentive perception.
Indeed, so thoroughly did the humility of the Incarnation
and the charity of the Passion
occupy his mind
that he scarcely wanted to think of anything else.

1,251,254

22 December

A reading from 'The Lauds', by Jacopone da Todi.

Hail, Virgin, more than woman, holy, blessèd Mary!
More than woman, I say: for humankind,
as scripture teaches us, is born in sin;
in you, holiness preceded birth.
Womb-hidden, a mighty presence enfolded you
and shielded you from all contagion.

The sin that Adam sowed did not take root in you;
no sin, great or small, has place in you.
High above all others is your virginity and your consecration.
Your secret virgin vow leads you,
all unaware of charity's intent,
to a wedding feast, to your spouse.

The high-born messenger's annunciation strikes fear in your heart:
'If you accept the counsel I bring, you will conceive a son without peer.'
'O Virgin, assent, assent!', the multitude cries out.
'If aid does not come quickly, we shall hurtle to our doom.'
You consented, and so conceived the loving Christ
and gave him to those who had lost their way.

Conception by a word stuns worldly wisdom –
to conceive without corruption, untouched, intact!
Reason and experience know nothing of such a possibility;
never was woman made pregnant without seed. You alone,
Mary Immaculate, you alone; in you the Word, *creans omnia*,
residing in majesty, becomes flesh, God Incarnate.   *IX,70*

23 December

A reading from 'The Lauds', by Jacopone da Todi.

Hail, Virgin, holy, blessèd Mary!
You carry God within you, God and man,
and the weight does not crush you.
Unheard-of birth, the child issuing from the sealed womb!
The infant joyously leaving the castle, through locked gates,
for it would not be fitting for God to do violence
to the womb that sheltered him.

O Mary, what did you feel when you first saw him?
Did love nearly destroy you?
As you gazed upon him, how could you sustain such love?
When you gave him suck, how could you bear such excess of joy?
When he turned to you and called you Mother,
how could you bear being called the Mother of God?

O Lady, I am struck mute
when I think of how you looked on him,
as you fondled him and ministered to his needs.
What did you feel then
when you held him at your breast?
The love that bound you makes me weep!

O salamander-heart, living in flame,
how is it that love did not consume you utterly?
Fortitude sustained you, and steadied the burning heart.
Yet the humility of the child dwarfed yours:
with your acceptance you ascended in glory;
he, instead, abased himself, descended to wretched state.

Compared to his humility in becoming a man,
all other humility is nothing but pride.
Come, one and all, come running!
Come and see Eternal Life in swaddling clothes!
Take him in your arms, he cannot run away;
he has come to redeem those who have lost all hope.   *IX,70f*

24 December — Christmas Eve

A reading from 'The Major Legend of Saint Francis', by Saint Bonaventure.

It happened, three years prior to his death, that blessèd Francis decided to celebrate at the town of Greccio the memory of the birth of the child Jesus with the greatest possible solemnity, in order to arouse devotion.

He had a manger prepared,
hay carried in and an ox and an ass led to the spot.
The brothers are summoned,
the people arrive,
the forest amplifies with their cries,
and that venerable night is rendered
brilliant and solemn
by a multitude of bright lights
and by resonant and harmonious hymns of praise.
The man of God stands before the manger,
filled with piety,
bathed in tears, and overcome with joy.
A solemn Mass is celebrated over the manger,
with Francis, a levite of Christ, chanting the holy gospel.
The he preaches to the people standing around him
about the birth of the poor King,
whom, whenever he means to call him,
he called in his tender love,
the Babe of Bethlehem.

A certain virtous and truthful knight,
Sir John of Greccio,
who had abandoned worldly, military activity out of love of Christ
and had become an intimate friend of the man of God,
claimed that he saw a beautiful little child asleep in that manger
whom the blessèd father Francis embraced in both his arms
and seemed to wake it from sleep.

The hay from the crib
was kept by the people
and miraculously cured sick animals
and drove away different kinds of pestilence.
Thus God glorified his servant in every way
and demonstrated the efficacy of his holy prayer
by the evident signs of wonderful miracles.   *II,610f>*

Christmas

25 December — Christmas Day

A reading from the 'Later Admonition and Exhortation, to the Brothers and Sisters of Penance', by Saint Francis.

In the name of the Father and of the Son and of the Holy Spirit. Amen. Brother Francis, their servant and subject, sends esteem and reverence, true peace from heaven and sincere love in the Lord to all Christian religious people: clergy and laity, men and women, and to all who live in the whole world.

Because I am the servant of all, I am obliged to serve all and to administer the fragrant words of my Lord to them. Therefore, realizing that I could not visit each one of you personally because of sickness and the weakness of my body, I decided to offer you in this letter and message the words of our Lord Jesus Christ, who is the Word of the Father, and the words of the Holy Spirit, who are spirit and life.

The Most High Father made known from heaven through his holy angel Gabriel this Word of the Father – so worthy, so holy and glorious – in the womb of the holy and glorious Virgin Mary, from whose womb he received the flesh of our humanity and frailty. Though he was rich, he wished, together with the most Blessèd Virgin, his mother, to choose poverty in the world beyond all else.

Let every creature
in heaven, on earth, in the sea and in the depths,
give praise, glory, honour and blessing
to him who suffered so much,
who has given and will give in the future every good,
for he is our power and strength,
who alone is good, who alone is almighty,
who alone is omnipotent, wonderful, glorious
and who alone is holy, worthy of praise and blessing
through endless ages.
Amen.   *1,45f,49f*

26 December

A reading from the 'Later Admonition and Exhortation, to the Brothers and Sisters of Penance', by Saint Francis.

We must never desire to be above others but, instead, we must be servants and subject to every human creature for God's sake.

And the Spirit of the Lord will rest upon all those men and women who have done and persevered in these things and the Spirit will make a home and dwelling place in them. And they will be the children of the heavenly Father, whose works they do. And they are spouses, brothers and mothers of our Lord Jesus Christ.

We are spouses when the faithful soul is united by the Holy Spirit to our Lord Jesus Christ. We are brothers, moreover, when we do the will of his Father, who is in heaven; mothers when we carry him in our heart and body through love and pure and sincere conscience, and give him birth through a holy activity, which must shine before others by example.

O how glorious and holy and great to have a Father in heaven! O how holy, consoling, beautiful and wonderful to have such a Spouse! O how holy and how loving, gratifying, humbling, peace-giving, sweet, worthy of love, and above all things desirable it is to have such a Brother and such a Son, our Lord Jesus Christ. *1,48f*

27 December

A reading from 'The Legend of Saint Clare'.

Just as the memory of her Christ was present to Clare in her sickness, so too Christ visited her in her sufferings. At that hour of the nativity when the world rejoices with the angels at the newly born child, all the ladies went to the oratory for matins and left their mother alone weighted down by her illnesses. When she began to think about the infant Jesus and was greatly sorrowing that she could not participate in his praises, she sighed and said, 'Lord God, look at how I have been left alone in this place for you!' Behold that wonderful concert that was taking place in the church of Saint Francis suddenly began to resound in her ears. She heard the jubilant psalmody of the brothers, listened to the harmonies of their songs, and even perceived the very sounds of the instruments.

The nearness of the place was in no way such that a human being could have heard this unless either that solemnity had been divinely amplified for her or her hearing had been strengthened beyond human means. But what totally surpasses this event: she was worthy to see the very crib of the Lord!

In the morning when her daughters came to her, blessèd Clare said, 'Blessèd be the Lord Jesus Christ, who did not leave me after you did. In fact, I heard, by the grace of Christ, all those solemnities that were celebrated this night in the church of Saint Francis.'   *V,282f*

28 December

A reading from 'The First Letter of Saint Clare to Blessèd Agnes of Prague'.

If so great and good a Lord, then, on coming into the Virgin's womb, chose to appear despised, needy, and poor in this world, so that people who were in utter poverty, want and absolute need of heavenly nourishment might become rich in him by possessing the kingdom of heaven, be very joyful and glad! Be filled with a remarkable happiness and a spiritual joy! Because, since contempt of the world has pleased you more than its honours, poverty more than earthly riches, and you have sought to store up greater treasures in heaven rather than on earth, where rust does not consume nor moth destroy nor thieves break in and steal, your reward is very rich in heaven! And you have truly merited to be called a sister, spouse and mother of the Son of the Most High Father and of the glorious Virgin.

You know, I believe, that the kingdom of heaven is promised and given by the Lord, only to the poor, for she who loves temporal things loses the fruit of love. Such a person cannot serve God and money, for either the one is loved and the other hated, or the one is served and the other despised.

What a great and praiseworthy exchange:
> to leave the things of time for those of eternity,
> to choose the things of heaven for the goods of earth,
> to receive the hundred-fold in place of one,
> and to possess a blessèd, eternal life!   *V,37f*

29 December

A reading from 'The Fourth Letter of Saint Clare to Blessèd Agnes of Prague'.

Happy, indeed, is she
  to whom it is given to share in this sacred banquet
  so that she might cling with all her heart
to him
  whose beauty all the blessèd hosts of heaven unceasingly admire,
  whose affection excites,
  whose contemplation refreshes,
  whose kindness fulfils,
  whose delight replenishes,
  whose remembrance delightfully shines,
  by whose fragrance the dead are revived,
  whose glorious vision will bless
  all the citizens of the heavenly Jerusalem:
  which, since it is the splendour of eternal glory, is
      the brilliance of eternal light
      and the mirror without blemish.

Gaze upon that mirror each day, O Queen and Spouse of Jesus Christ, and continually study your face within it, that you may adorn yourself within and without with beautiful robes, covered, as is becoming the daughter and most chaste bride of the Most High King, with the flowers and garments of all the virtues. Indeed, blessèd poverty, holy humility, and the inexpressible charity are reflected in that mirror, as, with the grace of God, you can contemplate them throughout the entire mirror.

Look at the border of this mirror, that is, the poverty of him who was placed in a manger and wrapped in swaddling clothes.
      O marvellous humility!
        O astonishing poverty!
    The King of angels,
        the Lord of heaven and earth,
           is laid in a manger!   *V,50f*

30 December

A reading from 'The Assisi Compilation'.

One day, a Minister of the brothers came to blessèd Francis, who was then staying in that same place, in order to celebrate the feast of Christmas with him. It happened that the brothers of that place on Christmas day itself prepared the table elaborately because of that Minister, covering it with lovely white tablecloths which they obtained for the occasion, and vessels of glass for drinking.

Blessèd Francis came down from the cell to eat and, when he saw the table set on a dais and finely prepared, he went secretly and took the hat of a poor man who had arrived there that very day, and the staff he carried in his hand. He called one of his companions in a whisper and went outside the door of the hermitage, unnoticed by the other brothers of the house.

His companion closed the door, remaining next to it on the inside. Blessèd Francis knocked on the door and he immediately opened it for him. He entered with his hat on his back and with staff in hand, like a pilgrim. When he came to the door of the house, where the brothers were eating, he called out to the brothers like a poor man, 'For the love of the Lord God, give alms to this poor, sick pilgrim.'

That Minister and the other brothers recognised him at once. The Minister told him, 'Brother, we are also poor and, because we are so many, we need these alms we are eating. But, for the love of that Lord you invoked, come into the house, and we will give you some of the alms which the Lord has given to us.'

When he came in and stood in front of the brothers' table, the Minister gave him the bowl from which he was eating and some bread. Taking it, he sat down on the floor beside the fire, facing the brothers who sat at the elevated table. Sighing, he said to the brothers, 'When I saw the table, finely and elaborately prepared, I considered that this was not a table of poor Religious, who go door-to-door each day. For more than other Religious, we should follow the example of poverty and humility in all things, because we have been called to this and have professed this before God and humanity. So, now it seems to me that I am seated like a brother.'   *II,175f>*

31 December

A reading from 'The Assisi Compilation'.

Saturday evening before nightfall, after vespers, when blessèd Francis passed to the Lord, many birds called larks flew low above the roof of the house where blessèd Francis lay, wheeling in a circle and singing.

We who were with blessèd Francis, and who wrote these things about him, bear witness that we often heard him say, 'If I ever speak to the emperor, I will beg him, for the love of God and by my entreaties, to enact a written law forbidding anyone to catch our sister larks or do them any harm. Likewise, all mayors of cities and lords of castles and villages should be bound to oblige people each year on the Nativity of the Lord to scatter wheat and other grain along the roads outside towns and villages, so that all the birds, but especially our sister larks, may have something to eat on such a solemn feast. Also, out of reverence for the Son of God, whom his Virgin Mother on that night laid in a manger between an ox and an ass, everyone should have to give brother ox and brother ass a generous portion of fodder on that night. Likewise, on the Nativity of the Lord, all the poor should be fed their fill by the rich.'

II,129

1 January — Naming & Circumcision of Christ

A reading from 'The Life of Saint Francis', by Thomas of Celano.

The brothers who lived with Francis know
that daily, constantly, talk of Jesus was always on his lips,
sweet and pleasant conversations about him,
kind words full of love.
Out of the fullness of the heart, his mouth spoke.
So the spring of radiant love
that filled his heart within
gushed forth.
He was always with Jesus:
Jesus in his heart, Jesus in his mouth,
Jesus in his ears, Jesus in his eyes,
Jesus in his hands,
he bore Jesus always in his whole body.
Often he sat down to dinner
but on hearing or saying or even thinking 'Jesus'
he forgot bodily food,
as we read about another saint,
'Seeing, he did not see; hearing, he did not hear.'
Often as he walked along a road,
thinking and singing of Jesus,
he would forget his destination
and start inviting all the elements
to praise Jesus.
With amazing love he bore
in his heart and always held onto
Christ Jesus and him crucified.
For this reason,
he, above others, was stamped with Christ's brilliant seal
as, in rapture of spirit,
he contemplated in unspeakable and incomprehensible glory
the One sitting at the right hand of the Father,
the Most High Son of the Most High,
who, with the Father, in the unity of the Holy Spirit,
is alive and reigns, conquers and commands,
God eternally glorified throughout all the ages.
Amen.

I,283f

2 January

A reading from 'Vespers of the Lord's Birth' from 'The Office of the Passion', by Saint Francis.

Exult in God our help!
  Shout to the Lord God, living and true, with cries of gladness!
Because the Lord, the Most High,
  the Awesome, is the Great King over all the earth.
Because the Most Holy Father of heaven, our King before all ages,
  sent his belovèd Son from on high
        and he was born of the Blessèd Virgin Mary.
He called to me, You are my Father
  and I will place him, my firstborn, as the Highest,
        above all the kings of the earth.
On that day, the Lord sent his mercy
  and at night his song.
This is the day the Lord has made,
  let us rejoice and be glad in it.
For the Most Holy Child has been given to us
  and has been born for us on the way
        and placed in a manger
        because he did not have a place in the inn.
Glory to the Lord God in the highest
  and peace on earth to those of good will.
Let the heavens rejoice and the earth exult,
  let the sea and its fullness resound,
        let the fields and all that is in them be joyful.
Sing a new song to the Lord,
  sing to the Lord all the earth.
Because the Lord is great and worthy of praise,
  he is awesome beyond all gods.
Give to the Lord, you families of nations,
  give to the Lord glory and praise,
        give to the Lord the glory due to his name.
Take up your bodies and carry his holy cross
  and follow his most holy commands even to the end.   *I,156f*

3 January

A reading from 'The Earlier Rule' of Saint Francis.

All-powerful, Most Holy,
Almighty and supreme God,
holy and just Father,
Lord King of heaven and earth:
we thank you for yourself
for through your holy will
and through your only Son
with the Holy Spirit
you have created everything spiritual and corporal
and, after making us in your own image and likeness,
you placed us in paradise.

Through our own fault, we fell.

We thank you
for as through your Son you created us,
so through your holy love
with which you loved us
you brought about his birth
as true God and true man
by the glorious, ever-virgin, most blessèd, holy Mary,
and you willed to redeem us captives
through his cross and blood and death.

Because all of us, wretches and sinners,
are not worthy to pronounce your name,
we humbly ask
our Lord Jesus Christ,
your belovèd Son,
in whom you were well pleased,
together with the Holy Spirit,
the Paraclete,
to give you thanks,
for everything
as it pleases you and him,
who always satisfies you in everything,
through whom you have done so much for us.
Alleluia!

I,81ff

4 January

A reading from 'The Lauds', by Jacopone da Todi.

Honour and praise to the Love made flesh,
who came to give himself to us!

Honour him, O my soul, for he comes to save you.
Come, hasten to greet him!
He does not hold back – all of himself he gives
in his desire to be one with you.
Will you not give all of yourself to him?
Will you not hasten to embrace him?

Think of what he gives you, and what he demands –
that you be as generous as he.
Leaving heaven behind, all alone,
without the trappings of wealth or glory,
no servants to minister to him, no palace to house him,
he manifested himself on earth in a stable.

'Why did you leave the golden throne resplendent with gems,
why did you put aside the dazzling crown?
Why did you leave the order of cherubim,
the seraphim, that joyous court of ardent love,
the honoured servants and courtiers you loved as brothers –
why did you leave them all, O Lord?

'In place of your glorious throne,
a manger and a little straw;
in place of a starry crown,
poor swaddling clothes
and the warm breath of an ox and an ass;
in place of a glorious court, Mary and Joseph.

'Were these the actions of someone drunk, or out of his senses?
How could you abdicate kingdom and riches,
a renunciation promise that verges on madness?
Did someone promise you other and greater treasure?
O measureless love that would cede
such glory as yours for such humble estate!'

IX,196

5 January

A reading from 'The Lauds', by Jacopone da Todi.

'High-born Love, who is it you love
so deeply and tenaciously and wildly?
Love holds you bound so tightly
you give all of yourself – this you can hardly deny.
And this love will lead you to your death,
for it gives no signs of diminishing or cooling.

'Such disproportionate love has never been known,
so powerful from the moment of birth!
You sold yourself for us even before you were born;
it was Love that purchased you, and you held back nothing.
The decision was made – you would die of love,
suffer death in agony on the cross.

'Love imposed these terms when first it wounded you;
it struck with such force, it stripped you of all –
stripped you of wisdom, life and strength,
drawing them to itself as a magnet draws iron.
From such heights, you were drawn to such wretched depths,
to a stable, not repelled by stench or poverty.

'It was almost as if you did not grasp or sense
the depth of the descent, when you came among us.
it was almost as if your understanding was darkened,
your power and insight lost. Wounded by Love,
you did nothing to defend yourself;
surrendering to Love, you gave it your strength.

'I know that all knowledge and power were yours
even when still a child; how could so much be contained
in such a tiny frame, made of common clay?
There is no limit to your charity,
for your wisdom, strength and worth
you kept concealed within you.

'Wrapped in poor swaddling clothes,
you were utterly dependent.
Dear humble cloth, in which the Most High God
was wound and bound, as if he had nothing –
humble cloth which enfolded treasure
that puts to shame all gems and gold!'   *IX,197f*

Epiphany

6 January — The Epiphany

A reading from 'The Tree of Life', by Saint Bonaventure.

You soul devoted to God,
whoever you are,
run
with living desire
to this Fountain of life and light
and with the innermost power of your heart
cry out to him,
'O inaccessible beauty of the Most High God
and the pure brightness of the eternal light,
life vivifying all life,
light illuming every light
and keeping in perpetual splendour
a thousand times a thousand lights
brilliantly shining
before the throne of your Divinity
since the primeval dawn!
O eternal and inaccessible,
clear and sweet stream from the fountain
hidden from the eyes of all mortals,
whose depth is without a floor,
whose height is without limit,
whose breadth cannot be bounded,
whose purity cannot be disturbed.
From this Fountain
flows the stream of the oil of gladness,
which gladdens the city of God,
and the powerful fiery torrent,
the torrent, I say, of the pleasure of God,
from which the guests at the heavenly banquet
drink to joyful inebriation
and sing without ceasing
hymns of jubilation.

Anoint us
with this sacred oil
and refresh
with the longed-for waters of this torrent
the thirsting throat of our parched hearts
so that amid shouts of joy and thanksgiving
we may sing to you
a canticle of praise,
proving by experience that
with you
is the fountain of life,
and in your light
we shall see
light.   *VI,171f*

7 January *(if before Epiphany 1)*

A reading from 'The Five Feasts of the Child Jesus', by Saint Bonaventure.

We come now to the fourth feast, the Adoration of the Magi. After the soul by God's grace has spiritually conceived, brought forth and named this dear child, the three kings, understood here as the three powers of the soul, resolve to go in search of the child already revealed to them in the royal city, that is, in the structure of the created universe.

The powers of the soul, [memory, understanding and will,] are rightly described as 'kings', because now they rule the flesh, have dominion over the senses, and are taken up entirely, as is fitting, with the pursuit of divine things.

They seek the child through meditation, go in search of him in heart-felt longings and inquire about him in prayerful reflections, 'Where is he who has been born king of the Jews? We have seen his star in the East.' We have seen his splendour shining in the devout mind, we have seen his radiance lighting up the inner recesses of the soul. We have heard his voice and it is soft and tender; we have tasted his sweetness and it is delightful; we have caught his fragrance and it is alluring; we have felt his embrace and it is irresistible.

Now, Herod, give us the answer, tell us where the Belovèd is to be found, show us the little child we are yearning to see. He is the one we seek and long for.

Where are you? We are looking for you. Where are you? We are searching for you in all things and above all else. Where are you who have been born king of the Jews, law of believers, light of the blind, leader of the poor, life of the dead, eternal salvation of all who live forever?

Scripture gives us the true answer: 'In Bethlehem of Judah.' Bethlehem means 'house of bread' and Judah 'one who praises'.

Christ is found when we have confessed our sins and listened attentively to the teaching of the gospel, the bread of everlasting life, meditated upon it and rooted it firmly in our hearts, so that we may fulfil it by good works and proclaim it to others that they may observe it also.   *VIII,147f>*

8 January *(if before Epiphany 1)*

A reading from 'The Five Feasts of the Child Jesus', by Saint Bonaventure.

We find the child Jesus with Mary his mother when we taste the sweetness of divine contemplation, sometimes accompanied by abundant tears of consolation, after we have shed tears of sorrow and made fruitful confession of our sins. We find the child when prayer, which at the outset saw us almost despairing, leaves us rejoicing and assured of forgiveness. How happy such a 'Mary' by whom Jesus is conceived, from whom he is born, and with whom he is found in tenderness and delight.

You also, native powers of the soul, whom I have called kings, must go in search of the child Jesus as did the three Magi, to worship him and offer him your gifts. Worship him with reverence, for he is the Creator, the Redeemer, and the Rewarder of all. Worship him as the Creator, for he fashioned our very being; as the Redeemer, for he restored life to our spirit; as the Rewarder, for he grants us eternal life.

Adore him with reverence, you kings, for he is the most powerful king; adore him with veneration, for he is the most wise teacher; adore him with gladness, for he is the most generous prince. Do not be content to adore him, offer him gifts as well. Offer him the gold of ardent love, the frankincense of devout contemplation, the myrrh of bitter sorrow. Offer him the gold of love for the graces he has bestowed on you, the frankincense of devotion, for the joys he has prepared for you, and the myrrh of sorrow for the sins you have committed. Offer gold in honour of Christ's eternal godhead, frankincense in honour of the holiness of his soul, and myrrh in honour of his bodily sufferings.

Devout soul, in this way seek the Child Jesus, adore him and offer him your gifts.   *VIII,148f*

9 January *(if before Epiphany 1)*

A reading from 'The Tree of Life', by Saint Bonaventure.

Finally, when the face of the earth has been renewed,
when the light of the moon will be
like the light of the sun
and the light of the sun will be seven times greater,
like the light of seven days,
that holy city of Jerusalem,
which had come down from heaven
like a bride adorned
now prepared for the marriage of the Lamb,
clothed with a double stole,
will be led into the palace of the heavenly court
and introduced into
that sacred and secret bridal chamber
and will be united to that heavenly Lamb
in so intense a covenant
that bride and groom will become
one spirit.
Then Christ will be clothed
with all the beauty of the elect
as if with a many-coloured tunic
in which he will shine forth richly adorned
as if covered with all manner of precious stones.
Then the sweet wedding song will resound
and throughout all the quarters of Jerusalem
Alleluia will be sung!   *VI,168*

10 January *(if before Epiphany 1)*

A reading from 'The Tree of Life', by Saint Bonaventure.

The glory and nobility of God's eternal kingdom have to be estimated from the dignity of its King, since a king is not derived from a kingdom but a kingdom from a king. And he indeed is King who has on his garment and on his thigh a name written: King of kings and Lord of lords, whose power is an everlasting power that shall not be taken away, whose kingdom will not be destroyed and whom all tribes and peoples and tongues will serve throughout eternity. He is truly a peaceable King, whose countenance both heaven and all the earth desire to look upon.

O how glorious is the kingdom
of this most excellent King
where all the just reign with him!
Its law is
truth, peace, charity, life, eternity.
It is not divided
by the number of those who reign;
nor lessened by being shared,
nor disturbed by its multitude,
nor disordered by its inequality of ranks,
nor circumscribed by space,
nor changed by motion,
nor measured by time.   *VI,169*

11 January *(if before Epiphany 1)*

A reading from 'The Tree of Life', by Saint Bonaventure.

For the glory of the kingdom to be perfect, there is required not only exalted power but also resplendent wisdom so that the government of the kingdom is directed not by arbitrary decision but by the brilliant rays of the eternal laws emanating without deception from the light of wisdom. And this wisdom is written in Christ Jesus as in the book of life, in which God the Father has hidden all the treasures of wisdom and knowledge. Therefore, the only-begotten Son of God, as the uncreated Word, is the book of wisdom and the light that is full of living eternal principles in the mind of the supreme Craftsman, as the inspired Word in the angelic intellects and the blessèd, as the incarnate Word in rational minds united with the flesh. Thus throughout the entire kingdom the manifold wisdom of God shines forth from him and in him, as in a mirror containing the beauty of all forms and lights and as in a book in which all things are written according to the deep secrets of God.

O, if only I could find this book
whose origin is eternal,

whose essence is incorruptible,
whose knowledge is life,
whose script is indelible,
whose study is desirable,
whose teaching is easy,
whose knowledge is sweet,
whose depth is inscrutable,
whose words are ineffable;
yet all are a single Word!
Truly, whoever finds this book
will find life and will draw salvation
from the Lord.   *VI,169f*

12 January *(if before Epiphany 1)*

A reading from 'The Tree of Life', by Saint Bonaventure.

It is true that the end of all desires is happiness, which is a perfect state
with the presence of all goods. No one reaches this state except by an
ultimate union with him who is the fountain and origin of goods that are
both natural and gratuitous, both bodily and spiritual, both temporal and
eternal. And this is the one who said of himself, 'I am the Alpha and the
Omega, the beginning and the end.' As all things are produced through
the word eternally spoken, so all things are restored, advanced and
completed through the Word united to flesh. Therefore he is truly and
properly called Jesus, because there is no other name under heaven given
to us by which we can obtain salvation.

Believing, hoping and loving
with my whole heart, with my whole mind
and with my whole strength,
may I be carried
to you, belovèd Jesus,
as to the goal of all things,
because you alone are sufficient,
you alone are good and pleasing
to those who seek you and love your name.
For you, my good Jesus,
are the redeemer of the lost,
the saviour of the redeemed,
the hope of exiles,

the strength of labourers,
the sweet solace of anguished spirits,
the crown and imperial dignity of the triumphant,
the unique reward and joy of all the citizens of heaven,
the renowned offspring of the supreme God
and the sublime fruit of the virginal womb,
the abundant fountain of all graces,
of whose fullness we have all received. *VI,172f*

First Sunday of Epiphany

Epiphany 1 — Sunday

Note that this reading is apposite to the feast of the Baptism of Christ: should that feast be celebrated on another date, this reading should be transferred to it and another (unused) reading used on Epiphany 1 in its stead.

A reading from 'The Tree of Life', by Saint Bonaventure.

When the Saviour reached the age of thirty, wishing to work out our salvation, he began first to act before he taught. And beginning with baptism as the doorway of the sacraments and the foundation of virtues, he wished to be baptised by John, in order to show us an example of perfect justice and to confer regenerative power on water by contact with his most pure flesh.

You also, accompany him faithfully;
and once regenerated in him,
explore his secrets so that
on the banks of the Jordan
you may discern
the Father in the voice,
the Son in the flesh
and the Holy Spirit in the dove,
and when the heaven of the Trinity
is opened to you,
you will be taken up
into God. *VI,133*

Epiphany 1 — Monday

A reading from 'The Legend of the Three Companions' of Saint Francis.

As we have said, while Lord Bernard was giving all his possessions to the poor, blessèd Francis was at his side assisting him, glorifying and praising the Lord in his heart, in awe at the astounding work of the Lord. A priest named Sylvester, from whom the blessèd Francis had purchased stones for the repair of the church of San Damiano, came. Seeing so much money being given away on the man of God's advice, he was consumed by a burning passion of greed, and said to him, 'Francis, you did not completely pay me for the stones which you bought from me.' The scorner of greed, hearing him complaining unjustly, approached Lord Bernard, and putting his hand into his cloak where the money was, in great fervour of spirit, filled it with a handful of coins, and gave them to the disgruntled priest. He filled his hand with money a second time, and said to him, 'Do you now have full payment, Lord Priest?' 'I have it completely, brother,' he replied. Overjoyed, he returned home with his money.

But after a few days that same priest, inspired by the Lord, began to reflect on these things blessèd Francis had done, and he said to himself, 'Am I not a miserable man? Old as I am, do I not still covet and desire the things of this world? And this young man despises and scorns them all for the love of God!'

The following night he saw in a dream an immense cross. Its top reached to the heavens, its base rested fixed in the mouth of the blessèd Francis, and its arms stretched from one part of the world to the other.

When he woke, therefore, the priest understood and resolutely believed that Francis was indeed Christ's friend and servant, and the religion which he founded would spread all over the world. From then on he began to fear God and to do penance in his own home. At last, after a little while, he entered the Order in which he lived excellently and ended gloriously.   *II,86f*

Epiphany 1 — Tuesday

A reading from 'The Legend of the Three Companions' of Saint Francis.

The man of God, Francis, accompanied by his two brothers, had no place to stay, so he moved with them to a poor little abandoned church, which was called Saint Mary of the Portiuncula. And there they built a little hut in which they would live from time to time.

After a few days, an Assisian, named Giles, came to them and, on his knees, begged the man of God with great reverence and devotion to accept him into his company. When the man of God saw how unusually faithful and devout the man was, realizing that he was able to obtain great grace from God, as later became clear by his success, he received him with open arms. These four, united in immense happiness and the joy of the Holy Spirit, separated for greater spiritual advantage.

Blessèd Francis, taking Brother Giles with him, went into the Marches of Ancona; the other two went into another area. While going to the Marches, they rejoiced enthusiastically in the Lord; the holy man, however, sang with a loud and clear voice, in French, the praises of the Lord, blessing and glorifying the goodness of the Most High. There was as much happiness in them as if they had found a great treasure in the evangelical field of Lady Poverty, for whose love they gladly and willingly disdained all worldly things as dung.

The saint told Brother Giles, 'Our religion will be like a fisherman who casts his nets into the water catching a great number of fish, and, leaving the small ones in the water, he puts the large ones into his basket.' Thus he prophesied that the Order would expand.

Even though the man of God did not yet fully preach to the people, when he went through cities and towns, he encouraged everyone to fear and love God and to do penance for their sins. Brother Giles, on the other hand, exhorted his listeners to believe him because he gave them the best advice.   *II,87f*

Epiphany 1 — Wednesday

A reading from 'The Legend of the Three Companions' of Saint Francis.

Those who heard the blessèd Francis and Brother Giles would say, 'Who are these men?' and 'What are these words they're saying?' For, at that time, love and fear of God were non-existent almost everywhere, and the way of penance was not only completely unknown, but it was also considered folly. Lust for the flesh, greed for the world, and pride of life was so widespread, that the whole world seemed to be engulfed in these three malignancies.

There was a diversity of opinions about these evangelical men. Some declared that they were fools or drunkards, while others maintained that such words did not come from fools. One of those listening said, 'Either they cling to the Lord for the sake of the highest perfection, or they are demented for sure, because their life seems reckless: they use little food, walk barefoot, and wear wretched clothes.'

Although some among them were struck with fear at seeing the form of their holy way of life, others would not as yet follow them. Instead, young ladies seeing them would run far away and tremble at perhaps being carried away by foolishness and madness.

After they had travelled around that province, they returned to the place called Saint Mary's. After a few days had elapsed, however, three other men from Assisi, Sabbatino, Morico, and John de Capella, came to them, begging blessèd Francis to receive them as brothers. He received them humbly and kindly.   *II,88*

Epiphany 1 — Thursday

A reading from 'The Legend of the Three Companions' of Saint Francis.

When the brothers were begging alms throughout the city, hardly anyone would give to them; instead they denounced them for disposing of their possessions so that they could live off others and, therefore, they suffered extreme want. Even their own relatives and families would persecute those men, and others in the city mocked them as senseless and stupid, because no one at that time would abandon what was his to go begging alms from door to door.

The Bishop of the city of Assisi, to whom Francis, the man of God, would frequently go for counsel, receiving him kindly, told him, 'It seems to me that your life is very rough and hard, especially in not possessing anything in this world.' To which the saint said, 'Lord, if we had possessions, we would need arms for our protection. For disputes and lawsuits usually arise out of them, and, because of this, love of God and neighbour are greatly impeded. Therefore, we do not want to possess anything in this world.' The man of God's response greatly pleased the Bishop. For Francis scorned all worldly goods, but money most of all; so much so, that in all his Rules he most forcefully commended poverty and repeated that the brothers be eager to avoid money.

For he composed several Rules and tested them, before writing that which he ultimately left to the brothers. In one of them he expressed his scorn of money: 'May we who have left all things, then, be careful of not losing the kingdom of heaven for so little. If we find coins anywhere, let us pay no more attention to them than to the dust we trample underfoot.'   *II,88f*

Epiphany 1 — Friday

A reading from 'The Legend of the Three Companions' of Saint Francis.

Calling together the six brothers, Saint Francis, since he was full of the grace of the Holy Spirit, predicted to them what was about to happen. 'Dearest brothers,' he said, 'let us consider our vocation, to which God has mercifully called us, not only for our own good, but for the salvation of many. We are to go throughout the world, encouraging everyone, more by deed than by word, to do penance for their sins and to recall the commandments of God. Do not be afraid that you seem few and uneducated. With confidence, simply proclaim penance, trusting in the Lord, who conquered the world. Because by his spirit, he is speaking through and in you, encouraging everyone to be converted to him and to observe his commandments.

'You will find some faithful people, meek and kind, who will receive you and your words with joy. You will find many others, faithless, proud, and blasphemous, who will resist and reject you and what you say. Therefore, resolve in your hearts to bear these things with patience and humility.'

When the brothers heard this, they began to be afraid. The saint told them, 'Do not fear, because after not much time many learnèd and noble men will come to us, and will be with us preaching to kings and rulers and great crowds. Many people will be converted to the Lord, who will multiply and increase his family throughout the entire world.' *II,89f*

Epiphany 1 — Saturday

A reading from 'The Legend of the Three Companions' of Saint Francis.

Whenever the brothers came upon a church or a cross, they bowed in prayer and said with devotion, 'We adore you, Christ, and we bless you in all your churches throughout the whole world, because, by your holy cross, you have redeemed the world.' For they believed they would find a place of God wherever they found a cross or a church.

Those who saw them, however, were greatly amazed that they differed from all others by their habit and life and seemed almost like wild men. In fact, whenever they entered especially a city, estate, town, or home, they announced peace, encouraging everyone to fear and love the Creator of heaven and earth and to observe the commandments.

Some people listened to them willingly; others, on the other hand, mocked them; and many tired them out with questions by saying to them, 'Where do you come from?' Others wanted to know which was their Order. Although it was tiresome answering so many questions, they responded simply that they were penitents originally from the city of Assisi. At that time their religion was not yet called an Order.

In fact, many judged them impostors or fools, and were unwilling to receive them into their homes lest, as thieves, they might slyly take their belongings. Therefore, in many places, after they had suffered a number of insults, they sought lodging in the porticos of churches and homes.

II,90

Second Sunday of Epiphany

Epiphany 2 — Sunday

A reading from 'The Legend of the Three Companions' of Saint Francis.

About this time, there were two of the brothers in Florence, unable to find lodging as they were begging throughout the city. When they came upon a house having a portico and, in the portico, a bread-oven, they told each other, 'We can stay here.' Therefore, asking the lady of the house to accept them into her home and having her make an excuse, they humbly said that she at least might let them spend that night near the oven.

She allowed them to do this. When her husband came and found them in the portico, he called his wife and told her, 'Why did you offer lodging to those two scoundrels in our portico?' She answered that she did not want them inside the house, but she did let them stay outside in the portico where they could steal nothing but firewood. Considering them scoundrels and thieves, he was opposed to giving them any kind of shelter, although the weather was bitterly cold.

That night, they rested near the oven in a sound sleep, warmed only by the glow of divine love and covered with the blanket of Lady Poverty. In the morning they went to the nearest church to hear the office of matins.

When morning came, the woman went to the same church and, seeing those brothers devoutly steadfast in prayer, she said to herself, 'If these men were scoundrels and thieves, as my husband claimed, they would not be persevering in prayer so reverently.' So she approached them and told them that she would gladly receive them into her home if they wanted lodging there. The brothers answered humbly, 'May the Lord reward you for your good will.'

II,90ff>

Epiphany 2 — Monday

A reading from 'The Legend of the Three Companions' of Saint Francis.

A man named Guido was distributing alms to the poor who were in the church. When he came to the brothers and wanted to give money to each one of them, as he had done to the others, they refused the money and did not want to accept it. But he said to them, 'Since you are poor, why do you not accept the coins like the others?' Brother Bernard answered, 'While it is true that we are poor, poverty is not burdensome for us as it is for other poor people. For, by the grace of God, we have willingly made ourselves poor. It is his counsel we fulfilled.' Astonished at these things and asking if they had ever possessed anything, he heard from them that they had indeed possessed much. For the love of God, though, they had given everything to the poor. The one who answered in this way was Brother Bernard, the first disciple of blessèd Francis, whom today we truly believe to be a most holy father. He was the first to run after the holy one of God, embracing the delegation of peace and penance. Selling everything he possessed and giving to the poor, according to the counsel of gospel perfection, he persevered to the end in most holy poverty. *II,91*

Epiphany 2 — Tuesday

A reading from 'The Legend of the Three Companions' of Saint Francis.

Although the brothers were treated kindly by some, they were often considered good-for-nothings, so that many, the small and the great, abused and harmed them, at times taking away from them even the cheapest clothing they had. Whenever the servants of God remained naked, because they wore only one tunic, according to the pattern of the gospel, they did not demand back what had been taken from them. If some, moved by piety, did want to return what was taken from them, they willingly accepted.

They did these and similar things to them, regarding them as so worthless that they brazenly afflicted them as they chose. In addition, they endured immense hardship and suffering from hunger and thirst, from cold and nakedness. Suffering all these things steadfastly and patiently, as blessèd Francis had admonished them, they did not become dejected or disturbed, nor did they curse those who brought evil upon them. On the contrary, as perfectly evangelical men, placed at a great advantage, they greatly exulted in the Lord, considering it pure joy when they fell into temptations and trials of this sort. According to the word of the gospel, they prayed carefully and enthusiastically for their persecutors.

II,92

Epiphany 2 — Wednesday

A reading from 'The Legend of the Three Companions' of Saint Francis.

People saw that the brothers rejoiced in their tribulations, persisted in prayer with eagerness and devotion, neither accepted nor carried money and possessed a great love for one another; and through this they were known really to be the Lord's disciples. Many came to them with heart-felt sorrow, asking pardon for the offences they had committed against them. They forgave them from their hearts, saying, 'May the Lord forgive you,' and encouraged them soundly about their eternal salvation.

Some asked those brothers to receive them into their company. And because of the small number of the brothers – all six of them possessed authority from blessèd Francis to receive others into the Order – they accepted some of them into their company. After they were received, they all returned at a predetermined time to Saint Mary of the Portiuncula.

When they saw one another again, however, they were filled with such delight and joy, as if they did not remember anything of what they had endured at the hands of the wicked.

Each day they were conscientious in prayer and working with their hands to avoid all idleness, the enemy of the soul. They rose conscientiously in the middle of the night, and prayed most devoutly with copious tears and sighs. They loved each other deeply, served one another, and took care of each other as a mother for an only and belovèd child. Charity burned so ardently in them that it seemed easy for them to give their bodies to death, not only for the love of Christ, but also for the salvation of the soul or the body of their confreres.

II,92f

Epiphany 2 — Thursday

A reading from 'The Legend of the Three Companions' of Saint Francis.

One day, when two of the brothers were walking along, they came across a simpleton who began to throw rocks at them. One of them, noticing that stones were being thrown at the other, ran directly in front of him, preferring that the stones strike him rather than his brother. Because of the mutual charity with which they burned, they were prepared to lay down their life in this way, one for the other.

They were so rooted and grounded in humility and love, that one respected the other as father and master, while those who excelled by way of the office of prelate or some grace, seemed humble and more self-effacing than the others. They all dedicated themselves wholeheartedly to obedience, ever prepared for the will of the one giving orders. They did not distinguish between a just and an unjust command because they considered whatever they were ordered to be the Lord's will. Fulfilling commands, therefore, was pleasant and easy for them. They abstained from carnal desires, judging themselves carefully and taking care that in no way would one offend the other.

If it ever happened that one uttered an annoying word to another, his conscience troubled him, so much so that he could not rest until he admitted his fault. In this way, with the grace of Jesus Christ anticipating and helping them, they strove to banish all ill will and malice from their midst, to preserve among them always perfect love, and, to combat, as far as possible, each vice by practicing a corresponding virtue. *II,93f>*

Epiphany 2 — Friday

A reading from 'The Legend of the Three Companions' of Saint Francis.

The brothers did not appropriate anything as their own, but used books or other items in common according to the pattern handed down and observed by the apostles. Although there was real poverty in and among them, they were generous and openhanded with everything given them for God's sake. The alms freely given to them out of his love, they gave to all those who begged from them, especially to the poor.

In fact, if they were travelling along the road and found the poor begging from them for the love of God, when they had nothing to offer them, they would give them some of their clothing even though it was shabby. Sometimes they gave their capuce, tearing it from the tunic; at other times they gave a sleeve, or tore off a part of their habit, that they might fulfil that gospel passage: 'Give to all who beg from you.' One day, however, a poor man begging alms came to the church of Saint Mary of the Portiuncula, near where the brothers sometimes stayed. There was a cloak there that a brother wore while in the world. When blessèd Francis told him to give it to that poor man, he gave it to him freely and quickly.

And immediately, because of the reverence and devotion which that brother had in giving the cloak to the poor man, it seemed to him that the alms rose up into heaven and he felt himself inundated by a new happiness.　　　　*II,94*

Epiphany 2 — Saturday

A reading from 'The Legend of the Three Companions' of Saint Francis.

Seeing that the Lord would increase his brothers in number and merit, since there were already twelve most perfect men expressing the same belief, blessèd Francis said to the eleven, he being the twelfth, their leader and father, 'Brothers, I see that the Lord mercifully wants to increase our congregation. Then, going to our mother, the holy Roman Church, let us inform the Supreme Pontiff what the Lord has begun to do through us, that, with his will and command, we may continue doing what we have undertaken.'

And since the proposal of their father pleased the other brothers, and they had embarked together with him on the journey to the Curia, he said to them, 'Let us make one of us our leader and consider that man a kind of vicar of Jesus Christ, so that wherever he wants to go, we will go, and whenever he wants to rest, we will rest.' And they chose Brother Bernard, the first after blessèd Francis, and, as the father said, they served him.

They, then, made their way rejoicing and spoke about the words of the Lord, not daring to say anything except for the praise and glory of God and the benefit of the soul, and they frequently spent time in prayer. The Lord, on the other hand, prepared lodging for them, doing what was necessary to minister to them.　　　　*II,95*

Third Sunday of Epiphany

Epiphany 3 — Sunday

A reading from 'The Legend of the Three Companions' of Saint Francis.

When blessèd Francis and the other brothers arrived in Rome and found the Bishop of the city of Assisi there, they were received with immense joy, for he honoured blessèd Francis and all the brothers with special affection. Not knowing the reason for their arrival, he began to be apprehensive, fearing that they might want to leave their native land, where the Lord had begun to do marvellous things through them. For he rejoiced to have in his diocese such men whose life and conduct he greatly appreciated. After he learned their purpose and understood their plan, however, he was overjoyed and promised them his counsel and help.

The Bishop was known to the Cardinal Bishop of Sabina, named Lord John of Saint Paul, a man truly full of God's grace, who loved, in particular, servants of God. The Bishop of Assisi made the life of blessèd Francis and his brothers clear to him. On this account, he was eager to meet the man of God and some of his brothers. Hearing that they were in the city, he sent for those men and welcomed them with great reverence and love. *II,95f*

Epiphany 3 — Monday

A reading from 'The Legend of the Three Companions' of Saint Francis.

During the few days that the brothers were staying in Rome with Cardinal John of Saint Paul, they so edified him with their holy words and example, that, seeing what he had heard about them to shine in deed, he commended himself humbly and devoutly to their prayers. He even asked them, as a special grace, to be considered one of their brothers. Then asking blessèd Francis the reason why he came and hearing from him their entire proposal and intention, he offered to be their procurator at the Curia.

That Cardinal then went to the Curia and told the Lord Pope Innocent III, 'I found a most perfect man, who wishes to live according to the form of the holy gospel, and to observe evangelical perfection in all things. I believe that the Lord wills, through him, to reform the faith of the holy church throughout the world.' Hearing this, the Lord Pope was greatly amazed and had the Cardinal bring blessèd Francis to him. *II,96*

Epiphany 3 — Tuesday

A reading from 'The Legend of the Three Companions' of Saint Francis.

On the following day, therefore, [after Cardinal John of Saint Paul had told the Lord Pope Innocent III about the blessèd Francis,] the man of God was presented by that Cardinal to the Pope, to whom he revealed his entire holy proposal. The Pope, a man of extraordinary discernment, in due fashion assented to Francis's request, and encouraged him and his brothers in many ways. He blessed them saying, 'Go with the Lord, brothers, and as he will see fit to inspire you, preach penance to everyone. When almighty God increases you in number and grace, come back to us. We will grant you more, and entrust you with a greater charge.'

Before the saint left his presence, the Lord Pope wanted to know whether what had been, and what would be conceded, was according to the Lord's will. And so, he said to him and his companions, 'My dear young sons, your life seems to us exceptionally hard and severe. While we believe there can be no question about your living it because of your great zeal, we must take into consideration those who will come after you lest this way of life seem too burdensome.'

The Pope saw that their constancy of faith and the anchor of their hope were so firmly grounded in Christ, that they did not want to be shaken from their enthusiasm. So he said to blessèd Francis, 'My son, go and pray that God will reveal to you whether what you ask proceeds from his will. In this way, knowing the Lord's will, we may accede to your desires.'   *II,96f*

Epiphany 3 — Wednesday

A reading from 'The Legend of the Three Companions' of Saint Francis.

Once Saint Francis had prayed [that God would reveal his will to him], as the Lord Pope suggested, the Lord spoke figuratively to him in spirit, 'There was a little, poor and beautiful woman in a desert, whose beauty fascinated a great king. He wanted to take her as his wife, because he thought that, from her, he would have handsome sons. After the marriage was celebrated and consummated, there were many sons born and raised. Their mother spoke to them in this way, 'My sons, do not be ashamed, for you are sons of the king. Therefore, go to his court and he will provide for all your needs.' When they went to see the king, he was struck by their good looks, and noticing a resemblance to himself in them, he asked them, 'Whose sons are you?' When they answered that they were the sons of the little poor woman living in the desert, the king embraced them with great joy. 'Do not be afraid,' he said, 'for you are my sons. If strangers are fed at my table, how much more will you, who are my lawful sons.' He then ordered the woman to send to his court all of the children she had borne to be fed.'

When these things had been shown to blessèd Francis while he was praying, the man of God understood that the poor woman signified him. After he completed his prayer, he presented himself to the Supreme Pontiff and narrated point-by-point the story that the Lord had revealed to him. 'My lord,' he said, 'I am that little poor woman whom the loving Lord, in his mercy, has adorned, and through whom he has been pleased to give birth to legitimate sons. The King of kings has told me that he will nourish all the sons born to me, because, if he feeds strangers, he must provide for his own. For if God gives temporal goods to sinful men out of love for providing for his children, how much more will he give to gospel men who deserve these things out of merit.' *II,97*

Epiphany 3 — Thursday

A reading from 'The Legend of the Three Companions' of Saint Francis.

Before the arrival of blessèd Francis [in Rome], the Pope had seen in a vision the church of Saint John Lateran threatening to collapse, and a Religious, small and of shabby appearance, supporting it on his own shoulders. When he awoke, stunned and shaken, as a discerning and wise man, he pondered what this vision meant to tell him. A few days later, blessèd Francis came to him, made known his proposal [that the brothers continue their work with the Pope's blessing], as we have said, and asked him to confirm the Rule he had written in simple words, using the words of the holy gospel, for whose perfection he fully longed.

As he was reflecting on how enthusiastic blessèd Francis was in God's service, and comparing his vision with that shown to the man of God, he began to say to himself, 'This is indeed that holy and religious man through whom the church of God will be sustained and supported.'

So he embraced him and approved the Rule he had written. He also gave him and his brothers permission to preach penance everywhere, with the stipulation that the brothers who preach obtain permission from blessèd Francis. Afterwards he approved this in a consistory. *II,97f*

Epiphany 3 — Friday

A reading from 'The Legend of the Three Companions' of Saint Francis.

After obtaining these favours, [the approval of the Rule and permission to preach penance,] blessèd Francis thanked God, and on bended knees, promised obedience and reverence to the Lord Pope humbly and devoutly. The other brothers, in accordance with the precept of the Lord Pope, promised obedience and reverence to blessèd Francis in a similar way.

After receiving a blessing from the Supreme Pontiff and visiting the tombs of the Apostles, blessèd Francis and the other eleven brothers were given the tonsure, as the lord Cardinal had arranged, wanting all twelve of them to be clerics.

As he was leaving the city, the man of God, with his brothers, set out into the world, greatly surprised at how easily his desire had been granted. He was growing each day in the hope and trust of the Saviour, who had earlier shown him by holy revelations what was to happen.

For before he had obtained these things, one night when he had gone to sleep, it seemed to him that he was making his way down a road beside which there was a lovely, strong and thick tree that was exceedingly high. As he approached and stood under it, marvelling at its height and beauty, the holy man suddenly rose to so great a height, that he touched the top of the tree and very easily bent it even to the ground.

It really happened this way, when the Lord Innocent, a very high, lovely and strong tree in the world, bent himself so kindly to his wish and request.   *II,98f*

Epiphany 3 — Saturday

A reading from 'The Legend of the Three Companions' of Saint Francis.

From then on, [after receiving the blessing of the Pope,] blessèd Francis, going around the cities and villages, began to preach more widely and more perfectly proclaiming the kingdom of God with confidence, not in the persuasive words of human wisdom, but in the learning and power of the Holy Spirit.

Strengthened by apostolic authority, he was a forthright preacher of truth, not using fawning words or seductive flattery, because he first convinced himself by action and then convinced others by word, so that he spoke the truth with the greatest fidelity. Even a very great number of learnèd and well-educated people marvelled at his power and truth, which no human had taught, and they hurried to see and hear him as if he were a person of another age.

Drawn by divine inspiration, many people, well-born and lowly, cleric and lay, began to cling to the footsteps of blessèd Francis, and, after they had abandoned the concerns and vanity of this world, to live under his discipline.   *II,99*

Fourth Sunday of Epiphany

Epiphany 4 — Sunday

A reading from 'The Legend of the Three Companions' of Saint Francis.

The blessèd father Francis, together with his sons, were staying in a place near Assisi called Rivo Torto, where there was a hut abandoned by all. The place was so cramped that they could barely sit or rest. Very often, for lack of bread, their only food was the turnips that they begged in their need, here and there.

The man of God would write the names of the brothers on the beams of that hut, so that anyone wishing to rest or pray would know his place, and so that any unusual noise would not disturb the mind's silence in such small and close quarters.

One day while the brothers were staying in that place, a peasant came with his donkey, wanting to stay in that hut with it. And so that he would not be driven away by the brothers, on walking into the hut, he said to his donkey, 'Go in, go in, because we will do well in this place.'

When the holy father heard the peasant's words and realised his intention, he was annoyed at him, most of all because he made quite an uproar with his donkey, disturbing all the brothers who were then immersed in silence and prayer. Then the man of God said to his brothers, 'I know, brothers, that God did not call us to prepare a lodging for a donkey, nor to have dealings with people. While we are preaching the way of salvation to people and are giving them wise counsel, we should dedicate ourselves most of all to prayer and thanksgiving.'

They left that hut for the use of poor lepers, moving to a small dwelling near Saint Mary of the Portiuncula where they stayed from time to time before acquiring that church. *II,99f*

Epiphany 4 — Monday

A reading from 'The Life of Saint Francis', by Thomas of Celano.

At that time, [while the brothers were still living in the hut at Rivo Torto,] the emperor Otto passed through that area, travelling in great pomp and circumstance to receive the crown of an earthly empire. The most holy father Francis and his followers were staying in that small hut next to the very parade route. He did not go outside to look and did not allow the others to do so, except for one who, without wavering, proclaimed to the emperor that his glory would be short-lived. The glorious holy one, living within himself and walking in the breadth of his heart, prepared in himself a worthy dwelling place of God. That is why the uproar outside did not seize his ears, nor could any cry intrude, interrupting the great enterprise he had in hand. Apostolic authority resided in him; so he altogether refused to flatter kings and princes.   *I,221*

Epiphany 4 — Tuesday

A reading from 'The Legend of the Three Companions' of Saint Francis.

[After the brothers had moved to the church of Saint Mary of the Portiuncula,] blessèd Francis, in accordance with God's will and inspiration, obtained it from the abbot of the monastery of Saint Benedict on Mount Subasio near Assisi. The saint, in a special and affectionate way, commended this place to the Minister General and to all the brothers, as the place loved by the glorious Virgin more than any other place or church in this world.

A vision one of the brothers had, while in the world, contributed much to the commendation and love of this place. Blessèd Francis loved this brother with unique affection as long as he was with him, by showing him extraordinary affection. This man, wanting to serve God – as he later did so faithfully in religion – saw in a vision that all the people of the world were blind and were kneeling in a circle around the church of Saint Mary of the Portiuncula with their hands joined and their faces raised to heaven. In a loud and sobbing voice, they were begging the Lord in his mercy to give them sight. While they were praying, it seemed that a great light came from heaven and, resting on them, enlightened all of them with its wholesome radiance.

On awakening, the man resolved to serve God more faithfully, and, shortly thereafter, leaving the world with its seductions, he entered religion where he persevered in the service of God with humility and dedication.   *II,100*

Epiphany 4 — Wednesday

A reading from 'The Legend of the Three Companions' of Saint Francis.

At that time, as blessèd Francis was with his brothers whom he had then, he was of such purity that, from the hour the Lord revealed to him that he and his brothers should live according to the form of the holy gospel, he desired and strove to observe it to the letter during his whole lifetime.

Therefore he told the brother who did the cooking for the brothers, that when he wanted the brothers to eat beans, he should not put them in warm water in the evening for the next day, as people usually do. This was so the brothers would observe the words of the holy gospel, 'Do not be concerned about tomorrow.' So that brother used to put them in water to soften after the brothers said matins.

Because of this, for a long time many brothers observed this in a great many places where they stayed on their own, especially in cities. They did not want to collect or receive more alms than were enough for them for one day. *II,151f*

Epiphany 4 — Thursday

A reading from 'A Mirror of the Perfection of a Lesser Brother'.

Once when blessèd Francis was at Saint Mary of the Portiuncula, a very spiritual poor man was coming back along the road from Assisi with a bag of alms. As he drew near the church of Saint Mary, praising God as he went his way in a loud voice with great joy, blessèd Francis heard him.

Immediately, with the greatest fervour and delight, he ran up to him on the road and, with great joy, kissed his shoulder on which he was carrying the bag with the alms. Taking the bag from his shoulder and putting it on his own shoulder, he carried it to the home of the brothers. He said to the brothers, 'This is how I want a brother of mine to go for alms and to return happy and joyful praising God.' *III,275f*

Epiphany 4 — Friday

A reading from 'The Assisi Compilation'.

Once when blessèd Francis had returned to Saint Mary of the Portiuncula, he found there Brother James the Simple with a leper covered with sores who had come there that day. The holy father had entrusted this leper to him, and especially all the other lepers who had severe sores. For in those days, the brothers stayed in the leper hospitals. That Brother James was like the doctor for those with severe sores, and he gladly touched, changed, and treated their wounds.

As if reproving Brother James, blessèd Francis told him, 'You should not take our Christian brothers about in this way since it is not right for you or for them.' Blessèd Francis used to call lepers 'Christian brothers.'

Although he was pleased that Brother James helped and served them, the holy father said this because he did not want him to take those with severe sores outside the hospital. This was especially because Brother James was very simple, and he often went with a leper to the church of Saint Mary, and especially because people usually abhorred lepers who had severe sores.

After he said these things, blessèd Francis immediately reproached himself, and he told his fault to Brother Peter of Catanio, who was then Minister General, especially because blessèd Francis believed that in reproving Brother James he had shamed the leper.

Blessèd Francis said, 'Let this be my penance: I will eat together with my Christian brother from the same dish.'

While blessèd Francis was sitting at the table with the leper and other brothers, a bowl was placed between the two of them. The leper was completely covered with sores and ulcerated, and especially the fingers with which he was eating were deformed and bloody, so that whenever he put them in the bowl, blood dripped into it.

Brother Peter and the other brothers saw this, grew very sad, but did not dare say anything out of fear of the holy father.

The one who wrote this, saw it and bore witness to it.   *II,166f>*

Epiphany 4 — Saturday

A reading from 'The Little Flowers of Saint Francis'.

It once happened that at a place where Saint Francis was staying at that time the brothers were serving sick lepers in a hospital. One of the lepers there was so impatient, so unbearable and obstinate that everyone believed as certain that he was possessed by the demon, and so he was. He so rudely insulted anyone who served him with words and blows and, what is worse, he hurled such angry blasphemies against the blessèd Christ and his most holy mother the Virgin Mary, that no one at all could be found who could or would serve him. Although the brothers strove to bear patiently the insults and harm to themselves, in order to increase the merit of patience, nevertheless their consciences could not bear those against Christ and his Mother, so they decided to abandon that leper entirely. But they did not want to do this until they explained this in detail to Saint Francis, who was then staying in a place near there.

After they explained this, Saint Francis went to that perverse leper and, coming up to him, greeted him, saying, 'My dear brother, may God give you peace.' The leper responded, 'What peace can I have from God? He has taken from me peace and every good thing, and has made me all decayed and stinking!' Saint Francis said, 'My son, be patient, because the illnesses of the body are given to us by God in this world for salvation of the soul, so they have great value, when they are borne patiently.' The sick man replied, 'How can I patiently bear the constant pain that torments me night and day? And I am suffering not only from my illness, but the brothers you gave me to serve me make me worse, and do not serve me as they should.' Then Saint Francis said, 'My son, I want to serve you myself, since you are not content with the others.' The sick man said, 'I like that. But what more can you do than the others?' Saint Francis answered, 'I will do whatever you want.' The leper said, 'I want you to wash me all over. I stink so badly I cannot bear myself.' Then Saint Francis quickly had some water heated with many fragrant herbs. He undressed the man, and began to wash him with his holy hands, while another brother poured the water. By a divine miracle, where Saint Francis touched him with his holy hands the leprosy went away, and there remained only perfectly healed flesh. And as the flesh began to heal, the soul also began to heal. When the leper saw himself being cured, he began to weep very bitterly. So while externally the body was being cleansed of leprosy by washing with water, so internally his soul was being cleansed of sin by contrition and tears.   *III,607ff*

2 February — The Presentation of Christ in the Temple (Candlemass)

A reading from 'The Tree of Life', by Saint Bonaventure.

It was not enough for Christ, the teacher of perfect humility, who was equal to the Father in all things, to submit himself to the humble Virgin. He must submit himself also to the Law, that he might redeem those who were under the Law and free them from the slavery of corruption to the freedom of the glory of the children of God. He wished that his mother, although she was most pure, should observe the law of purification. And he wished that he himself, the redeemer of all, should be redeemed as a firstborn son and should be presented to God in the temple and that an offering should be given for him in the presence of the just who were rejoicing.

Rejoice, then,
with that blessèd old man and the aged Anna;
walk forth
to meet the mother and Child.
Let overcome your bashfulness;
let affection dispel your fear.
Receive the Infant
in your arms
and say with the bride,
'I took hold of him
and would not let him go.'
Dance with the holy old man
and sing with him,
'Now dismiss your servant, Lord,
according to your word in peace.'   *VI,131*

*For the weeks after Candlemass and before The Sunday Next Before Lent,
see the Weeks in Ordinary Time, page 141ff.*

The Sunday Next Before Lent

A reading from 'The Considerations on the Holy Stigmata'.

[Once, when they were in retreat together on Mount Alverna,] Brother Leo went one night at the usual time to say matins with Saint Francis. And after he had called from the end of the bridge, as he usually did, Saint Francis did not answer. Now Brother Leo did not go back, as Saint Francis had instructed him, but with a good and holy intention he went across the bridge and quietly entered the saint's cell. By the bright moonlight shining in through the door, he saw that he was not in the cell. Not finding him, he thought that he might be praying outside somewhere in the woods. So he came out and silently walked among the trees looking for him by the light of the moon.

And at last he heard the voice of Saint Francis speaking, and he went closer to hear what he was saying. In the moonlight he saw Saint Francis on his knees, with his face lifted towards the sky and his hands held out to God, saying these words with fervour of spirit, 'Who are you, my dearest God? And what am I, your vilest little worm and useless little servant?' And he repeated those words over and over, and he said

Sunday Next Before Lent

nothing else.

Brother Leo marvelled greatly at this, and he looked up and gazed at the sky. And while he was looking, he saw come down from the heights of heaven a torch of flaming fire that was very beautiful and bright and pleasing to the eyes and that descended and rested on Saint Francis' head. And he heard a voice come out of the flame and speak with Saint Francis, and the Saint answered the speaker.

But seeing this and thinking himself unworthy to be so close to that holy spot where this marvellous apparition was taking place, and also fearing to offend Saint Francis or to disturb him in his contemplation of such holy secrets, in case the saint should hear him, he silently went back so that he could not hear what was said. And he stood at a distance, waiting to see the end. And finally, after a long time, he saw the flame return to heaven. So Brother Leo went away, felling reassured and joyful, and began to return quietly to his cell, so that the saint should not hear him.

IV>,1444f

Monday before Lent

A reading from 'The Assisi Compilation'.

One of the brothers, a spiritual man, to whom blessèd Francis was very close, was staying in a hermitage. Considering that if blessèd Francis came there at some time he would not have a suitable place to stay he had a little cell built in a remote place near the place of the brothers, where blessèd Francis could pray when he came. After a few days, it happened that blessèd Francis came. When the brother led him to see it, blessèd Francis said to him, 'This little cell seems too beautiful to me. But, if you want me to stay in it for a few days, have it covered inside and out with ferns and tree-branches.'

That little cell was not made of stonework but of wood, but because the wood was planed, made with hatchet and axe, it seemed too beautiful to blessèd Francis. The brother immediately had it changed as blessèd Francis had requested.

For the more the house and cells of the brothers were poor and religious, the more willingly he would see them and sometimes be received as a guest there. As he stayed and prayed in it for a few days, one day, outside the little cell near the place of the brothers, a brother who was at that place came to where blessèd Francis was staying. Blessèd Francis said to him, 'Where are you coming from, brother?' He told him, 'I am coming for your little cell.' 'Because you said it is mine,' blessèd Francis said, 'someone else will stay in it from now on; I will not.'

We who were with him often heard him repeat the saying of the holy gospel: 'Foxes have dens and the birds of the air have nests; but the Son of Man has nowhere to lay his head.'   *II,158f*

Shrove Tuesday

A reading from a medieval Franciscan manuscript.

Once in the early days of the Order, the blessèd Francis, with the holy Brother Bernard, his first disciple, came to a certain town where they hoped to beg alms, and both sat down, tired, by a stone. As it was dinner-time and the pangs of hunger were torturing these 'poor men of Christ', the holy father said to his companion, 'By this stone, my dearest brother, let us meet again when we have both collected something to eat for the love of God.'

So they parted, and each went his way in the city, knocking on the doors of the houses, standing on the doorsteps, boldly asking for alms and reverently taking what was given to them.

But that holy man Brother Bernard became so hungry with walking about that he collected together nothing at all, for, as soon as he was given any crumbs or crusts or scraps he immediately ate them, so that when he returned to the stone where they had agreed to meet he brought nothing whatever with him in the way of alms.

When Father Francis came, carrying with him the food which he had collected, he showed it to his companion and said, 'See, brother, what alms God in his goodness has given me. Now set down what you have got so that we may eat together in the name of God.' Then Brother Bernard was greatly perturbed and, flinging himself at the feet of the holy father, exclaimed, 'O my father, let me confess my sin. Alas, I have brought nothing here, for all that I was given I ate, for I was very hungry.'

When Saint Francis heard this, he wept for joy and, embracing Brother Bernard, cried out with a loud voice, 'Indeed, my sweetest son, you are a much holier man than I am. You are a perfect follower of the holy gospel, for you have laid up no store, neither have you taken any thought for the morrow, but you have cast all your care upon God.'   *IV,1834f*

Lent

Ash Wednesday

A reading from 'The Remembrance of the Desire of a Soul', by Thomas of Celano.

While the holy father Francis was staying at San Damiano, he was pestered by the superior with repeated requests that he should present the word of God to his spiritual daughters, and he finally gave in to his insistence. The Ladies gathered as usual to hear the word of God, but no less to see their father, and he raised his eyes to heaven, where he always had his heart, and began to pray to Christ. Then he had ashes brought and made a circle with them round himself on the floor, and then put the rest on his own head.

As they waited, the blessèd father remained in silence within the circle of ashes, and real amazement grew in their hearts. Suddenly he got up and, to their great surprise, recited the 'Have mercy on me, God', instead of a sermon. As he finished it, he left quickly. The handmaids of God were so filled with contrition by the power of this mime that they were flowing with tears and could hardly restrain their hands from punishing themselves. By his action, he taught them to consider themselves ashes, and that nothing else was close to his heart except what was in keeping with that view. *II,379f*

Thursday after Ash Wednesday

A reading from 'The Earlier Rule of Saint Francis'.

Whenever it pleases them, all my brothers can announce this or similar exhortation and praise among all peoples with the blessing of God:

> Fear and honour,
> praise and bless,
> give thanks and adore
> the Lord God Almighty in Trinity and in Unity,
> Father, Son and Holy Spirit,
> the Creator of all.
> Do penance,
> performing worthy fruits of penance
> because we shall soon die.

Give and it will be given to you.
Forgive and you shall be forgiven.
If you do not forgive people their sins,
the Lord will not forgive you yours.
Confess all your sins.
Blessèd are those who die in penance,
for they shall be in the kingdom of heaven.
Woe to those who do not die in penance,
for they shall be children of the devil
whose works they do
and they shall go into everlasting fire.
Beware of and abstain from every evil
and persevere in good till the end.   *I,78*

Friday after Ash Wednesday

A reading from the 'Earlier Exhortation [of Saint Francis] to the Brothers and Sisters of Penance'.

In the name of the Lord!

All those who love the Lord with their whole heart, with their whole soul and mind, with their whole strength, and love their neighbours as themselves, who hate their bodies with their vices and sins, who receive the Body and Blood of our Lord Jesus Christ, and who produce worthy fruits of penance: O how happy and blessèd are these men and women while they do such things and persevere in doing them, because the Spirit of the Lord will rest upon them and make its home and dwelling place among them, and they are children of the heavenly Father whose works they do, and they are spouses, brothers and mothers of our Lord Jesus Christ.

We are spouses when the faithful soul is joined by the Holy Spirit to our Lord Jesus Christ. We are brothers to him when we do the will of the Father who is in heaven. We are mothers when we carry him in our heart and body through a divine love and a pure and sincere conscience and give birth to him through a holy activity which must shine as an example before others.

O how glorious it is to have a holy and great Father in heaven! O how holy and consoling to have such a beautiful and wonderful Spouse! O how holy and loving, gratifying, humbling, peace-giving, sweet, worthy of love and, above all things, desirable, to have such a Brother and such a

Son, our Lord Jesus Christ, who laid down his life for his sheep and prayed to his Father, saying:
'Bless and sanctify them; I sanctify myself for them. I pray not only for them, but for those who will believe in me through their word that they might be sanctified in being one as we are. Amen.'   *I,41f*

Saturday after Ash Wednesday

A reading from the 'Earlier Exhortation [of Saint Francis] to the Brothers and Sisters of Penance'.

All those men and women who are not living in penance, who do not receive the Body and Blood of our Lord Jesus Christ, who practice vice and sin and walk after the evil concupiscence and the evil desires of their flesh, who do not observe what they have promised to the Lord, and who in their body serve the world through the desires of the flesh, the concerns of the world and the cares of this life: they are held captive by the devil, whose children they are, and whose works they do. They are blind because they do not see the true light, our Lord Jesus Christ. They do not possess spiritual wisdom because they do not have the Son of God, the true wisdom of the Father. It is said of them: 'Their wisdom has been swallowed up' and 'Cursed are those who turn away from your commands.' They see and acknowledge, know and do evil, and knowingly lose their souls.

In the love which is God, we beg all those whom these words reach to receive those fragrant words of our Lord Jesus Christ written above with divine love and kindness. And let whoever does not know how to read have them read to them frequently. Because they are spirit and life, they should preserve them together with a holy activity to the end.

And whoever has not done these things will be held accountable before the tribunal of our Lord Jesus Christ on the day of judgement.   *I,43f*

The First Sunday of Lent

Lent 1 — Sunday

A reading from 'The Life of Saint Francis', by Thomas of Celano.

Day by day the blessèd father Francis was being filled with the consolation and the grace of the Holy Spirit and, with all vigilance and concern, he was forming his new sons with new instruction, teaching them to walk with steady steps the way of holy poverty and blessèd simplicity.

One day, he was marvelling at the Lord's mercy in the kindness shown to him. He wished that the Lord would show him the course of life for him and for his brothers, and he went to a place of prayer, as he so often did. He remained there a long time with fear and trembling before the Ruler of the whole earth. He recalled in the bitterness of his soul the years he had spent badly, frequently repeating the phrase, 'Lord, be merciful to me, a sinner.' Gradually, an indescribably joy and tremendous sweetness began to well up deep in his heart.

He began to lose himself;
his feelings were pressed together;
and that darkness disappeared
which fear of sin had gathered in his heart.
Certainty of the forgiveness of all his sins poured in
and the assurance of being revived in grace was given to him.
Then he was caught up above himself and totally engulfed in light
and, with his inmost soul opened wide,
he clearly saw the future.
As that sweetness and light withdrew,
renewed in spirit,
he now seemed to be changed into another man.   *1,205*

Lent 1 — Monday

A reading from the 'Later Admonition and Exhortation' of Saint Francis.

The Lord Jesus Christ wishes all of us to be saved through him and receive him with our heart pure and our body chaste. But, even though his yoke is easy and his burden light, there are few who wish to receive him and be saved through him. Those who do not wish to taste how sweet the Lord is and who love the darkness more than the light, not wishing to fulfil God's commands, are cursed; it is said of them by the prophet: 'Cursed are those who stray from your commands.'

But how happy and blessèd are those who love God and do as the Lord himself says in the gospel: 'You shall love the Lord your God with all your heart and all your mind, and your neighbour as yourself.' Let us love God, therefore, and adore him with a pure heart and a pure mind, because he who seeks this above all things has said: True adorers adore the Father in Spirit and Truth. For all who adore him must adore him in the Spirit of truth. And day and night let us direct praises and prayers to him, saying, 'Our Father in heaven ...' for we should pray always and not become weary.

We must, of course, confess all our sins to a priest and receive the Body and Blood of our Lord Jesus Christ from him. Whoever does not eat his flesh and drink his blood cannot enter the kingdom of God. But let him eat and drink worthily because anyone who receives unworthily, not distinguishing, that is, not discerning, the Body of the Lord, eats and drinks judgement on himself.   *I,46f*

Lent 1 — Tuesday

A reading from the 'Later Admonition and Exhortation' of Saint Francis.

Let us love our neighbours as ourselves. And if anyone does not want to love them as himself, let him at least not do them any harm, but let him do good.

Let whoever has received the power of judging others pass judgement with mercy, as they would wish to receive mercy from the Lord. For judgement will be without mercy for those who have not shown mercy.

Let us, therefore, have charity and humility and give alms because it washes the stains of our sins from our souls. For, although people lose everything they leave behind in this world, nevertheless, they carry with them the rewards of charity and the alms they have given, for which they will receive a reward and a fitting repayment from the Lord.

We must also fast and abstain from vices and sins and from an excess of food and drink and be Catholics.

We much also frequently visit churches and venerate and revere the clergy, not so much for themselves, if they are sinners, but because of their office and administration of the most holy Body and Blood of Christ which they sacrifice upon the altar, receive and administer to others. And let all of us know for certain that no one can be saved except through the holy words and Blood of our Lord Jesus Christ which the clergy pronounce, proclaim and minister. And they alone must minister and not others. Religious, however, who have left the world, are bound to do more and greater things, but not to overlook these.   *I,47f*

Lent 1 — Wednesday

A reading from the 'Later Admonition and Exhortation' of Saint Francis.

We must hate our bodies with their vices and sins because the Lord says in the gospel: 'All evils, vices and sins come from the heart.'

We must love our enemies and do good to those who hate us.

We must observe the commands and counsels of our Lord Jesus Christ.

We must also deny ourselves and place our bodies under the yoke of servitude and holy obedience as each one has promised to the Lord. And let no one be bound to obey another in anything in which a crime or sin would be committed. Instead, let the one to whom obedience has been entrusted and who is considered the greater be the lesser and the servant of the other brothers. And let him have and show mercy to each of his brothers as he would want them to do to him were he is a similar position. Let him not become angry at the fault of a brother but, with all patience and humility, let him admonish and support him.

We must not be wise and prudent according to the flesh but, instead, we must be simple, humble and pure. And let us hold our bodies in scorn and contempt because, through our own fault, we are all wretched and corrupt, disgusting and worms, as the Lord says through the prophet: 'I am a worm and no man, the scorn of men and the outcast of the people.'

We must never desire to be above others but, instead, we must be servants and subjects to every human creature, for God's sake.

And the Spirit of the Lord will rest upon all those men and women who have done and persevered in these things, and the Spirit will make a home and dwelling place in them. And they will be the children of the heavenly Father, whose works they do. And they are spouses, brothers and mothers of our Lord Jesus Christ.   *I,48f*

Lent 1 — Thursday

A reading from the 'Later Admonition and Exhortation' of Saint Francis.

See, you blind ones, deceived by your enemies, that is, the flesh, the world and the devil; for it is sweet for the body to commit sin and bitter to serve God, because every evil, vice and sin flow and proceed from people's hearts, as the Lord says in the gospel. And you have nothing in this world or in that to come. You think you possess the vanities of the world for a long time, but you are deceived, because a day and an hour are coming of which you do not think, do not know and are not aware.

The body becomes weak, death approaches, relatives and friends come saying, 'Put your affairs in order.' Look, his wife and children, relatives and friends pretend to cry. Glancing about, he sees them weeping and is moved by an evil impulse. He says, thinking to himself, 'See, I place my soul and body, all that I have in your hands.' In fact, they are cursed who entrust and place their souls and bodies and all they have in such hands; for, as the Lord says through the prophet, 'Cursed are they who trust in another.'

And immediately they make a priest come. The priest says to him, 'Do you want to receive penance for all your sins?' 'I do,' he responds. 'Do you wish to make satisfaction, as far as you can, out of your wealth, for what you have done and the ways in which you have cheated and deceived people?' 'No,' he responds. 'Why not?', the priest asks. 'Because I have placed everything in the hands of my relatives and friends.' And the wretched man begins to lose his speech, and so dies.

I.50f

Lent 1 — Friday

A reading from the 'Later Admonition and Exhortation' of Saint Francis.

Let everyone know that whenever and however someone dies in mortal sin without making amends when he could have done so and did not, the devil snatches his soul from his body with such anguish and distress that no one can know what it is like except the one experiencing it.

And every talent and power and knowledge that he thought he had will be taken away from him. And he leaves his relatives and friends and they take and divide the wealth and afterwards they say, 'Let his soul be cursed because he could have given us more and acquired more than he distributed to us!' Worms eat his body and so he loses his body and soul in this brief world and goes to hell, where he will be tortured without end.

In the name of the Father and of the Son and of the Holy Spirit. Amen.

I, brother Francis, your lesser servant, with a wish to kiss your feet, beg and implore you in the love that is God, to receive, to put into practice and to observe, as you should, these words and the others of our Lord Jesus Christ, with humility and love. And may the Father and the Son and the Holy Spirit bless all those men and women who receive them with kindness, understand them and send copies of them to others, if they have persevered to the end in them. Amen. *I,51*

Lent 1 — Saturday

A reading from 'A Letter to the Rulers of the Peoples', by Saint Francis.

Brother Francis, your little and looked-down-upon servant in the Lord God, wishes health and peace to all mayors and consuls, magistrates and governors throughout the world and to all others to whom these words may come.

Reflect and see that the day of death is approaching. With all possible respect, therefore, I beg you not to forget the Lord because of this world's cares and preoccupations and not to turn away from his commandments, for all those who leave him in oblivion and turn away from his commandments are cursed and will be left in oblivion by him.

When the day of death does come, everything they think they have shall be taken from them. The wiser and more powerful they may have been in this world, the greater will be the punishment they will endure in hell.

Therefore I strongly advise you, my Lords, to put aside all care and pre-occupation and receive the most holy Body and Blood of our Lord Jesus Christ with fervour, in holy remembrance of him. May you foster such honour to the Lord among the people entrusted to you that, every evening, an announcement may be made by a messenger, or some other sign, that praise and thanksgiving may be given by all people to the all-powerful Lord God. If you do not do this, know that, on the day of judgement, you must render an account before the Lord your God, Jesus Christ.

Let those who keep this writing with them and observe it know that they will be blessed by the Lord God. *I,58f*

The Second Sunday of Lent

Lent 2 — Sunday

A reading from 'The Life of Saint Francis', by Thomas of Celano.

The man of God, the blessèd Francis,
had been taught not to seek his own salvation,
but what he discerned would help the salvation of others.
More than anything else he desired
to be set free to be with Christ.
Thus his chief object of concern
was to live free from all things that are in the world,
so that his inner serenity would not be disturbed
even for a moment
by contact with any of its dust.
He made himself insensible to all outside noise,
gathering his external senses into his inner being
and checking the impetus of his spirit,
he emptied himself for God alone.

In the clefts of the rock he would build his nest
and in the hollow of the wall his dwelling.
With blessèd devotion he visited the heavenly mansions;
and, totally emptied of himself,
he rested for a long time in the wounds of the Saviour.
That is why he often chose solitary places
to focus his heart entirely on God.

But he was not reluctant,
when he discerned the time was right,
to involve himself in the affairs of his neighbours,
and attend to their salvation.
For his safest haven was prayer;
not prayer of a fleeting moment, empty and proud,
but prayer that was prolonged,
full of devotion, peaceful in humility.
If he began at night,
he was barely finished in the morning.
Walking, sitting, eating, drinking,
he was focussed on prayer.

He would spend the night alone praying
in abandoned churches and in deserted places
where,
with the protection of divine grace,
he overcame his soul's many fears and anxieties.   *I,243f*

Lent 2 — Monday

A reading from 'The Remembrance of the Desire of a Soul', by Thomas of Celano.

Francis celebrated the canonical Hours with no less awe than devotion. Although he was suffering from diseases of the eyes, stomach, spleen and liver, he did not want to lean against a wall or partition when he was chanting the psalms. He always fulfilled his Hours standing up straight and without a hood, without letting his eyes wander and without dropping syllables.

When he was travelling the world on foot, he always would stop walking in order to say the Hours, and when he was on horseback he would dismount to be on the ground. So, one day when he was returning from Rome and it was raining constantly, he got off his horse to say the Office and, standing for quite a while, he became completely soaked. He would sometimes say, 'If the body calmly eats its food, which along with itself will be food for worms, the soul should receive its food, which is its God, in great peace and tranquility.'   *II,311*

Lent 2 — Tuesday

A reading from 'The Remembrance of the Desire of a Soul', by Thomas of Celano.

When Francis returned from his private prayers, in which he was changed almost into a different man, he tried his best to resemble the others; lest, if he appeared glowing, the breeze of favour might cancel what he had gained.

Often he would say to those close to him, 'When a servant of God is praying, and is visited by the Lord in some new consolation, he should lift his eyes up to heaven before he comes away from prayer, fold his hands and say to the Lord, "Lord, you have sent this sweetness and consolation from heaven to me, an unworthy sinner, and I send it back to you so that you may save it for me, because I am a thief of your treasure." And also, "Lord, take away your gift from me in this world and keep it for me in the next." This is the way it should be,' he said. 'When one comes away from prayer he should appear to others a poor sinner, who had not obtained any new grace.' He also used to say, 'It happens that one loses something priceless for the sake of a small reward and may easily provoke the giver not to give again.'

Finally, his custom was to be so secret and quiet in rising for prayer that none of his companions would notice his rising or praying. But in the evening, he made a good loud noise in going to bed, so that everyone would hear him as he went to rest. *II,312f*

Lent 2 — Wednesday

A reading from 'The Remembrance of the Desire of a Soul', by Thomas of Celano.

Once, the abbot of the monastery of San Giustino in the diocese of Perugia happened to meet Saint Francis and, quickly dismounting from his horse, conversed for a short time with him about the salvation of his soul. Finally, as he left him, he humbly asked him to pray for him, and Saint Francis replied, 'My lord, I will willingly pray.' Now, when the abbot had ridden away a short distance, the saint said to his companion, 'Wait for me a little while, brother, for I want to pay that debt I promised.' For this was always his custom, that when he had a request for prayer he never did toss it behind his back but rather fulfilled his promise quickly. As the saint entreated God, the abbot suddenly felt in spirit unusual warmth and sweetness like nothing he had felt before, and carried into ecstasy, he seemed to faint away. This lasted for a short time and then he returned to his senses and realized the power of Saint Francis' prayer. From that time on, he always burned with even greater love for the Order, and told many about this miraculous event.

These small gifts are the kind
that servants of God should give each other;
among them,
this is the proper communion of giving and receiving.
This holy love, sometimes called 'spiritual',
is content with the fruit of prayer:
charity holds earthly gifts in low esteem.
To help and be helped in spiritual warfare,
to commend and be commended

before Christ's judgement seat,
that is what I believe is characteristic of holy love.
How far do you think Francis rose in prayer,
if he could raise up someone else this way by his merits? *II,313f*

Lent 2 — Thursday

A reading from 'The Legend of Saint Clare'.

Truly dead to the flesh, Clare was thoroughly a stranger to the world, continually occupying her soul with sacred prayers and divine praises. She had already focused the most fervent attention of her entire desire on the Light and she opened more generously the depths of her mind to the torrents of grace that bathe a world of turbulent change.

Clare would pray with the sisters for long periods of time after compline and the torrents of tears that burst forth in her excited them in others. But after the others went to their hard beds to rest their tired bodies, she remained in prayer, thoroughly vigilant and invincible, so that she could then secretly receive the divine whispers while sleep occupied the others. Very frequently while she was prostrate on her face in prayer, she flooded the ground with tears and caressed it with kisses, so that she might always seem to have her Jesus in her hands, on whose feet her tears flowed and her kisses were impressed.

Once in the depth of night, while she was sleeping, an angel of darkness stood by her in the form of a child and warned her, saying, 'You should not cry so much because you will become blind.' But when she replied immediately, 'Whoever sees God will not be blind,' he departed confused. That same night, after matins, while Clare was praying, bathed as usual in a stream of tears, the deceitful admonisher approached. 'You should not cry so much,' he said, 'otherwise your brain will dissolve and flow through your nose, because you will have a crooked nose.' To which she responded quickly, 'Whoever knows the Lord suffers nothing that is twisted.' Immediately he fled and vanished. *V,273*

Lent 2 — Friday

A reading from 'The Assisi Compilation'.

Once, when blessèd Francis was at [Saint Mary of the Angels], he stayed at prayer in the cell that was in the back, behind the house. One day while he was staying in it, the Bishop of Assisi came to see him. It happened that as he came into the house, he knocked on the door to approach blessèd Francis. He opened the door himself, and immediately entered the cell in which there was another small cell made of mats where blessèd Francis stayed. And because he knew that the holy father treated him with friendliness and love, he entered without hesitation, and opened for himself the little cell of mats to see him. As he quickly put his head inside the little cell, all of a sudden, by the will of the Lord, because he was not worthy to see him, he was forcefully pushed outside, willy-nilly, stumbling backwards. He immediately came outside the cell, trembling and stunned, and told the brothers his fault, and said he was sorry for coming there that day. *II,152f*

Lent 2 — Saturday

A reading from 'The Book of the Blessèd Angela of Foligno'.

We have not said anything yet about how the soul grants hospitality to God. Everything we have said thus far comes nowhere near to expressing what the soul knows when it grants hospitality to the Pilgrim.

When my soul knows that it has given hospitality to the Pilgrim, it reaches such a level of understanding of the goodness of God, indeed of his infinite goodness, that when I return to myself, I know with the utmost certainty that the more one feels God, the less is one able to say anything about him, for the very fact of feeling something of this infinite and unutterable Good renders one incapable of speaking about it.

Would that when you go to preach you could understand, as I understood when I knew I had given hospitality to the Pilgrim. For then you would be absolutely unable to say anything about God, and neither could anyone else. Then I would like to come to you and tell you, 'Brother, say something to me, now, about God.' And you would not be able to say anything at all or come up with any thought about God, his infinite goodness being so far beyond anything you could possibly say or think. In this state, I must add, the soul does not lose its self-awareness or the body the use of any of its senses; rather, one is in complete possession of oneself. And thus if you had attained this state, you would then say to the people with total self-assurance, 'Go with God, because about God I can say nothing.' *X,191f*

The Third Sunday of Lent

Lent 3 — Sunday

A reading from 'The Later Rule of Saint Francis'.

Let the brothers fast from the feast of All Saints until the Lord's Nativity.
May those be blessed by the Lord who fast voluntarily during that holy
Lent that begins at the Epiphany and lasts during the forty days which
our Lord consecrated for his own fast; but those who do not wish to
keep it will not be obliged. Let them fast, however, during the other Lent
until the Lord's Resurrection. At other times, they may not be bound to
fast except on Fridays. During a time of obvious need, however, the
brothers may not be bound by corporal fast.

I counsel, admonish and exhort my brothers in the Lord Jesus Christ
not to quarrel or argue or judge others when they go about in the world;
but let them be meek, peaceful, modest, gentle and humble, speaking
courteously to everyone, as is becoming. They should not ride horseback
unless they are compelled by an obvious need or an infirmity. Into whatever house they enter, let them first say, 'Peace be to this house!'
According to the holy gospel, let them eat whatever food is set before
them.   *I,101f*

Lent 3 — Monday

A reading from 'The Little Flowers of Saint Francis'.

Once, Saint Francis was alongside the Lake of Perugia on the day of the
Carnival, at the house of a man devoted to him, where he was lodged for
the night. He was inspired by God to go to make that Lent on an island
in the lake. So Saint Francis asked this devout man that, for love of
Christ, he carry him with his little boat to an island of the lake where no
one lived, and that he do this on the night of the Day of Ashes, so that
no one would notice. And this man, out of love – from the great
devotion he had for Saint Francis – promptly fulfilled his request and
carried him to that island. And Saint Francis took nothing with him
except two small loaves of bread. Arriving at the island, as his friend was
departing to return home, Saint Francis asked him kindly not to reveal to
anyone that he was there, and that he should not come for him until Holy
Thursday. And so the man departed, and Saint Francis remained alone.
Since there was no dwelling in which he could take shelter, he went

into some very thick brush that was formed like a little den or a little hut by many bushes and saplings. And in this place he put himself in prayer and contemplation of heavenly things. And there he stayed the whole of Lent without eating or drinking, except for half of one of those little loaves, as his devoted friend found on Holy Thursday when he returned for him; for of the two loaves he found one whole one and one half; the other half, it is supposed, Saint Francis ate, out of reverence for the fast of the blessèd Christ, who fasted for forty days and forty nights without taking any material food. And thus, with that half of a loaf, he drove away from himself vainglory, and after the example of Christ he fasted forty days and forty nights. *III,578f*

Lent 3 — Tuesday

A reading from 'The Assisi Compilation'.

Blessèd Francis stayed in the hermitage of the brothers at Fonte Colombo near Rieti, because of the disease of his eyes. One day, the eye doctor of that city visited him and stayed with him for some hours, as he often used to do. When he was ready to leave, blessèd Francis said to one of his companions, 'Go and give the doctor a good meal.' 'Father,' his companion answered, 'we are ashamed to say that, because we are poor now, we would be ashamed to invite him and give him anything to eat.' Blessèd Francis told his companions, 'O you of little faith! Do not make me tell you again!'

The doctor said to blessèd Francis and his companions, 'Brother, it is because the brothers are so poor that I am happy to eat with them.' The doctor was very rich and, although blessèd Francis and his companions had often invited him, he had refused to eat there.

The brothers went and set the table. With embarrassment, they placed the little bread and wine they had, as well as a few greens they had prepared for themselves.

When they had sat down at the table and eaten a bit, there was a knock at the door of the hermitage. One of the brothers arose, went, and opened the door. And there was a woman with a large basket filled with beautiful bread, fish, crabcakes, honey and freshly-picked grapes, which had been sent to brother Francis by a lady of the town about seven miles away from the hermitage.

After they saw this and considered the holiness of blessèd Francis, the brothers and the doctor were greatly amazed. 'My brothers,' the doctor said to them, 'neither you nor we sufficiently recognize the holiness of this saint.'   *II,171*

Lent 3 — Wednesday

A reading from 'The Assisi Compilation'.

Once, at the very beginning, that is, at the time when blessèd Francis began to have brothers, he was staying with them at Rivo Torto. One night, around midnight, when they were all asleep in their beds, one of the brothers cried out, saying, 'I am dying! I am dying!' Startled and frightened, all the brothers woke up.

Getting up, blessèd Francis said, 'Brothers, get up and light a lamp.' After the lamp was lit, blessèd Francis said, 'Who was it who said "I am dying"?'

'I am the one,' the brother answered.

'What is the matter, brother?', blessèd Francis said to him. 'Why are you dying?'

'I am dying of hunger,' he answered.

So that brother would not be ashamed to eat alone, blessèd Francis, a man of great charity and discernment, immediately had the table set and they all ate together with him. This brother, as well as the others, were newly converted to the Lord and afflicted their bodies excessively.

After the meal, blessèd Francis said to the other brothers, 'My brothers, I say that each of you must consider his own constitution, because, although one of you may be sustained with less food than another, I still do not want one who needs more food to try imitating him in this. Rather, considering his constitution, he should provide his body with what it needs. Just as we must be aware of over-indulgence in eating, which harms body and soul, so we must beware of excessive abstinence even more, because the Lord desires mercy and not sacrifice.'

And he said, 'Dearest brothers, great necessity and charity compelled me to do what I did, namely that, out of love for our brother, we ate together with him, so he would not be embarrassed to eat alone. But I tell you, in the future, I do not wish to act this way because it would not be religious or decent. Let each one provide his body with what it needs as our poverty will allow. This is what I wish and command you.'

II,149f

Lent 3 — Thursday

A reading from 'The Assisi Compilation'.

Once, Francis was staying in a hermitage for the Lent of Saint Martin. Because of his illness, the brothers cooked the food they gave him to eat in lard, because oil was very bad for him in his illnesses. When the forty days had ended, and he was preaching to a large crowd of people, gathered not far from that hermitage, in the opening words of his sermon he told them, 'You came to me with great devotion and believe me to be a holy man. But I confess to God and to you that, during this Lent, in that hermitage, I have eaten food flavoured with lard.'

Indeed, if the brothers or the friends of the brothers, with whom he would eat, occasionally prepared a special dish for him because of his illnesses or the obvious need of his body, it frequently happened that he would immediately tell this to the brothers or lay people who did not know about it, whether inside the house or outside, saying publicly, 'I ate such and such foods.' He did not wish to conceal from people what was known to God.

Moreover, if his soul were ever tempted to vainglory, pride or any vice, no matter where he was, or in whose presence, whether they be Religious or lay, he would immediately and openly confess it to them, without concealing anything. This is why he told his companions one day, 'I want to live before God, in hermitages and other places where I stay, just as the people see and know me. If they believe that I am a holy man and do not lead a life becoming a holy man, I would be a hypocrite.'   *II,182f*

Lent 3 — Friday

A reading from 'The Third Letter of Saint Clare to Blessèd Agnes of Prague'.

Now concerning those matters that you have asked me to clarify for you: which are the specific feasts our most glorious father Saint Francis urged us to celebrate in a special way by a change of food – feasts of which, I believe, you already have some knowledge – I propose to respond to your love.

Your prudence should know, then, that except for the weak and the sick, for whom Saint Francis advised and admonished us to show every possible discretion in matters of food, none of us who are healthy and strong should eat anything other than Lenten fare, either on ferial days or on feast days. Thus, we must fast every day except Sundays and the Nativity of the Lord, on which days we may have two meals. And on ordinary Thursdays everyone may do as she wishes, so that she who does not wish to fast is not obliged. However, we who are well should fast every day except on Sundays and on Christmas.

During the entire Easter week, as the writing of Saint Francis tells us, and on the feasts of the Blessèd Virgin Mary and of the holy Apostles, we are not obliged to fast, unless these feasts occur on a Friday. And, as I have already said, let we who are well and strong always eat Lenten fare.

But our flesh is not bronze nor is our strength that of stone. No, we are frail and inclined to every bodily weakness! I beg you, therefore, dearly belovèd, to refrain wisely and prudently from an indiscreet and impossible austerity in the fasting that you have undertaken. And I beg you in the Lord to praise the Lord by your very life, to offer the Lord your reasonable service and your sacrifice always seasoned with salt.

May you do well in the Lord, as I hope I myself do. And remember me and my sisters in your prayers.   *V,47f*

Lent 3 — Saturday

A reading from 'The Acts of the Process of Canonization' of Saint Clare.

This witness also said the blessèd mother Clare kept vigil so much of the night in prayer, and kept so many abstinences that the sisters lamented and were alarmed. She said that because of this she herself had sometimes wept.

Asked how she knew this, she replied: because she saw when Lady Clare lay on the ground and had a rock from the river for her head, and heard her when she was in prayer.

She said she was so very strict in her food that the sisters marvelled at how her body survived. She also said blessèd Clare fasted much of the time. Three days of the week, Monday, Wednesday, and Friday, she did not eat anything. She said on other days she kept such abstinences she developed a certain illness so Saint Francis together with the Bishop of Assisi commanded her to eat on those three days at least a half a roll of bread, about one and a half ounces.

She also said the blessèd mother was assiduous and careful in her prayers, lying a long time upon the ground, remaining humbly prostrate. When she came from her prayer, she admonished and comforted her sisters always speaking the words of God who was always in her mouth, so much so that she did not want to speak or hear of vanities.

When she returned from her prayer, the sisters rejoiced as though she had come from heaven.

Asked how she knew these things, she replied she lived with her.

V,138

The Fourth Sunday of Lent

Lent 4 — Sunday

A reading from 'The Remembrance of the Desire of a Soul', by Thomas of Celano.

What tongue could
tell of this man's compassion for the poor?
He certainly had an inborn kindness,
doubled by the piety poured out on him.
Therefore,
the soul of Francis melted for the poor,
and to those to whom he could not extend a hand,
he extended his affection.
Any need,
any lack he noticed in anyone,
with a rapid change of thought, he turned back to Christ.
In that way
he read the Son of our Poor Lady in every poor person.
As she held him naked in her hands
so he carried him naked in his heart.
Although he had driven away all envy from himself,
he could not give up his envy of poverty.
If he saw people poorer than himself,
he immediately envied them and,
contending with a rival for poverty
was afraid he would be overcome.

It happened one day when the man of God was going about preaching he met a poor man on the road. Seeing the man's nakedness, he was deeply moved and, turning to his companion said, 'This man's need brings great shame on us; it passes a harsh judgement on our poverty.' 'How so, brother?' his companion replied. The saint answered in a sad voice, 'I chose Poverty for my riches and for my Lady, but look: she shines brighter in this man. Do you not know that the whole world has heard that we are the poorest of all for Christ? But this poor man proves it is otherwise!' *II,302*

Lent 4 — Monday

A reading from 'The Legend of the Three Companions'.

[When Francis was still a young man living with his parents], although he had been for some time a benefactor of the poor, he proposed in his heart never to deny alms to any poor person begging from him for God's sake, but rather to give more willingly and abundantly than usual. When away from home, if he could, he always gave money to any poor person requesting alms. If he had no money, he gave him his hat or belt, making sure never to send him away empty-handed. If he lacked even these things, he would go to a deserted place, take off his shirt, and give it to the poor man, begging him to take it for the love of God. He would even purchase furnishings for adorning churches, and would secretly send them to poor priests.

When his father was away and he was at home alone with his mother, although only two of them took their meals, he filled the table with loaves of bread as if he were preparing for an entire family. When his mother asked why he put so much food on the table, he answered that it would be given as alms for the poor, since he had resolved to give to anyone begging alms for God's sake. Because his mother loved him more than the other children, she tolerated him in such matters, noticing the things he did and admiring in his heart many more. For his whole heart was intent on seeing the poor, listening to them, and giving them alms. *II,72f*

Lent 4 — Tuesday

A reading from 'The Assisi Compilation'.

When blessèd Francis went to a hermitage of the brothers near Rocca di Brizio to preach to the people of that region, it happened that on the very day that he was to preach, a poor sick man came to him. When he saw him and noticed his poverty and illness, he was moved to piety for him and he began to speak to his companion about the man's nakedness and illness. 'It is true, brother,' his companion said to him, 'that he is poor, but perhaps there is no one in the whole province who desires riches more.'

Blessèd Francis rebuked him for not speaking well and he admitted his fault. Blessèd Francis told him, 'Do you want to do the penance I will tell you?' 'Willingly' he replied. 'Go, strip off your tunic,' he said, 'and go to that poor man naked, throw yourself at his feet, and tell him how you sinned against him, how you slandered him, and ask him to pray for you that God may forgive you.'

So he went and did everything blessèd Francis had told him. When he finished, he got up, put on his tunic, and returned to blessèd Francis. And blessèd Francis said to him, 'Do you want me to tell you how you sinned against him, and even against Christ?'

And he said, 'Whenever you see a poor person you ought to consider him in whose name he comes, that is, Christ, who came to take on our poverty and weakness. This man's poverty and weakness is a mirror for us in which we should see and consider lovingly the poverty and weakness of our Lord Jesus Christ which he endured in his body for the salvation of the human race.'   *II,220f*

Lent 4 — Wednesday

A reading from 'The Remembrance of the Desire of a Soul', by Thomas of Celano.

Once when blessèd Francis was coming back from Siena he met a poor man, and the saint said to his companion, 'Brother, we must give back to this poor man the mantle that is his. We accepted in on loan until we should happen to find someone poorer than we are.' The companion, seeing the need of his pious father, stubbornly objected that he should not provide for someone else by neglecting himself. But the saint said to him, 'I do not want to be a thief; we will be accused of theft if we do not give to someone in greater need.' So his companion gave in, and he gave up the mantle.

A similar thing happened at 'Le Celle' of Cortona. Blessèd Francis was wearing a new mantle which the brothers had gone to some trouble to find for him. A poor man came to the place weeping for his dead wife and his poor little family which was left desolate. The saint said to him, 'I'm giving you this cloak for the love of God, but on the condition that you do not hand it over to anyone unless they pay well for it.' The brothers immediately came running to take the mantle away and prevent this donation. But the poor man, taking courage from the father's look, clutched it with both hands and defended it as his own. In the end the brothers had to redeem the mantle, and the poor man left after getting his price. *II,304f*

Lent 4 — Thursday

A reading from 'The Remembrance of the Desire of a Soul', by Thomas of Celano.

In Celano in winter time Saint Francis was wearing a piece of folded cloth as a cloak, which a man from Tivoli, a friend of the brothers, had lent him. While he was at the palace of the Bishop of the Marsi, an old woman came up to him begging for alms. He quickly unfastened the cloth from his neck, and, although it belonged to someone else, he gave it to the poor old woman, saying, 'Go and make yourself a tunic; you really need it.' The old woman laughed; she was stunned – I do not know if it was out of fear or joy – and took the piece of cloth from his hands. She ran off quickly, so that delay might not bring the danger of having to give it back, and cut it with scissors. But when she saw that the cut cloth would not be enough for a tunic, she returned to the saint, knowing his earlier kindness, and showed him that the material was not enough. The saint turned his eyes on his companion, who had just the same cloth covering his back. 'Brother,' he said, 'do you hear what this old woman is saying? For the love of God, let us bear with the cold! Give the poor woman the cloth so she can finish her tunic.' He gave his, the companion offered his as well, and both were left naked so the old woman could be clothed.

With the same fervour, as he was going through the city of Assisi, another old woman met him and asked him for something. As he had nothing except his mantle, he offered it with quick generosity. But then he felt an impulse of empty congratulations, and at once he confessed before everyone that he felt vainglory. *II,304,333*

Lent 4 — Friday

A reading from 'The Remembrance of the Desire of a Soul,' by Thomas of Celano.

The mother of two of the brothers once came to the saint, confidently asking for alms. Sharing her pain the holy father said to Brother Peter of Catanio, 'Can we give some alms to our mother?' He used to call the mother of any brother his mother and the mother of all the brothers.

Brother Peter replied, 'There is nothing left in the house which we could give her.' Then he added, 'We do have one New Testament, for reading the lessons at matins, since we do not have a breviary.' Blessèd Francis said to him, 'Give our mother the New Testament so she can sell it to care for her needs, for through it we are reminded to help the poor. I believe that God will be pleased more by the giving than by the reading.' So the book was given to the woman, and the first Testament in the Order was given away through this sacred piety.   *II,306*

Lent 4 — Saturday

A reading from 'The Remembrance of the Desire of a Soul,' by Thomas of Celano.

At the time when Saint Francis was staying at the palace of the Bishop of Rieti to be treated for his eye disease, a poor woman from Machilone who had the same disease as the saint came to see the doctor.

Then the saint, speaking familiarly to his Guardian, nudged him a bit, 'Brother Guardian, we have to give back what belongs to someone else.' And he answered, 'Father, if there is such a thing with us, let it be returned.' And he said, 'Yes, there is this mantle, which we received as a loan from that poor woman; we should give it back to her, because she has nothing in her purse for her expenses.' The Guardian replied, 'Brother, this mantle is mine, and nobody lent it to me! Use it as long as you like, and when you do not want to use it any longer, return it to me.' In fact the Guardian had recently bought it because Saint Francis needed it. The saint then said to him, 'Brother Guardian, you have always been courteous to me; now, I beg you, show your courtesy.' And the Guardian answered him, 'Do as you please, father, as the Spirit suggests to you.' The saint called a very devout layman and told him, 'Take this mantle and twelve loaves of bread, and go and say to that poor woman, "The poor man to whom you lent this mantle thanks you for the loan, but now take what is yours."' The man went and said what he was told, but the woman thought she was being mocked, and replied to him, all embarrassed, 'Leave me in peace, you and your mantle! I do not know what you are talking about!' The man insisted, and put it all in her hands. She saw that this was in fact no deception, but fearing that such an easy gain would be taken away from her, she left the place by night and returned home with the mantle, not caring about caring for her eyes.   *II,306f*

The Fifth Sunday of Lent

Lent 5 — Sunday

A reading from 'The Major Legend of Saint Francis', by Saint Bonaventure.

The man of God, Francis, gathered with his companions in an abandoned hut near the city of Assisi, where they kept themselves alive according to the pattern of holy poverty in much labour and want, drawing their nourishment more from the bread of tears than of delights.

They spent their time there praying incessantly, directing their effort mentally rather than vocally to devoted prayers, because they did not yet have liturgical books from which to chant the canonical Hours. In place of these they had the book of Christ's cross which they studied continually day and night, taught by the example and words of their father who spoke to them constantly about the cross of Christ.

When the brothers asked him to teach them to pray, he said, 'When you pray, say "Our Father ..." and "We adore you, O Christ, in all your churches throughout the whole world, and we bless you, for by your holy cross you have redeemed the world."' He also taught them to praise God in all and with all creatures, to honour priests with a special reverence, and to believe with certainty and to confess with simplicity the truth of the faith, as the holy Roman Church holds and teaches. They observed the holy father's teaching in every detail and prostrated themselves humbly before every church and crucifix which they were able to see from a distance, praying the formula he had taught them.   *II,551*

Lent 5 — Monday

A reading from 'The Assisi Compilation'.

Once, a few years after his conversion, blessèd Francis was walking alone one day along the road not too far from the church of Saint Mary of the Portiuncula, crying loudly and wailing as he went. As he was walking along, a spiritual man met him, someone we know and from whom we learned about this incident, who had shown him great mercy and consolation, both before he had any brothers and afterwards. Moved by piety towards him, he asked him, 'Brother, what's wrong?' He thought that blessèd Francis was suffering some painful illness. But he answered, 'I should go through the whole world this way, without any shame, crying

and bewailing the Passion of my Lord.' At this, the man began to weep
and cry aloud together with him.   *II,180f*

Lent 5 — Tuesday

A reading from 'A Mirror of the Perfection of a Lesser Brother'.

Intoxicated by love and compassion for Christ, blessèd Francis sometimes did this: a sweet melody of the spirit bubbling up inside him would
frequently become on the outside a French tune; the thread of a divine
whisper which his ears heard secretly would break out in a French song.

At other times, picking up a stick from the ground and putting it over
his left arm, he would draw another stick across it with his right hand like
a bow on a viola or some other instrument. Performing all the right
movements, he would sing in French about the Lord Jesus.

All of this dancing often ended in tears, and the cry of joy dissolved
into compassion for Christ's suffering. Then he would sigh without stop-
ping and sob without ceasing. Forgetful of what he was holding in his
hands, he was caught up to heaven.   *III,340*

Lent 5 — Wednesday

A reading from 'The Admonitions', by Saint Francis.

Consider in what great excellence the Lord God has placed you, for he
created and formed you to the image of his belovèd Son, according to the
body and to his likeness according to the Spirit.

And all creatures under heaven serve, know, and obey their Creator,
each according to its own nature, better than you. And even the demons
did not crucify him, but you, together with them, have crucified him and
are still crucifying him by delighting in vices and sins.

In what, then, can you boast? Even if you were so skilful and wise that
you possessed all knowledge, knew how to interpret every kind of language, and to scrutinize heavenly matters with skill: you could not boast
in these things. For, even though someone may have received from the
Lord a special knowledge of the highest wisdom, one demon knew about
heavenly matters and now knows more about those of earth than all
humanity.

In the same way, even if you were more handsome and richer than
everyone else, and even if you worked miracles so that you put demons
to flight: all these things are contrary to you; nothing belongs to you; you

can boast in none of these things.

But we can boast in our weaknesses and in carrying each day the holy cross of our Lord Jesus Christ. *I,131*

Lent 5 — Thursday

A reading from 'The Major Legend of Saint Francis', by Saint Bonaventure.

The man of God, Francis,
remaining more alone and at peace
would fill the forest with groans,
water the places with tears,
strike his breast with his hand,
and, as if finding a more secret hiding place,
would converse with his Lord.
There he replied to the Judge,
there he entreated the Father,
there he conversed with the Friend.
There too the brothers who were devoutly observing him
heard him on several occasions groan with loud cries,
imploring the divine clemency for sinners,
and weeping over the Lord's passion
as if it were before him.
There he was seen praying at night,
with his hands outstretched in the form of a cross,
his whole body lifted up from the ground
and surrounded by a sort of shining cloud,
so that the extraordinary illumination around his body
was a witness to the wonderful light that shone within his soul.
There too,
as is proven by certain evidence,
the unknown and hidden secrets of divine wisdom
were opened up to him,
although he never spoke of them outside
except when the love of Christ urged him
and the good of his neighbour demanded.
For he used to say,
'It happens that one loses something priceless
for the sake of a small reward,
and easily provokes the giver not to give again.' *II,607f*

Lent 5 — Friday

A reading from 'The Book of the Blessèd Angela of Foligno'.

Once I was at Vespers and was gazing at the cross. And while I was thus gazing at the cross with the eyes of the body, suddenly my soul was set ablaze with love; and every member of my body felt it with the greatest joy. I saw and felt that Christ was within me, embracing my soul with the very arm with which he was crucified. This took place right at the moment when I was gazing at the cross or shortly afterward. The joy that I experienced to be with him in this way and the sense of security that he gave me were far greater than I had ever been accustomed to.

Henceforth my soul remained in a state of joy in which it understood what this man, namely Christ, is like in heaven, that is to say, how we will see that through him our flesh is made one with God. This was a source of delight for my soul beyond words and description, and it was a joy that was abiding. From it I was left with such security that even if all that we have written were not true, there would not remain any doubt whatever in me that it was God at work in me and that, most certainly, he is responsible for this state. I was so completely certain that God was at work in me that even if everyone in the world were to say that I ought to doubt this, I would not believe them. This is why I am amazed now when I recall how I sought reassurance in the past and relief from my doubts, for now there can be no doubt whatever within me concerning the certainty that it was God at work.

My delight at the present is to see that hand which he shows me with the marks of the nails on it, and to hear him say, 'Behold what I have suffered for you and for others.' The joy which seizes my soul in this moment can in no way be spoken of. And in no way whatever can I be sad concerning the passion; on the contrary, my joy is in seeing this man, and to come to him. All my joy now is in this suffering God-man.

X,175f

Lent 5 — Saturday

A reading from 'The Legend of Saint Clare'.

Crying over the Lord's passion was well known to Clare.
At times she poured out feelings of bitter myrrh at the sacred wounds.
At times she imbibed sweeter joys.
The tears of the suffering Christ made her quite inebriated
and her memory continually pictured him

whom love had profoundly impressed upon her heart.

She taught the novices to weep over the crucified Christ and, at the same time, what she taught with her words, she expressed with her deeds. For frequently when she would encourage them in private in such matters, a flow of tears would come before the passage of her words.

During the Hours of the day, at Sext and None, she was usually afflicted with a greater sorrow as she was immolated with her immolated Lord.

Once, in fact, while she was praying None in her little cell, the devil struck her on the cheek, filled her eye with blood and her cheek with a bruise.

She repeated more frequently the Prayer of the Five Wounds of the Lord so that she might nourish her mind on the delights of the Crucified without any interruption. She learned the 'Office of the Cross' as Francis, a lover of the cross, had established it and recited it with similar affection. Underneath her habit she girded her flesh with a small cord marked with thirteen knots, a secret reminder of the wounds of the Saviour. *V,283*

Holy Week

Palm Sunday

A reading from 'The Major Legend of Saint Francis', by Saint Bonaventure.

Who would be competent to describe the burning charity
with which Francis, the friend of the Bridegroom, was aflame?
Like a thoroughly burning coal,
he seemed totally absorbed in the flame of the divine love.

Aroused by everything to divine love,
he rejoiced in all the works of the Lord's hands
and through their delightful display
he rose into their life-giving reason and cause.
In beautiful things he discerned Beauty itself
and through the footprints impressed in things
he followed his Belovèd everywhere,
out of them all making for himself a ladder
through which he could climb up to lay hold of him
who is utterly desirable.
With an intensity of unheard devotion
he savoured
in each and every creature
- as in so many rivulets –
that fontal Goodness,
and discerned
an almost celestial choir
in the chords of power and activity
given to them by God,
and, like the prophet David,
he sweetly encouraged them to praise the Lord.

Jesus Christ crucified
always rested like a bundle of myrrh in the bosom of his soul,
into whom
he longed to be totally transformed
through an enkindling of ecstatic love.
And as a sign of his special devotion to him,
he found leisure

from the feast of the Epiphany through forty successive days
- that period when Christ was hidden in the desert –
resting in a place of solitude,
shut up in a cell,
with as little food and drink as possible,
fasting, praying, and praising God without interruption.
He was borne aloft into Christ
with such burning intensity,
but the Belovèd repaid him with such intimate love
that it seemed to that servant of God
that he was aware
of the presence of the Saviour before his eyes.   *II,596f*

Monday in Holy Week

A reading from 'The Second Letter of Saint Clare to Blessèd Agnes of Prague'.

As a poor virgin,
  embrace the poor Christ.
Look upon him who became contemptible for you,
  and follow him, making yourself contemptible in this world for him.

Your Spouse, though more beautiful than all born in this world, became, for your salvation, the lowest of men, was despised, struck, scourged untold times throughout his entire body, and then died amid the suffering of the Cross.

O most noble Queen,
gaze upon him,
consider him,
contemplate him,
as you desire to imitate him.
If you suffer with him, you will reign with him.
If you weep with him, you shall rejoice with him.
If you die with him on the cross of tribulation,
  you shall possess heavenly mansions in the splendour of the saints
  and, in the Book of Life,
    your name shall be called glorious among all people.

Because of this you shall share always and forever the glory of the king-

dom of heaven in place of earthly and passing things, and everlasting
treasures instead of those that perish, and you shall live forever.   *V,42*

Tuesday in Holy Week

A reading from 'The Letter of Saint Clare to Ermentrude of Bruges'.

Be faithful, dearly belovèd, till death
   to him to whom you have promised yourself,
   for you shall be crowned by him with the garland of life.
Our labour here is brief, the reward eternal;
   may the excitements of the world,
   fleeing like a shadow,
   not disturb you.
May the false delights of the deceptive world not deceive you.
   Close your ears to the whisperings of hell
   and bravely oppose its onslaughts.
Gladly endure whatever goes against you
   and do not let your good fortunes lift you up:
   for these things destroy faith and those demand it.
Offer faithfully what you have vowed to God
   and he shall reward you.
Look to heaven that invites us, O dearly belovèd,
   and take up the cross and follow Christ
   who goes before us,
for through him
   we shall enter into his glory
   after many different trials.
Love God
   and Jesus, his Son, who was crucified for us sinners,
   from the depths of your heart,
   and never let the thought of him leave your mind.
Meditate constantly on the mysteries of the cross
   and the agonies of his mother standing at the foot of the cross.
Pray and always be vigilant.
The work you have begun well, complete immediately
   and the ministry you have assumed,
   fulfil in holy poverty and sincere humility.
Do not be afraid, daughter.
   God, who is faithful in all his words

and holy in all his deeds,
will pour his blessings upon you and your sisters;
and he will be your helper and the best consoler;
he is our redeemer and our eternal reward.
Let us pray to God for one another,
for by carrying each other's burden of charity in this way
we will easily fulfil the law of Christ.   *V,53ff*

Wednesday in Holy Week

A reading from 'The Book of the Blessèd Angela of Foligno'.

On Wednesday of Holy Week, I was meditating on the death of the Son
of God incarnate, and trying to empty my soul of everything else so I
could be more recollected in his passion and death. I had only one care,
only one desire, and that was to find the best way to empty my soul from
everything else in order to have a more vivid memory of the passion and
death of the Son of God.

Suddenly, while I was engrossed in this effort and desire, a divine word
sounded in my soul: 'My love for you has not been a hoax.' These words
struck me a mortal blow. For immediately the eyes of my soul were
opened and I saw that what he had said was true. I saw his acts of love,
everything that the Son of God had done, all that he had endured in life
and in death – this suffering God-man – because of his inexpressible and
visceral love. Seeing in him all the deeds of true love, I understood the
perfect truth of what he had said, that his love for me had not been a
hoax, but that he had loved me with a most perfect and visceral love. I
saw, on the other hand, the exact opposite in myself, because my love for
him had never been anything but playing games, never true. Being made
aware of this was a mortal blow and caused such intolerable pain that I
thought I would die.

I perceived all the signs and marks of the truest love in him; how he
had given himself wholly and totally to me, in order to serve me; how he
had come so close to me: he had become human in order to truly feel and
carry my sufferings in himself. When, on the other hand, I perceived the
exact opposite in me, I had such suffering and pain that I thought I
would die. I felt my ribs dislocate in my chest under the weight of my
pain, and it seemed as though my heart would burst.   *X,280f>*

Maundy Thursday

A reading from 'The Legend of Saint Clare'.

Once, the day of the most sacred supper arrived, in which the Lord loved his own until the end. Near evening, as the agony of the Lord was approaching, Clare, sad and afflicted, shut herself up in the privacy of her cell.

While in her own prayer she was accompanying the praying Saviour and when saddened even to death she experienced the effect of his sadness, she was filled at once with the memory of his capture and of the whole mockery and she sank down on her bed.

All that night and the following day, she was so absorbed that she remained out of her senses. She seemed to be joined to Christ and to be otherwise totally insensible, always focusing the light of her eyes on one thing.

A certain sister close to her often went to see if she might want something and always found her the same way. But with Friday night coming on, the devoted daughter lit a candle and, with a sign not a word, reminded her mother of the command of Saint Francis. For the saint had commanded her that no day should pass without some food. With that sister standing by, Clare, as if returning from another world, offered this word: 'What need is there for a candle? Is it not daytime?' 'Mother,' she replied, 'the night has gone and a day has passed, and another night has returned!' To which Clare said, 'May that vision be blessed, most dear daughter! Because after having desired it for so long, it has been given to me. But, be careful not to tell anyone about that vision while I am still in the flesh.'

V,284

Good Friday

A reading from 'The Office of the Passion', by Saint Francis.

I cried to the Lord with all my voice;
  with all my voice I begged the Lord.
I pour out my prayer in his sight
  and I tell the Lord of all my trouble.
When my spirit failed me
  you knew my ways.
On the path where I walked,
  the proud hid a trap for me.

I looked to my right and saw:
  there was no one who knew me.
I have no means of escape:
  there is no one who cares for my life.
I have borne abuse because of you
  and confusion covers my face.
I have become an outcast to my brothers,
  a stranger to the children of my mother.
Holy Father, zeal for your house has consumed me;
  and the insults of those who blasphemed you have fallen on me.
They rejoiced and united together against me.
  Blows were heaped on me and I knew not why.
More numerous than the hairs of my head
  are those who hate me without cause.
My enemies, who persecuted me unjustly, have been strengthened;
  I then repaid what I did not steal.
The wicked witnesses who rise up
  asked me about things of which they are ignorant.
They repaid me evil for good and harassed me
  because I pursued good.
You are my most holy Father
  my King and my God.
Come to my aid,
  Lord, God of my salvation.   *I,144f*

Easter Eve

A prayer used by Saint Francis.

I beg you, Lord,
let the glowing and honey-sweet force
of your love
draw my mind away
from all things
that are under heaven,
that I may die
for love of the love of you,
who thought it a worthy thing
to die
for love
of the love of me.   *III,190f*

Easter

Easter Day

'The praises of God', given to Brother Leo on Mount La Verna by Saint Francis.

You are holy, Lord God; you do wonderful things.
You are strong. You are great. You are the Most High.
  You are the almighty King. You, holy Father,
  King of heaven and earth.

You are three and one, the Lord God of gods;
  you are good, all good, the highest good,
  Lord God, living and true.

Your are love, charity; you are wisdom, you are humility,
  you are patience, you are beauty, you are meekness,
  you are security, you are rest,
  you are gladness and joy, you are our hope, you are justice,
  you are moderation, you are all our riches to sufficiency.

You are beauty, you are meekness,
  you are the protector, you are our custodian and defender,
  you are strength, you are refreshment. You are our hope,
  you are our faith, you are our charity,
  you are all our sweetness, you are our eternal life:
  great and wonderful Lord, Almighty God, Merciful Saviour.

I,109

Monday in Easter Week

A reading from 'The Office of the Passion' of Saint Francis.

All you nations clap your hands
  shout to God with a voice of gladness.
For the Lord, the Most High,
  the Awesome, is the Great King over all the earth.
For the Most Holy Father of heaven, our King before all ages,
  sent his Belovèd Son from on high
  and has brought salvation in the midst of the earth.
Let the heavens rejoice and the earth exult

let the sea and all that is in it be moved
let the fields and all that is in them be glad.
Sing a new song to him;
sing to the Lord all the earth.
Because the Lord is great and highly to be praised,
awesome beyond all gods.
Give to the Lord, you families of nations,
give to the Lord glory and honour,
give to the Lord the glory due to his name.
Take up your bodies and carry his holy cross
and follow his most holy commands even to the end.
Let the whole earth tremble before his face
tell among the nations that the Lord has ruled from a tree. *I,147*

Tuesday in Easter Week

A reading from 'The Book of the Blessèd Angela of Foligno'.

[I heard God say to me], 'I want to show you something of my power.'
And immediately the eyes of my soul were opened, and in a vision I
beheld the fullness of God in which I beheld and comprehended the
whole of creation, that is, what is on this side and what is beyond the sea,
the abyss, the sea itself, and everything else. And in everything that I saw,
I could perceive nothing except the presence of the power of God, and
in a manner totally indescribable. And my soul in an excess of wonder
cried out, 'This world is pregnant with God!' Wherefore I understood
how small is the whole of creation – that is, what is on this side and what
is beyond the sea, the abyss, the sea itself, and everything else – but the
power of God fills it all to overflowing. He then said to me, 'I have just
manifested to you something of my power.' From this I comprehended
that henceforth I would be able to better understand other things.

Then he added, 'Behold now my humility.' I saw then the great depths
of God's humility towards us. And because I had understood the power
of God and perceived now his deep humility, my soul was filled with
wonder and esteemed itself to be nothing at all – indeed, saw in itself
nothing except pride. Also, as a result, I started to say that I did not
want to receive communion, because it seemed to me that I was totally
unworthy, and at that moment, I was, in fact, totally unworthy. He
had also told me after he had shown me his power and humility, 'My
daughter, no creature can come to the point of seeing what you have

seen, except by divine grace. And you have come to that point.'

And close to the moment of the elevation of the body of Christ, he said, 'Behold, the divine power is now present on the altar. I am within you. You can now receive me because you have already done so. Receive communion therefore with the blessing of God the Father, the Son, and the Holy Spirit. I who am worthy make you worthy.'

The great joy and the indescribable sweetness that was mine as a result of that communion were such that I think they will remain with me for the rest of my life.   *X,169f*

Wednesday in Easter Week

A reading from 'The Book of the Blessèd Angela of Foligno'.

In this state [of joy and gladness], I did not want to hear anything at all about the passion, nor did I want to hear God's name mentioned in my presence, for my experience of him was so delightful that anything else would be an impediment, for it would be less than that experience. And whatever is said about the gospel or about any other divine revelation seems to me as nothing, for what I saw of God was incomparably greater.

When that love leaves me, I nonetheless remain so totally contented, so angelic, that I can love reptiles, toads, serpents, and even devils. Whatever I see happening, even mortal sin, does not disturb me; that is, it causes me no displeasure, for I believe that God in his justice permits it. And even if a dog were to devour me, I would not care, and it seems to me that I would not feel the pain or suffer from it. This state is higher than standing at the foot of the cross as blessèd Francis did. My soul moves from one state to the other. Seeing the flesh of the one who died for us increases my soul's desire to see more of it, and come closer to it. These states are sources for me of supreme and joy-filled love, without any sorrow over the passion.   *X,184*

Thursday in Easter Week

A reading from 'The Lauds', by Jacopone da Todi.

My heart and will and feeling
can no longer endure the created
but cry out in longing for the Creator.
The earth and the heavens have no sweetness;
compared to Christ, all is stench.

His shining countenance makes sunlight seem dark;
the wisdom of the cherubim and ardour of the seraphim
are but a faded memory to one who beholds the Lord.

Let no one mock me, then,
if that Love drives me to madness.
Once captured, no heart can shield itself,
or escape Love's hold.
How can it withstand the searing flame
without turning to ashes?
Where can I find someone who can understand
who can take pity on me in my agony?

For heaven and earth and all things created
cry out insistently that I should love:
'Make haste to embrace the Love
that made us all, love with all your heart!
Because that Love so desires you
he uses all things to draw you to himself.'
I see all goodness and beauty and gentleness
spilling out of this super-abundance of holy light.

Oh, that my heart would not stumble and sag;
that I were able to love more intensely,
that I had more than myself to give
to that measureless light,
that sweet splendour!
I have given all that I have
to possess the Lover who constantly renews me,
that ancient Beauty forever new!

At the sight of such beauty I am swept up
out of myself to who knows where;
my heart melts, like wax before the fire.
Christ puts his mark on me, and stripped of myself
(O wondrous exchange!) I put on Christ.
Robed in this precious garment,
crying out its love,
the soul drowns in ecstasy!   *IX,258f*

Friday in Easter Week

A reading from 'The Lauds', by Jacopone da Todi.

When you no longer love yourself
but love Goodness,
you and your Belovèd will become one.
When you love him, he must love you in return;
in his charity you are drawn to him
and the two are made one.
This is a true union
that admits no divisions.

You have passed through death to true life,
safe forever from attacks or violence;
leaving yourself behind, you live in God,
in infinity, without opposition.
No one can comprehend you
or know how you are fashioned
except the One who created you
and raised you up.

From humble station
you are raised on high,
seated at the right hand of God,
as your wretchedness sinks from sight
in the depths of the abyss of God.
One who has no experience
of this fusion of rise and fall
can never understand.   *IX,269,273* >

Saturday in Easter Week

A reading from 'The Tree of Life' by Saint Bonaventure.

This most beautiful flower of the root of Jesse, which had blossomed in
the incarnation and withered in the passion, thus blossomed again in the
resurrection so as to become the beauty of all. For that most glorious
body – subtle, agile and immortal – was clothed in glory so as to be truly
more radiant than the sun, showing an example of the beauty destined for
the risen human bodies. Concerning this, the Saviour himself said, 'Then
the just will shine forth like the sun into the kingdom of their Father,' that

is, in eternal beatitude. And if the just will shine forth like the sun, how great do you think is the radiance of the very Sun of justice himself?: so great is it, I say, that it is more beautiful than the sun and surpasses every constellation of the stars; compared to light, his beauty is deservedly judged to be pre-eminent.

Happy the eyes that have seen!
But you will be truly happy
if there will be remnants of your seed
to see
both interiorly and exteriorly
that most-desired splendour.   *VI,160f*

The Second Sunday of Easter

Easter 2 — Sunday

A reading from 'The Life of Saint Francis', by Thomas of Celano.

How handsome,
how splendid!
How gloriously Francis appeared
in innocence of life,
in simplicity of words,
in purity of heart,
in love of God,
in fraternal charity,
in enthusiastic obedience,
in agreeable compliance,
in angelic appearance.

Friendly in behaviour,
serene in nature,
affable in speech,
generous in encouragement,
faithful in commitment,
prudent in advice,
tireless in prayer,
he was fervent in everything!

Firm in intention,

consistent in virtue,
persevering in grace,
he was the same in everything!

Swift to forgive,
slow to grow angry,
free in nature,
remarkable in memory,
subtle in discussing,
careful in choices,
he was simple in everything!

Strict with himself,
kind with others,
he was discerning in everything!

He was very eloquent, with a cheerful appearance and a kind face; free of laziness and arrogance. He was of medium height, closer to short, his head was of medium size and round. His face was somewhat long and drawn, his forehead small and smooth, with medium eyes black and clear. His hair was dark; his eyebrows were straight, and his nose even and thin; his ears small and upright, and his temples smooth. His tongue was peaceable, fiery and sharp; his voice was powerful, but pleasing, clear and musical. His teeth were white, well set and even; his lips were small and thin; his beard was black and sparse; his neck was slender, his shoulders straight; his arms were short, his hands slight, his fingers long and his nails tapered. He had thin legs, small feet, fine skin and little flesh. His clothing was rough, his sleep was short, his hand was generous. *1,252f*

Easter 2 — Monday

A reading from 'The Assisi Compilation'.

While blessèd Francis was staying at Saint Mary [of the Portiuncula], it happened that a very serious temptation of the spirit was inflicted on him for the benefit of his soul. He was tormented inside and out, in body and spirit, so much that he sometimes withdrew from the close company of the brothers, especially since he could not be his usual cheerful self because of that temptation. He inflicted upon himself not only abstinence from food, but also from talking. He would often go to pray in the woods near the church, so that he could better express his pain and could more abundantly pour out his tears before the Lord, so that the

Lord who is able to do all things, would be kind enough to send him a remedy from heaven for this great trial.

He was troubled by this temptation day and night for more than two years. One day while he was praying in the church of Saint Mary, he happened to hear in spirit that saying of the holy gospel, 'If you have faith like a mustard seed, and you tell that mountain to move from its place and move to another place, it will happen.' Saint Francis replied, 'What is that mountain?' He was told, 'That mountain is your temptation.' 'In that case, Lord,' said blessèd Francis, 'be it done to me as you have said.'

Immediately he was freed in such a way that it seemed to him that he had never had that temptation.   *II,165f*

Easter 2 — Tuesday

A reading from 'The Assisi Compilation'.

There was a certain brother, a spiritual man, an elder in religion, and close to blessèd Francis. It happened once that for many days he suffered the most severe and cruel suggestions of the devil, so that he was almost cast into the depths of despair. And even though he was tormented daily, he was ashamed to confess it every time. And, because of this, he afflicted himself with fasting, with vigils, with tears, and with beatings.

While he was being tormented daily for many days, blessèd Francis came to that place by divine guidance. And when blessèd Francis was walking one day not too far from that place with one brother and with the brother who was so tormented, he left the other brother behind and walked with the one who was being tempted. He said to him, 'My dearest brother, I wish and tell you that from now on you are not bound to confess these suggestions and intrusions of the devil to anyone. Don't be afraid, because they have not harmed your soul. But I give you my permission just to say seven Our Father's as often as you are troubled by these suggestions.'

That brother was overjoyed at what he said to him, that he was not bound to confess those things, especially because, since he would have had to confess daily, he was quite upset, and this was the main reason for his suffering. He marvelled at the holiness of the holy father, how he knew his temptations through the Holy Spirit, since he had not confessed to anyone except priests. And he would frequently switch priests because of shame, since he was ashamed that one priest would know all his weakness and temptation.

From the very moment blessèd Francis spoke to him, he was immediately freed both in spirit and body from that great trial which he endured for such a long time. And, through the grace of God and the merits of blessèd Francis, he remained in great serenity and peace of soul and body.
II,153

Easter 2 — Wednesday

A reading from 'The Remembrance of the Desire of a Soul', by Thomas of Celano.

Not only was Saint Francis attacked by Satan with temptations, he even had to struggle with him hand to hand. On one occasion Lord Leo, the Cardinal of Santa Croce, invited him to stay with him for a little while in Rome. He chose to stay in a detached tower, which offered nine vaulted chambers like the little rooms of hermits. The first night, when he had poured out his prayer to God and wanted to go to sleep, demons came and fiercely attacked the holy one of God. They beat him long and hard, and finally left him half dead. When they left and he had caught his breath, the saint called his companion who was sleeping under another vault of the roof. When he came over he said to him, 'Brother, I want you to stay by me, because I am afraid to be alone. A moment ago demons were beating me.' The saint was trembling and quaking in every limb, as if he had a high fever.

They spent a sleepless night, and Saint Francis said to his companion, 'Demons are the police of our Lord, whom he assigns to punish excesses. It is a sign of special grace that he does not leave anything in his servant unpunished while he still lives in the world. I do not recall my offence which, through God's mercy, I have not washed away by reparation. For he has always acted towards me with such fatherly kindness, that in my prayer and meditation he shows me what pleases or displeases him. But it could be that he allowed his police to burst in on me because my staying at the courts of the great doesn't offer good example to others. When my brothers who stay in poor little places hear that I'm staying with cardinals, they might suspect that I am living in luxury. And so, brother, I think that one who is set up as an example is better off avoiding courts, strengthening those who suffer want by putting up with the same things.' So in the morning they went to the Cardinal, told him the whole story, and said goodbye to him.
II,326f

Easter 2 — Thursday

A reading from 'The Little Flowers of Saint Francis'.

A boy who was very pure and innocent was received into the Order while Saint Francis was living; and he was staying in a small place where the brothers, out of necessity, slept outside on the ground. Saint Francis once came to this place and in the evening after saying compline, he went off to sleep as he usually did, so he could get up at night to pray when the other brothers were asleep. The boy had in mind to spy attentively on Saint Francis' movements in order to find out about his holiness and especially to know what the saint did at night when he arose. To make sure that sleep would not overcome him, he lay down to sleep at Saint Francis' side and tied his cord to that of Saint Francis, so he would feel when the saint arose. And Saint Francis did not feel any of this. That night, during the first time of sleep, when all the other brothers were sleeping, Saint Francis got up and found his cord tied that way. He gently untied it so that the boy did not feel it, and Saint Francis went alone into the woods near the place, entering a little cell there and set himself to pray. The boy awoke after a while and found the cord untied and Saint Francis gone, so he got up to look for him. When he found the gate to the woods open, he thought that Saint Francis had gone out there, so he entered the woods. Reaching the place where Saint Francis was praying, he began to hear a great sound of voices. Going closer so that he might see and understand what he heard, he saw a wonderful light surrounding Saint Francis on all sides, and in it he saw Christ and the Virgin Mary and Saint John the Baptist and the Evangelist and a great multitude of angels speaking with Saint Francis. When the boy saw and heard this, he fell to the ground as if dead. Then, when the mystery of that holy apparition ended, Saint Francis was returning to the place. And his foot bumped into the boy lying almost dead on the path. Out of compassion, he lifted him up, took him in his arms and carried him back, as a good shepherd does with his little sheep.

Learning from him later about how he saw the vision, he ordered him never to tell anyone, that is, while he lived. The boy, growing in the grace of God and devotion to Saint Francis, was an important man in the Order, and, after the death of Saint Francis, he revealed that vision to the brothers. *III,594f*

Easter 2 — Friday

A reading from 'The Assisi Compilation'.

Once blessèd Francis was travelling with a spiritual brother from Assisi who came from a great and powerful family. Because he was weak and ill, blessèd Francis rode on a donkey. Feeling tired from walking, that brother began to think to himself, 'His parents were never at the same level as mine, and here he is riding, while I'm worn out, walking behind him, prodding the beast.'

While he was thinking this, blessèd Francis got off the donkey and said to him, 'No, brother, it's not right or proper for me to ride while you go on foot, for in the world you were nobler and more influential than I.' The brother, stunned and ashamed, fell down at his feet and, in tears, confessed his thought and then said his penance. He was greatly amazed at his holiness, for he immediately knew his thought.   *II,174*

Easter 2 — Saturday

A reading from 'The Assisi Compilation'.

At one time blessèd Francis was staying at the hermitage of Sant' Eleuterio, near the town of Condigliano in the district of Rieti. Since he was wearing only one tunic, one day because of the extreme cold, and out of great necessity, he patched his tunic and that of his companion with scraps of cloth on the inside, so that his body began to be comforted a little. A short while afterwards, when he was returning from prayer one day, he said with great joy to his companion, 'I must be the form and example of all the brothers; so, although it is necessary for my body to have a tunic with patches, nevertheless I must take into consideration my brothers who have the same need, but perhaps do not and cannot have this. Therefore, I must stay down with them, and I must suffer those same necessities they suffer so that in seeing this, they may be able to bear them more patiently.'

We who were with him could not say how many and how great were the necessities that he denied his body in food and clothing, to give good example to the brothers and so that they would endure their necessities in greater patience. At all times, especially after the brothers began to multiply and he resigned the office of prelate, blessèd Francis had as his highest and principal goal to teach the brothers more by actions than by words what they ought to do and what they ought to avoid.   *II,218*

The Third Sunday of Easter

Easter 3 — Sunday

A reading from 'The Little Flowers of Saint Francis'.

The first companion of Saint Francis was Brother Bernard of Assisi, who was converted in this way. Saint Francis was still in secular clothing, though he had already despised the world, and was going about all despised and mortified by penance, so that many considered him a fool, and he was scorned as a madman and driven away with rocks and mud by relatives and strangers, and he remained patient as if deaf and mute to every injury and insult. Sir Bernard of Assisi, who was one of the noblest and richest and wisest people of the city, wisely began to consider Saint Francis: his great scorn for the world; his great patience in injuries. Even after being so despised and scorned by everyone for two years, he always seemed even more constant and patient. He began to think and say to himself, 'It cannot be that this Francis does not have great grace from God.' And he invited him for the evening for supper and lodging; and Saint Francis accepted and dined with him in the evening and lodged there.

Then Sir Bernard decided in his heart to examine his holiness. He had a bed prepared in his own chamber, in which a lamp always burned at night. And Saint Francis, to conceal his holiness, as soon as he entered the chamber jumped into bed and gave the appearance of sleeping. And Sir Bernard also, after a little while, lay down and began to snore loudly, as if were sleeping very deeply. Then Saint Francis, truly believing that Sir Bernard was sleeping, during the first time of sleep, got up from the bed and set himself to praying, lifting his eyes and his hands to heaven, and with great devotion and fervour said, 'My God, my God.' Saying this, and sobbing, he remained like this until early morning, constantly repeating, 'My God, my God,' and nothing else. As Sir Bernard saw by the light of the lamp the very devout acts of Saint Francis, and considering devoutly the words he said, he was touched and inspired by the Holy Spirit to change his life.

Thus, when morning came, he called Saint Francis and said, 'Brother Francis, I am fully prepared in my heart to abandon the world and to follow you in what you will command me.' *III,567f>*

Easter 3 — Monday

A reading from 'The Little Flowers of Saint Francis'.

At the beginning and foundation of the Order, when the brothers were few and places had not yet been taken, Saint Francis in his devotion went to Santiago in Galicia, and took with him some brothers, among whom was Brother Bernard. And as they were going together along the road, in a certain village he came upon a sick little poor man. Having compassion for him, he said to Brother Bernard, 'My son, I want you to remain here to serve this sick man.' And Brother Bernard, humbly kneeling and bowing his head, accepted the holy father's obedience and remained in that place. And Saint Francis with the other companions went to Santiago. When they arrived there, remaining in prayer during the night in the Church of Saint James, God revealed to Saint Francis that he must take many places throughout the world since his Order was to expand and grow into a great multitude of brothers. And because of this revelation Saint Francis began to take places in those regions. As Saint Francis was returning by the way he took earlier, he again found Brother Bernard; and the sick man, with whom he had left him, was perfectly healed. So Saint Francis allowed Brother Bernard to go to Santiago the following year. *III,571f*

Easter 3 — Tuesday

A reading from 'The Little Flowers of Saint Francis'.

It happened, at the beginning of the Religion, that Saint Francis sent Brother Bernard to Bologna and there, according to the grace God gave him, he should produce fruit for God. Brother Bernard, making the sign of the most holy Cross, departed out of holy obedience, and arrived at Bologna. When the children saw him in an odd and rough habit, they made many jokes at him and insults, the way people do with someone crazy. Brother Bernard patiently and joyfully bore it all for love of Christ. In fact, so that he could be insulted more easily, he deliberately placed himself in the city's piazza. As he was sitting there many children and adults gathered around him, and they pulled his capuce, one backwards, one forward; some threw stones, and others, dirt; and they pushed him here and there. Brother Bernard, always with the same manner, and with the same patience, and with a happy expression, did not complain and did not move. What is more, he returned to that same place, just to endure similar things. Because patience is a work of perfection and a proof of virtue, a wise doctor of law, seeing and considering such constancy and virtue in Brother Bernard, who could not be disturbed by any annoyance or insult after so many days, said to himself, 'It's impossible that he's not a holy man.' Drawing near to him he asked him, 'Who are you and why have you come here?' And Brother Bernard answered by putting his hand to his chest and taking out the Rule of Saint Francis, and gave it to him to read. On reading it, considering its most high state of perfection, with great surprise and wonder the man turned to his companions and said, 'Truly this is the highest state of religion that I ever heard of; so this one and his companions are some of the holiest men in this world. And whoever insults them commits the greatest of sins. He should instead be honoured most highly, since he's a friend of God.' And he said to Brother Bernard, 'If you want to take a place in which you can serve God fittingly, I'll gladly give it to you for the good of my soul.' Brother Bernard replied, 'Sir, I believe that our Lord Jesus Christ inspired you to do this. Therefore I gladly accept your offer, for the honour of Christ.' Then, with great joy and charity that judge took Brother Bernard to his house. And then he gave him the place he promised, and he prepared it all and finished it at his own expense. From that moment on he became the father and special defender of Brother Bernard and his companions.

And Brother Bernard began to be greatly honoured by the people because of his holy way of living, so much so, that whoever could touch or see him considered himself blessed. But he, as a true disciple of Christ and of the humble Francis, fearing that the honour of the world might be an obstacle to the peace and health of his soul, left one day and returned to Saint Francis. *III,575f*

Easter 3 — Wednesday

A reading from 'The Little Flowers of Saint Francis'.

The great grace that God showed many times to the evangelical poor who abandoned the world for love of Christ was shown in Brother Bernard of Quintavalle who, after he had taken the habit of Saint Francis, was very frequently rapt in God through contemplation of heavenly things.

Brother Bernard was so lifted up in spirit to this heavenly treasure, promised to lovers of God, that continually for fifteen years he always went about with his spirit and his face lifted towards heaven. And during that time he never relieved his hunger at table, though he ate a little of what was placed before him, because he said that we do not practice perfect abstinence from things if we do not taste them; true abstinence is refraining from things that taste good to the mouth. And with this he had come to such clarity and light of intelligence that even great clerics came to him for solutions to the most difficult questions and obscure passages of scripture; and he enlightened them on every difficulty.

Because his spirit was entirely set free and removed from earthly things, like the swallows he flew very high through contemplation, and sometimes for twenty days, sometimes for thirty days, he remained alone on the peaks of high mountains, contemplating heavenly things. For this reason Brother Giles used to say about him that others had not received this gift, which had been given to Brother Bernard of Quintavalle, that is, like a swallow, finding food for himself while flying. And because of this outstanding grace that he had from God, Saint Francis often and willingly talked with him by day and by night, so that sometimes they were found together rapt in God the whole night long in the woods where both of them met to speak with God.   *III,616f>*

Easter 3 — Thursday

A reading from 'The Remembrance of the Desire of a Soul', by Thomas of Celano.

Another time Saint Francis spoke prophetically about Brother Bernard, who was the second brother in the Order, saying, 'I tell you, Brother Bernard has been given the most cunning devils to test him, the worst among all the other evil spirits. They constantly strive to make this star fall from heaven, but the outcome will be something else. He will be troubled, tormented, and harassed, but in the end he will triumph over all.' And he added, 'Near the time of his death, with every storm calmed, every temptation overcome, he will enjoy wonderful tranquillity and peace. The race finished he will pass over happily to Christ.'

And in fact it happened just like that: his death was lit up with miracles, and everything happened exactly as the man of God foretold. That is why the brothers said when he died, 'This brother was not really recognised while he lived!'   *II,280*

Easter 3 — Friday

A reading from 'The Assisi Compilation'.

Sitting next to the bed where blessèd Francis was lying [close to death], Brother Bernard said, 'Father! I beg you, bless me and show me your love. I believe that, if you show me your love with fatherly affection, God himself and the other brothers of the religion will love me more.'

Blessèd Francis was not able to see him, since many days earlier he had lost his sight. Extending his right hand, he placed it on the head of Brother Giles, the third of the first brothers, who at that moment was sitting next to Brother Bernard. Feeling the head of Brother Giles, like a person going blind, he immediately recognised him by the Holy Spirit, and said, 'This is not the head of my Brother Bernard.'

Brother Bernard immediately drew closer to him. Blessèd Francis, placing his hand on his head, blessed him. 'Write what I tell you,' he then said to one of his companions. 'Brother Bernard was the first brother the Lord gave me. He began first and most perfectly fulfilled the perfection of the holy gospel, distributing all his goods to the poor. Because of this and his many other prerogatives, I am bound to love him more than any other brother in the whole religion. As much as I am able, it is my will and command that whoever becomes Minister General should love and honour him as he would me. Let the other Ministers Provincial and the brothers of the whole religion hold him in my place.' Because of this, Brother Bernard was greatly consoled as were the other brothers who saw this. *II,126f*

Easter 3 — Saturday

A reading from 'The Little Flowers of Saint Francis'.

After the death of Saint Francis the brothers loved and revered Brother Bernard as a venerable father. And as he approached death, many brothers from diverse regions of the world came to him. Among them came that hierarchic and divine Brother Giles. When he saw Brother Bernard, he said with great joy, 'Sursum corda, Brother Bernard, sursum corda!' And the holy Brother Bernard secretly told a brother to prepare for Brother Giles a place suitable for contemplation, and so it was done. As Brother Bernard was at the last hour of death, he had himself raised, and spoke to the brothers in front of him, saying, 'Dearest brothers, I don't want to say many words to you, but you must consider that the state of the religion that I have had, you have; and what I have now, you will also have. And I know this in my soul: even for a thousand worlds equal to this one I would not wish to have served another lord besides our Lord Jesus Christ. And for every offence I have done, I accuse myself and declare myself at fault, to my Saviour Jesus Christ and to you.' And after these words and other good instructions, he lay down again on the bed, and his face became radiant and happy beyond measure, and all the brothers marvelled greatly at this. And in that joy his most holy soul, crowned with glory, passed from the present life to the blessèd life of the angels.   *III,577f*

The Fourth Sunday of Easter

Easter 4 — Sunday

A reading from 'The Little Flowers of Saint Francis'.

Once at the beginning of the Order Saint Francis was with Brother Leo in a place where they did not have books for saying the Divine Office. When the time for matins came, Saint Francis said to Brother Leo, 'Dearest brother, we do not have a breviary with which we can say matins; but so that we may spend the time in praising God, I'll speak and you'll respond as I teach you. And be careful that you don't change the words into something different from what I teach you. I'll say this, "O, Brother Francis, you have done so many evil things and so many sins in the world that you are worthy of hell." And you, Brother Leo, will respond, "That's true: you deserve the lowest place in hell." ' And Brother Leo with dove-like simplicity responded, 'Of course, Father, begin, in the name of God.' Then Saint Francis began to say, 'O Brother Francis, you have done so many evil things and so many sins in the world that you are worthy of hell.' And Brother Leo responded, 'God will do so many good things for you that you will go to Paradise.' Saint Francis said, 'Don't say that, Brother Leo! When I say, "Brother Francis, you have done so many evil things against God that you deserve to be cursed by God," you will respond like this, "Truly, you deserve to be put among the cursed."' And Brother Leo responded, 'Of course, Father.' Then Saint Francis, with many tears and groans and beating his breast said in a loud voice, 'O my Lord of heaven and earth, I have committed so many iniquities and sins against you, that I thoroughly deserve to be cursed by you.' And Brother Leo responded, 'O Brother Francis, God will do so much for you that you will be singularly blessed among the blessèd.' And Saint Francis, surprised that Brother Leo responded the opposite of what he had told him, rebuked him in this way, 'Why don't you respond the way I teach you? I command you by holy obedience to respond as I teach you. I will say this, "O evil little Brother Francis, do you think God will have mercy on you? You have committed so many sins against the Father of mercy and God of every consolation, that you don't deserve to find mercy." And you, Brother Leo, little lamb, will respond, "You in no way deserve to find mercy."' But when Saint Francis said, 'O evil little Brother Francis,' etc., Brother Leo responded, 'God the Father, whose mercy is infinitely more than your sin, will have great mercy on you, and on top of this he will add many graces.' At this response, Saint Francis, sweetly angered and patiently upset, said to Brother Leo, 'And why have you got the presumption to act contrary to obedience? You've already responded several times the opposite of what I've ordered you!' Brother Leo responded very humbly and reverently, 'God knows, my Father: each time I tried in my heart to respond as you commanded me, but God makes me speak as it pleases him, not as it pleases me.' Saint Francis was surprised by this, and said to Brother Leo, 'I beg you most dearly that you respond this time as I've told you.' Brother Leo responded, 'In the name of God, say it, and this time for sure I will respond as you want.' And Saint Francis said tearfully, 'O evil little Brother Francis, do you think that God has mercy on you?' Brother Leo responded, 'More than that, you will receive great grace from God and he will exalt you and glorify you forever, since whoever humbles himself will be exalted. And I cannot say anything else, since God speaks through my mouth.' And so, in this humble contest, with many tears and much spiritual consolation, they kept vigil until daybreak.   *III,581f*

Easter 4 — Monday

A reading from a medieval Franciscan manuscript.

Once when Saint Francis was going on a preaching tour with Brother Leo it happened that Brother Leo began to lose heart through utter exhaustion. So, as they were passing a certain vineyard, Saint Francis went in and seized a bunch of grapes which he gave to Brother Leo to eat. But while he was so doing an angry countryman appeared on the scene and most violently beat Saint Francis with many blows.

As they were going on their way afterwards Saint Francis complained bitterly of the hard knocks which he had received on Brother Leo's account, finding it quite impossible to give thanks to God for his sufferings. When he spoke he said to Brother Leo, 'Brother Leo has well eaten, but Brother Francis has been well beaten. Brother Leo has had a good meal, but Brother Francis has, with his body, well paid for it.'

IV,1833

Easter 4 — Tuesday

A reading from a medieval Franciscan manuscript.

Brother Leo, the companion of the Blessèd Francis, said that there was once a friar of such holiness that he seemed to be on an equality with the Apostles themselves. Yet in the end he yielded to temptation and left the Order. But, living in the world afterwards, he still gave the appearance of being of such virtue that he seemed almost to attain to apostolic perfection.

One day when Brother Leo and some other friars were walking along a road with the Blessèd Francis, the question was raised by some of the brethren as to why that brother had left the Order. But the saint replied, 'I want to read something and to ask myself some questions which I shall myself answer. Let no one speak to me until I have done.' And then he said the word 'Humility', which he repeated three or four times. Then 'Chastity', 'Abstinence', 'Poverty'. And in this way he ran through a number of virtues, mentioning each one several times. And with each one he asked himself, 'Do you know that?' and answered, 'Yes, I know that.' Finally he said, several times over, the word 'Fear'. And when he asked himself, 'Do you know that?' he answered, 'No.' Then again he cried out, 'Fear,' repeating the word over and over again. But when he asked himself, 'Do you know that?' again he answered, 'No.' So yet again he cried, 'Fear,' and at last whispered to himself, 'Yes, I know Fear.' Then he added these words, 'It is useless for a man to seek all virtues and leave out Fear; yet few have it, and therefore it is hard to teach them.' And finally, 'It was because he had no Fear that that good brother fell and left the Order.'

IV,1836f

Easter 4 — Wednesday

A reading from 'The Little Flowers of Saint Francis'.

Once when Saint Francis was seriously ill and Brother Leo was taking care of him, that same Brother Leo was near Saint Francis and was praying, and he was rapt in ecstasy and led in spirit to a very great river, wide and turbulent. As he was watching those crossing over, he saw some brothers with heavy loads entering that river, and some as far as the middle of the river, and some as far as the shore; but all of them, because of the force of the river and the loads they carried with them, finally fell in and drowned. Brother Leo, seeing this, felt great compassion for them; and suddenly, as he stood there, a great multitude of brothers arrived, without any loads or burdened by anything at all, and in whom shone holy poverty. They entered the river and crossed it without any harm at all. Having seen this, Brother Leo returned to himself.

Then Saint Francis, sensing in spirit that Brother Leo had seen a vision, called him to himself, and asked him what he had seen. And the same Brother Leo told him the whole vision in detail, and Saint Francis said, 'What you saw is true. The great river is this world; the brothers who drowned in the river are those who do not follow their evangelical profession especially in regard to the highest poverty. Those who crossed without danger are those brothers who neither seek nor possess anything earthly or anything of the flesh, but are content having only basic food and clothing, following Christ naked on the Cross and willingly and happily carrying the burden and the gentle yoke of Christ and of holy obedience; and therefore they cross easily from temporal life to eternal life.' *III,627*

Easter 4 — Thursday

A reading from 'The Remembrance of the Desire of a Soul', by Thomas of Celano.

While Saint Francis was secluded in a cell on Mount La Verna, [Brother Leo,] one of his companions, was yearning with great desire to have something encouraging from the words of our Lord, commented on briefly by Saint Francis and written with his own hand. He believed that by this means he would be set free from, or at least could bear more easily, a serious temptation which oppressed him, not in the flesh but in the spirit. Though growing weary with this desire, he feared to express it to the most holy father. But what man did not tell him, the Spirit revealed. One day Saint Francis called this brother and said, 'Bring me paper and ink, because I want to write down the words of the Lord and his praises upon which I have meditated in my heart.' What he had asked for was quickly brought to him. He then wrote down with his own hand the Praises of God and the words he wanted and, at the end, a blessing for that brother, saying, 'Take this paper for yourself and keep it carefully to your dying day.' The whole temptation disappeared immediately. The letter was preserved; and later it worked wonders. *II,280*

Easter 4 — Friday

A reading from 'A Letter to Brother Leo', by Saint Francis.

Brother Leo, health and peace from Brother Francis!
I am speaking, my son, in this way – as a mother would – because I am putting everything we said on the road in this brief message and advice. If, afterwards, you need to come to me for counsel, I advise you thus: In whatever way it seems better to you to please the Lord God and to follow his footprint and poverty, do it with the blessing of the Lord God and my obedience. And if you need and want to come to me for the sake of your soul or for some consolation, Leo, come. *I,122*

Easter 4 — Saturday

A reading from 'A Mirror of the Perfection of a Lesser Brother'.

Once, the Lord Jesus Christ said to Brother Leo, the companion of blessèd Francis, 'Brother Leo, I have a complaint about the brothers.' 'About what, Lord?' Brother Leo replied. And the Lord said, 'About three things. They do not recognise my gifts which, as you know, I generously and abundantly bestow on them daily, since they neither sow nor reap. All day long they are idle and complain. And they often provoke one another to anger, and do not return to love, and do not pardon the injury they receive.' *III,295f*

The Fifth Sunday of Easter

Easter 5 — Sunday

A reading from 'The Legend of Saint Clare'.

A woman, admirable by name,
Clare, illustrious by designation and in virtue
took her origin from a lineage already sufficiently illustrious
in the city of Assisi:
at first a fellow citizen with blessèd Francis on earth,
afterwards reigning with him in heaven.

Her father was a knight, as were all her relatives on both sides of the knightly class. Her home was well-endowed and had abundant means following the same fashion of her native place. Her mother, Ortulana, who would give birth to a fruitful plant in the garden of the church, was herself overflowing in no small way with good fruits. Even though she was bound by the bond of marriage and was burdened with the cares of the family, she, nonetheless, devoted herself as much as possible to divine worship and applied herself to works of piety. She, therefore, devoutly travelled with pilgrims beyond the sea and, after surveying those places which the God-Man had consecrated with his sacred footprints, she afterwards returned home filled with joy. She set out again to pray to Saint Michael the Archangel and visited with even more devotion the basilicas of the Apostles.

While the pregnant woman, already near delivery, was attentively praying to the Crucified before the cross in a church to bring her safely through the danger of childbirth, she heard a voice saying to her, 'Do not be afraid, woman, for you will give birth in safety to a light which will give light more clearly than light itself.' Taught by this oracle, when the child was born and then reborn in sacred baptism, she ordered that she be called Clare, hoping that the brightness of the promised light would in some way be fulfilled according to the divine pleasure.   *V,252ff>*

Easter 5 — Monday

A reading from 'The Legend of Saint Clare'.

Hardly had she been brought into the light, than the little Clare began to shine sufficiently in the darkness of the world and to be resplendent in her tender years through the propriety of her conduct. From the mouth of her mother she first received with a docile heart the fundamentals of the faith and, with the Spirit inflaming and moulding her interiorly, she became known as a most pure vessel, a vessel of graces. She freely stretched out her hand to the poor and satisfied the needs of many out of the abundance of her house. In order that her sacrifice would be more pleasing to God, she would deprive her own body of delicate foods and, sending them secretly through intermediaries, she would nourish the bodies of the poor.

Thus, from her infancy,
as mercy was growing with her,
she bore a compassionate attitude,
merciful towards the miseries of the destitute.
She held the pursuit of holy prayer as a friend
and after she was frequently sprinkled with its holy fragrance,
she gradually entered a celibate life.

When she did not have a chaplet with which to count the Our Father's, she would count her little prayers to the Lord with a pile of pebbles. When she began to feel the first stirrings of holy love, she judged that the passing scene of worldly pride should be condemned, being taught by the unction of the Spirit to place a worthless price upon worthless things. Under her costly and soft clothes she wore a hairshirt, blossoming externally to the world, inwardly putting on Christ. Finally, when her family desired that she be married in a noble way, she would in no way consent, but feigning that she would marry a mortal at a later date, she entrusted her virginity to the Lord. *V,254f*

Easter 5 — Tuesday

A reading from 'The Legend of Saint Clare'.

Such were the offerings of Clare's virtue in her paternal home,
such the beginnings of the Spirit,
such the preludes of her holiness!

As a chest of so many perfumes,
even though closed,
reveals its content by its fragrance,
so she unknowingly began to be praised
by the mouth of her neighbours
and, when the true recognition of her secret deeds appeared,

the account of her goodness
was spread about among the people.

Hearing of the then celebrated name of Francis,
who, like a new man,
was renewing with new virtues
the way of perfection forgotten by the world,
she was moved by the Father of the spirits,
whose initiatives each one had already accepted
although in different ways,
and immediately desired to see and hear him.

No less did he desire to see and speak with her,
impressed by the widespread fame of so gracious a young lady,
so that, in some way,
he, who was totally longing for spoil
and who had come to depopulate the kingdom of the world,
would be also able to wrest this noble spoil from the evil world
and win her for his Lord.

He visited her and she more frequently him, moderating the times of
their visits so that this divine pursuit could not be perceived by anyone
nor objected to by gossip. For, with only one close companion accompanying her, the young girl, leaving her paternal home, frequented the
clandestine meetings with the man of God, whose words seemed to her
to be on fire and whose deeds were seen to be beyond the human.

V,255ff

Easter 5 — Wednesday

A reading from 'The Legend of Saint Clare'.

The Solemnity of the Day of the Palms was at hand when the young girl
Clare went with a fervent heart to the man of God, asking him about her
conversion and how it should be carried out. The father Francis told her
that on the day of the feast, she should go, dressed and adorned, together
with the crowd of people, to receive a palm, and, on the following night,
leaving the camp she should turn her worldly joy into mourning the
Lord's passion.

Therefore, when Sunday came, the young girl, thoroughly radiant with
festive splendour among the crowd of women, entered the church with
the others. Then something occurred that was a fitting omen: as the

others were going to receive the palms, while Clare remained immobile in her place out of shyness, the bishop, coming down the steps, came to her and placed a palm in her hands. On that night, preparing to obey the command of the saint, she embarked upon her long desired flight with a virtuous companion. Since she was not content to leave by way of the usual door, marvelling at her strength, she broke open – with her own hands – that other door that is customarily blocked by wood and stone.

And so she ran to Saint Mary of the Portiuncula, leaving behind her home, city, and relatives. There the brothers, who were observing sacred vigils before the little altar of God, received the virgin Clare with torches. There, immediately after rejecting the filth of Babylon, she gave the world 'a bill of divorce'. There, her hair shorn by the hands of the brothers, she put aside every kind of her fine dress.   *V,259*

Easter 5 — Thursday

A reading from 'The Legend of Saint Clare'.

After Clare received the insignia of holy penance before the altar of the blessèd Virgin and, as if before the throne of this Virgin, the humble servant was married to Christ, Saint Francis immediately led her to the church of San Paolo to remain there until the Most High would provide another place.

But after the news reached her relatives, they condemned with a broken heart the deed and proposal of the virgin and, banding together as one, they ran to the place, attempting to obtain what they could not. They employed violent force, poisonous advice, and flattering promises, persuading her to give up such a worthless deed that was unbecoming to her class and without precedence in her family. But, taking hold of the altar cloths, she bared her tonsured head, maintaining that she would in no way be torn away from the service of Christ. With the increasing violence of her relatives, her spirit grew and her love – provoked by injuries – provided strength. So, for many days, even though she endured an obstacle in the way of the Lord and her own relatives opposed her proposal of holiness, her spirit did not crumble and her fervour did not diminish. Instead, amid words and deeds of hatred, she moulded her spirit anew in hope until her relatives, turning back, were quiet.

After a few days, she went to the church of San Angelo in Panzo, where her mind was not completely at peace, so that, at the advice of Saint Francis, she moved to San Damiano.   *V,260f*

Easter 5 — Friday

A reading from 'The Legend of Saint Clare'.

There [at San Damiano],
as if casting the anchor of her soul in a secure site
Clare no longer wavered
due to further changes of place,
nor did she hesitate because of its smallness,
nor did she fear its isolation.

This is that church
for whose repair Francis sweated with remarkable energy
and to whose priest he offered money for its restoration.

This is the place where,
while Francis was praying,
the voice spoke to him from the cross,
'Francis, go and repair my house,
which, as you see, is totally destroyed.'

In this little house of penance
the virgin Clare enclosed herself
for love of her heavenly spouse.

Remaining enclosed
Clare began to enlighten the whole world
and her brilliance dazzled it
with the honours of her praises.

Certainly the wonderful power of her prayer
should not be buried in silence,
which in the very beginning of her conversion
turned one soul to God
and then defended her convert.

In fact, she had a sister, tender in age,
a sister by flesh and by purity.
In her desire for her conversion,
among the first prayers that she offered to God with all her heart,
she more ardently begged this grace that,
just as she had an affinity of spirit with her sister in the world,
she might also have now a unity of will in the service of God.

Sixteen days after the conversion of Clare, Agnes, inspired by the divine spirit, ran to her sister, revealed the secret of her will, and told her that she wished to serve God completely. Embracing her with joy, Clare said, 'I thank God, most sweet sister, that he has heard my concern for you.'

A defence no less marvellous followed this conversion. For while the joyous sisters were clinging to the footprints of Christ in the church of San Angelo in Panzo and she who had heard more from the Lord was teaching her novice sister, new attacks by relatives were quickly flaring up against the young girls.   *V,261f,264f,278f*>

Easter 5 — Saturday

A reading from 'The Legend of Saint Clare'.

Hearing that Agnes had gone off to Clare, twelve men, burning with anger and hiding outwardly their evil intent, ran to the place and pretended to make a peaceful entrance. Immediately they turned to Agnes – since they had long ago lost hope of Clare – and said, 'Why have you come to this place? Get ready to return immediately with us!' When she responded that she did not want to leave her sister Clare, one of the knights in a fierce mood ran towards her and, without sparing blows and kicks, tried to drag her away by her hair, while the others pushed her and lifted her in their arms. At this, as if she had been captured by lions and been torn from the hands of the Lord, the young girl cried out, 'Dear sister, help me! Do not let me be taken from Christ the Lord!' While the violent robbers were dragging the young girl along the slope of the mountain, ripping her clothes and strewing the path with the hair they had torn out, Clare prostrated herself in prayer with tears, begged that her sister would be given constancy of mind and that the strength of humans would be overcome by divine power.

Suddenly, in fact, Agnes' body lying on the ground seemed so heavy that the men, many as there were, exerted all their energy and were not able to carry her beyond a certain stream. Even others, running from their fields and vineyards, attempted to give them some help, but they could in no way lift that body from the earth. When they failed, they shrugged off the miracle by mocking, 'She has been eating lead all night; no wonder she is so heavy!'

Then Lord Monaldus, her enraged uncle, intended to strike her a lethal blow; but an awful pain suddenly struck the hand he had raised and for a long time the anguish of pain afflicted it.

But, notice how after the long struggle, Clare came to the place and asked her relatives to give up such a conflict and to entrust Agnes, half-dead on the ground, to her care. After they departed with a bitter spirit at their unfinished business, Agnes got up joyfully and, already rejoicing in the cross of Christ for which she had struggled in this first battle, gave herself perpetually to the divine service. In fact, Blessèd Francis cut off her hair with his own hand and directed her, together with her sister, in the way of the Lord.   *V,280*

The Sixth Sunday of Easter

Easter 6 — Sunday

A reading from 'The Bull of Canonization' of Saint Clare.

O the wonderful brilliance of blessèd Clare!
The more eagerly she is sought after for particular favours
the more brilliant she is found in each!
This woman, I say, grew bright in the world,
dazzled in her Religious life;
spread as a ray of the sun in her home,
shimmered as lightning in the enclosure.

O how great is the power of this light
and how intense is the brilliance of its illumination!
While this light remained certainly in a hidden enclosure,
it emitted sparkling rays outside.
Placed in the confined area of the monastery,
yet it was spread throughout the wide world.

Hidden within,
she extended herself abroad.
In fact,
Clare was hidden,
yet her life was visible.
Clare was silent,
yet her reputation became widespread.
She was kept hidden in a cell,
but was known throughout the world.   *V,239f>*

Easter 6 — Monday

A reading from 'The Legend of Saint Clare'.

There was only one loaf of bread in the monastery when both hunger and the time for eating arrived. After calling the refectorian, Saint Clare told her to divide the bread and to send part of it to the brothers, keeping the rest for the sisters. From this remaining part, she told her to cut fifty pieces according, to the number of ladies, and to place them on the table of poverty. When the devoted daughter replied to her, 'It would be necessary to have the ancient miracles of Christ occur to receive fifty pieces from such a small piece of bread,' the mother responded by saying, 'Confidently do whatever I say, my child.' The daughter hurried to fulfil the command of her mother; the mother hurried to direct her pious aspirations for her sisters to her Christ. Through a divine gift, that little piece of bread increased in the hands of the one breaking it and a generous portion existed for each one in the convent.   *V,270*

Easter 6 — Tuesday

A reading from 'The Acts of the Process of Canonization' of Saint Clare.

Sister Angeluccia, daughter of Messer Angelico of Spoleto, nun of the monastery of San Damiano, said under oath that it had been twenty-eight years that she, the witness, had been in the monastery of San Damiano and, for all this time in the monastery under the direction of Lady Clare of holy memory, she saw so many and such great good things in her she could truthfully say of her what could be said about any saint in heaven.

The witness also saw when the door of the piazza, that is, of the monastery fell upon Lady Clare. The sisters believed that door had killed her and, thereupon, raised a great moan. But the Lady remained unharmed and said that she had not felt in any way the weight of that door which was so heavy three brothers could barely return it to its place.

Asked how she knew this, she replied: because she saw it and was present. Asked how long ago this was, she replied: almost seven years ago. Asked about the day, she said: during the octave of Saint Peter, a Sunday evening. At that time, at the cry of the witness, the sisters immediately came and found the door still lying upon her since she, the witness, could not lift it by herself.

She also said when the most holy mother used to send the serving sisters outside the monastery, she reminded them to praise God when they saw beautiful trees, flowers and bushes; and, likewise, always to praise him for and in all things when they saw all peoples and creatures.

V,177f>

Easter 6 — Wednesday

A reading from 'The Little Flowers of Saint Francis'.

Saint Clare, a most devoted disciple of the Cross and noble plant of Saint Francis, was of such holiness that not only the bishops and cardinals but even the Pope desired with great affection to see her and listen to her, and often visited her personally.

Once, the Holy Father went to her at the monastery to hear her speak of heavenly and divine things; and as they were speaking together about various things, Saint Clare had the tables prepared and bread placed on them, so that the Holy Father might bless it. So, when their spiritual conversation was finished, Saint Clare knelt down with great reverence, and asked him to be kind enough to bless the bread placed on the table. The Holy Father replied, 'My most faithful Sister Clare, I want you to bless this bread, and make over it the sign of the most holy Cross, to which you have given your whole self.' And Saint Clare said, 'Most Holy Father, forgive me, because I would be worthy of the greatest rebuke if in front of the Vicar of Christ I, who am a vile little woman, should presume to give such a blessing.' And the Pope replied, 'So that this may not be attributed to presumption but to the merit of obedience, I command you under holy obedience to make the sign of the most holy Cross over this bread and bless it in the name of God.' Then Saint Clare, as a true daughter of obedience, very devoutly blessed that bread with the sign of the most holy Cross of Christ. An amazing thing happened! Immediately the sign of the Cross appeared, beautifully cut into each loaf. And then some of these loaves were eaten and others were kept because of the miracle. And the Holy Father, having seen the miracle, took some of that bread and, giving thanks to God, departed, leaving Saint Clare with his blessing.

At that time living in that monastery were Sister Ortulana, mother of Saint Clare, and Sister Agnes, her sister, both together, with Saint Clare, filled with virtues and with the Holy Spirit, and many other holy nuns. To them Saint Francis sent many sick people; and with their prayers and the sign of the most holy Cross they returned them all to health.

III,624

Ascension Day

A reading from 'The Office of the Passion', by Saint Francis.

Sing a new song to the Lord,
    for he has done wonderful things.
His right hand and holy arm
    have sacrificed his belovèd Son.
The Lord has made his salvation known;
    has revealed his justice in the sight of the nations.
On that day the Lord has sent his mercy,
    and at night his song.
This is the day the Lord has made;
    let us rejoice and be glad in it.
Blessèd is the one who comes in the name of the Lord,
    the Lord is God, and has enlightened us.
Let the heavens rejoice and the earth exult,
    let the sea and all that is in it be moved,
    let the fields and all that is in them be glad.
Give to the Lord, you families of nations,
    give to the Lord glory and honour,
    give to the Lord the glory due to his name.

Sing to the Lord, kingdoms of the earth,
    sing psalms to the Lord.
Sing psalms to God who ascends above the heights
                        of the heavens
    to the rising of the sun.
Behold, the Lord will give his voice the voice of power;
    give glory to God!
    whose greatness is over Israel;
    whose power is in the skies.
God is marvellous in his holy ones;
    the God of Israel himself will give power and strength
                        to his people.
Blessèd be God!   *I,149*

Easter 6 — Friday

A reading from 'The Tree of Life', by Saint Bonaventure.

We pray to the most kind Father
through you, his only-begotten Son,
who for us became man, was crucified and glorified,
that he sends us,
out of his treasures,
the Spirit of sevenfold grace
who rested upon you in all fullness:
the Spirit, I say, of WISDOM,
that we may taste the life-giving flavours
of the fruit of the tree of life,
which you truly are;
the gift also of UNDERSTANDING,
by which the intentions of our mind are illumined;
the gift of COUNSEL,
by which we may follow in your footsteps
on the right paths;
the gift of FORTITUDE,
by which we may be able to weaken the violence
of our enemies' attacks;
the gift of KNOWLEDGE,
by which we may be filled with the brilliant light
of your sacred teaching
to distinguish good and evil;
the gift of PIETY,
by which we may acquire a merciful heart;
the gift of FEAR,
by which we may draw away from all evil
and be set at peace
by submitting in awe to your eternal majesty.
For you have wished
that we ask for these things
in that sacred prayer which you have taught us;
and now we ask to obtain them,
through your cross,
for the praise of your most holy name.
To you,

with the Father and the Holy Spirit,
be honour and glory,
thanksgiving, beauty and power,
forever and ever.
Amen. *VI,174f*

Easter 6 — Saturday

A reading from 'The Major Legend of Saint Francis', by Saint Bonaventure.

At Siena, a Religious, who was a Doctor of Sacred Theology, once asked Francis about certain questions that were difficult to understand.

Francis brought to light the secrets of divine wisdom with such clarity in teaching that the learnèd man was absolutely dumbfounded. With admiration, he responded, 'Truly, the theology of this holy father, borne aloft, as it were, on the wings of purity and contemplation, is a soaring eagle; while our learning crawls on its belly on the ground.'

For although he was unskilled in word,
nevertheless, full of knowledge,
he often untangled the ambiguities of questions
and brought the hidden into light.
Nor is it inconsistent!
If the holy man had received from God
an understanding of the Scriptures,
it is because,
through his imitation of Christ,
he carried in his activity the perfect truth described in them and,
through a full anointing of the Holy Spirit,
held their Teacher in his heart.' *II,613*

The Seventh Sunday of Easter

Easter 7 — Sunday

'The Salutation of the Virtues', by Saint Francis.

Hail, Queen Wisdom!
May the Lord protect you,
with your Sister, holy pure Simplicity!
Lady holy Poverty,
may the Lord protect you,
with your Sister, holy Humility!
Lady holy Charity,
may the Lord protect you,
with your Sister, holy Obedience!
Most holy Virtues,
may the Lord protect all of you,
from whom you come and proceed.

There is surely no one in the whole world
who can possess any one of you
without dying first.
Whoever possesses one
and does not offend the others
possesses all.
Whoever offends one
does not possess any
and offends all.
And each one confounds vice and sin.
Holy Wisdom confounds
Satan and all his cunning.
Pure holy Simplicity confounds
all the wisdom of this world
and the wisdom of the body.
Holy Poverty confounds
the desire for riches,
greed,
and the cares of this world.
Holy Humility confounds
pride,
all people who are in the world

and all that is in the world.
Holy Charity confounds
every diabolical and carnal temptation
and every carnal fear.
Holy Obedience confounds
every corporal and carnal wish,
binds its mortified body
to obedience of the Spirit
and obedience to one's brother,
so that it is
subject and submissive
to everyone in the world,
not only to people
but to every beast and wild animal too
that they may do whatever they want with it
insofar as it has been given to them
from above by the Lord.   *I,164f*

Easter 7 — Monday

A reading from 'The Major Legend of Saint Francis', by Saint Bonaventure.

Once, a noble woman, devoted to God, came to Saint Francis to explain her trouble to him and to ask for help. She had a very cruel husband whom she endured as an antagonist to her service of Christ. So she begged the saint to pray for him so that God in his goodness would soften his heart. When he heard this, he said to her, 'Go in peace, and without any doubt be assured that you will soon have consolation from your husband.' And he added, 'You may tell him for God and for me, that now is the time of clemency, and later it will be the time of justice.'

After receiving his blessing, the lady returned home, found her husband and relayed the message. The Holy Spirit came upon him and he was changed from the old to the new man, prompting him to reply very meekly, 'My lady, let us serve the Lord and save our souls.' At the suggestion of his holy wife, they lived a celibate life for many years. On the same day, they both departed to the Lord.

The power of the prophetic spirit in the man of God
was certainly extraordinary,
which restored vigour to dried-up limbs

and impressed piety on hardened hearts.
The transparency of his spirit
was no less wondrous;
for he could foresee future events
and even probe obscurity of conscience,
as if another Elisha rivalling the twofold spirit of Elijah. *II,616f*

Easter 7 — Tuesday

A reading from 'The Major Legend of Saint Francis', by Saint Bonaventure.

A certain brother, devoted to God and to Christ's servant, Francis, frequently turned over in his heart the idea: whomsoever the holy man embraced with intimate affection would be worthy of divine favour. Whosoever he excluded, on the other hand, he would not regard among God's chosen ones. He was obsessed by the repeated pressure of this thought and intensely longed for the intimacy of the man of God, but never revealed the secret on his heart to anyone. The devoted father called him and spoke gently to him in this way, 'Let no thought disturb you, my son, because, holding you dearest among those very dear to me, I gladly lavish upon you my intimacy and love.' The brother was amazed at this and became even more devoted. Not only did he grow in his love of the holy man but, through the grace of the Holy Spirit, he was also filled with still greater gifts. *II,617f*

Easter 7 — Wednesday

A reading from 'The Major Legend of Saint Francis', by Saint Bonaventure.

The Spirit of the Lord,
who had anointed and sent Francis,
and also Christ,
the power and wisdom of God,
were with their servant Francis wherever he went
so that he might abound with words of sound teaching
and shine with miracles of great power.
For his word was like a blazing fire,
reaching the deepest parts of the heart,
and filling the souls of all with wonder,

since it made no pretence
at the elegance of human composition,
but exuded the breath of divine revelation.

Once, when Francis was to preach before the Pope and the Cardinals at the suggestion of the Lord of Ostia, he memorized a sermon which he had carefully composed. When he stood in their midst to offer his edifying words, he went completely blank and was unable to say anything at all. This he admitted to them in true humility and directed himself to invoke the grace of the Holy Spirit. Suddenly, he began to overflow with such effective eloquence, and to move the minds of those high-ranking men to compunction with such force and power, that it was clearly evident it was not he, but the Spirit of the Lord who was speaking.

II,625f

Easter 7 — Thursday

A reading from 'The Major Legend of Saint Francis', by Saint Bonaventure.

People of all ages and both sexes hurried
to see and hear this new man
given to the world by heaven.
Moving about through various regions,
he preached the gospel ardently,
as the Lord worked with him
and confirmed his preaching with the signs that followed.
For in the power of his name
Francis, the herald of truth,
cast out devils and healed the sick,
and, what is greater,
he softened the obstinate minds of sinners
and moved them to penance,
restoring at the same time health to the bodies and hearts,
as his miracles prove,
a few of which we will cite below as examples.

In the city of Toscanella, he was warmly taken in as a guest by a knight whose only son had been crippled since birth. At the father's insistent entreaties, he lifted the child up with his hand and cured him instantly, so that all the limbs of his body at once got back their strength in view of all. The boy became healthy and strong and immediately rose, walking and leaping and praising God.

In the city of Narni, at the request of the bishop, Francis made the sign of the cross from head to foot over a paralytic who had lost the use of all his limbs, and restored him to perfect health.

There was a woman in the town of Gubbio whose hands were both so withered and crippled that she could do nothing with them. When he made the sign of the cross over them in the name of the Lord, she was so perfectly cured that she immediately went home and prepared with her own hands food for him and for the poor, like Peter's mother-in-law.

In the village of Bevagna he marked the eyes of a blind girl with his saliva three times in the name of the Trinity and restored the sight she longed for. *II,626f>*

Easter 7 — Friday

A reading from 'The Acts of the Process of Canonization' of Saint Clare.

Sister Benvenuto of Perugia, nun of the monastery of San Damiano, also said that a certain brother of the Order of Friars Minor, Stephen by name, was mentally ill. Saint Francis sent him to the monastery of San Damiano, so Saint Clare would make the sign of the cross over him. After she had done this, the brother went to sleep a little bit in the place where the holy mother usually prayed. Upon waking, he ate a little and then departed cured.

Asked who was present at this event, she replied the sisters of the monastery were, some still living, others dead.

Asked if she had known that brother beforehand, how many days she had seen him ill, and how much time well, she replied she did not know all these things, because she was enclosed. Brother Stephen, once cured, went on his way.

She also said a young boy of the city of Spoleto, Mattiolo, three or four years old, had put a small pebble up one of the nostrils of his nose, so it could in no way be extricated. The young boy seemed to be in danger. After he was brought to Saint Clare and she made the sign of the cross over him, that pebble immediately fell from his nose. The young boy was cured. *V,141,144f>*

Easter 7 — Saturday

A reading from 'The Acts of the Process of Canonization' of Saint Clare.

Sister Cecilia, a nun of the monastery of San Damiano, said under oath that she knew of Lady Clare of holy memory, former abbess of the monastery. It could have been forty-three years or so that the Lady had been governing the sisters. She herself entered religion three years after the Lady had, because of the preaching of Saint Francis.

She said the Lord had given Lady Clare the grace that, when she made the sign of the cross with her hand, she cured many sisters of their illnesses. The other sisters, who gave testimony before, had also said this.

She saw others who had been brought to the monastery to be cured by the holy mother. She made the sign of the cross over them and they were cured.

She also said Lady Clare had the spirit of prophecy. Once when, one day, Saint Francis had sent five women to be received in the monastery, Saint Clare lifted herself up and said she would receive four of them. But she said that she did not want to receive the fifth because she would not persevere in the monastery, even if she stayed there for three years. After she did receive her because of great pressure, the woman stayed hardly half a year. *V,158ff>*

Day of Pentecost — Whit Sunday

A reading from 'The Office of the Passion', by Saint Francis.

Cry out with joy to the Lord, all the earth,
  chant a psalm to his name
    give glory to his praise.
Say to God: How awesome are your works, O Lord,
  your enemies shall fawn upon you
    in the greatness of your strength.
Let all the earth adore you and sing a psalm to you,
  let us chant a psalm to your name.
Come, listen, and I will tell you, all you who fear God,
  how much he has done for my soul.
I cried with my mouth to him
  and I have exulted with my tongue.
From his holy temple, he heard my voice
  and my cry reached his ears.
Bless our Lord, you peoples,
  make the voice of his praise heard.
May all the tribes of the Lord be blessed in him
  and all nations will glorify him.
Blessèd be the Lord, the God of Israel,
  who alone does great wonders.
Blessèd forever be the name of his majesty,
  and may all the earth be filled with his majesty.
          So be it. So be it.   *I,151*

For the weekdays after Pentecost, see the dated week in Ordinary Time, page 147ff.
For Trinity Sunday, Corpus Christi, Divine Compassion/Sacred Heart and Dedication Festival, see pages immediately following this.

Ordinary Time

Trinity Sunday — *Sunday after Pentecost*

'The Praises to be said at all the Hours', by Saint Francis.

Holy, holy, holy Lord God Almighty,
　　who is, and who was and who is to come:
　　　　And let us praise and glorify him for ever.
O Lord our God, you are worthy to receive
　　praise, glory and honour and blessing.
　　　　And let us praise and glorify him for ever.
The Lamb who was slain is worthy to receive
　　power and divinity, wisdom and strength,
　　honour and glory and blessing.
　　　　And let us praise and glorify him for ever.
Let us bless the Father and the Son with the Holy Spirit:
　　　　And let us praise and glorify him for ever.
Bless the Lord, all you works of the Lord.
　　　　And let us praise and glorify him for ever.
Sing praise to our God, all you his servants
　　and you who fear God, the small and the great.
　　　　And let us praise and glorify him for ever.
Let heaven and earth praise him who is glorious.
　　　　And let us praise and glorify him for ever.
Every creature in heaven, on earth and under the earth;
　　and in the sea and those which are in it.
　　　　And let us praise and glorify him for ever.
Glory to the Father and to the Son and to the Holy Spirit.
　　　　And let us praise and glorify him for ever.
As it was in the beginning, is now, and shall be for ever.
　　　　And let us praise and glorify him for ever.

All powerful, Most Holy, Most High, supreme God:
all good, supreme good, totally good, you who alone are good,
may we give you all praise, all glory, all thanks, all honour, all blessing,
and all good.
So be it! So be it! Amen.　　　　　　　　　　　　　　　*I,161f*

Corpus Christi — *Thursday after Trinity Sunday*

A reading from 'A Letter to the Entire Order', by Saint Francis.

Let everyone be struck with fear,
let the whole world tremble,
and let the heavens exult
when Christ, the Son of the living God,
is present on the altar in the hands of a priest!
O wonderful loftiness and stupendous dignity!
O sublime humility!
O humble sublimity!
The Lord of the universe,
God and the Son of God,
so humbles himself
that for our salvation
he hides himself
under an ordinary piece of bread!
Brothers, look at the humility of God,
and pour out your hearts before him!
Humble yourselves
that you may be exalted by him!
Hold back nothing of yourselves for yourselves,
that he who gives himself totally to you
may receive you totally!   *I,118*

Divine Compassion ● Sacred Heart of Jesus
— *Friday after Trinity 1*

A reading from 'The Remembrance of the Desire of a Soul', by Thomas of Celano.

Perhaps it would be useful and worthwhile to touch briefly on the special devotions of Saint Francis. Although this man was devout in all things, since he enjoyed the anointing of the Spirit, there were special things that moved him with special affection.

Among other expressions used in common speech, he could not hear the words 'the love of God' without a change in himself. As soon as he heard the words 'the love of God' he was excited, moved, and on fire, as if these words from the outside were a pick strumming the strings of his heart on the inside.

He used to say that it was a noble extravagance to offer such a treasure for alms, and that those who considered it less valuable than money were complete fools. As for himself, he kept until his death the resolution he made while still entangled in the things of this world: he would never refuse any poor person who asked something 'for the love of God'.

Once, a poor man begged something of him 'for the love of God', and since he had nothing, he secretly picked up scissors and hurried to cut his small tunic in two. And he would have done just that, except that he was caught by the brothers and they had the poor man supplied with a different compensation.

He said,
'The love of him who loved us greatly
is greatly to be loved!'   *II,373*

Dedication Festival

2 August or 30 October, if actual date not known

A reading from 'A Mirror of the Perfection of a Lesser Brother'.

Holy of Holies is this place of places,
rightly deemed worthy of the highest honours!
Happy its surname 'of the holy Angels',
happier its dedication to 'Saint Mary':
and now the third name of 'The little portion'
foretells the Mother House of all the Order.
Here the fair presence of the holy Angels
sheds light around it, filling it with splendour;
here in the long night-watches of the brothers
praises soar upwards, piercing the heavens.
Once long abandoned, fallen into ruin,
Francis restored it to its former honour;
of the three churches which the holy father
raised with his own hands, this is best and dearest.
This place our Father chose for his own dwelling,
here in stern penance clad his limbs in sackcloth,
subdued his body and its errant passions,
made it obedient to the Spirit's bidding.
This holy temple God chose as the birthplace
of the Friars Minor, humble, poor and joyful,

while the example of the holy father
drew a great army, walking in his footsteps.
Here for the tonsure of her golden tresses
came the sweet virgin Clare, the spouse of Jesus,
casting behind her all the pomps and pleasures
loved by the worldly, and embracing penance.
Here did the Orders of the Friars and Ladies
spring into being, born of one fair Mother,
Mary, most holy, who in her new offspring
gave to the world new patterns for her First-born.
Here the broad highway of the old world changed
into the narrow way of life eternal;
and to the faithful, called from every nation,
new grace was given freely by the Father.
Here was the Holy Rule to guide the Order
written by Francis; Poverty exalted;
Pride was cast headlong, and the Cross upraised
once more among us for the world's salvation.
Whenever Francis, worn and frail in body,
in the sweet silence of this sanctuary
here he found healing, comfort and refreshment.
And when the Devil doubting and confusion
sowed in his spirit, here was Truth revealed;
here, too, was granted to the holy father
all that he asked for in his intercession.   *IV,1216f*

Weeks in Ordinary Time

The following readings are used either between 3 February and up to the Sunday Next Before Lent (for which readings can be found on pages 60ff) or between the Monday after the Day of Pentecost and the Saturday before Advent Sunday. Proper readings are provided for Trinity Sunday, Corpus Christi and Divine Compassion/Sacred Heart, (see previous pages) and on various Sanctorale days.

Week of Sunday between 3 & 9 February inclusive
if before Lent

Sunday — DEL Week 5

A reading from 'The Sacred Exchange between Saint Francis and Lady Poverty'.

Among the other outstanding and exceptional virtues which prepare in us an abode and a dwelling for God and which show an excellent and unencumbered path of going to and arriving before him, holy Poverty shines with a certain prerogative before them all. By a unique grace, it excels the claims of the others. For it is the foundation and guardian of all virtues and enjoys a principal place and name among the gospel virtues. As long as they have been firmly placed on this foundation, the others need not fear the downpour of rains, the rush of floods and the blast of winds that threaten ruin.

This is certainly appropriate since the Son of God, the Lord of virtue and the King of glory, fell in love with this virtue with a special affection. He sought, found and embraced it while achieving our salvation in the midst of the earth. At the beginning of his preaching he placed it as a light of faith in the hands of those entering the gate, and even set it as the foundation stone of the house. While the other virtues receive the kingdom of heaven only by way of promise from him, poverty is invested with it by him without delay. He said, 'Blessèd are the poor in spirit, for the kingdom of heaven is theirs.'

At the beginning of his conversion, therefore, blessèd Francis, as the Saviour's true imitator and disciple, gave himself with all eagerness, all longing, all determination to searching for, finding, and embracing holy poverty. He did so neither wavering under adversity nor fearing injury, neither shirking effort nor shunning bodily discomfort, in order to achieve his desire: to reach her to whom the Lord had entrusted the keys of the kingdom of heaven.   *1,529f>*

Monday — *DEL Week 5*

A reading from 'The Sacred Exchange between Saint Francis and Lady Poverty'.

Francis eagerly began to go about the streets and piazzas of the city, as a curious explorer diligently looking for her whom his soul loved. He asked those standing about and inquired of those who came near him, 'Have you seen her whom my soul loves?' But that saying was hidden from them as though it was barbaric. Not understanding him, they told him, 'We do not know what you are saying. Speak to us in our own language and we will answer you.'

Afterwards he left the city, and blessèd Francis quickly came to a certain field in which, as he looked from afar, he saw two old men wasted away from great sorrow. One of them spoke in this way: 'Whom shall I respect except the one who is poor and contrite in spirit and the one who trembles at my words?' 'We brought nothing into the world,' the other said, 'and, without a doubt, we can take nothing out of it; but having food and whatever covers us, we are content with these.'

When blessèd Francis reached them, he said to them, 'Tell me, I beg you, where does Lady Poverty dwell? Where does she eat? Where does she rest at noon, for I languish with love for her?'

They answered, 'Brother, she has now gone up to a great and high mountain where God has placed her. If, then, you wish to reach her, take off your clothes of rejoicing, and put aside every burden and sin clinging to you; for, unless you are naked, you will not be able to climb to her who lives in so high a place. Yet, because she is kind, she will easily be seen by those who love her and be found by those who search for her. To think about her, brother, is perfect understanding, and whoever keeps vigil for her will quickly be secure. Take faithful companions so that during the mountain's ascent you will have their advice and be strengthened by their help. For woe to the one who is alone! If he falls, he will have no one to lift him up. For if anyone falls, he should have someone to help him!'

1,530ff>

Tuesday — *DEL Week 5*

A reading from 'The Sacred Exchange between Saint Francis and Lady Poverty'.

Blessèd Francis came and chose some faithful companions for himself with whom he hurried to the mountain. He said to his brothers, 'Come, let us climb the mountain of the Lord and the dwelling of Lady Poverty, that she might teach us her ways and we might walk in her paths.'

Because of its great height and difficulty, they studied the ascent of the mountain from every angle. Some of them said to one another, 'Who can climb this mountain and who can reach its summit?'

Blessèd Francis understood this and said to them, 'The road is difficult, brothers, and the gate that leads to it is narrow. There are few who find it. Be strengthened in the Lord and in the power of his virtue, for everything difficult will be easy for you. Cast off the burdens of your own will, get rid of the weight of your sins, and gird yourselves as powerful men. Forgetting whatever is in the past, stretch yourselves as much as you can for what lies ahead. I tell you that wherever you place your foot will be yours. For the Spirit is before your face, Christ the Lord, who draws you to the heights of the mountain in bonds of love. The espousal of Poverty, brothers, is wonderful, yet we will be able to enjoy her embraces easily because the lady of the nations has been made as it were a widow, the queen of the virtues worthless and contemptible to all. There is no one of our region who would dare to cry out, no one who would oppose us, no one who would be able to prohibit by law this salvific exchange. All her friends have spurned her and have been made her enemies.'

After he said these things, they all began to follow the holy Francis.

1,532f

Wednesday — *DEL Week 5*

A reading from 'The Sacred Exchange between Saint Francis and Lady Poverty'.

While blessèd Francis and his faithful companions were hastening to the summit at a very easy pace, Lady Poverty, standing at the top of the mountain, looked down its slopes. She was greatly astonished at seeing these men climbing so ably, almost flying. 'Who are these men,' she asked, 'who fly like clouds and like doves to their windows? It has been a long time since I have seen such people or gazed upon those so unencumbered, all their burdens set aside. Therefore I will speak to them about what engages my heart so that, when staring down at the abyss that lies about them, they do not, like others, have second thoughts about such a climb. I know they cannot take hold of me without my consent, but there will be a reward for me before my heavenly Father if I give them saving advice.'

'We have come to you, our Lady,' said Francis and his companions, 'and beg you: receive us in peace! We wish to become servants of the

Lord of hosts, because he is the King of glory. We have heard that you are the queen of virtues and, to some extent, we have learned this from experience. Casting ourselves at your feet, then, we humbly ask you to agree to be with us. Be for us the way of arriving at the King of glory, just as you were for him when he, the Daybreak from on high, agreed to visit those sitting in darkness and in the shadow of death. For we know that yours is the power, yours is the kingdom. Established as queen and lady by the King of kings, you are above all powers. Simply make peace with us and we will be saved. In that way, he who redeemed us through you may receive us through you. If you decide to save us, immediately we will be set free.'   *I,533f>*

Thursday — *DEL Week 5*

A reading from 'The Sacred Exchange between Saint Francis and Lady Poverty'.

Lady Poverty responded with a joyful heart, a radiant face and a gentle voice: 'Brothers and very dear friends, I admit that, from the moment you began to speak, I was filled with joy, with an over-flowing happiness, as I observed your fervour and learned of your holy intention. Your words became more desirable to me than gold and a very precious jewel and sweeter than honey and the comb. For it is not you who have spoken, but the Holy Spirit who has spoken in you. That anointing teaches you everything you have uttered about the Most High King who, by his grace alone, took me as his belovèd, taking away my reproach from the earth, and glorified me among the most celebrated in heaven.

'Therefore, if it is not too much of a burden for you to hear, I want to tell you the long but no less useful tale of my condition. In this way, you might learn how you should walk and please God, being careful of any hint of looking back, you who want to put your hand to the plough.

'I am not uneducated, as many think, but I am quite old and abounding in days, knowing the nature of things, the varieties of creatures, the changes of times. I have known the fluctuations of the human heart, in part by the experience of time, in part by the insight of nature, in part through the nobility of grace.'   *I,537*

Friday — *DEL Week 5*

A reading from 'The Sacred Exchange between Saint Francis and Lady Poverty'.

At Lady Poverty's words, the blessèd Francis and his brothers fell flat on the ground and gave thanks to God. 'What you say pleases us, our Lady,' they said. 'There can be no fault in anything you have said. What we heard in our land about your words and your wisdom is true. Your wisdom is so much greater than the rumour we had heard. Your men and your servants are blessed, those who are always before you and listen to your wisdom. May the Lord God be blessed forever whom you have pleased and who has loved you forever and placed you as queen to show mercy and judgement upon his servants. O how good and sweet is your spirit, correcting the erring and admonishing sinners!

'Lady, by the eternal King's love with which he loved you and by the love with which you love him, we beg you not to cheat us of our desire. Deal with us, instead, according to your kindness and mercy. For your deeds are great and ineffable. For this reason those who lack discipline have strayed from you! Because you march over rocky ground, like an army of soldiers set in array, the foolish cannot stay with you. But we are your servants and the sheep of your pasture. For all eternity and age upon age we promise and resolve to keep the judgements of your justice.'

These words deeply moved Lady Poverty. Always accustomed to being merciful and forgiving, she ran, incapable of containing herself any more, and embraced them. She placed a kiss of peace on each one. 'Look, I am coming to you, my brothers and sons,' she shouted. 'I know many will acquire me as profit because of you.'

Blessèd Francis, unable to contain himself out of joy, with a loud voice began to praise the All-powerful who did not abandon those who hope in him. 'Bless the Lord,' he said, 'all you his chosen ones. Keep days of joy and confess to him because he is good, because his mercy is forever!'

As they came down from the mountain, they led Lady Poverty to the place where they were staying, for it was nearly the sixth hour.   *1,550f*

Saturday – *DEL Week 5*

A reading from 'The Sacred Exchange between Saint Francis and Lady Poverty'.

After they had prepared everything, blessèd Francis and his faithful companions persuaded Lady Poverty to eat with them. But she said, 'First, show me your oratory, chapter room, enclosure, refectory, kitchen, dormitory and stable; your beautiful chairs, polished tables and larger houses. I do not see any of these. I only notice that you are cheerful and happy, overflowing with joy, filled with consolation, as if you expect that everything will be given to you at your request.'

They answered, 'Our Lady and Queen, we, your servants, are tired from the long journey and you, coming with us, have expended no little effort. Let us first eat. Once we are strengthened, if you direct, we will do everything as you wish.'

'I am pleased at what you say,' she said. 'But bring some water that we might wash our hands and some towels to dry them.' They brought her immediately a cracked earthen bowl – because there was not a whole one – filled with water. Pouring the water over her hands they looked here and there for a towel. When they could not find one, one of them offered her the tunic he was wearing that she could dry her hands with it. Accepting it with thanks, she then gave, in her heart, glory to God, who had brought her into association with such men.

Then they led her to where they had prepared the table. When they had led her there, she saw that there was nothing more than three or four crusts of barley- or bran-bread set upon the grass. She was greatly astonished and said to herself, 'Who has ever seen in past generations such things as these! Blessèd are you, Lord God, who cares for all things! Everything is possible when you wish. You have taught your people to please you through such deeds.' They then sat down together, thanking God for all his gifts.

When they were satisfied, more by the glory of such want than by an abundance of all things, they blessed the Lord in whose sight they found such grace and led her to a place where she would rest because she was tired. And so she laid down naked upon the naked earth. She even asked for a pillow for her head. They immediately brought a stone and placed it under her head. After enjoying a very quiet and healthy sleep, she quickly arose and asked to be shown the enclosure. Taking her to a certain hill, they showed her all the world they could see and said, 'This, Lady, is our enclosure.'   *I,551f>*

Week of Sunday between 10 & 16 February inclusive
if before Lent, or
Week of Sunday between 8 & 14 May inclusive
if after Pentecost

Sunday — *RCL Proper 1 / DEL Week 6*

A reading from 'A letter to friends in Liège', 1216, by Jacques de Vitry.

After I had been at the Curia for a while, I encountered a great deal that was repugnant to me. They were so occupied with worldly affairs, with rulers and kingdoms, with lawsuits and litigation, that they hardly let anyone speak of spiritual things. I did find, however, one source of consolation in those parts. Many well-to-do secular people of both sexes, having left all things for Christ, had fled the world. They were called 'Lesser Brothers' and 'Lesser Sisters'. They are held in a great reverence by the Lord Pope and the Cardinals. They are in no way occupied with temporal things but, with fervent desire and ardent zeal, they labour each day to draw from the vanities of the world souls that are perishing, and draw them to their way of life. Thanks be to God, they have already reaped great fruit and have converted many. Those who have heard them, say, 'Come!', so that one group brings another.

They live according to the form of the primitive Church, about whom it was written: 'The community of believers were of one heart and one mind.' During the day they go into the cities and villages giving themselves over to the active life in order to gain others; at night, however, they return to their hermitage or solitary places to devote themselves to contemplation. The women dwell together near the cities in various hospices, accepting nothing, but living by the work of their hands. They are grieved, indeed troubled, by the fact that they are honoured by both clergy and laity more than they would wish.

With great profit, the brothers of this Order assemble once a year in a designated place to rejoice in the Lord and eat together; with the advice of good men they draw up and promulgate holy laws and have them confirmed by the Lord Pope. After this, they disperse again for the whole year throughout Lombardy and Tuscany, Apulia and Sicily. Not long ago, Brother Nicholas, a provincial administrator for the Lord Pope and a holy and religious man, left the Curia and took refuge with these men, but because he was so needed by the Lord Pope, he was recalled by him. I believe, however, that the Lord desires to save many souls before the end of the world through such simple and poor men in order to put to shame our prelates, who are like dumb dogs not able to bark. *1,579f*

Monday — *RCL Proper 1 / DEL Week 6*

A reading from 'The History of the West', by Jacques de Vitry.

As we have seen, up to now there have been three Religious Orders: hermits, monks and canons. But in order that the state of those living according to a Rule might rest firmly on a solid foundation, the Lord in these days has added a fourth form of Religious Life, the embellishment of a new Order, and the holiness of a new Rule.

But if we carefully consider the form and condition of the primitive church, the Lord has not so much added a new way of living as renewed an old one; he lifted up one that was being cast aside and revived one that was almost dead. Thus, in the twilight of the world that is tending to its end, at a time when the son of perdition is soon to arrive, he might prepare new athletes to confront the perilous times of the Antichrist, fortifying and propping up the church.

This is the Religious way of life of the true poor of the Crucified One and of the order of preachers whom we call Lesser Brothers. They are truly Minors, for they are more humble than all present-day Religious in their habit, in their poverty and in their contempt of the world. They have one general Superior, whose commands and regulations the lesser Superiors and the other brothers of the same Order obey; he sends them throughout the various provinces of the world to preach and to save souls. *1,582*

Tuesday — *RCL Proper 1 / DEL Week 6*

A reading from 'The History of the West', by Jacques de Vitry.

The Lesser Brothers diligently strive to renew in themselves the way of life of the primitive church, its poverty and humility. They drink of the pure waters of the fountain of the gospel with such thirst and ardour of spirit that they work hard at carrying out not only the evangelical precepts but the counsels as well, thus imitating more explicitly the life of the apostles. They renounce everything they possess; they deny themselves and take up their cross and, naked, follow the naked Christ. Like Joseph, they leave their cloak behind; like the Samaritan woman, their water jar. They run their race unburdened. They walk before his face and do not turn back; forgetful of the past, they are always straining with tireless gait towards what is ahead, flying like clouds, and like doves to their windows, on guard with all diligence and caution, lest death enter in.

The Lord Pope confirmed their Rule and gave them authority to preach at any church they came to, although out of reverence having first obtained the consent of the local prelates. They are sent two by two to preach as if before the face of the Lord and before his Second Coming.

1,582f

Wednesday — *RCL Proper 1 / DEL Week 6*

The papal bull of Honorius III, 'Pro dilectis'.

Honorius, Bishop, servant of the servants of God, to our venerable brothers, the archbishops and bishops; and to our belovèd sons, the abbots, priors and other prelates of the churches, established throughout the kingdom of France: health and apostolic benediction.

We recall that we sent you a letter on behalf of our belovèd sons of the Order of Lesser Brothers in order that you might consider them as having been recommended in the sight of the love of God. But, as we now understand, some of you seemingly have a doubtful conscience about this same Order. We also gather from other reports, in which we can place full trust, that others of you do not even allow these brothers to stay in their dioceses, although the very fact that we have granted these brothers our letter shows that you should not consider them suspect in any way.

Therefore, we want all of you to take note that we hold their Order to be among those approved by us, and that we regard the brothers of this Order as truly Catholic and devout men. We therefore take this occasion through these apostolic letters to warn and exhort you, indeed we prescribe and command you, to admit them into your dioceses as true believers and Religious and to hold them, out of reverence for God and for us, as having been favourably recommended.

> Given at Viterbo, the twenty-ninth day of May,
> in the fourth year of our pontificate [1220].   *1,559f*

Thursday — RCL Proper 1 / DEL Week 6

The papal bull of Honorius III, 'Quia populares'.

Honorius, Bishop, servant of the servants of God, to our belovèd sons, the brothers of the Order of Minors: greetings and apostolic benediction.

Fleeing the tumult of the crowds as something that impedes your proposed way of life, you eagerly seek separate places so that you can give yourselves more freely to the sacred quiet of prayer. Because of this, we are most attentive to this opportune request of your many prayers. For your intercession before God will be all the more efficacious to the extent that, living perfectly, you become all the more worthy of graces from him.

We consider that what does not take away from anyone else's rights should not be denied to you, while genuine religion entreats us to concede to you even those things which are a special favour. Furthermore, since you have professed and embraced holy poverty, you are not seeking any temporal favour from us, but a spiritual one for your devotion. Therefore, favourable to your petitions, by authority of these present letters, we concede to you this privilege: that in your places and oratories you may celebrate solemn Mass with a portable altar, as well as the other divine offices, without prejudice to the rights of parochial churches.

No one, therefore, is in any way permitted to tamper with this decree of our concession and indult or rashly dare to oppose it. If anyone shall have presumed to attempt this, let him know that he will incur the wrath of Almighty God and of his holy apostles Peter and Paul.

> Given at Rieti, the third day of December,
> in the ninth year of our pontificate [1224]. *1,562f*

Friday — RCL Proper 1 / DEL Week 6

A reading from 'The Chronicle of Lauterberg' (circa 1224).

Two Orders, having a new way of Religious Life, began to settle in the province, especially in the city of Magdeburg. One of them was called the Holy Preachers; the other, the Lesser Brothers. It is reported that they were founded about twenty years before this time and were confirmed by Pope Innocent. The first of these is made up of clerics; the second receives both clerics and laymen, and it is said that it was begun by a merchant.

But why are such novelties introduced, if not as a kind of reproach against the neglected and indolent manner of Religious Life of those of us living in Orders on which the Church was first founded? In fact, the most blessèd Augustine and Benedict lived as they taught, and it is known to what great heights of sanctity they climbed by living their way of Religious life. Certainly, if anyone had the will to follow their precepts obediently, it would seem that he would need no new institutions. For if these new institutions are seeking after holiness, then that holiness at which those two most holy fathers arrived by living according to their Rules should be enough. It is not easy to believe that anyone from the Order of Holy Preachers or from the Order of Lesser Brothers will become holier than Augustine or Benedict!

Now far be it from me, when I say these things, to disparage anyone's zealous endeavours. But I am saying that one must deplore, yes vigorously deplore, the fact that the ancient Orders have been led into such disrepute by the disordered way of life of those who profess them, that they are no longer believed to suffice for salvation by those wishing to renounce the world. For if they were still considered sufficient, new ones would never be sought. *I,592*

Saturday — *RCL Proper 1 / DEL Week 6*

A reading from the 'World Chronicle' of Burchard of Ursperg.

At that time, when the world was already growing old, there arose two Religious orders in the Church, whose youth is continually renewed like the eagle's, and which were approved by the Apostolic See, namely the Lesser Brothers and the Friars Preachers. Perhaps they were approved at that time because two sects, which had previously sprung up in Italy, were still around; one was called the Humiliati and the other the Poor Men of Lyons. Pope Lucius had not long before listed them among the heretics, for among them had been found superstitious teachings and observances. Furthermore, in their clandestine preaching, which for the most part took place in their secret haunts, the Church of God and the priesthood were disparaged.

At that time we saw some of their number, who were called the Poor Men of Lyons, at the Apostolic See, with one of their Ministers whose name, I think, was Bernard. He was seeking to have his sect confirmed and given privileges by the Apostolic See. In fact, they went about through towns and villages, saying that they were living the life of the apostles, not wishing to possess anything or to have a definite place to live. But the Lord Pope took them to task for certain irregular practices in their way of life, namely, that they cut off their shoes above the foot and went about walking as if barefooted. Besides, while they wore mantles like Religious, they had their hair cut just like the lay people. But what was most shameful about them was that men and women would walk together on the road and often stay in the same house, even – so it was reported of them – sleeping together in the same bed! Nevertheless, they claimed that all these practices came down from the apostles.

In place of these, the Lord Pope approved certain others then on the rise who called themselves 'Poor Minors'. These rejected the above-mentioned superstitious and scandalous practices, but travelled about both in winter and in summer absolutely barefoot; they accepted neither money nor anything else besides food, and occasionally a needed garment that someone might spontaneously offer them, for they could not ask anything from anyone. However, later on, these men realized that their name could possibly lead to self-glorification under the cover of great humility and that, as many bear the title 'poor' to no purpose, they could boast in vain before God; therefore, obedient to the Apostolic See in all things, they preferred to be called Lesser Brothers instead of Poor Minors. *1,593f*

Week of Sunday between 17 & 23 February inclusive
if before Lent, or
Week of Sunday between 15 & 21 May inclusive
if after Pentecost

Sunday — *RCL Proper 2 / DEL Week 7*

A reading from 'The Legend of the Three Companions' of Saint Francis.

After blessèd Francis had obtained the place of Saint Mary of the Portiuncula from the Abbot of Saint Benedict, he ordered that a chapter be held there twice a year: that is, on Pentecost and on the Dedication of Saint Michael.

At Pentecost, all the brothers used to gather at the church of Saint Mary and discuss how they could better observe the Rule. They appointed brothers throughout the various provinces who would preach to the people, and assigned other brothers in their provinces. Saint Francis, however, used to give admonitions, corrections and directives as it seemed to him to be according to the Lord's counsel. Everything that he said to them in word, however, he would show them in deed with eagerness and affection.

He used to revere prelates and priests of the holy Church, and honoured the elderly, the noble and the wealthy. Moreover, he intimately loved the poor, suffering deeply with them, and he showed himself subject to all.   *II,100f*

Monday — *RCL Proper 2 / DEL Week 7*

A reading from 'The Legend of the Three Companions' of Saint Francis.

Blessèd Francis admonished the brothers not to judge anyone, nor to look down upon those who live with refinement and dress extravagantly or fashionably. For, he would say, their God is ours, the Lord who is capable of calling them to himself and justifying those called. He also used to tell them he wanted the brothers to show reverence to these people as their brothers and lords. They are brothers, because we were all created by one Creator; they are lords, because they help the good to do penance by providing them with the necessities of life. He added, 'The brothers' way of life among the people should be such that whoever hears or sees them glorifies and praises the heavenly Father with dedication.'

For his great desire was that he, as well as his brothers, would abound in such good deeds for which the Lord would be praised. He used to tell them, 'As you announce peace with your mouth, make sure that greater peace is in your hearts. Let no one be provoked to anger or scandal through you, but may everyone be drawn to peace, kindness and harmony through your gentleness. For we have been called to this: to heal the wounded, bind up the broken, and recall those who err. In fact, many who seem to us to be members of the devil will yet be disciples of Christ.'   *II,101f*

Tuesday — *RCL Proper 2 / DEL Week 7*

A reading from 'The Legend of the Three Companions' of Saint Francis.

The pious father Francis used to reprove his brothers who to him were too austere, exerting too much effort in those vigils, fasts and corporal punishments. Some of them afflicted themselves so harshly, to repress within them every impulse of the flesh, that they seemed to hate themselves. The man of God forbade them, admonishing them with kindness, reprimanding them with reason, and binding up their wounds with the bandages of wholesome precepts.

Among the brothers who had come to chapter, no one dared to discuss worldly matters, but they spoke of the lives of the holy fathers, and how they could better and more perfectly find the grace of the Lord Jesus Christ. If some of the brothers who came to the chapter experienced any temptation or tribulation, upon hearing blessèd Francis speaking so sweetly and fervently, and on seeing his penance, they were freed from their temptations and were miraculously relieved of the tribulations. For, while suffering with them, he spoke to them, not as a judge but as a merciful father to his children, or a good doctor to the sick, knowing how to be sick with the sick and afflicted with the afflicted. Nevertheless, he duly rebuked all delinquents, and restrained the obstinate and rebellious with an appropriate punishment. *II,102*

Wednesday – *RCL Proper 2 / DEL Week 7*

A reading from 'The Legend of the Three Companions' of Saint Francis.

When a chapter had ended, blessèd Francis would bless all the brothers and assign each of them to individual provinces. To anyone possessing the Spirit of God and an eloquence suitable for preaching, whether cleric or lay, he gave permission to preach. When those men received his blessing with great joy of spirit, they went throughout the world as pilgrims and strangers, taking nothing on their way except the books in which they could say their Hours. Whenever they found a priest, rich or poor, good or bad, bowing humbly they paid him their respect. When it was time to seek lodging, they more willingly stayed with priests rather than with seculars.

When they were unable to stay with priests, they would seek more spiritual and God-fearing persons with whom they could more suitably be welcomed. After this, in each city and town that the brothers wanted to visit, the Lord inspired some God-fearing people to offer them hospitality, until some places were built for them in cities and towns.

Not only were men converted to the Order; but also many virgins and widows, struck by their preaching, on their advice secluded themselves in cities and towns in monasteries established for doing penance. One of the brothers was appointed their visitator and corrector. Similarly, both married men and women given in marriage, unable to separate because of the law of matrimony, committed themselves to more severe penance in their own homes on the wholesome advice of the brothers. And thus, through blessèd Francis, a perfect worshipper of the Holy Trinity, the Church of God was renewed in three orders, just as the earlier repair of the three churches foreshadowed. Each one of these orders was in its time approved by the Supreme Pontiff. *II,102f>*

Thursday — *RCL Proper 2 / DEL Week 7*

A reading from 'The Assisi Compilation'.

When blessèd Francis was at the general chapter called the Chapter of Mats, held at Saint Mary of the Portiuncula, there were five thousand brothers present. Many wise and learnèd brothers told the Lord Cardinal, who later became Pope Gregory, who was present at the chapter, that he should persuade blessèd Francis to follow the advice of those same wise brothers and allow himself to be guided by them for the time being. They cited the Rule of blessèd Benedict, of blessèd Augustine and of blessèd Bernard, which teach how to live in such order in such a way.

Then blessèd Francis, on hearing the Cardinal's advice about this, took him by the hand and led him to the brothers assembled in chapter, and spoke to the brothers in this way, 'My brothers! My brothers! God has called me by the way of simplicity and showed me the way of simplicity. I do not want you to mention to me any Rule, whether of Saint Augustine, or of Saint Bernard, or of Saint Benedict. And the Lord told me what he wanted: he wanted me to be a new fool in the world. God did not wish to lead us by any way other than this knowledge, but God will confound you by your knowledge and wisdom. But I trust in the Lord's police that through them he will punish you, and you will return to your state, to your blame, like it or not.'

The Cardinal was shocked, and said nothing, and all the brothers were afraid. *II,132f*

Friday — *RCL Proper 2 / DEL Week 7*

A reading from 'The Assisi Compilation'.

Once when the time for the chapter of the brothers was approaching, to be held at the church of Saint Mary of the Portiuncula, blessèd Francis said to his companion, 'It seems to me that I am not a Lesser Brother unless I have the attitude I will tell you.' And he said, 'The brothers come to me with great devotion and veneration, invite me to the chapter and, touched by their devotion, I go to the chapter with them. After they assemble, they ask me to proclaim the word of God among them and I rise and preach to them as the Holy Spirit instructs me.

'After the sermon, suppose that they reflect and speak against me, saying, "We do not want you to rule over us. You are not eloquent and you are too simple. We are very ashamed to have such a simple and contemptible prelate over us. From now on, do not presume to call yourself our prelate." And so, with insults, they throw me out.

'It seems to me that I am not a Lesser Brother unless I am just as happy when they insult me and throw me out in shame, refusing that I be their prelate, as when they honour and revere me, if in both cases the benefit to them is equal. If I am happy about their benefit and devotion when they praise and honour me, which can be a danger to the soul, it is even more fitting that I should rejoice and be happy at my benefit and the salvation of my soul when they revile me as they throw me out in shame, which is profit for the soul.'   *II,217*

Saturday — *RCL Proper 2 / DEL Week 7*

A reading from 'The Assisi Compilation'.

Blessèd Francis wanted to be humble among his brothers. To preserve greater humility, a few years after his conversion he resigned the office of prelate before all the brothers during a chapter held at Saint Mary of the Portiuncula. 'From now on,' he said, 'I am dead to you. But here is Brother Peter di Catanio: let us all, you and I, obey him.' Then all the brothers began to cry aloud and weep profusely, but blessèd Francis bowed down before Brother Peter and promised him obedience and reverence.

From that time on, until his death, he remained a subject, like one of the other brothers. He wished to be subject to the Minister General and the Ministers Provincial, so that in whatever province he stayed or preached, he obeyed the Minister of that province.

He likewise said, 'There is no prelate in the whole world who would be as feared by his subjects and brothers as the Lord would make me feared by his subjects, if I wished. But the Most High gave me this grace: that I want to be content with all, as one who is lesser in the religion.'

We who were with him witnessed this often with our own eyes. Frequently, when some of the brothers did not provide for his needs, or said something to him that would ordinarily offend a person, he would immediately go to prayer. On returning, he did not want to remember it by saying 'Brother so-and-so did not provide for me,' or 'He said such-and-such to me.'

The closer he approached death, the more careful he became in complete perfection to consider how he might live and die in complete humility and poverty. *II,125f>*

Week of Sunday between 24 February & 2 March inclusive *if before Lent, or*
Week of Sunday between 22 & 28 May inclusive
if after Pentecost

Sunday — *RCL Proper 3 / DEL Week 8*

A reading from 'The Earlier Rule' of Saint Francis.

Let no brother preach contrary to the rite and practice of the Church or without the permission of his Minister. Let the Minister be careful of granting it without discernment to anyone. Let all the brothers, however, preach by their deeds. No Minister or preacher may make a ministry of the brothers or the office of preaching his own but, when he is told, let him set it aside without objection.

In the love that is God, therefore, I beg all my brothers – those who preach, pray or work, cleric or lay – to strive to humble themselves in everything, not to boast or delight in themselves or inwardly exalt them-selves because of the good words and deeds or, for that matter, because of any good that God sometimes says or does or works in and through them, in keeping with what the Lord says: Do not rejoice because the spirits are subject to you. We may know with certainty that nothing belongs to us except our vices and sins. We must rejoice, instead, when we fall into various trials and, in this world, suffer every kind of anguish or distress of soul and body for the sake of eternal life.

Therefore, let all the brothers, beware of all pride and vainglory. *I,75*

Monday — RCL Proper 3 / DEL Week 8

A reading from 'The Life of Saint Francis', by Thomas of Celano.

Francis was extremely determined and paid no attention to anything beyond what was of the Lord. Though he often preached the word of God among thousands of people, he was as confident as if he were speaking with a close friend. He used to view the largest crowd of people as if it were a single person, and he would preach fervently to a single person as if to a large crowd. Out of the purity of his mind he drew his confidence in preaching and, even without preparation, he used to say the most amazing things to everyone. Sometimes he prepared for his talk with some meditation, but once the people gathered he could not remember what he had meditated about and had nothing to say. Without any embarrassment, he would confess to the people that he had thought of many things before, but now he could not remember a thing. Sometimes he would be filled with such great eloquence that he moved the hearts of his hearers to astonishment. When he could not think of anything, he would give a blessing and send the people away, with this act alone as a very good sermon.   *I,244f*

Tuesday — RCL Proper 3 / DEL Week 8

A reading from 'The Life of Saint Francis', by Thomas of Celano.

Once, blessèd Francis came to the city of Rome on a matter concerning the Order, and he greatly yearned to speak before the Lord Pope Honorius and the venerable Cardinals. Lord Hugo, the renowned Bishop of Ostia, venerated the holy man of God with special affection. When he learned of his arrival, Lord Hugo was filled with fear and joy, admiring the holy man's fervour yet aware of his simple purity. Trusting to the mercy of the Almighty, that never fails the faithful in time of need, he led the holy man before the Lord Pope and the venerable Cardinals.

As he stood in the presence of so many princes of the Church, blessèd Francis, after receiving permission and a blessing, fearlessly began to speak.

He was speaking with such fire of spirit
that he could not contain himself for joy.
As he brought forth the word from his mouth,
he moved his feet as if dancing,
not playfully but burning with the fire of divine love,

not provoking laughter but moving them to tears of sorrow.
For many of them were touched in their hearts,
amazed at the grace of God
and the great determination of the man.   *1,245*

Wednesday — *RCL Proper 3 / DEL Week 8*

A reading from 'The Life of Saint Francis', by Thomas of Celano.

The blessèd father Francis was travelling through the Spoleto valley. He reached a place near Bevagna, in which a great multitude of birds of different types gathered, including doves, crows, and others commonly called monaclae. When Francis, the most blessèd servant of God, saw them, he ran swiftly towards them, leaving his companions on the road. He was a man of great fervour, feeling much sweetness and tenderness even towards lesser, irrational creatures. When he was already very close, seeing that they awaited him, he greeted them in his usual way. He was quite surprised, however, because the birds did not take flight, as they usually do. Filled with great joy, he humbly requested that they listen to the word of God.

Among many other things, he said to them, 'My brother birds, you should greatly praise your Creator, and love him always. He gave you feathers to wear, wings to fly, and whatever you need. God made you noble among his creatures and gave you a home in the purity of the air, so that, though you neither sow nor reap, he nevertheless protects and governs you without your least care.' He himself, and those brothers who were with him, used to say that, at these words, the birds rejoiced in a wonderful way according to their nature. They stretched their necks, spread their wings, opened their beaks and looked at him. He passed through their midst, coming and going, touching their heads and bodies with his tunic. Then he blessed them and, having made the sign of the cross, gave them permission to fly off to another place. The blessèd father, however, went with his companions along their way rejoicing and giving thanks to God.   *1,234*

Thursday — *RCL Proper 3 / DEL Week 8*

A reading from 'The Life of Saint Francis', by Thomas of Celano.

One day, blessèd Francis came to a village called Alviano to preach the word of God. Going up to a higher place where all could see him, he called for silence. All remained silent and stood reverently. But a large number of swallows nesting there were shrieking and chirping. Since blessèd Francis could not be heard by the people, he said to the noisy birds, 'My sister swallows, now it is time for me also to speak, since you have already said enough. Listen to the word of the Lord and stay quiet and calm until the word of the Lord is completed.' Immediately, those little birds fell silent – to the amazement and surprise of all present – and did not move from that place until the sermon was over. Those men who saw this sign were filled with great wonder, saying, 'Truly, this man is holy, and a friend of the Most High.' *I,235*

Friday — *RCL Proper 3 / DEL Week 8*

A reading from 'The Remembrance of the Desire of a Soul', by Thomas of Celano.

Although the evangelist Francis
preached to the simple,
in simple, concrete terms,
since he knew that virtue
is more necessary than words,
still, when he was among spiritual people
with greater abilities
he gave birth to life-giving and profound words.
With few words he would suggest
what was inexpressible
and, weaving movement with fiery gestures,
he carried away all his hearers towards the things of heaven.
He did not use the keys of distinctions,
for he did not preach about things he had not himself discovered.
Christ, true Power and Wisdom,
made his voice a voice of power.

A physician, a learnèd and eloquent man, once said, 'I remember the sermons of other preachers word for word, only what the saint, Francis, says eludes me. Even if I memorize some of his words, they do not seem to me like those that originally poured from his lips.' *II,318*

Saturday — *RCL Proper 3 / DEL Week 8*

A reading from 'The Legend of Saint Clare'.

> Clare provided for her children,
> through dedicated preachers,
> the nourishment of the Word of God
> and from this she did not take a poorer portion.

> She was filled with such rejoicing at hearing a holy sermon;
> she delighted at such a remembrance of her Jesus
> that, once, when Brother Philip of Atri was preaching,
> a very splendid child stood by the Virgin Clare
> and during the greater part of the sermon
> delighted her with his sighs of joy.
> That sister who merited to see such a thing in her mother
> experienced an indescribable sweetness
> from the sight of this apparition.

Although she was not educated in the liberal arts, she nevertheless enjoyed listening to the sermons of those who were, because she believed that a nucleus lay hidden in the text that she would subtly perceive and enjoy with relish. She knew what to take out of the sermon of any preacher that might be profitable to the soul, while knowing that to pluck a flower from a wild thorn was no less prudent than to eat the fruit of a noble tree.

Once when Lord Pope Gregory forbade any brother to go to the monasteries of the Ladies without permission, the pious mother, sorrowing that her sisters would more rarely have the food of sacred teaching, sighed, 'Let him now take away from us all the brothers since he has taken away those who provide us with the food that is vital.' At once she sent back to the Minister all the brothers, not wanting to have the questors who acquired corporal bread when they could not have the questors for spiritual bread. When Pope Gregory heard this, he immediately mitigated that prohibition into the hands of the Minister General. *V,289f*

Week of Sunday between 29 May & 4 June inclusive

Sunday — *RCL Proper 4 / DEL Week 9*

A reading from 'The Founding of the Order', by John of Perugia.

The Lord inspired one of the Cardinals, Hugolino, the Bishop of Ostia, who loved blessèd Francis and his brothers very much, not merely as a friend, but even more as a father. When blessèd Francis heard of his reputation, he approached him. When the Cardinal saw him he received him with joy and said, 'I offer myself to you for counsel, assistance and protection, as you wish, and I want you to have me remembered in your prayers.'

Blessèd Francis gave thanks to the Most High for inspiring that man's heart to offer advice, assistance and protection, and told him, 'I gladly want to have you as the father and lord of me and of all my brothers. And I want all my brothers to be bound to pray to the Lord for you.' Then he invited him to come to the chapter of the brothers at Pentecost. He agreed and came each year.

Whenever he came, all the brothers gathered at the chapter would go in procession to meet him. As they were coming, he would dismount from his horse and go on foot with the brothers to the church because of the devotion he had for them. Afterwards, he would preach to them and celebrate mass, during which blessèd Francis would chant the gospel.

II,55f

Monday — *RCL Proper 4 / DEL Week 9*

A reading from 'The Legend of the Three Companions' of Saint Francis.

Blessèd Francis proposed to ask the Lord Pope Honorius that one of the Cardinals of the Roman Church be a sort of pope of his Order: that is, the Lord Bishop of Ostia, to whom the brothers could have recourse in their dealings.

For blessèd Francis had had a vision which led him to ask for the Cardinal, and to entrust the Order to the Roman Church. He saw a hen that was small and black, with feathered legs and the feet of a domestic dove. It had so many chicks that it was unable to gather them all under its wings, and so they wandered all around her in circles.

Waking from sleep, he began to think about this vision and,

immediately, he perceived by means of the Holy Spirit that the hen symbolized him. 'I am that hen,' he said, 'short in stature and dark by nature. I must be simple like a dove, flying up to heaven with the feathered strokes of virtue. The Lord in his mercy has given, and will give me, many sons whom I will be unable to protect with my own strength. I must, therefore, commend them to the holy Church who will protect and guide them under the shadow of her wings.'   *II,105*

Tuesday — *RCL Proper 4 / DEL Week 9*

A reading from 'The Remembrance of the Desire of a Soul', by Thomas of Celano.

Saint Francis once visited Pope Gregory of venerable memory, at that time holding a lesser office. When it was time for dinner, he went out for alms and, on his return, he placed some crusts of black bread on the bishop's table. When the bishop saw this, he was rather embarrassed, especially since there were dinner guests he had invited for the first time. The father, however, with a smile on his face, distributed the alms he had received to the knights and chaplains who were his table companions, and they all accepted them with remarkable devotion. Some ate the crusts, while others saved them out of reverence.

When the meal was over, the bishop got up from the table and, taking the man of God aside to a private place, lifting up his arms he embraced him. 'My brother,' he said, 'why did you shame me in a house, which is yours and your brothers, by going out for alms?' The saint replied, 'I showed you honour instead, while I honoured a greater Lord. For the Lord is pleased by poverty, and especially when one freely chooses to go begging. As for me, I consider it a royal dignity and an outstanding nobility to follow that Lord who, though he was rich, became poor for our sake.' And he added, 'I get greater delight from a poor table, set with some little alms, than from a great table with so many dishes that they can hardly be numbered.'

The bishop, greatly edified, said to the saint, 'My son, do what seems good in your eyes, for the Lord is with you.'   *II,296*

Wednesday — *RCL Proper 4 / DEL Week 9*

A reading from 'The Remembrance of the Desire of a Soul', by Thomas of Celano.

Once, when Francis was returning from Verona and wished to pass through Bologna, he heard that a new house of the brothers had been built there. And just because he heard the words 'house of the brothers', he changed course and went by another route, avoiding Bologna. Furthermore, he commanded the brothers to leave the house quickly. For this reason the house was abandoned; and even the sick could not stay, but were thrown out with the rest of them. And they did not get permission to return there until Lord Hugo, who was then Bishop of Ostia and Legate in Lombardy, declared while preaching in public that this house was his. And he who writes this and bears witness to it was at that time thrown out from that house while he was sick.   *II,286*

Thursday — *RCL Proper 4 / DEL Week 9*

A reading from 'The Assisi Compilation'.

When blessèd Francis reached Florence, he found there Lord Hugolino, the Bishop of Ostia, who later became Pope. He had been sent by Pope Honorius as a legate for the Duchy of Tuscany, and Lombardy, and the Marches of Treviso as far as Venice. The Lord Bishop greatly rejoiced at his arrival, but when he heard from blessèd Francis that he wanted to go to France, he prohibited him from going, telling him, 'Brother, I do not want you to go beyond the mountains, because there are many prelates and others who would willingly block the religion's interests in the Roman Curia. The other Cardinals and I, who love your religion, can protect and help it more willingly if you stay within the confines of this region.'

But blessèd Francis said to him, 'Lord, it is a great shame to me, if I remain in these regions when I send my brothers to remote and far away regions.' The Lord Bishop, however, said to him as if rebuking him, 'Why did you send your brothers so far away to die of hunger and to so many other trials?' In great fervour of spirit, and in the spirit of prophecy, blessèd Francis answered him, 'My Lord Bishop, do you think or believe that the Lord sent the brothers only for these regions? But I tell you in truth that the Lord chose and sent the brothers for the benefit and salvation of the souls of all people in the whole world and they should be received not only in the land of believers, but also in that of non-believers. As long as they observe what they promised the Lord, the Lord will minister to them in the land of non-believers as well as in the countries of believers.'

The Lord Bishop marvelled at his words and admitted that he spoke the truth. But the Lord Bishop did not allow him to go to France. Instead, blessèd Francis sent Brother Pacifico there with other brothers, and he returned to the valley of Spoleto.   *II,216*

Friday — *RCL Proper 4 / DEL Week 9*

A reading from 'The Assisi Compilation'.

Those two bright lights of the world, namely Saint Francis and Saint Dominic, were once in the City with the Lord Bishop of Ostia, who later became Supreme Pontiff. As they took turns pouring out honey-sweet words about the Lord God, the Bishop finally said to them, 'In the early church, the church's shepherds were poor, and men of charity, not on fire with greed. Why do we not make bishops and prelates of your brothers who excel in teaching and example.'

There arose a disagreement between the saints about answering, neither wishing to go first, but rather each deferring to the other. Each urged the other to reply. Each seemed superior to the other, since each was devoted to the other. At last, humility conquered Francis as he did not speak first, but it also conquered Dominic, since in speaking first, he humbly obeyed Francis. Blessèd Dominic therefore answered the Bishop, 'My lord, my brothers are already raised to a good level, if they will only realize it, and as much as possible I would not allow them to obtain any other appearance of dignity.' As this brief response ended, blessèd Francis bowed to the Bishop and said, 'My lord, my brothers are called "lesser" precisely so they will not presume to become "greater". They have been called this to teach them to stay down to earth, and to follow the footprints of Christ's humility, which in the end will exalt them above others in the sight of the saints. If you want them to bear fruit in the Church of God, keep them in the status in which they were called and hold them to it. Bring them back down to ground level even against their will. Never allow them to rise to become prelates.'

When they finished their replies, the Lord Bishop of Ostia was greatly edified by the words of both and gave unbounded thanks to God.

II,148

Saturday — *RCL Proper 4 / DEL Week 9*

A reading from the writings of Bartholomew of Pisa.

When the blessèd Francis was once staying in the place now known as 'Saint Francis' Cell', he was visited by the Lord Cardinal Ugolino, who was afterwards Bishop of Ostia, and finally Pope Gregory IX. When the blessèd Francis saw him coming, he took to his heels and fled into the very heart of the mountains. The Cardinal followed him alone and eventually managed to catch up with him. When they were together, Ugolino asked the blessèd Francis why he had run away from him, seeing that he loved him and the Order so dearly. To which Francis replied, 'My lord and father, the reason why I fled was that I am but a poor man, wretched and worthless, and am put to great confusion when so noble a lord as you are condescends to speak to so poor a creature as I.' Then, after much talk together about holy things, the Cardinal said, 'Tell me now, Brother Francis, for the love of God, what I ought to do; for I cannot decide whether to remain as a Cardinal or whether to join your Order and throw over all worldly ambition. As the Lord lives, I will do whatever you tell me.'

Then Saint Francis said to him, 'O my lord, you are a man of great wisdom and can do much good to the world by remaining as a Cardinal. Yet, at the same time, were you to join the Order it would act as a great example to the world, inspiring the hearts of many to serve Christ; for you are also a great preacher and by your eloquence many would be turned to Christ. So, as God at present gives me no guidance in this matter, I fear I am unable to tell you which of the two things you ought to do.' And so Saint Francis had to leave him still undecided as to whether he should join the Order or not. But Francis prophesied that, in the fullness of time, Ugolino would become Pope; as indeed happened.

Moreover, when he had become Pope, he once put on a habit, cord and sandals and went with the friars to visit the holy places in the city of Rome. One Maundy Thursday, thus attired, he went to carry out our Lord's commandment that we should wash the feet of the poor. And while he was so doing, some of the poor men, not recognising who he was, drove him away, saying, 'You do not know how to wash feet! Go away, and send some of the other brothers who can make a better job it it!' And the Holy Father got up and meekly obeyed.   *IV,1860f*

Week of Sunday between 5 & 11 June inclusive

Sunday — *RCL Proper 5 / DEL Week 10*

A reading from 'The Admonitions' of Saint Francis.

All those who saw the Lord Jesus according to the humanity, therefore, and did not see and believe according to the Spirit and the Divinity that he is the true Son of God were condemned. Now in the same way, all those who see the sacrament sanctified by the words of the Lord upon the altar at the hands of the priest in the form of bread and wine, and who do not see and believe according to the Spirit and the Divinity that it is truly the Body and Blood of our Lord Jesus Christ, are condemned. This is affirmed by the Most High himself who says, 'This is my body and the blood of my new covenant, which will be shed for many;' and 'Whoever eats my flesh and drinks my blood will have eternal life.' It is the Spirit of the Lord, therefore, that lives in its faithful, that receives the Body and Blood of the Lord. All others who do not share in this same Spirit and presume to receive him eat and drink judgement on themselves.

Therefore: children, how long will you be hard of heart? Why do you not know the truth and believe in the Son of God? Behold, each day he humbles himself as when he came from the royal throne into the Virgin's womb; each day he himself comes to us, appearing humbly; each day he comes down from the bosom of the Father upon the altar in the hands of a priest.

As he revealed himself to the holy apostles in true flesh, so he reveals himself to us now in sacred bread. And as they saw only his flesh by an insight of their flesh, yet believed that he was God as they contemplated him with their spiritual eyes, let us, as we see bread and wine with our bodily eyes, see and firmly believe that they are his most holy Body and Blood living and true. And in this way the Lord is always with his faithful, as he himself says: 'Behold, I am with you until the end of the age.'

I,128f

Monday — *RCL Proper 5 / DEL Week 10*

A reading from 'A Mirror of the Perfection of a Lesser Brother'.

Blessèd Francis had such reverence and devotion to the Body of Christ that he wanted it written in the Rule that the brothers, in the regions where they stay, exercise great care and solicitude about this, admonishing clerics and priests to reserve the Body of Christ in a good and fitting place. And, if they neglect to do so, the brothers should do it.

For he wanted it put into the Rule that wherever the brothers should find the names of the Lord or those words through which the Body of the Lord is made present not well and honourably kept, they should collect them and store them decently, thus honouring the Lord in his words. And although he did not write these things in the Rule, because it did not seem good to the Ministers that the brothers have these as a command, nevertheless in his Testament and in some of his other writings he wanted to leave for the brothers his will in these matters.

Moreover, once, he wanted to send throughout every region some brothers who would carry many beautiful and decorated pyxes. And wherever they would find the Body of the Lord carelessly lying around, they were to place it fittingly in them. He also wanted to send throughout every region other brothers with good and beautiful wafer irons for making fine and pure hosts. *III,309*

Tuesday — *RCL Proper 5 / DEL Week 10*

A reading from 'The First Letter to the Custodians', by Saint Francis.

With all that is in me and more I beg you that, when it is fitting and you judge it expedient, you humbly beg the clergy to revere above all else the most holy Body and Blood of our Lord Jesus Christ and his holy name and the written words that sanctify his Body. They should hold as precious the chalices, corporals, appointments of the altar, and everything that pertains to the sacrifice. If the most holy Body of the Lord is very poorly reserved in any place, let it be placed and locked up in a precious place according to the command of the Church. Let it be carried about with great reverence and administered to others with discernment. Let the names and written words of the Lord, whenever they are found in sullied places, be also gathered up and kept in a becoming place.

In every sermon you give, remind people about penance and that no one can be saved unless he receives the most holy Body and Blood of the Lord. When it is sacrificed on the altar by a priest and carried anywhere, let all peoples praise, glorify and honour, on bended knee, the Lord God living and true. May you announce and preach his praise to all nations in such a way that praise and thanks may always be given to the all-powerful God by all people throughout the world at every hour and whenever bells are rung. *I,56f*

Wednesday — *RCL Proper 5 / DEL Week 10*

A reading from 'The Acts of the Process of Canonization' of Saint Clare.

The evidence of the ninth witness:

Sister Francesca, daughter of Messer Capitaneo of Col de Mezzo, a nun of the monastery of San Damiano, said under oath that she, the witness, had been in the monastery more than twenty-one years or so this May during which time Lady Clare had been Abbess. She said if she had as much wisdom as Solomon and as much eloquence as Saint Paul, she did not believe she could tell fully of the goodness and holiness that she saw in Lady Clare throughout all the said time.

Asked what she saw in her, she replied that once, when the Saracens entered the cloister of the said monastery, the Lady made them bring her to the entrance of the refectory and bring a small box where there was the Blessèd Sacrament of the Body of our Lord Jesus Christ. Throwing herself prostrate on the ground in prayer, she begged with tears, saying among other things, 'Lord, look upon these servants of yours, because I cannot protect them.' Then the witness heard a voice of wonderful sweetness, 'I will always defend you!' The Lady then prayed for the city, saying, 'Lord, please defend the city as well!' The same voice resounded and said, 'The city will endure many dangers but it will be defended.' Then the Lady turned to the sisters and told them, 'Do not be afraid, because I am a hostage for you so that you will not suffer any harm now, nor at any other time, as long as you wish to obey God's command-ments.' Then the Saracens left in such a way that they did not do any harm or damage. *V,165*

Thursday — *RCL Proper 5 / DEL Week 10*

A reading from 'The Tree of Life', by Saint Bonaventure.

Among all the memorable events of Christ's life, the most worthy of remembrance is that last banquet, the most sacred supper. Here, not only was the paschal lamb was presented to be eaten but also the immaculate Lamb, who takes away the sin of the world. Under the appearance of bread, having all delight and the pleasantness of every taste, he was given as food. In this banquet, the marvellous sweetness of Christ's goodness shone forth when he dined at the same table and on the same plates with those poor disciples and the traitor Judas. The marvellous example of his humility shone forth when, girt with a towel, the King of Glory diligently washed the feet of the fishermen and even of his betrayer. The marvellous richness of his generosity was manifest when he gave to those first priests, and as a consequence to the whole Church and the world, his most sacred body and his true blood as food and drink so that what was soon to be a sacrifice pleasing to God and the priceless price of our redemption would be our viaticum and sustenance. Finally, the marvellous outpouring of his love shone forth when, loving his own to the end, he strengthened them in goodness with a gentle exhortation, especially forewarning Peter to be firm in faith and offering to John his breast as a pleasant and sacred place of rest.

O how marvellous are all these things,
how full of sweetness,
but only for that soul
who, having been called to so distinguished a banquet,
runs with all the ardour of his spirit
so that he may cry out
with the Prophet:
As the deer longs for the water brooks,
so longs my soul for you, O God.   *VI,139*

Friday — *RCL Proper 5 / DEL Week 10*

A reading from 'The Remembrance of the Desire of a Soul', by Thomas of Celano.

Towards the sacrament of the Lord's Body
Francis burned with fervour to his very marrow,
and with unbounded wonder
of that loving condescension
and condescending love.
He considered it disrespectful
not to hear, if time allowed, at least one Mass a day.
He received Communion frequently
and so devoutly
that he made others devout.
Following that which is so venerable with all reverence
he offered the sacrifice of all his members,
and receiving the Lamb that was slain
he slew his own spirit
in the fire which always burned

upon the altar of his heart.

Because of this, he loved France as a friend of the Body of the Lord, and even wished to die there, because of its reverence for sacred things.

He wanted great reverence shown to the hands of priests, since they have the divinely-granted authority to bring about this mystery. He often used to say, 'If I should happen at the same time to come upon any saint coming from heaven and some little poor priest, I would first show honour to the priest, and hurry more quickly to kiss his hands. For I would say to the saint, ' Saint Lawrence, wait! His hands may handle the Word of Life, and possess something more than human!'   *II,375f>*

Saturday – *RCL Proper 5 / DEL Week 10*

A reading from 'The Book of the Blessèd Angela of Foligno'.

One goes to this Good, beyond and outside of which there is no other good. O neglected, unknown, unloved Good, discovered by those who totally desire you and yet cannot possess you totally. If one looks and ponders with the utmost care the small piece of bread which the body eats, how much more should the soul not look and ponder before receiving this eternal and infinite good, created and uncreated, this sacramental food which is the sustenance, treasure, and fountain for the life of both soul and body. This is truly the Good which in itself contains every good. One must, therefore, approach such a table, and such a great and wonderful Good with great respect, purity, fear, and love. The soul must approach it all cleansed and adorned, because it is going to that which, and the one who, is the Good of all glory. It is going to that which, and the one who, is perfect blessèdness, eternal life, beauty, loftiness, sweetness, all love and the sweetness of love.

Why should one go to this mystery? I will tell you what I think. One should go to receive in order to be received, go pure in order to be purified, go alive in order to be enlivened, go as just in order to be justified, go united and conjoined to Christ in order to be incorporated through him, with him, and in him, God uncreated and God made man, who is given in this most holy and most high mystery through the hands of the priest. Thanks be to God always.   *X,298f*

Week of Sunday between 12 & 18 June inclusive

Sunday — *RCL Proper 6 / DEL Week 11*

A reading from 'The Testament of Saint Clare'.

In the name of the Lord! Amen.

Among the other gifts that we have received and do daily receive from our benefactor, the Father of mercies, and for which we must express the deepest thanks to the glorious Father of Christ, there is our vocation, for which, all the more by way of its being more perfect and greater, do we owe the greatest thanks to him. Therefore the Apostle Paul writes, 'Know your vocation'. The Son of God has been made for us the Way, which our blessèd father Francis, his true lover and imitator, has shown and taught us by word and example.

Therefore, belovèd sisters, we must consider the immense gifts that God has bestowed on us, especially those that he has seen fit to work in us through his belovèd servant, our blessèd father Francis, not only after our conversion but also while we were still living among the vanities of the world. In fact, almost immediately after his conversion, when he had neither brothers nor companions, while he was building the church of San Damiano, where he was totally visited by divine consolation and impelled to completely abandon the world, through the great joy and enlightenment of the Holy Spirit, the holy man made a prophecy about us that the Lord later fulfilled.

For at that time, climbing the wall of that church, he shouted in French to some poor people who were standing nearby, 'Come and help me in the work of building the monastery of San Damiano, because ladies are yet to dwell here who will glorify our heavenly Father throughout his holy, universal church by their celebrated and holy manner of life.'

We can consider in this, therefore, the abundant kindness of God to us. Because of his mercy and love, he saw fit to speak these words through his saint about our vocation and choice through his saint. And our most blessèd father prophesied not only for us, but also for those who would come to this same holy vocation to which the Lord has called us. *V,56f*

Monday — *RCL Proper 6 / DEL Week 11*

A reading from 'The Testament of Saint Clare'.

After the Most High, heavenly Father saw fit in his mercy and grace to enlighten my heart, that I should do penance according to the example and teaching of our most blessèd father Francis, a short while after his conversion, I, together with a few sisters whom the Lord had given me after my conversion, willingly promised him obedience, as the Lord gave us the light of his grace through his wonderful life and teaching. When the blessèd Francis saw, however, that, although we were physically weak and frail, we did not shirk deprivation, poverty, hard work, trial, or the shame or contempt of the world – rather, we considered them as great delights, as he had frequently examined us according to the example of the saints and his brothers – he greatly rejoiced in the Lord. And moved by compassion for us, he bound himself, both through himself and through his Order, to always have the same loving care and special solicitude for us as for his own brothers.

And thus, by the will of God and our most blessèd father Francis, we were to dwell in the Church of San Damiano where, in a little while, the Lord, through his mercy and grace, made our number increase so that he would fulfil what he had foretold through his saint. In fact, we had stayed in another place before this, but only for a short while.

Afterwards he wrote a form of life for us, especially that we always persevere in holy poverty. While he was living he was not content to encourage us with many words and examples to the love of holy poverty and its observance, but he gave us many writings that, after his death, we would in no way turn away from it, as the Son of God never wished to abandon this holy poverty while he lived in the world. And our most blessèd father Francis, having imitated his footprints, never departed either in example or in teaching from this holy poverty that he had chosen for himself and his brothers. *V,58*

Tuesday — *RCL Proper 6 / DEL Week 11*

A reading from 'The Little Flowers of Saint Francis'.

While Saint Francis was staying in Assisi, he visited Saint Clare many times, giving her holy instruction. She greatly desired to eat once with him and she asked him for this many times, but he never wanted to grant this consolation. So his companions, seeing the desire of Saint Clare, said to Saint Francis, 'Father, it does not seem to us that this rigidity is in accord with divine charity, that you do not grant to Sister Clare such a small thing as eating with you, as she is such a holy virgin, belovèd of God; especially considering that she abandoned the riches and vanities of the world because of your preaching. Truly, even if she were to ask you a greater favour than this, you should do it for your spiritual plant.' Then Saint Francis replied, 'It seems to you that I should grant her request?' The companions responded, 'Yes, Father, it is only right that you grant her this favour and consolation.' Then Saint Francis said, 'Since it seems this way to you, it also seems that way to me. But so that she may be even more consoled, I want this meal to be held at Saint Mary of the Angels, since she has been enclosed for a long time in San Damiano, and it will do her good to see the place of Saint Mary, where she was tonsured and became the spouse of Jesus Christ; and there we will eat together in the name of God.'

When the appointed day arrived, Saint Clare with a companion came out from the monastery, was accompanied by companions of Saint Francis, and came to Saint Mary of the Angels. After she devoutly greeted the Virgin Mary in front of her altar, where she had been tonsured and veiled, they took her around to see the place until it was time to eat. And in the meantime, Saint Francis had the table prepared on the bare ground, as he usually did. When it was time to eat they sat down together: Saint Clare with Saint Francis; one of the companions of Saint Francis with the companion of Saint Clare; then all the other companions gathered humbly at the table. And as a first course Saint Francis began to speak of God so sweetly, so deeply, and so wonderfully that the abundance of divine grace descended upon them, and all were rapt into God.

And while they were enraptured this way, their eyes and hands lifted up to heaven, the people of Assisi and Bettona, and those of the surrounding area, saw Saint Mary of the Angels burning brightly, along with the whole place and the forest, which was next to the place. It seemed that a great fire was consuming the church, the place and the forest together. For this reason, the Assisians, in a great hurry, ran down there to put out the fire, believing that everything really was burning. But on arriving at the place, not finding anything burning, they went inside and found Saint Francis with Saint Clare and all their companions sitting around that humble table, rapt into God through contemplation. From this they clearly understood that that was divine, not material fire, which God had made appear miraculously, to demonstrate and signify the fire of divine love, burning in the souls of these holy brothers and holy nuns. Then they departed with great consolation in their hearts and with holy edification.

Then, after a long time, Saint Francis and Saint Clare, together with the others returned to themselves; and feeling themselves well comforted by spiritual food, they had little concern for bodily food. And thus finishing that blessèd meal, Saint Clare, well accompanied, returned to San Damiano.   *III,590f*

Wednesday — *RCL Proper 6 / DEL Week 11*

A reading from 'The Remembrance of the Desire of a Soul', by Thomas of Celano.

As earlier foretold by the Holy Spirit,
an Order of holy virgins was to be established
to be brought one day
as a polished collection of living stones
for the restoration of the heavenly house.
The virgins of Christ
had begun to gather in that place,
assembled from diverse regions of the world,
professing the greatest perfection
in the observance of the highest poverty
and the beauty of every virtue.
Though the father Francis gradually withdrew
his bodily presence from them,
he still offered in the Holy Spirit
his affection to care for them.
The saint recognized that they were marked
with many signs of the highest perfection,
and that they were ready to bear any loss
and undergo any labour for Christ
and did not ever want to turn aside
from the holy commandments.
Therefore, he firmly promised them,
and others who professed poverty
in a similar way of life,
that he and his brothers
would perpetually offer them help and advice.

And he carried this out carefully
as long as he lived,
and when he was close to death
he commanded it to be carried out without fail always,
saying that
one and the same Spirit
had led the brothers and those little poor ladies
out of this world.

The brothers were sometimes surprised that he did not often visit such holy handmaids of Christ in his bodily presence, but he would say, 'Do not imagine, dear brothers, that I do not love them fully. For if it were a crime to cherish them in Christ, would it not be even worse to have joined them to Christ? Not calling them would not have been harmful, but not to care for them after calling them would be the height of cruelty. But I am giving you an example, that as I do, so should you do also. I do not want one volunteering to visit them, but rather command that those who are unwilling and very reluctant should be assigned to their service, as long as they are spiritual men tested by a long-standing, worthy way of life.'   *II,378f*

Thursday — *RCL Proper 6 / DEL Week 11*

A reading from 'The Little Flowers of Saint Francis'.

Once, when Saint Francis had a serious eye disease, Sir Hugolino, Cardinal Protector of the Order, because of the great tenderness he had for him, wrote to tell him to go to Rieti where there were excellent eye doctors. Saint Francis, after he had received the letter of the Cardinal, went first to San Damiano, where Saint Clare was, the most devout spouse of Christ, to give her some consolation and then to the Cardinal. While he was there, that night his eyes became so much worse that he was unable to see any light. So, since he could not depart, Saint Clare made him a little cell of reeds, where he could rest more easily. But Saint Francis, because of the pain of the illness and because of the many mice that troubled him greatly, could not rest at all by night or by day. Bearing that pain and disturbance for several days, he began to think and under-stood this as a punishment from God for his sins, and he began to give thanks to God with his whole heart and voice, and cried out in a loud voice and said, 'Lord, my God, I am worthy of this and of much worse. O Lord Jesus Christ, good shepherd, who have shown your mercy to us sinners in different bodily pains and sufferings, give grace and strength to me, your little lamb, that I may not turn away from you because of any illness or tribulation or suffering.' After he made this prayer, a voice came to him from heaven, saying, 'Francis, answer me: if the whole world were gold, and all the seas and springs and rivers were balsam, and all the mountains, hills and stones were precious stones; and if you found another treasure more noble than all these things, as much as gold is more noble than the earth, balsam more than water, precious stones more than mountains and rocks, and that more noble treasure were given to you for this illness, would you not be happy and quite joyful?' Saint Francis answered, 'Lord, I am not worthy of such a precious treasure.' And the voice of God said to him, 'Rejoice, Francis, because that is the treasure of eternal life, which I have kept for you, and from now on I invest you with it. This illness and affliction is the pledge of that blessèd treasure.' Then Saint Francis called his companion with the greatest joy over such a glorious promise, and said, 'Let us go to the Cardinal.' And first consoling Saint Clare with holy words, and humbly taking leave of her, he started his journey towards Rieti.   *III,598f*

Friday — *RCL Proper 6 / DEL Week 11*

A reading from 'The Assisi Compilation'.

Blessèd Francis, after he had composed the *Praises of the Lord* for his creatures, also composed some holy words with chant for the greater consolation of the Poor Ladies of the Monastery of San Damiano. He did this especially because he knew how much his illness troubled them.

And since he was unable to console and visit them personally because of that illness, he wanted those words to be proclaimed to them by his companions. In these words, he wanted to reveal his will to them briefly, for then and for always, how they should be of one mind and how they should live in charity towards one another. He wanted to do this because they were converted to Christ by his example and preaching when the brothers were still few. Their conversion and manner of living is the glory and edification not only of the religion of the brothers, whose little plant they are, but also of the entire Church of God.

Therefore, since blessèd Francis knew that from the beginning of their conversion they had led, and were still leading, a strict and poor life by free choice and by necessity, his spirit was always moved to piety for them.

With these words, then, he begged them that, as the Lord had gathered them as one from many different regions in holy charity, holy poverty, and holy obedience, so in these they should live and die. And he begged them particularly to provide for their bodies with discernment from the alms which the Lord would give them, with cheerfulness and thanksgiving. And he especially asked them to remain patient: the healthy, in the labours which they endure for their sick sisters; and the sick in their illnesses and the needs they suffer.   *II,188f*

Saturday — *RCL Proper 6 / DEL Week 11*

A reading from 'The Assisi Compilation'.

During the week in which blessèd Francis died, Lady Clare was seriously ill. She feared that she would die before blessèd Francis. She wept in bitterness of spirit and could not be comforted, because she would not be able before her death to see her only father after God, that is, blessèd Francis.

She sent word of this to blessèd Francis through one of the brothers. Blessèd Francis heard this and was moved to piety, since he loved her and her sisters with fatherly affection. He considered that what she desired, that is, to see him, could not be done then since they were both seriously ill. To console her, he wrote his blessing in a letter and also absolved her from any failings, if she had any, regarding his commands and wishes or the commands and wishes of the Son of God. Moreover, so that she would put aside all her grief and be consoled in the Lord, he, or rather the Spirit of God speaking through him, spoke to the brother she had sent. 'Go and take this letter to the Lady Clare, and tell her to put aside all her grief and sorrow over not being able to see me now. Let her be assured that before her death, both she and her sisters will see me and will receive the greatest consolation from me.'

Soon afterwards blessèd Francis passed away during the night. In the morning, all the people of the city of Assisi, men and women, with all the clergy, took the holy body from the place where he had died. With hymns and praises, all carrying tree branches, they carried him to San Damiano at the Lord's will, in order to fulfil that word which the Lord had spoken through his saint to console his daughters and servants.

The iron grille was removed from the window through which the servants of Christ usually receive communion and sometimes hear the word of God. The brothers lifted his holy body from the stretcher and, raising him in their arms, they held him in front of the window for over an hour. By then, Lady Clare and her sisters had received the greatest consolation from him, although they wept profusely and were afflicted with great grief, because, after God, he was their one consolation in this world.

II>,128f

Week of Sunday between 19 & 25 June inclusive

Sunday — *RCL Proper 7 / DEL Week 12*

A reading from 'The Little Flowers of Saint Francis'.

The humble servant of Christ, Saint Francis, a short time after his conversion, having already gathered and received many companions into the Order, was greatly preoccupied and in serious doubt about what to do: whether to dedicate himself solely to prayer, or sometimes to preach; and he greatly desired to know the will of God about this. Since the holy humility in him did not allow him to rely on himself or his own prayers he decided to seek the divine will with the prayers of others. So he called Brother Masseo and said to him, 'Go to Sister Clare and tell her for me that she, with some of her more spiritual companions, should devoutly pray to God that he be pleased to show me what is better: to dedicate myself to preaching or only to prayer. Then go to Brother Sylvester and tell him the same.' Now in the world, this man had been Sir Sylvester, the one who had seen coming out of the mouth of Saint Francis a golden cross as tall as the sky and as wide as the ends of the earth. And this Brother Sylvester was a man of so much devotion and holiness that whatever he asked and begged of God was granted, and he often spoke with God, and therefore Saint Francis had great devotion towards him.

Brother Masseo went and, following the command of Saint Francis, delivered the message first to Saint Clare, then to Brother Sylvester. And he, as soon as he received the message, knelt down in prayer and, as he prayed, he received God's answer. He turned to Brother Masseo and said, 'God says this: tell Brother Francis that God did not call him to this state only for himself, but to bear fruit, the fruit of souls, that through him many may be saved.' On receiving this response, Brother Masseo returned to Saint Clare to learn what she had received from God. And she replied that she and the other companions had received from God the same response that Brother Sylvester had received.

At that, Brother Masseo returned to Saint Francis, and Saint Francis received him with the greatest charity, washing his feet and preparing him something to eat. After the meal, Saint Francis called Brother Masseo into the forest and there knelt down in front of him and pulled back his capuce, making a cross with his arms, and asked him, 'What does my Lord Jesus Christ command me to do?' Brother Masseo replied, 'Christ answered both Brother Sylvester and Sister Clare with the sisters, and revealed that it is his will that you go through the world to preach, because he has not chosen you only for yourself, but rather for the salvation of others.' Then Saint Francis, having heard this answer and knowing Christ's will by it, got up with great fervour and said, 'Let us go, in the name of God.'   *III,591f*

Monday — *RCL Proper 7 / DEL Week 12*

A reading from 'The Little Flowers of Saint Francis'.

One day, Saint Francis was travelling with Brother Masseo, and the same Brother Masseo was walking a little bit ahead. When he reached a three-way crossroads, by which they could go to Florence, to Siena or Arezzo, Brother Masseo said, 'Father, which road should we take?' Saint Francis answered, 'The one that God wills.' Brother Masseo said, 'And how will we know the will of God?' Saint Francis answered, 'By the sign that I will show you. I command you, by virtue of holy obedience, that in this crossroads, in the place where you have your feet placed, you turn round and round, as children do, and do not stop turning yourself until I tell you to do so.' So Brother Masseo started to twirl around, and he turned so much that, because of dizziness in his head, which is normal with such turning, he fell down on the ground several times. But since Saint Francis did not tell him to stop and he wanted to obey faithfully, he kept getting up. Finally, while he was spinning quickly, Saint Francis said, 'Stop! Do not move!' And he stopped, and Saint Francis asked him, 'Where is your face pointing?' Brother Masseo answered, 'Towards Siena.' Saint Francis said, 'That is the way that God wants us to go.'

Travelling along that road, Brother Masseo was greatly amazed at what Saint Francis had made him do, like a child, in front of lay people who were passing by. But, out of reverence, he did not dare to say anything to the holy father.   *III,584*

Tuesday — *RCL Proper 7 / DEL Week 12*

A reading from 'The Little Flowers of Saint Francis'.

As Saint Francis and Brother Masseo neared Siena, the people of the city heard of the coming of the saint, and went out to meet him. Out of devotion they carried him and his companion to the Bishop's palace, and his feet did not touch the ground at all. At that time, many men of Siena were fighting each other, and two of them had already died. Arriving there, Saint Francis preached to them in such a devout and holy way, that he returned them all to peace and great humility and harmony with each other. Because of this, when the Bishop of Siena heard of the holy deed that Saint Francis had done, he invited him home, and received him with great honour that day, and also for the night. And the next morning Saint Francis, truly humbled, who sought only the glory of God in his deeds, got up early with his companions, and left without the Bishop's knowledge.

Along the road, Brother Masseo grumbled within himself about this, saying, 'What is this that this good man has done? He made me twirl around like a child, and to the Bishop, who did him so much honour, he did not even say a kind word or thank him.' And it seemed to Brother Masseo that Saint Francis acted in this way without discernment. But then, by divine inspiration, returning to himself and reproving himself, he said within his heart, 'Brother Masseo, you are too proud, you judge the works of God and you are worthy of hell for your indiscreet pride. Yesterday, Brother Francis did such holy deeds that if they had been done by an angel of God they would not have been more marvellous. So if he should command you to throw stones, you would have to do it and obey him, since what he has done on this road came from divine operation, as demonstrated by the good end that followed. If he had not brought peace to those who were fighting, not only would many bodies be dead from the sword, as had already begun to happen, but even more than that, the devil would have carried many souls off to hell. But you are very stupid and proud, grumbling about what clearly comes from the will of God.'

And all these things that Brother Masseo was saying in his heart, while walking ahead, were revealed by God to Saint Francis. So Saint Francis drew up to him and said, 'Hold onto those things that you are thinking now, because they are good and useful and inspired by God. But that first grumbling you were doing was blind and vain and proud and it was put into your mind by the demon.' Then Brother Masseo clearly saw that Saint Francis knew the secrets of his heart, and understood surely that the spirit of divine Wisdom guided the holy faith in all his actions.

To the praise of Jesus Christ
and the little poor man, Francis.
Amen.   *III,584f*

Wednesday — *RCL Proper 7 / DEL Week 12*

A reading from 'The Little Flowers of Saint Francis'.

One day, coming to a village feeling quite hungry, Saint Francis and Brother Masseo went begging bread for the love of God, according to the Rule.   And Saint Francis went through one neighbourhood and Brother Masseo through another.   But since Saint Francis was such a worthless-looking man and small of body, and for that reason was considered a lowly, little poor man by those who did not know him, he only got a few mouthfuls and some little pieces of dry bread.   But Brother Masseo, since he was a big man and handsome of body, was given good, large portions, and plenty of them, and whole loaves of bread.

Having received these, they met together in a place outside the town to eat, where there was a beautiful spring, with a good big rock next to it, upon which each placed all the alms he had received.   And when Saint Francis saw that Brother Masseo's pieces of bread were greater in number, in beauty and in size than his own, he expressed great joy and said, 'O Brother Masseo, we do not deserve such a great treasure.'   And as he was repeating these words several times, Brother Masseo replied, 'Father, how can you call this a treasure, where there is such poverty and lack of essentials?   Here there is no table-cloth, no knife, no dishes, no bowls, no house, no table, no waiter, no maid.'   Saint Francis said, 'And this is what I consider the great treasure, where there is not a single thing prepared by human skill; but what there is here is prepared by divine providence, as you can see clearly in the bread we received, in such a beautiful table of rock, and such a clear spring.   But I want God to make us love whole-heartedly the treasure of holy poverty, so noble as to have God for a servant.'   And having said these words and made a prayer and taken bodily nourishment with these pieces of bread and that water, they got up to walk to France.   *III,587f*

Thursday — *RCL Proper 7 / DEL Week 12*

A reading from 'The Major Legend of Saint Francis', by Saint Bonaventure.

In the sixth year of his conversion, burning with the desire of martyrdom, Francis decided to take a ship to the region of Syria in order to preach the Christian faith and penance to the Saracens and other non-believers. When he boarded a ship to go there, he was driven by contrary winds to land on the shore of Slavonia. He spent a little while there and could not find a ship that would cross the sea at that time. Feeling that he had been cheated of his desire, he begged some sailors going to Ancona to take him with them for the love of God. When they stubbornly refused because he could not pay them, the man of God, completely trusting the Lord's goodness, secretly boarded the ship with his companion. A man arrived, sent by God for the poor man, as it is believed, who brought with him the food needed. He called over a person from the ship, a God-fearing man, and spoke to him in this way: 'Keep all these things faith-fully for the poor brothers hiding on your ship and distribute them in a friendly fashion in their time of need.' And it so happened that, when the crew was unable to land anywhere for many days because of the force of the winds, they used up all their food. Only the alms given from above to the poor Francis remained. Since this was only a very small amount, by God's power it was multiplied so much that while they were delayed at sea for many days by the relentless storm, it fully supplied their needs until they reached the port of Ancona. When the sailors realized that they had escaped many threats of death through God's servant, as those who had experienced the horrifying dangers of the sea and had seen the wonderful works of the Lord in the deep, they gave thanks to almighty God, who is always revealed through his friends and servants as awesome and lovable.   *II,600f*

Friday — *RCL Proper 7 / DEL Week 12*

A reading from 'The Major Legend of Saint Francis', by Saint Bonaventure.

When Francis left the sea [at the port of Ancona], he began to walk the earth and to sow in it the seed of salvation, reaping fruitful harvests. But, because the fruit of martyrdom had attracted his heart to such an extent, he desired a precious death for the sake of Christ more intensely than all the merits of the virtues. So he took the road to Morocco to preach the gospel of Christ to the Miramamolin and his people, hoping to attain in this way the palm of martyrdom he so strongly desired. He was so carried away with the desire that, although he was physically weak, he would race ahead of his companion on the journey and hurry to carry out his purpose, flying along, as if intoxicated in spirit. But after he had gone as far as Spain, by the divine design, which had other things in store for him, he was overtaken by a very grave illness which hindered him from achieving what he desired.

Realizing, then,
that his physical life was still necessary
for the children he had begotten,
the man of God,
while he considered death as gain for himself,
returned to feed the sheep entrusted to his care.   *II,601*

Saturday — *RCL Proper 7 / DEL Week 12*

A reading from the writings of Bartholomew of Pisa.

In the thirteenth year after his conversion, the blessèd Francis proposed to go to Syria to preach to the Sultan, and many of the friars accompanied him as far as Ancona, being anxious to go with him. But Francis thought it over and realised how difficult it would be to take so many brothers overseas, though at the same time he hated to disappoint any of them. So, when they reached the harbour at Ancona, he addressed them thus: 'My dearest brothers, I wish that I could satisfy you all and take you all with me, but the sailors will not hear of it. And since to start choosing one and rejecting another would only cause trouble and division, let us try to find out the will of God.' Then he beckoned to a little boy, who knew none of them, and said to the brothers, 'If you are agreeable, we will ask this little boy.' And when the brothers showed their consent, Francis said to the child, 'Is it God's will, my son, that all these brothers should go abroad with me?' To which the boy said, 'No.' 'Which, then,' said the Saint, 'does God wish to go with me?' Then the little boy touched one or two of the brothers, saying, 'This, and this, and that one.' In this way he touched altogether eleven brothers and said to the blessèd Francis, 'These are the ones to go with you. That is God's will.' Then all the brothers who had not been touched were perfectly satisfied, recognising that such was the will of God.   *IV,1841f*

Week of Sunday between 26 June & 2 July inclusive

Sunday — *RCL Proper 8 / DEL Week 13*

A reading from 'The Major Legend of Saint Francis', by Saint Bonaventure.

With the ardour of his charity
urging his spirit on towards martyrdom,
Francis tried yet a third time to set out to the non-believers,
hoping to shed his blood
for the spread of the faith in the Trinity.

In the thirteenth year of his conversion, he journeyed to the regions of Syria, constantly exposing himself to many dangers in order to reach the presence of the Sultan of Babylon. For at that time there was a fierce war between the Christians and the Saracens, with their camps situated in close quarters opposite each other in the field, so that there was no way of passing from one to the other without danger of death. A cruel edict had been issued by the Sultan that whoever would bring back the head of a Christian would receive as a reward a gold piece. But Francis, the intrepid knight of Christ, hoping to be able to achieve his purpose, decided to make the journey, not terrified by the fear of death, but rather drawn by desire for it. After praying, strengthened by the Lord, he confidently chanted that prophetic verse: 'Even if I should walk in the midst of the shadow of death, I shall not fear evil because you are with me.'

II,601f

Monday — *RCL Proper 8 / DEL Week 13*

A reading from 'The Major Legend of Saint Francis', by Saint Bonaventure.

The spirit of prophecy so shone forth in Francis
that he foresaw the future,
contuited the secrets of the heart,
knew of events from afar as if they were present
and miraculously appeared present to those who were absent.

For at the time when the Christian army was besieging Damietta, the man of God was there, armed not with weapons, but with faith. When Christ's servant heard that the Christians were preparing for war, on the day of the battle he sighed deeply and said to his companion, 'If a clash of battle is attempted, the Lord has shown me that it will not go well for the Christians. But if I say this, they will take me for a fool; if I keep silent, my conscience will not leave me alone. What do you think I should do?' His companion replied, 'Brother, do not give the least thought to how people judge you. This will not be the first time people took you for a fool. Unburden your conscience and fear God rather than mortals.

When he heard this, the herald of Christ leapt to his feet and rushed to the Christians, crying out warnings to save them, forbidding war and threatening disaster. But they took the truth as a joke. They hardened their hearts and refused to turn back. The whole Christian army charged, attacked and retreated, fleeing from the battle, carrying not triumph but shame. The number of Christians was diminished by such a great massacre, that about six thousand were either dead or captured.   *II,614*

Tuesday — *RCL Proper 8 / DEL Week 13*

A reading from 'The Major Legend of Saint Francis', by Saint Bonaventure.

Taking a companion with him, a brother named Illuminato, a virtuous and enlightened man, after he had begun his journey, Francis came upon two lambs. Overjoyed to see them, the holy man said to his companion, 'Trust in the Lord, brother, for the gospel text is being fulfilled in us: Behold, I am sending you out like sheep in the midst of wolves.' When they proceeded further, the Saracen sentries fell upon them like wolves swiftly taking sheep, savagely seizing the servants of God, and cruelly and contemptuously dragging them away, treating them with insults, beating them with whips, and putting them in chains.

Finally, after they had been maltreated in many ways and were exhausted, by divine providence they were led to the Sultan, just as the man of God had wished. When that ruler inquired by whom, why and how they had been sent and how they had got there, Christ's servant, Francis, answered with an intrepid heart that he had been sent not by man but by the Most High God in order to point out to him and his people the way of salvation and to announce the gospel of truth.

He preached to the Sultan
the Triune God and the one Saviour of all, Jesus Christ,
with such firmness,
such strength of soul

and such fervour of spirit
that the words of the gospel appeared
to be truly fulfilled in him:
'I will give you utterance and wisdom
which all your adversaries will not be able to resist or answer back.'

For the Sultan, perceiving in the man of God a fervour of spirit and a courage that had to be admired, willingly listened to him and invited him stay longer with him.   *II,602f*

Wednesday — *RCL Proper 8 / DEL Week 13*

A reading from 'A Book of Exemplary Stories'.

While Francis was at the Sultan's court, the latter wanted to test the faith and devotion that Francis showed to our crucified Lord. So one day he had a beautiful, multi-coloured carpet laid out in his audience hall; it was almost entirely decorated with a geometric pattern of crosses. He said to his attendants, 'Now fetch this man who seems to be an authentic Christian. If he comes towards me, he will have to tread on the crosses that cover this carpet, so then I will accuse him of insulting his Lord. But if he is unwilling to come towards me, I will ask him why he is insulting me by refusing to approach me.'

So Francis was called in. Now he was filled with the Spirit of God and, from this plenitude he was well instructed on what he should do and say, so he walked across the carpet to greet the Sultan. Then the Sultan, thinking he had good reason to berate the man of God for showing disrespect for his Lord, Jesus Christ, said to him, 'You Christians adore the cross as a special sign of your God. Why then do you have the audacity to tread on those crosses?' Saint Francis replied, 'You should know that along with our Lord, two thieves were also crucified. We possess the cross of our God and Saviour Jesus Christ, and that cross we adore and surround with total devotion. So, while that true cross of God has been entrusted to us, you have been left with the crosses of the thieves. That is why I did not fear to walk on the signs of the thieves. For among you there is nothing of the sacred cross of the Saviour.'

III,798f

Thursday — *RCL Proper 8 / DEL Week 13*

A reading from 'The Major Legend of Saint Francis', by Saint Bonaventure.

Inspired from heaven, Francis, Christ's servant, said to the Sultan, 'If you wish to be converted to Christ along with your people, I will most gladly stay with you for love of him. But if you hesitate to abandon the law of Mohammed for the faith of Christ, then command that an enormous fire be lit and I will walk into the fire, along with your priests, so that you will recognize which faith deserves to be held as the holier and more certain.' 'I do not believe,' the Sultan replied, 'that any of my priests would be willing to expose himself to the fire to defend his faith or to undergo any kind of torment.' For he had seen immediately one of his priests, a man full of authority and years, slipping away from his view when he heard Francis' words.

'If you wish to promise me that if I come out of the fire unharmed,' the saint said to the Sultan, 'you and your people will come over to the worship of Christ, then I will enter the fire alone. And if I shall be burned, you must attribute it to my sins. But if God's power protects me, you will acknowledge Christ, the power and wisdom of God, as the true God and the Saviour of all.' The Sultan replied that he did not dare to accept this choice, because he feared a revolt among his people. Nevertheless, he offered him many precious gifts, which the man of God, greedy not for worldly possessions but the salvation of souls, spurned as if they were dirt. Seeing that the holy man so completely despised worldly possessions, the Sultan was overflowing with admiration, and developed an even greater respect for him. Although he refused, or perhaps did not dare, to come over to the Christian faith, he nevertheless devoutly asked Christ's servant to accept the gifts and give them to the Christian poor or to churches for his salvation. But, because he was accustomed to flee the burden of money and did not see a root of true piety in the Sultan's soul, Francis would in no way accept them.

When he saw that he was making no progress
in converting these people
and that he could not achieve his purpose,
namely martyrdom,
he went back to the lands of the faithful
as he was advised by a divine revelation. *II, 603f*

Friday — RCL Proper 8 / DEL Week 13

A reading from a Letter of Jacques de Vitry, Bishop of Acre.

The Lord Rayner, Prior of Saint Michael's [Church in Acre], has entered the Order of Lesser Brothers. This Order is multiplying rapidly throughout the world, because it expressly imitates the pattern of the primitive Church and the life of the apostles in everything. But to our way of thinking, this Order is quite risky, because it sends out two by two throughout the world, not only formed Religious, but also immature young men who should first be tested and subjected to conventual discipline for a time. The head of these brothers, who also founded the Order, came into our camp. He was so inflamed with zeal for the faith that he did not fear to cross the lines to the army of our enemy. For several days he preached the Word of God to the Saracens and made a little progress. The Sultan, the ruler of Egypt, privately asked him to pray to the Lord for him, so that he might be inspired by God to adhere to that religion which most pleased God. Colin, the Englishman, our clerk, also has joined this Order, as well as two more of our company, namely, Master Michael and Lord Matthew, to whom I had committed the care of the Church of the Holy Cross. I am having a difficult time holding on to the cantor and Henry and several others.   *1,580f*

Saturday — RCL Proper 8 / DEL Week 13

A reading from 'The Earlier Rule' of Saint Francis.

The Lord says, 'Behold, I am sending you like sheep in the midst of wolves. Therefore, be wise as serpents and simple as doves.' Let any brother, then who desires by divine inspiration to go among the Saracens and other non-believers, go with the permission of his Minister and servant. If he sees they are fit to be sent, the Minister may give them permission and not oppose them, for he will be bound to render an accounting to the Lord if he has proceeded without discernment in this and other matters.

As for the brothers who go, they can live spiritually among the Saracens and non-believers in two ways. One way is not to engage in arguments or disputes but to be subject to every human creature for God's sake and to acknowledge that they are Christians. The other way is to announce the Word of God, when they see it pleases the Lord, in order that unbelievers may believe in Almighty God, the Father, the Son and the Holy Spirit, the Creator of all, the Son, the Redeemer and Saviour, and be baptized and become Christians because no one can enter the kingdom of God without being born of water and the Holy Spirit.

They can say to them and the others these and other things which please God because the Lord says in the gospel, 'Whoever acknowledges me before others I will acknowledge before my heavenly Father. Whoever is ashamed of me and of my words, the Son of Man will be ashamed of when he comes in his glory and in the glory of the Father.'

Wherever they may be, let all my brothers remember that they have given themselves and abandoned their bodies to the Lord Jesus Christ. For love of him, they must make themselves vulnerable to their enemies, both visible and invisible, because the Lord says, 'Whoever loses his life for my sake will save it to eternal life. Blessèd are they who suffer persecution for the sake of justice, for theirs is the kingdom of heaven.'

I,74

Week of Sunday between 3 & 9 July inclusive

Sunday — *RCL Proper 9 / DEL Week 14*

A reading from 'The Later Rule' of Saint Francis.

I strictly command all my brothers not to receive coins or money in any form, either personally or through intermediaries. Nevertheless, the Ministers and Custodians alone may take special care, through their spiritual friends, to provide for the needs of the sick and the clothing of the others according to places, seasons and cold climates, as they judge necessary, saving always that, as stated above, they do not receive coins or money.

Let the brothers not make anything their own: neither house, nor place, nor anything at all. As pilgrims and strangers in this world, serving the Lord in poverty and humility, let them go seeking alms with confidence, and they should not be ashamed because, for our sakes, our Lord made himself poor in this world. This is that sublime height of most exalted poverty which has made you, my most belovèd brothers, heirs and kings of the Kingdom of Heaven, poor in temporal things but exalted in virtue. Let this be your portion which leads into the land of the living. Giving yourselves totally to this, belovèd brothers, never seek anything else under heaven for the name of our Lord Jesus Christ.

Wherever the brothers may be and meet one another, let them show that they are members of the same family. Let each one confidently make known his need to the other, for if a mother loves and cares for her son according to the flesh, how much more diligently must someone love and care for his brother according to the Spirit! When any brother falls sick, the other brothers must serve him as they would wish to be served themselves.   *I,102f*

Monday — *RCL Proper 9 / DEL Week 14*

A reading from 'The Life of Saint Francis', by Thomas of Celano.

As followers of most holy poverty, since the brothers had nothing, they loved nothing; so they feared losing nothing. They were satisfied with a single tunic, often patched both inside and out. Nothing about it was refined; rather it appeared lowly and rough, so that in it they seemed completely crucified to the world. They wore crude trousers with a cord for a belt. They held firmly to the holy intention of remaining this way and having nothing more. So they were safe wherever they went. Disturbed by no fears, distracted by no cares, they awaited the next day without any worry. Though frequently on hazardous journeys, they were not anxious about where they might stay the next day. Often, they need-ed a place to stay in extreme cold, and a baker's oven would receive them; or they would hide for the night humbly in caves or crypts.

During the day, those who knew how worked with their own hands, staying in the houses of lepers or in other suitable places, serving every-one humbly and devoutly. They did not want to take any job that might give rise to scandal; but rather always doing what was holy and just, honest and useful, they inspired all they dealt with to follow their example of humility and patience.   *I,218*

Tuesday — *RCL Proper 9 / DEL Week 14*

A reading from 'The Assisi Compilation'.

While Francis, this true friend of God, completely despised all worldly things, he detested money above all. From the beginning of his conversion, he despised money particularly and encouraged his followers to flee from it always as from the devil himself. He gave his followers this observation: money and manure are equally worthy of love.

Now it happened one day that a layman came to pray in the church of

Saint Mary of the Portiuncula and placed some money by the cross as an offering. When he left, one of the brothers simply picked it up with his hand and threw it on the window-sill. What the brother had done reached the saint and he, seeing he had been caught, ran to ask forgiveness, threw himself to the ground, and offered himself to be whipped.

The saint rebuked him and reprimanded him severely for touching coins. He ordered him to pick up the money from the window-sill with his mouth, take it outside the fence of that place, and with his mouth to put it on the donkey's manure pile. While that brother was gladly carrying out this command, fear filled the hearts of the rest who heard it. From then on, all of them held in even greater contempt what had been so equated with manure and were encouraged to despise it by new examples every day.   *II,137*

Wednesday — *RCL Proper 9 / DEL Week 14*

A reading from 'The Remembrance of the Desire of a Soul', by Thomas of Celano.

The holy man Francis, would often repeat this: 'As far as the brothers will withdraw from poverty, that far the world will withdraw from them; they will seek,' he said, 'but will not find. But if they would only embrace my Lady Poverty, the world would nourish them, for they are given to the world for its salvation.' He would also say: 'There is an exchange between the brothers and the world: they owe the world good example and the world owes them the supply of necessities of life. When they break faith and withdraw their good example, the world withdraws its helping hand, a just judgement.'

Concerned about poverty, the man of God feared large numbers; they give the appearance, if not the reality, of wealth. Because of this he used to say: 'Oh, if it were possible, I wish the world would only rarely get to see Lesser Brothers, and should be surprised at their small number!' Joined by an unbreakable bond to Lady Poverty, he expected her dowry in the future, not in the present. He also sang with warmer feeling and livelier joy the psalms that praise poverty, such as, 'The patience of the poor will not perish in the end,' and 'Let the poor see this and rejoice.'   *II,294*

Thursday — RCL Proper 9 / DEL Week 14

A reading from 'The Testament of Saint Clare'.

Therefore I, Clare, a handmaid of Christ and of the Poor Sisters of the Monastery of San Damiano, although unworthy, and the little plant of the holy father, consider, together with my sisters, so lofty a profession and the command of such a father and also the frailty of some others that we feared in ourselves after the passing of our holy father Francis, who was our pillar of strength and, after God, our one consolation and support. Time and again we willingly bound ourselves to our Lady, most holy Poverty, that after my death, the sisters, those present and those to come, would never turn away from her.

And as I have always been most zealous and solicitous to observe and to have the others observe the holy poverty that we have promised to the Lord and our holy father Francis, so, too, the others who will succeed me in office should be always bound to observe holy poverty with the help of God and have it observed by the other sisters. Moreover, for greater security, I took care to have our profession of the most holy poverty that we promised our father strengthened with privileges by the Lord Pope Innocent, during whose pontificate we had our beginning, and by his other successors, that we would never nor in any way turn away from her.

For this reason, on bended knees and bowing low with both body and soul, I commend all my sisters, both those present and those to come, out of love of the God who was placed poor in the crib, lived poor in the world, and remained naked on the cross, to observe the holy poverty that we have promised to God and our most blessèd father Saint Francis.

V,59>

Friday — RCL Proper 9 / DEL Week 14

A reading from 'The Testament of Saint Clare'.

As the Lord gave us our most blessèd father Francis as a founder, planter, and helper in the service of Christ and in those things we have promised to God and to our blessèd father who, while he was living, was always solicitous in word and in deed to cherish and take care of us, his plant, so I commend and leave my sisters, both those present and those to come, to the successor of our blessèd father Francis and to the entire Order, that they may always help us to progress in serving God more perfectly and, above all, to observe more perfectly most holy poverty.

If the sisters spoken of ever leave and go elsewhere, let them be bound after my death, wherever they may be, to observe that same form of poverty that we have promised God and our most blessèd father Francis.

Nevertheless, let both the sister who is in office, as well as the other sisters, exercise such care and farsightedness that they do not acquire or receive more land about the place than extreme necessity requires for a vegetable garden. But if, for the integrity and privacy of the monastery, it becomes necessary to have more land beyond the limits of the garden, no more should be acquired than extreme necessity demands. This land should not be cultivated or planted but remain always untouched and undeveloped.

In the Lord Jesus Christ, I admonish and exhort all my sisters, both those present and those to come, to strive always to imitate the way of holy simplicity, humility and poverty and to preserve the integrity of our holy way of living, as we were taught from the beginning of our conversion by Christ, and our blessèd father Francis.   *V,59f*

Saturday – *RCL Proper 9 / DEL Week 14*

A reading from 'The First Letter of Saint Clare to Blessèd Agnes of Prague'.

Therefore, most belovèd sister, or should I say, Lady, worthy of great respect; because you are the spouse and the mother and the sister of my Lord Jesus Christ, and have been beautifully adorned with the sign of an undefiled virginity and a most holy poverty: Be strengthened in the holy service which you have undertaken out of a burning desire for the Poor Crucified, who for the sake of all of us took upon himself the passion of the cross, delivered us from the power of the prince of darkness to whom we were enslaved because of the disobedience of our first parent, and so reconciled us to God the Father.

O blessèd poverty,
> who bestows eternal riches
>> on those who love and embrace her!

O holy poverty,
> God promises the kingdom of heaven
>> and, in fact, offers eternal glory and a blessèd life
>> to those who possess and desire you!

O God-centred poverty,
> whom the Lord Jesus Christ
>> who ruled and now rules heaven and earth,

who spoke and things were made,
condescended to embrace before all else!   *V,36*

Week of Sunday between 10 & 16 July inclusive

Sunday — *RCL Proper 10 / DEL Week 15*

A reading from 'The Assisi Compilation'.

Francis used to pierce eyes that are not chaste with this parable. 'A powerful and pious king sent two messengers to his queen, one after the other. The first returned and simply reported her words verbatim. Truly, the eyes of the wise man stayed in his head and did not dart elsewhere. The other returned and, after reporting in brief words, launched into a long story about the lady's beauty. 'Truly, my lord, I saw a lovely woman; happy is he who enjoys her!' And the king said, 'You evil servant, you cast your shameless eyes on my wife? It is clear that you would like to buy what you inspected so carefully!' He then called back the first messenger and asked, 'What did you think of the queen?' And he answered, 'I thought very highly of her, for she listened gladly and then replied wisely.' 'And do you not think she is beautiful?', the king said. 'My lord,' he said, 'this is for you to see; my job was simply to deliver messages.'

And the king then pronounced his sentence: 'You, chaste of eyes, even more chaste in body, stay in my chamber. Let that other man leave my house, so that he does not defile my marriage bed.'

Francis used to say, 'Who would not fear to look at the bride of Christ?'

II,141f

Monday — *RCL Proper 10 / DEL Week 15*

A reading from 'The Remembrance of the Desire of a Soul', by Thomas of Celano.

In the brothers' hermitage at Sarteano, that evil one who always envies the progress of God's children dared to attempt something against Francis. Seeing that the holy man was becoming even holier, and not overlooking today's profit because of yesterday's, as the saint gave himself one night to prayer in his cell, the devil sent into him a violent temptation to lust but, as soon as the blessèd father felt it, he took off his clothes and lashed himself furiously with the cord, saying, 'Come on, Brother Ass, that is the way you should stay, under the whip! The tunic belongs to religion: no stealing allowed! If you want to leave, leave!'

However, when he saw that the temptation did not leave even after the discipline, though he painted welts all over limbs black and blue, he opened his cell, went out to the garden and threw himself naked into the deep snow. Taking snow by the handful, he packed it together into balls and made seven piles. Showing them to himself, he began to address his body: 'Here, this large one is your wife, and those four over there are your two sons and your two daughters; the other two are your servant and your maid who are needed to serve them. So hurry,' he said, 'get all of them some clothes, because they are freezing to death! But if complicated care of them is annoying, then take care to serve one Master!' As that, the devil went away in confusion, and the saint returned to his cell praising God.

A certain spiritual brother was giving himself to prayer at that time, and he saw it all in the bright moonlight. When the saint later learned that the brother had seen him that night, he was very disturbed, and ordered him not to reveal it to anyone as long as he lived in the world. *II,324f>*

Tuesday — *RCL Proper 10 / DEL Week 15*

A reading from 'The Remembrance of the Desire of a Soul', by Thomas of Celano.

Francis strove to hide the good things of the Lord in the secrecy of his heart, not wanting to display for his own glory what could be the cause of ruin. Often, when many were calling him blessèd, he would reply with these words: 'Do not praise me as if I were safe; I can still have sons and daughters! No one should be praised as long as his end is uncertain. Whenever something is on loan and the lender wants it back, all that is left is body and soul – and even non-believers have that much!' This he would say to those who praised him. But he would say to himself, 'If the Most High had given so much to a thief, he would be more grateful than you, Francis!' *II,333f*

Wednesday — *RCL Proper 10 / DEL Week 15*

A reading from 'The Assisi Compilation'.

One day, [when he was close to death,] blessèd Francis called his companions to himself: 'You know how faithful and devoted Lady Jacoba dei Settesoli was and is to me and to our religion. Therefore, I believe she would consider it a great favour and consolation if you notified her about my condition. Above all, tell her to send you some cloth for a tunic of religious cloth the colour of ashes, like the cloth made by Cistercian monks in the region beyond the Alps. Have her also send some of that confection which she often made for me when I was in the City.' This confection, made of almonds, sugar and honey, and other things, the Romans call *mostacciolo.*

After the letter was written, as dictated by the holy father, while one brother was looking for another one to deliver the letter, there was a knock at the door. When one of the brothers opened the gate, he saw Lady Jacoba who had hurried from the City to visit blessèd Francis. With great joy the brother immediately went to tell blessèd Francis that Lady Jacoba had come to visit him, with her son and many other people. 'What shall we do, Father,' he said, 'shall we allow her to enter and come in here?' He said this because blessèd Francis a long time ago had ordered that in that place no women should enter that cloister out of respect and devotion for that place. Blessèd Francis answered him, 'This command need not be observed in the case of this lady, whose faith and devotion made her come here from so far away.' And in this way, she came in to see blessèd Francis, crying many tears in his presence.

II,121f>

Thursday — *RCL Proper 10 / DEL Week 15*

A reading from the 'Exposition of the Rule', by Hugh of Digne.

'Wherever the brothers may be and meet one another, let them show that they are members of the same family. Let each one confidently make known his need to the other, for if a mother loves and cares for her son according to the flesh, how much more diligently must someone love and care for his brother according to the Spirit!' By these words [of Saint Francis in his Rule] it is clearly demonstrated how perfect the love must be among the friars; namely, in its manifestation, in its intensity, and in deed.

With regard to the manifestation of love, it does not suffice for a Friar Minor to refrain from hating his brother; for that much is demanded of every Christian, however imperfect. But every friar owes to his confreres such an external show of familiarity and such signs of family love, that one may manifest his necessity to another as he would to a member of the same family.

How great should be the intensity of love is described by the example of a mother who is most strongly drawn to her child.

The above-mentioned love was most fervent among the early friars. Offering themselves and all they had with a wonderful mutual readiness, they cared not only for those who lived with them, but also for all strangers that came along. For the friars received all guests – whether known or unknown – as if they were angels from God, and they did this with the greatest possible love. As soon as their guests arrived, they hastened to wash their feet and hurriedly prepared whatever was needed by the weary pilgrims. They did not look upon them as strangers, but considered them their brothers, and in a true family spirit generously offered them food and all other necessities, as if they were members of the same household. And in their works of charity and mercy, which they had to exercise, there was no false show or fraud, but all was hidden under the cover of genuine love. *XI,90ff>*

Friday – *RCL Proper 10 / DEL Week 15*

A reading from 'The First Letter of Saint Clare to Blessèd Agnes of Prague'.

To the esteemed and most holy virgin, Lady Agnes, daughter of the most excellent and illustrious King of Bohemia; Clare, an unworthy servant of Jesus Christ and a useless servant of the enclosed Ladies of the Monastery of San Damiano, her subject and servant in all things, presents herself totally with a special reverence that she attain the glory of everlasting happiness.

As I hear of the fame of your holy conduct and irreproachable life, which is known not only to me but to the entire world as well, I greatly rejoice and exult in the Lord. I am not alone in rejoicing at such great news, but I am joined by all who serve and seek to serve Jesus Christ. For, though you, more than others, could have enjoyed the magnificence and honour and dignity of the world and could have been married to the illustrious emperor with splendour befitting you and his Excellency, you have rejected all these things and have chosen with your whole heart and soul a life of holy poverty and destitution. Thus you took a spouse of a more noble lineage, who will keep your virginity ever unspotted and unsullied, the Lord Jesus Christ.

When you have loved him, you are chaste;
when you have touched him, you become more pure;
when you have accepted him, you are a virgin.

Whose power is stronger,
whose generosity more abundant,
whose appearance more beautiful,
whose love more tender,
whose courtesy more gracious!

In whose embrace you are already caught up;
who has adorned your breast with precious stones
        and has placed priceless pearls on your ears
and has surrounded you with sparkling gems
        as though blossoms of springtime
        and placed on your head a golden crown
        as a sign of your holiness.   *V,34f*

Saturday — *RCL Proper 10 / DEL Week 15*

A reading from 'The Earlier Rule' of Saint Francis.

With our whole heart,
        our whole soul,
        our whole mind,
with our whole strength and fortitude
with our whole understanding
        with all our powers
        with every effort,
        every affection,
        every feeling,
        every desire and wish
    let us all love the Lord God
who has given and gives to each one of us
our whole body, our whole soul and our whole life,
who has created, redeemed and will save us by his mercy alone,
        who did and does everything good for us,
        miserable and wretched,

rotten and foul,
ungrateful and evil ones.

Therefore,
let us desire nothing else,
let us want nothing else,
let nothing else please us and cause us delight
except our Creator, Redeemer and Saviour,
the only true God,
who is the fullness of good,
all good, every good, the true and supreme good,
who alone is good,
merciful, gentle, delightful and sweet,
who alone is holy,
just, true, holy and upright,
who alone is kind, innocent, clean,
from whom, through whom and in whom
is all pardon, all grace, all glory
of all penitents and just ones,
of all the blessèd rejoicing together in heaven.

Therefore,
let nothing hinder us,
nothing separate us,
nothing come between us.

Wherever we are,
in every place,
at every hour,
at every time of the day,
every day and continually,
let all of us truly and humbly believe,
hold in our heart and love,
honour, adore, serve,
praise and bless,
glorify and exalt,
magnify and give thanks
to the most high and supreme Eternal God
Trinity and Unity,
Father, Son and Holy Spirit,
Creator of all,
Saviour of all
who believe and hope in him,
and love him, who,

without beginning and end,
is unchangeable, invisible,
indescribable, ineffable,
incomprehensible, unfathomable,
blessèd, praiseworthy,
glorious, exalted,
sublime, Most High,
gentle, lovable, delightful,
and totally desirable above all else
for ever.
Amen.   *I,84ff*

Week of Sunday between 17 & 23 July inclusive

Sunday — *RCL Proper 11 / DEL Week 16*

A reading from the writings of Bartholomew of Pisa.

Two young men once came to see the blessèd Francis, desiring to be received into the Order. But the Saint, anxious to test their obedience and to find out whether they were really willing to surrender their own wills, took them into the garden and said to them, 'Come, and let us plant some cabbages; and as you see me doing, so you must do also.' So the blessèd Francis began to plant, putting the cabbages with the roots up in the air and the leaves down under the ground. Then one of the two men did as Francis was doing, but the other said, 'That is not the way to plant cabbages, father; you are putting them in upside down!' But Francis turned and said to him, 'My son, I want you to do as I do.' And when the other still refused, thinking it all wrong, the blessèd Francis said to him, 'Brother, I see that you are a very learnèd man; but go your way: you will not do for my Order.' So he accepted the one and refused the other.
IV,1847

Monday — *RCL Proper 11 / DEL Week 16*

A reading from 'The Later Rule' of Saint Francis.

Let the brothers who are the Ministers and servants of the others visit and admonish their brothers and humbly and charitably correct them, not commanding them anything that is against their soul and our Rule. Let the brothers who are subject, however, remember that, for God's sake, they have renounced their own wills. Therefore, I strictly command them to obey their Ministers in everything they have promised the Lord to observe and which is not against their soul or our Rule.

Wherever the brothers may be who know and feel they cannot observe the Rule spiritually, they can and should have recourse to their Ministers. Let the Ministers, moreover, receive them charitably and kindly and have such familiarity with them as masters with their servants, for so it must be that the Ministers are the servants of all the brothers.   *I,105*

Tuesday — *RCL Proper 11 / DEL Week 16*

A reading from 'The Remembrance of the Desire of a Soul', by Thomas of Celano.

Francis not only resigned the office of Minister General but also, for the greater good of obedience, asked for a special Guardian to honour as his personal prelate. And so he said to Brother Peter of Catanio, to whom he had earlier promised obedience, 'I beg you for God's sake to entrust me to one of my companions, to take your place in my regard and I will obey him as devoutly as you. I know the fruit of obedience, and that no time passes without profit for one who bends his neck to the yoke of another.' His request was granted, and until death he remained a subject wherever he was, always submitting to his own Guardian with reverence.

Once, he said to his companions, 'Among the many things which God's mercy has granted me, he has given me this grace, that I would readily obey a novice of one hour, if he were given to me as my Guardian, as carefully as I would obey the oldest and most discerning. For a subject should not consider his prelate a human being, but rather the One for love of whom he is subject. And the more contemptibly he presides, the more pleasing is the humility of the one who obeys.'   *II,344f*

Wednesday — *RCL Proper 11 / DEL Week 16*

A reading from 'The Remembrance of the Desire of a Soul', by Thomas of Celano.

Once, when he was sitting with his companions, blessèd Francis let out a sigh: 'There is hardly a single Religious in the whole world who obeys his prelate perfectly!' His companions, disturbed, said to him, 'Tell us, father, what is the perfect and highest obedience?' And he replied, describing someone truly obedient using the image of a dead body. 'Take a lifeless corpse and place it wherever you want. You will see that it does not resist being moved, does not complain about the location, or protest if it is left. Sit in on a throne, and it will look down, not up; dress it in purple and it will look twice as pale. This,' he said, 'is someone who really obeys: he does not argue about why he is being moved; he does not care where he is placed; he does not pester you to transfer him. When he is raised to an office, he keeps his usual humility, and the more he is honoured, the more he considers himself unworthy.'

On another occasion, speaking about the same matter, he said that things granted because of a request were really 'permissions', but things that are ordered and not requested he called 'holy obediences'. He said that both were good, but the latter was safer.   *II,345*

Thursday — RCL Proper 11 / DEL Week 16

A reading from 'The Remembrance of the Desire of a Soul', by Thomas of Celano.

Francis' opinion was that only rarely should something be commanded under obedience, for the weapon of last resort should not be the first one used. As he said, 'The hand should not reach quickly for the sword.' He who does not hurry to obey what is commanded under obedience neither fears God nor respects anyone. Nothing could be truer. For, what is command in a rash leader, but a sword in the hands of a madman? And what could be more hopeless than a Religious who despises obedience?   *II,346*

Friday — RCL Proper 11 / DEL Week 16

A reading from 'The Testament of Saint Clare'.

I beg that sister, who will be in an office of the sisters, to strive to exceed the others more by her virtues and holy life than by her office, so that, stimulated by her example, they obey her not so much because of her office as because of love. Let her also be discerning and attentive to her sisters as a good mother is to her daughters, and let her take care especially to provide for them according to the needs of each one out of the alms that the Lord shall give. Let her also be so kind and available that they may safely reveal their needs and confidently have recourse to her at any hour, as they see fit, both for themselves and their sisters.

Let the sisters who are subjects, however, keep in mind that they have given up their own wills for the sake of the Lord. Therefore I want them to obey their mother of their own free will as they have promised the Lord, so that, seeing the charity, humility and unity they have towards one another, their mother might bear all the burdens of her office more easily, and, through their way of life, what is painful and bitter might be changed into sweetness.

And because the way and path is difficult and the gate through which one passes and enters to life is narrow, there are few who both walk it and enter through it. And if there are some who walk that way for a while, there are very few who persevere on it. But how blessèd are those to whom it has been given to walk and to persevere till the end. *V,60f*

Saturday — RCL Proper 11 / DEL Week 16

A reading from the writings of Thomas of Pavia.

Once, Brother Stephen said that he was staying in a hermitage for a few months with blessèd Francis and some other brothers. While he was there, he did the cooking and took care of the kitchen. By Francis' orders, the others devoted themselves to silence and prayer until Brother Stephen gave the signal for dinner by banging on a pan. Now it was Saint Francis' custom to come out of his cell at the hour of terce. If he did not see the fire lit yet in the kitchen, he would pick some greens with his own hands, saying quietly to Brother Stephen, 'Go now, and cook up these greens, and it will go well with the brothers.' Now many times, if he had also cooked some eggs or cheese that had been offered to the brothers, blessèd Francis would be totally happy, eating with the others and praising the skill of his cook. But other times, with a frown on his face, he would say, 'You made too much today, Brother. Tomorrow I do not want you to cook anything.' And since Brother Stephen was a little afraid of Saint Francis, he carried out his wishes. When he did so, the next day Francis would see the table with only a few motley pieces of bread and would sit down with the other brothers delighted. But now and then he would say, 'Brother Stephen, why have you not made us anything to eat?' And he would respond, 'Because that is what you ordered me to do.' And then Saint Francis would answer, 'Discretion is a good thing, for we should not always do what the superior says!' *III,795f*

Week of Sunday between 24 & 30 July inclusive

Sunday — *RCL Proper 12 / DEL Week 17*

A reading from 'The Remembrance of the Desire of a Soul', by Thomas of Celano.

Francis, the servant of God,
was small in stature,
humble in attitude,
and lesser by profession.
While living in the world
he chose a little portion of the world
for himself and his followers,
since he could not serve Christ
unless he had something of this world.
Since ancient times, prophetically,
this place was called 'The Little Portion',
since it was the lot ceded
to those who wished to hold nothing of this world.
In this place
there was a church built for the Virgin Mother,
who by her unique humility
deserved, after her Son, to be the head of all the saints.
It is here the Order of the Lesser Ones
had its beginning.
As their numbers increased,
there 'a noble structure arose
upon their solid foundation.'
The saint loved this place more than any other.
He commanded his brothers
to venerate it with special reverence.
He wanted it, like a mirror of the Order,
always preserved in humility and highest poverty,
and therefore kept its ownership in the hands of others,
keeping for himself and his brothers only the use of it.

There the most rigid discipline was kept in all things: as much in silence and in labour as in other religious observances. The entrance there was not open except to specially selected brothers, gathered from every region, whom the saint wanted to be truly devoted to God and perfect in every respect. Similarly, entrance was completely forbidden to any secular person. He did not want the brothers dwelling there – always kept below a certain number – to have their ears itching for worldly news and, interrupting their contemplation of heavenly things, to be dragged down to dealing with lower things by the talk of gossips. No one was allowed to speak idle words there, nor to repeat those spoken by others. And, if anyone happened to do this, punishment taught him to avoid further harm and not to repeat this in the future. Day and night, without interruption, those living in the place were engaged in the praises of God and, scented with a wonderful fragrance, they led the life of angels. This was only right! According to the stories of the old neighbours, that church used to be called by another name, 'Saint Mary of the Angels.' As the blessèd Father used to say, God revealed to him, that among all other churches built in her honour throughout the world, the blessèd Virgin cherished that church with special affection. For that reason the saint also loved it more than all others.   *II,256ff*

Monday — *RCL Proper 12 / DEL Week 17*

A reading from 'The Assisi Compilation'.

Once, close to a chapter that was to be held – which in those days was held annually at Saint Mary of the Portiuncula – the people of Assisi considered that, by the Lord's grace, the brothers had already increased and were increasing daily. Yet, especially when they all assembled there for a chapter, they had nothing but a poor, small hut covered with straw, and its walls were built with branches and mud, as the brothers had built when they first came to stay there. After a general meeting, within a few days, with haste and great devotion, they built there a large house with stone-and-mortar walls without the consent of blessèd Francis, while he was away.

When blessèd Francis returned from another region and came to the chapter, and saw that house built there, he was amazed. He considered that, seeing this house, the brothers would build or have built large houses in the places where they now stayed or where they would stay in the future. And especially because he wanted this place always to be a model and example for all the places of the brothers, before the chapter ended he got up one day, climbed onto the roof of that house, and ordered the brothers to climb up. And, intending to destroy the house, he, along with the brothers, began to throw the tiles covering it to the ground.

The knights of Assisi saw this, as well as others who were there on behalf of the city's Commune to protect that place from secular people and outsiders who were outside the place, arriving from all over to see the brothers' chapter. They saw that blessèd Francis and the other brothers wanted to destroy that house. They immediately approached them and said to blessèd Francis, 'Brother, this house belongs to the Commune of Assisi and we are here on behalf of the same Commune, and we are telling you not to destroy our house.' 'If the house belongs to you,' answered blessèd Francis, 'I do not want to touch it.' He and the brothers who were with him immediately came down. That is why for a long time the people of the city of Assisi decreed that every year their Podestà [or Mayor], whoever he is, is obliged to have it roofed and repair it if necessary.   *II,157f*

Tuesday – *RCL Proper 12 / DEL Week 17*

A reading from 'The Assisi Compilation'.

Once, the Minister General wanted to build a small house at Saint Mary of the Portiuncula for the brothers of that place where they could sleep and say their Hours. At that time especially, all the brothers of the religion, and those who were coming to the religion, were coming and going to that place. For this reason those brothers were being worn out almost daily. And because of the large number of brothers gathering in that place, they had no place where they could sleep and say their Hours, since they had to give up the places where they slept to others.

Because of this they frequently endured a lot of trouble because, after so much work, they could hardly provide for the necessities of their own bodies and the good of their own souls.

When that house was already almost finished, blessèd Francis returned to that place. While he was sleeping in a small cell one night, at dawn he heard the noise of the brothers who were working there. He began to wonder what this could be. 'What is that noise?' he asked his companion. 'What are those brothers doing?' His companion told him the whole story.

Blessèd Francis immediately sent for the Minister and said to him, 'Brother, this place is a model and example for the entire religion. And it is my will that the brothers of this place endure trouble and need for the love of the Lord God, so that the brothers of the whole religion who come here will take back to their places a good example of poverty, rather than have these brothers receive satisfaction and consolation. Otherwise, the other brothers of the religion will take up this example of building in their places. They will say, "At Saint Mary of the Portiuncula, which is the first place of the brothers, such and such buildings are built, so we can certainly build in our own places, because we do not have a suitable place to stay." ' *II,158*

Wednesday — *RCL Proper 12 / DEL Week 17*

A reading from 'The Assisi Compilation'.

Once when Francis was in Siena for treatment of the disease of his eyes, he was staying in a cell, where after his death a chapel was built out of reverence for him. Lord Bonaventure, who had donated to the brothers the land where the brothers' place had been built, said to him, 'What do you think of this place?' Blessèd Francis answered him, 'Do you want me to tell you how the places of the brothers should be built?' 'I wish you would, Father,' he answered.

And he told him, 'After receiving the bishop's blessing, let them go and have a big ditch dug around the land which they received for building the place, and as a sign of holy poverty and humility, let them place a hedge there, instead of a wall. Afterwards, they may have poor little houses built, of mud and wood, and some little cells where the brothers can sometimes pray and where, for their own greater decency and also to avoid idle words, they can work.

'They may also have churches made; however, the brothers must not have large churches made, in order to preach to the people there or for any other reason, for it is greater humility and better example when the brothers go to other churches to preach, so that they may observe holy poverty and their humility and decency.

'And if prelates and clerics, Religious or secular, should sometimes visit their places, their poor house, little cells and churches in that place will preach to them and edify them.

'The brothers often have large buildings made, breaking with our holy poverty, resulting in complaints and bad example to their neighbour. Afterwards, they abandon those places and buildings for the sake of better or healthier places, prompting those who gave alms there, as well as others who see or hear about this to be scandalized and greatly upset. It is, therefore, better that the brothers have small and poor places built, observing their profession, and giving their neighbour good example, rather than making things contrary to their profession and offering bad example to others. For, if it should ever happen that the brothers leave their little places and poor buildings for the sake of a more decent place, that would be a very bad example and a scandal.'   *II,159ff>*

Thursday — *RCL Proper 12 / DEL Week 17*

'A Rule for Hermitages', by Saint Francis.

Let those who wish to stay in hermitages in a religious way be three brothers or, at the most, four; let two of these be 'the mother' and have two 'sons' or at least one. Let the two who àre 'mothers' keep the life of Martha and the two 'sons' the life of Mary and let them have an enclosure in which each one may have his cell in which he may pray and sleep.

And let them always recite Compline of the day immediately after sunset and strive to maintain silence, recite their Hours, rise for Matins, and seek first the kingdom of God and his justice. And let them recite Prime at the proper hour and, after Terce, they may end their silence, speak with and go to the 'mothers'. And when it pleases them, they can beg alms from them as poor little ones out of love of the Lord God. And afterwards, let them recite Sext, None and, at the proper hour, Vespers.

And they may not permit anyone to enter or eat in the enclosure where they dwell. Let those brothers who are the 'mothers' strive to stay far from everyone and, because of obedience to their Minister, protect their 'sons' from everyone so that no one can speak with them. And those 'sons' may not talk with anyone except with their 'mothers' and with the Minister and his Custodian when it pleases them to visit with the Lord's blessing.

The 'sons', however, may periodically assume the role of the 'mothers', taking turns for a time as they have mutually decided. Let them strive to observe conscientiously and eagerly everything mentioned above.   *I,61f>*

Friday — *RCL Proper 12 / DEL Week 17*

A reading from 'The Remembrance of the Desire of a Soul', by Thomas of Celano.

Once, a Spaniard, a devout cleric, happened to enjoy some time seeing and talking with Saint Francis. Among other news about the brothers in Spain, he made the saint happy with this report: 'Your brothers in our country stay in a poor hermitage. They have set up the following way of life for themselves: half of them take care of the household chores and half remain free for contemplation. In this manner each week the active half moves to the contemplative, and the repose of those contemplating returns to the toils of labour. One day, the table was set and a signal called those who were away. All the brothers came together except one, who was among those contemplating. They waited a while, and then went to his cell to call him to table, but he was being fed by the Lord at a more abundant table. For they saw him lying on his face on the ground, stretched out in the form of a cross, and showing no signs of life; not a breath or a motion. At his head and at his feet there flamed twin candelabra, which lit up the cell with a wonderful, golden light. They left him in peace so as not to disturb his anointing. Suddenly the light disappeared and the brother returned to his human self. He got up at once, came to the table, and confessed his fault for being late. 'That is the kind of thing,' said the Spaniard, 'that happens in our country.'

Saint Francis could not restrain himself for joy; he was so pervaded by the fragrance of his sons. He suddenly rose up to give praise, as if his only glory was this: hearing good things about the brothers. He burst out from the depths of his heart, 'I give you thanks, Lord, Sanctifier and Guide of the poor, you who have gladdened me with this report about the brothers! Bless those brothers, I beg you, with a most generous blessing, and sanctify with a special gift all those who make their profession fragrant through good example!'   *II,361*

Saturday — *RCL Proper 12 / DEL Week 17*

A reading from 'The Remembrance of the Desire of a Soul', by Thomas of Celano.

Although we learn of the love which made Francis rejoice in the successes of those he loved, we believe this is also a great criticism of those who live in hermitages in a very different way.

Many turn the place of contemplation into a place of laziness, and turn the way of life in the hermitage, established for perfection of souls, into a cesspool of pleasure. This is the norm of those modern anchorites for each one to live as he pleases. This does not apply to all; we know saints living in the flesh who live as hermits by the best of rules. We also know that the fathers who went before us stood out as solitary flowers.

May the hermits of our times not fall away

from that earliest beauty;
may the praise of its justice remain forever!

As Saint Francis exhorted all to charity, he encouraged them to show a friendly manner and a family's closeness. 'I want my brothers,' he said, 'to show they are sons of the same mother, and that if one should ask another for a tunic or cord or anything else, the other should give it generously. They should share books and any pleasant thing; even more, one should urge the other to take them.'

And so that, even in this,
he might not speak of anything
that Christ has done through him,
he was the first to do all these things.   *II,362*

Week of Sunday between 31 July & 6 August inclusive

Sunday — *RCL Proper 13 / DEL Week 18*

'The Blessing of Clare of Assisi' to her sisters.

In the name of the Father and of the Son and of the Holy Spirit.

May the Lord bless you and keep you.

May he show his face to you and be merciful to you.

May he turn his countenance to you, my sisters and daughters, and give peace to you, and to all others who come and remain in your company, as well as to others now and in the future who have persevered in every other monastery of the Poor Ladies.

I, Clare, a servant of Christ, a little plant of our most holy father Francis, a sister and mother of you and the other poor sisters, although unworthy, beg our Lord Jesus Christ through his mercy and the intercession of his most holy mother Mary and blessèd Michael the Archangel and all the holy angels of God, of our blessèd father Francis, and all men and women saints, that the heavenly Father give you and confirm for you this most holy blessing in heaven and on earth. On earth, may he multiply you in his grace and his virtues among his servants and handmaids in his church militant. In heaven, may he exalt you and glorify you among his men and women saints in his church triumphant.

I bless you during my life and after my death, as I am able, out of all

See also readings for use around the feast of Saint Clare on page 350ff

the blessings with which the Father of mercies has and does bless his sons and daughters in heaven and on earth and a spiritual father and mother have blessed and bless their spiritual sons and daughters. Amen.

Always be lovers of your souls and those of all your sisters. And may you always be eager to observe what you have promised the Lord.

May the Lord always be with you and may you always be with him. Amen. *V,81f*

Monday – RCL Proper 13 / DEL Week 18

A reading from 'The Form of Life of Clare of Assisi'.

After the Most High, heavenly Father saw fit by his grace to enlighten my heart to do penance according to the example and teaching of our most blessèd father Saint Francis, I, together with my sisters, willingly promised him obedience shortly after his own conversion.

When the blessèd father saw we had no fear of poverty, hard work, trial, shame, or contempt of the world, but, instead, regarded such things as great delights, moved by compassion he wrote a form of life for us as follows:

'Because, by divine inspiration, you have made yourselves daughters and servants of the Most High King, the heavenly Father, and have espoused yourselves to the Holy Spirit, choosing to live according to the perfection of the holy gospel, I resolve and promise for myself and for my brothers always to have that same loving care and solicitude for you as I have for them.'

As long as he lived, he diligently fulfilled this and wished that it always be fulfilled by his brothers.

Shortly before his death he once more wrote his last will for us that we or those, as well, who would come after us would never turn aside from the holy poverty we had embraced. He said,

'I, little brother Francis, wish to follow the life and poverty of our most high Lord Jesus Christ and of his holy mother and to persevere in this until the end; and I ask and counsel you, my ladies, to live always in this most holy life and poverty. And keep most careful watch that you never depart from this by reason of the teaching or advice of anyone.'

As I, together with my sisters, have ever been solicitous to safeguard the holy poverty which we have promised the Lord God and blessèd Francis, so too the Abbesses who shall succeed me in office and all the sisters are bound to observe it inviolably to the end: that is, by not receiving or having possession or ownership either of themselves or through an intermediary, or even anything that might reasonably be called property, except as much land as necessity requires for the integrity and proper seclusion of the monastery, and this land may not be cultivated except as a garden for the needs of the sisters.   *V,71f*

Tuesday — *RCL Proper 13 / DEL Week 18*

A reading from 'The Form of Life of Clare of Assisi'.

Let the sisters, to whom the Lord has given the grace of working, work faithfully and devotedly after the Hour of Terce at work that pertains to a virtuous life and the common good. Let them do this in such a way that, while they banish idleness, the enemy of the soul, they do not extinguish the spirit of holy prayer and devotion to which all other things of our earthly existence must contribute.

At the Chapter, in the presence of all, the Abbess or her Vicaress is bound to assign the work that each should perform with her hands. Let the same be done if alms have been sent by some benefactors for the needs of the sisters, so that, in common, a recommendation may be made for them. All such alms may be distributed for the common good by the Abbess or her Vicaress with the advice of the discerning ones.

Let the sisters not appropriate anything, neither a house nor a place nor anything at all; instead, as pilgrims and strangers in this world who serve the Lord in poverty and humility, let them confidently send for alms. Nor should they be ashamed, since the Lord made himself poor in this world for us. This is that summit of the highest poverty which has established you, my dearest sisters, heiresses and queens of the kingdom of heaven; it has made you poor in the things of this world but exalted you in virtue. Let this be your portion which leads into the land of the living. Clinging totally to this, my most belovèd sisters, for the name of our Lord Jesus Christ and his most holy mother, do not ever wish to have anything else under heaven.   *V,73f*

Wednesday — *RCL Proper 13 / DEL Week 18*

A reading from 'The Form of Life of Clare of Assisi'.

Let no sister be permitted to send letters or to receive or give away anything outside the monastery without the permission of the Abbess. Let it not be permitted to have anything that the Abbess has not given or permitted. Should anything be sent to a sister by her relatives or others, let the Abbess give it lovingly to a sister who does need it. If, however, money is sent to her, the Abbess, with the advice of the discerning ones, may provide for the needs of the sister.

As for the sick sisters, let the Abbess be strictly bound to inquire with diligence, by herself and through other sisters, what their illness requires, both by way of counsel as well as food and other necessities, and let her provide for them charitably and kindly according to the resources of the place. Because everyone is bound to serve and provide for their sisters who are ill, let them do this as they would wish to be served if they were suffering from some illness. Let each one confidently manifest her needs to the other. For if a mother loves and cherishes her child according to the flesh, how much more diligently should a sister love and cherish her sister according to the Spirit.   *V,74*

Thursday — *RCL Proper 13 / DEL Week 18*

A reading from 'The Legend of Saint Clare'.

> Because she was clearly the teacher of the uneducated and,
> as it were, the director of young women in the palace of the King,
> Clare taught her sisters with such discipline
> and encouraged them with such love,
> that no word will describe it.

First of all she taught them to drive every noise away from the dwelling place of the mind so that they might be able to cling to the depths of God alone. She taught them not to be affected by a love of their relatives and to forget the homes of their families so that they might please Christ. She encouraged them to consider the demands of the flesh as insignificant and to restrain the frivolities of the flesh with the reins of reason. She showed them how the insidious enemy lays traps for pure souls, in one way tempting the holy, in another, the worldly. Finally she wanted them so to work with their hands during certain hours that, according to the desire of the founder, they would keep warm through the exercise of prayer and, fleeing the lukewarmness of neglect, would put aside the coldness of a lack of devotion by the fire of holy love.

> Nowhere was the strict rule of silence greater;
> nowhere was the brightness and the quality of every virtue
> more abundant.

There was no lax talk bespeaking a lax spirit
nor a frivolity of words producing a frivolous disposition of mind.
For the teacher herself was sparing in her words
and she abundantly compressed in few words
the desires of her mind. *V,288f*

Friday — *RCL Proper 13 / DEL Week 18*

A reading from 'The Legend of Saint Clare'.

Perhaps it would be better to be silent rather than to speak
of her marvellous mortification of the flesh,
since Clare did such things that would astonish
those who hear of them
and they would challenge the truth of these things.

For it was not unusual that she covered rather than warmed her frail body with a simple tunic and a poor mantle made of rough material. We should not marvel that she completely ignored the use of shoes. It was not out of keeping for her to fast continually or to use a bed without a mat. For in all these things, she perhaps does not merit any special praise since the other sisters of the enclosure did the same.

But what agreement could there be between the flesh of the virgin and a pigskin garment? For the most holy virgin obtained a pigskin garment which she secretly wore under her tunic with its sharp, cutting bristles next to her skin. At other times she would use a rough shirt woven from knotted horsehair which she would tie to her body with rough cords. Once she loaned this garment to one of her daughters who had asked for it; but, after three days, when that sister had worn it, immediately overwhelmed by such roughness, she not only gave it up far more quickly but also more joyfully than when she had asked for it.

The bare ground and sometimes branches of vines were her bed, and a hard piece of wood under her head took the place of a pillow. But in the course of time, when her body became weak, she placed a mat on the ground and indulged her head with a little bit of straw. After a long illness began to take hold of her weakened body and the blessèd Francis had commanded it, she used a sack filled with straw. *V,271f*

Saturday — *RCL Proper 13 / DEL Week 18*

A reading from 'The Versified Legend of Saint Clare'.

As God plans, it is believed that as Clare's vivacity
made her shine with the splendour of deeds,
she is more distinguished by her merits in suffering.
Suffering made her victorious, while a vigorous act
gave her a splendid crown after vanquishing the enemy.
Patience, the virtues' guardian, preserves her
extraordinary strength, and rejoices at adding new riches.
The patience of her sickness does not excel any less, preserving
other virtues as if they were the treasure-chest of virtue.
More than the others, it deserves to be made strongly one's own.
The reward of seeking equals preserving what has been sought.
Virtue is no less than seeking and protecting what was acquired.
Patience is the linchpin of the virtues, a friend of peace.
It shines with greater nobility than all others in the hall of virtue.
It is seen to be more distinguished among the virtues, and while it preserves
and accumulates the others' riches, it seeks the reward of praise for itself.
A noble kind of virtue may be rewarded by endurance:
to conquer while suffering. Nothing is more excellent than
this kind of virtue. A reward becomes more joyful in patience
as the suffering becomes sweeter. When someone afflicted suffers bodily,
her spirit is stronger. Virtue frequently is perfected
by the weakness of the flesh. Thus frailty becomes delectable,
sickness sweet, suffering light. Thus the joyful woman approaches all
evils that no complaint or grumbling is made. Not only courageously
but joyfully as if delicacies: thus she receives all her
illnesses. She seeks great rewards in them for herself.
The higher the merit, the more productive her
ailment. The greater the merit, the greater the glory.   *V,221f*

Week of Sunday between 7 & 13 August inclusive

Sunday — *RCL Proper 14 / DEL Week 19*

A Reading from 'The Life of Saint Francis', by Thomas of Celano

The first work that blessèd Francis undertook,
after he had gained his freedom
from the hands of his carnally-minded father,
was to build a house of God.
He did not try to build a new one,
but he repaired an old one,
restored an ancient one.
He did not tear out the foundation,
but he built upon it,
always reserving to Christ his prerogative,
although unaware of it,
for no one can lay another foundation,
but that which has been laid,
which is Christ Jesus.

When he had returned to the place mentioned where
the church of San Damiano had been built in ancient times,
he repaired it zealously within a short time,
aided by the grace of the Most High.
This is the blessèd and holy place where
the glorious religion and most excellent Order
of Poor Ladies and holy virgins
had its happy beginning,
about six years after the conversion of the blessèd Francis
and through that same blessèd man.
The Lady Clare,
a native of the city of Assisi,
the most precious and strongest stone of the whole structure,
stands as the foundation for all the other stones.
For after the beginning of the Order of Brothers,
when this lady was converted to God
through the counsel of the holy man,
she lived for the good of many

See also readings for use around the feast of Saint Clare on page 350ff

and as an example to countless others.
Noble by lineage, but more noble by grace,
chaste in body, most chaste in mind,
young in age, mature in spirit,
steadfast in purpose and most eager in her desire for divine love,
endowed with wisdom and excelling in humility,
bright in name, more brilliant in life, most brilliant in character.

I,196f

Monday — *RCL Proper 14 / DEL Week 19*

A reading from 'The Life of Saint Francis', by Thomas of Celano.

A noble structure of precious pearls arose above this woman, Clare,
whose praise comes not from mortals but from God,
since our limited understanding is not sufficient to imagine it,
nor our scanty vocabulary to utter it.

First of all,
the virtue of mutual and continual charity
that binds their wills together
flourishes among them.
Forty or fifty of them can dwell together in one place,
wanting and not wanting the same things
forming one spirit in them out of many.

Second,
the gem of humility,
preserving the good things bestowed by heaven
so sparkles in each one
that they merit other virtues as well.

Third,
the lily of virginity and chastity
diffuses such a wondrous fragrance among them
that they forget earthly thoughts
and desire to meditate only on heavenly things.
So great a love of their eternal Spouse arises in their hearts
that the integrity of their holy feelings keeps them
from every habit of their former life.

Fourth,
all of them have become so distinguished

by their title of highest poverty
that their food and clothing
rarely or never
manage to satisfy extreme necessity.

Fifth,
they have so attained the unique grace
of abstinence and silence
that they scarcely need to exert any effort
to check the prompting of the flesh
and to restrain their tongues.

Sixth,
they are so adorned with the virtue of patience
in all these things,
that adversity of tribulation,
or injury of vexation
never breaks or changes their spirit.

Seventh,
and finally,
they have so merited the height of contemplation
that they learn in it everything they should do or avoid,
and they know how to go beyond the mind to God with joy,
persevering night and day
in praising him and praying to him.   *I,197ff*

Tuesday – *RCL Proper 14 / DEL Week 19*

A reading from 'The Notification of the Death of Clare of Assisi'.

To all the sisters of the Order of San Damiano throughout the world, the sisters living in Assisi wish salvation in the Author of Salvation.

Since the sting of a darkening sadness has risen, we embark upon – not without tears – the narration of a report full of sadness. We break faith – not without the sorrowful sounds of mourning – to tell you that the mirror of the morning star, whose image we admired as a type of the true light, has vanished from our sight. The staff of our religion has perished! The vehicle of our profession, I am sorry to say, has departed from the stadium of the human pilgrimage!

Our Lady Clare, our leader, venerable mother, teacher, was called by the separating best man of carnal bond, that is destructive death, and ascended not long ago to the bridal chamber of her heavenly Spouse.

Her festive ascent from earth, from the shadow of darkness to brilliance, and her celebrated appearance in heaven – although spiritually suggesting joy to the senses – from a temporal point of view, has, nevertheless, over-whelmed our light with an outpouring of grief. While she has taken us from the slippery path of worldly desire and has directed us on the path of salvation, nevertheless, she has left our sight. For by the guilt of our imperfection, perhaps deserved, the Lord was pleased to make the glorious Clare more brilliant with heavenly rays rather than have her graciously remain any longer among her sisters in their earthly places.

Why proceed any further? The depth of this blessèdness does not know any explanation in human terms. But listen to that gift of the Divinity that she received towards the end of her time on earth. The Vicar of Christ with the venerable College of his brothers visited her when she was dying and, because he more graciously remained afterwards and did not pass up the funeral of the deceased, he honoured her body at her burial. *V,129ff>*

Wednesday – *RCL Proper 14 / DEL Week 19*

A reading from 'The Versified Legend of Saint Clare'.

After a period of a few days had passed,
Agnes, Clare's sister, followed her and made her way
to the Lamb's banquet. God had planned for them, sisters
by birth, by nature, by a life of merit, and by the kingdom,
to rejoice with Christ and to enjoy heaven eternally.
What her sister promised before her departure,
her death reveals. Thus she, who had followed
her, who was shimmering with the light of virtue,
in contempt of the world, would in dying follow
her brightness to Christ with signs, harmonious in life
and reigning with her in the kingdom.
O Virgin, renowned charioteer of your daughters,
pray to Christ for us. Your holy manner of life
drew many from their faults and, by a certain
newness of life, led those new ones to life.
We, who rejoice that you have reached the highest kingdom
and proclaim an account of your praise, pray that you
would take away the predator's world, restoring it to heaven. *V,229*

Thursday — RCL Proper 14 / DEL Week 19

A reading from 'The Versified Legend of Saint Clare'.

Let our mind keep vigil in praise of this virgin
and let our voice sound Clare's praise, extolling her
brilliant virtues with praises, sing of her mellifluous conduct,
proclaim her radiant deeds.
Her excellence puts bodily ailments to flight,
drives away the spirits' frenzies, mitigates the soul's rage,
and compels the wild beasts to be tame.
Let us commend ourselves to her exalted merits and blessèd prayers,
and let us beg the Lord that he would enlighten all the soul's senses
by this virgin's help and, by her holy prayers,
grant serenity to our mind and purify our deeds; that,
after the clouds of this world,
after the darkness of the present life,
he would breathe into tomorrow's morn,
and he would instill the joys of a heavenly life.   *V,237*

Friday — RCL Proper 14 / DEL Week 19

A reading from 'The Letter of Brother Bonaventure to the Abbess and Sisters of the Monastery of Saint Clare in Assisi'.

To his belovèd daughters in Jesus Christ, the Abbess of the Poor Ladies of Assisi in the monastery of Saint Clare, and to all its sisters, Brother Bonaventure, Minister General and servant of the Order of Friars Minor, sends his greeting and wish that you, together with the holy virgins, follow the Lamb and his attendants wherever he goes.

Dear daughters in the Lord, I have recently learned from our dear Brother Leo, once a companion of our holy Father, how eager you are, as spouses of the eternal King, to serve the poor crucified Christ in total purity. I was filled with a very great joy at this, so that I now wish, through this letter, to encourage your devotion and your generous following of the virtuous footprints of your holy mother, who, by means of the little poor man Francis, was taught by the Holy Spirit.

May you desire to have nothing else under heaven, except what that mother taught, that is, Jesus Christ and him crucified. My dear daughters, may you run after the fragrance of his blood according to the example of your mother. May you strongly hold on to the mirror of poverty, the pattern of humility, the shield of patience, the insignia of obedience. And, inflamed by the fire of divine love, may you totally give your heart to him who on the cross offered himself to God the Father for us. Thus you will be clothed with the light of your mother's example and on fire with the delightful burning flames that last forever. Imbued with the fragrance of all the virtues, you will be the perfume of Christ, the virgin's Son and the Spouse of the prudent virgins, among those who have been saved and those who are perishing.   *V,340f*

Saturday — *RCL Proper 14 / DEL Week 19*

A reading from 'The Letter of Brother Bonaventure to the Abbess and Sisters of the Monastery of Saint Clare in Assisi'.

Be so attentive in continuing your affections and fervent in the spirit of devotion that when the cry is raised, 'the Bridegroom is coming,' you will be able to meet him with faithfulness and with the lamps of your souls filled with the oil of charity and joy. While the foolish virgins are left outside, you will go in with him to the wedding of eternal happiness. Christ will have his spouses sit down there with his angels and chosen ones, will minister to them, and offer them the bread of life and the meat of the Lamb that was slain, roast fish cooked on the cross upon the fire of love, that burning love with which he loved you. Then he will give you a cup of spiced wine, that is, of his humanity and divinity, from which his friends drink and his dearly belovèd, while miraculously maintaining their sobriety, drink deeply. While enjoying that abundance of sweetness reserved for those who fear him, you will gaze upon him who is not only the most beautiful of all children but also of all the thousands of angels. It is upon him, moreover, that the angels desire to look, for he is the brightness of eternal light, the unspotted mirror of God's majesty and the radiance of the glory of paradise.

Therefore, dearly belovèd daughters, as you continue to cling to him who is our everlasting good and when he had done good things for you, commend such a sinful person as me to his indescribable kindness. Keep up your prayers that, for the glory and honour of his wonderful name, he will be good enough to guide my steps mercifully in caring for the poor little flock of Christ entrusted to me.   *V,341*

Week of Sunday between 14 & 20 August inclusive

Sunday — *RCL Proper 15 / DEL Week 20*

A reading from 'The Assisi Compilation'.

When Francis washed his hands, he chose a place where the water would not be trampled underfoot after the washing. Whenever he had to walk over rocks, he would walk with fear and reverence out of love for him who is called 'the Rock'.

Whenever he recited the verse of the psalm: 'You have set me high upon the rock,' he would say, out of great reverence and devotion, 'You have set me high at the foot of the rock.'

He also told the brother who cut the wood for the fire not to cut down the whole tree, but to cut in such a way that one part remained while another was cut. He also ordered the brother in the place where he stayed to do the same.

He would tell the brother who took care of the garden not to cultivate all the ground in the garden for vegetables, but to leave a piece of ground that would produce wild plants that in their season would produce 'Brother Flowers'. Moreover, he used to tell the brother gardener that he should make a beautiful flower bed in some part of the garden, planting and cultivating every variety of fragrant plant and those producing beautiful flowers. Thus, in their time they would invite all who saw the beautiful flowers to praise God, for every creature announces and proclaims: 'God made me for you, O people!'

We who were with him saw him always in such joy, inwardly and outwardly, over all creatures, touching and looking at them, so that it seemed his spirit was no longer on earth but in heaven. This is evident and true, because of the many consolations he had and continued to have in God's creatures. Thus, shortly before his death, he composed the *Praises of the Lord* by his creatures to move the hearts of his listeners to the praise of God, and that in his creatures the Lord might be praised by everyone.

II,192

Monday — *RCL Proper 15 / DEL Week 20*

A reading from 'The Life of Saint Francis', by Thomas of Celano.

Once while Francis was staying near the town of Greccio, a certain brother brought to him a live rabbit caught in a trap. Seeing it, the most blessèd man was moved to tenderness. 'Brother rabbit,' he said, 'come to me. Why did you let yourself get caught?' As soon as the brother holding it let go, the rabbit, without any prompting, took shelter with the holy man, as in a most secure place, resting in his bosom. After it had rested there awhile, the holy father, caressing it with motherly affection, let it go, so that now free it would return to the woods. As often as it was put on the ground, it rushed back to the holy man's lap, so he told the brothers to carry it away to the nearby forest. Something similar happened with another little rabbit, a wild one, when he was on the island in the Lake of Perugia.

He had the same tender feeling towards fish. When he had the chance he would throw back into the water live fish that had been caught, and he warned them to be careful not to be caught again. Once while he was sitting in a little boat at the port on the Lake of Rieti, a fisherman caught a large fish, commonly called a *tinca*, and reverently offered it to him. He accepted it gladly and gratefully, calling it 'brother'. He put it back in the water next to the little boat, and with devotion blessed the name of the Lord. For some time that fish did not leave the spot but stayed next to the boat, playing in the water where he put it until, at the end of his prayer, the holy man of God gave it permission to leave. *1,235f*

Tuesday — *RCL Proper 15 / DEL Week 20*

A reading from 'The Life of Saint Francis', by Thomas of Celano.

On another occasion, blessèd Francis was travelling through the Marches and Brother Paul was gladly accompanying him when he came across a man on his way to market. The man was carrying over his shoulder two little lambs bound and ready for sale. When blessèd Francis heard the bleating lambs, his innermost heart was touched and, drawing near, he touched them as a mother does with a crying child, showing his compassion. 'Why are you torturing my brother lambs,' he said to the man, 'binding and hanging them this way?' 'I am carrying them to market to sell them, since I need the money,' he replied. The holy man asked, 'What will happen to them?' 'Those who buy them will kill them and eat them,' he responded. At that, the holy man said, 'No, this must not happen! Here, take my cloak as payment and give me the lambs.' The man readily gave him the little lambs and took the cloak since it was much more valuable. The cloak was one the holy man had borrowed from a friend on the same day to keep out the cold. The holy man of God, having taken the lambs, now was wondering what he should do with them. Asking for advice from the brother who was with him, he gave them back to the man, ordering him never to sell them or allow any harm to come to them, but instead to preserve, nourish and guide them carefully.   *I,249f*

Wednesday — *RCL Proper 15 / DEL Week 20*

A reading from 'The Assisi Compilation'.

Once during summer, blessèd Francis was at [Saint Mary of the Portiuncula], and he stayed in the last cell next to the hedge of the garden behind a house where, after his death, Brother Raineri, the gardener, stayed. It happened that one day, as he came down from that little cell, there was a cricket within on the branch of the fig tree next to that cell, and he could touch it. Stretching out his hand, he said, 'Sister Cricket, come to me.' It obeyed him at once and began to chirp. This consoled blessèd Francis greatly and he praised God. He held it in his hand that way for more than an hour. Afterwards he put it back on the branch of the fig tree from which he had taken it.

And in the same way, for eight days constantly, when he came down from the cell, he found it in the same place. And daily he would take it in his hand, and as soon as he told it to sing, touching it, it sang. After eight days, he said to his companions, 'Let us give permission to our sister cricket to go where she wants. She has consoled us enough; and the flesh might vainglory from this.' As soon as it had received permission, the cricket went away and never appeared there again. His companions admired how obedient and tame she was to him.

Blessèd Francis found so much joy in creatures because of love of the Creator, to console him in his inner and outer self, that the Lord made even those that are wild to people become tame to him.   *II,217f*

Thursday — RCL Proper 15 / DEL Week 20

A reading from 'The Little Flowers of Saint Francis'.

At the time that Saint Francis was staying in the city of Gubbio, in the district of Gubbio there appeared a very big wolf, fearsome and ferocious, which devoured not only animals but even human beings, so that all the citizens were in great fear, because many times he came near to the city.

Saint Francis had compassion on the people of the town, and decided to go out to this wolf, even though all the citizens advised against it. Making the sign of the most holy cross, he went out of the town, he and his companions, placing all his confidence in God. Then that wolf, seeing many citizens who had come to see this miracle, ran towards Saint Francis, who made the sign of the most holy cross on him and called him, 'Come here, Brother Wolf, I command you on behalf of Christ that you do no harm to me or to anyone.' Immediately, the fearsome wolf closed his mouth and stopped running; and came meekly as a lamb, and threw itself to lie at the feet of Saint Francis, who said, 'Brother Wolf, you do much harm in this area and you have done great misdeeds, destroying and killing the creatures of God without his permission. You are worthy of the gallows as a thief and the worst of murderers. But I want to make peace between you and these people, so that you do not offend them anymore, and that they may pardon you every past offence, and so that neither the people nor the dogs will persecute you anymore.' And after these words were said, the wolf showed that he accepted what Saint Francis said and wanted to observe it, by movement of his body and tail and ears and by bowing his head.

Then Saint Francis said, 'Brother Wolf, since it pleases you to make this pact of peace and keep it, I promise that I will have food given to you constantly, as long as you live, by the people of this town, so that you will no longer suffer hunger, since I know very well that you did all this harm because of hunger. But in order for me to obtain this grace for you, I want you to promise me that you will never harm any human person nor any animal. Do you promise me this?' Saint Francis reached out his hand to receive his guarantee, the wolf lifted his right paw in front of him and tamely placed it on top of the hand of Saint Francis, giving the only sign of a guarantee that he was able to make.

Immediately, this news was known throughout the whole city and all the people poured into the piazza to see the wolf with Saint Francis, who got up and preached to them saying that God allows such things and pestilences because of sins; and the flame of hell, which lasts forever for the damned, is much more dangerous than the fierceness of the wolf, which can only kill the body.

Afterwards, that same wolf lived in Gubbio for two years, and he tamely entered the houses without doing any harm to anyone and without any being done to him; and he was kindly fed by the people. Finally, after two years, Brother Wolf died of old age, at which the citizens grieved very much, because when they saw him going through the city so tamely, they better recalled the virtue and holiness of Saint Francis.   *III,601ff>*

Friday — *RCL Proper 15 / DEL Week 20*

A reading from a medieval Franciscan manuscript.

Brother Tebaldo once told us something that he himself had seen. When Saint Francis was preaching one day to the people of Trevi, a noisy and ungovernable ass went careering about the square, frightening the people out of their wits. And when it became clear that no one could catch it or restrain it, Saint Francis said to it, 'Brother Ass, please be quiet and allow me to preach to the people.' When the donkey heard this, it immediately bowed its head and, to everyone's astonishment, stood perfectly quiet. And the blessèd Francis, fearing that the people might take too much notice of this astonishing miracle, began saying funny things to make them laugh.   *IV,1882*

Saturday — *RCL Proper 15 / DEL Week 20*

A reading from a medieval Franciscan manuscript.

Brother Masseo has said that he was present with the blessèd Francis when he preached to the birds. Rapt in devotion, Francis once found by the roadside a large flock of birds, to whom he turned aside to preach, as he had done before to another flock. But when the birds saw him approaching they all flew away at the very sight of him. Then he came back and began to accuse himself most bitterly, saying, 'What effrontery you have, you impudent son of Pietro Bernardone' – and this because he had expected irrational creatures to obey him as if he, and not God, were their Creator.   *IV,1882f*

Week of Sunday between 21 & 27 August inclusive

Sunday — *RCL Proper 16 / DEL Week 21*

A reading from 'The Remembrance of the Desire of a Soul', by Thomas of Celano.

Francis always sought out a hidden place
where he could join to God
not only his spirit
but every member of his body.
When it happened that he was suddenly overcome in public
by a visitation of the Lord
so as not to be without a cell,
he would make a little cell out of his mantle.
Sometimes, when he had no mantle,
he would cover his face with his sleeve
to avoid revealing the hidden manna.
He would always place something between himself and bystanders
so they would not notice the Bridegroom's touch.
Even when crowded in the confines of a ship,
he could pray unseen.
Finally, when none of these things was possible,
he made a temple out of his breast.
Forgetful of himself,
he did not cough or groan;
and being absorbed in God
took away any hard breathing or external movement.

Thus it was at home.
But when praying in the woods or solitary places
he would fill the forest with groans,
water the places with his tears,
strike his breast with his hand
and, as if finding a more secret hiding place,
he often conversed out loud with his Lord.
There he replied to the Judge,
there he entreated the Father;
there he conversed with the Friend,

there he played with the Bridegroom.
Indeed, in order to make
all the marrow of his heart a holocaust in manifold ways,
he would place before his eyes
the One who is manifold and supremely simple.
He would often ruminate inwardly with unmoving lips
and, drawing outward things inward,
he raised his spirit to the heights.
Thus he would direct all his attention and affection
towards the one thing he asked of the Lord,
not so much praying as becoming totally prayer.
How deeply would you think he was pervaded with sweetness,
as he grew accustomed to such things?
He knows.
I can only wonder.   *II,309f*

Monday — *RCL Proper 16 / DEL Week 21*

A reading from 'The Inscription of Brother Leo' in the Breviary of Saint Francis.

Blessèd Francis acquired this breviary from his companions Brother Angelo and Brother Leo, and when he was well he wished always to say the Office, as is stated by the Rule. At the time when he was sick and not able to recite it, he wished to listen to it. And he continued to do this for as long as he lived. He also had the book of the gospels copied, and whenever he would be unable to hear Mass due to infirmity or any other manifest impediment, he had that gospel read to him, which on that day was read at Mass in Church. And he continued to do this until his death. For he used to say, 'When I do not hear Mass, I adore the Body of Christ in prayer with the eyes of my mind, just as I adore it when I see it during Mass.' After blessèd Francis read the gospel or listened to it, he always kissed the gospel out of the greatest reverence for the Lord. For this reason, Brother Angelo and Brother Leo, as much as they can, humbly beg the Lady Benedetta, the abbess of the Poor Ladies of the Monastery of Saint Clare, and all the abbesses of the same monastery who are to come after her, that in memory of and out of devotion to our holy father Francis, they always preserve in the Monastery of Saint Clare this book out of which he so many times read.   *II,309f*

Tuesday — *RCL Proper 16 / DEL Week 21*

A Prayer of Saint Francis, inspired by the Lord's Prayer.

O *Our Father* most holy:
our Creator, Redeemer, Consoler and Saviour:

Who are *in heaven:*
in the angels and the saints,
enlightening them to know, for you, Lord, are Light;
inflaming them to love, for you, Lord, are Love;
dwelling in them and filling them with happiness,
for you, Lord, are Supreme Good, the Eternal Good,
from whom all good comes
without whom there is no good.

Holy be your Name:
may knowledge of you become clearer in us
that we may know
the breadth of your blessings,
the length of your promises,
the height of your majesty,
the depth of your judgements.

Your kingdom come:
that you may rule in us through your grace
and enable us to come to your kingdom
where there is clear vision of you,
perfect love of you,
blessèd companionship with you,
eternal enjoyment of you.

Your will be done on earth as in heaven:
that we may love you
with our whole heart by always thinking of you,
with our whole soul by always desiring you,
with our whole mind by always directing all our intentions to you,
and by seeking your glory in everything,
with all our whole strength by exerting
all our energies and affections of body and soul
in the service of your love and of nothing else;
and we may love our neighbour as ourselves

by drawing them all to your love with our whole strength,
by rejoicing in the good of others as in our own,
by suffering with others at their misfortunes,
and by giving offence to no one. *I,158f*

Wednesday — *RCL Proper 16 / DEL Week 21*

A Prayer of Saint Francis, inspired by the Lord's Prayer.

Father, *give us this day:*
in remembrance, understanding and reverence
of that love which our Lord Jesus Christ had for us
and of those things that he said and did and suffered for us.

our daily bread:
your own belovèd Son, our Lord Jesus Christ.

Forgive us our trespasses:
through your ineffable mercy
through the power of the passion of your belovèd Son
and through the merits and intercession
of the ever-blessèd Virgin and all your elect.

As we forgive those who trespass against us:
and what we do not completely forgive,
make us, Lord, forgive completely
that we may truly love our enemies because of you
and we may fervently intercede for them before you,
returning no one evil for evil
and we may strive to help everyone in you.

And lead us not into temptation:
hidden or obvious,
sudden or persistent.

But deliver us from evil:
past,
present
and to come.

Glory to the Father and to the Son and to the Holy Spirit;
as it was in the beginning is now, and shall be forever.
Amen. *I,159f*

Thursday — RCL Proper 16 / DEL Week 21

A reading from 'The Legend of Saint Clare'.

The usual signs prove
how much strength Clare received in her furnace of ardent prayer,
how sweet the divine goodness was to her in that enjoyment.

For when she returned with joy from holy prayer,
she brought from the altar of the Lord burning words
that also inflamed the hearts of her sisters.

In fact, they marvelled
that such sweetness came from her mouth
and that her face shone more brilliantly than usual.

Surely, in his sweetness,
God has waited upon the poor,
and the True Light
which was already revealed outwardly in her body,
had filled her soul in prayer.

Thus in a fleeting world,
united unfleetingly to her noble spouse,
she delighted continuously in the things above.

Thus, on the wheel of an ever-changing world,
sustained by stable virtue
and hiding a treasure of glory in a vessel of clay,
her mind remained on high while her body lingered here below.

It was her custom to come to matins before the younger sisters,
whom she called to the praises by silently arousing them with signs.
She would frequently light the lamps while others were sleeping;
and she would frequently ring the bell with her own hand.

There was no place for tepidity,
no place for idleness,
where a sharp reproof prodded laziness
to prayer and service of the Lord.   *V,275f*

Friday — *RCL Proper 16 / DEL Week 21*

A reading from 'The Third Letter of Saint Clare to Blessèd Agnes of Prague'.

Therefore, dearly belovèd, may you too always rejoice in the Lord. And may neither bitterness nor a cloud of sadness overwhelm you, O dearly belovèd Lady in Christ, joy of the angels and crown of your sisters!

Place your mind before the mirror of eternity!
Place your soul in the brilliance of glory!
Place your heart in the figure of the divine substance!
And transform your entire being into the image
of the Godhead itself through contemplation.

So that you too may feel what his friends feel
as they taste the hidden sweetness
that God himself has reserved from the beginning
for those who love him.

And, after all who ensnare their blind lovers
in a deceitful and turbulent world
have been completely sent away,
you may totally love him
who gave himself totally for your love,
whose beauty the sun and the moon admire,
whose rewards and their preciousness and greatness
are without end.   *V,45f*

Saturday — *RCL Proper 16 / DEL Week 21*

A reading from 'A Mirror of the Perfection of a Lesser Brother'.

When blessèd Francis had chosen from those brothers the ones he wished to take with him, he said to them, 'Go, in the name of the Lord, two by two along the way, humbly and decently, in strict silence from dawn until terce, praying to the Lord in your hearts. And let no idle or useless words be mentioned among you. Although you are travelling, nevertheless, let your behaviour be as humble and as decent as if you were staying in a hermitage or a cell because wherever we are or wherever we travel, we always have a cell with us. Brother Body is our cell, and the soul is the hermit who remains inside the cell to pray to God and meditate on him. So if the soul does not remain in quiet in its cell, a cell made by hands does little good to a Religious.'   *III,309*

Week of Sunday between 28 August & 3 September inclusive

Sunday — *RCL Proper 17 / DEL Week 22*

A reading from 'The Remembrance of the Desire of a Soul', by Thomas of Celano.

Francis wanted ministers of the word of God to be intent on spiritual study and not hindered by other duties. He said that they were heralds chosen by a great king to deliver to the people the decrees received from his mouth. For he used to say, 'Preachers must first secretly draw in by prayer what they later pour out in sacred preaching; they must first of all grow warm on the inside, or they will speak frozen words on the outside.' He said that this office was worthy of reverence and that those who exercised it should be revered by all. As he said, 'They are the life of the body, the opponents of demons, the lamp of the world.'

He considered doctors of sacred theology to be worthy of even greater honour. Indeed, he once had it written as a general rule that 'We should honour and revere all theologians and those who minister to us the words of God, as those who minister to us spirit and life.' And once, when writing to Brother Antony, he had this written at the beginning of the letter: 'Brother Francis sends greetings to Brother Antony, my Bishop. I am pleased that you teach sacred theology to the brothers providing that, as is contained in the Rule, you "do not extinguish the spirit of prayer and devotion" during study of this kind.' *II,352;I,107*

Monday — *RCL Proper 17 / DEL Week 22*

A reading from 'The Assisi Compilation'.

There was once a brother novice who could read the psalter, but not very well. And because he enjoyed reading, he sought permission from the Minister General to have a psalter and the Minister granted it to him. But the brother did not wish to have it unless he first had permission from blessèd Francis, especially since he had heard that blessèd Francis did not want his brothers to be desirous of learning and books, but wanted and preached to the brothers to be eager to have and imitate pure and holy simplicity, holy prayer and Lady Poverty, on which the holy and first brothers had built. And he believed this to be the more secure path for the soul's well-being.

Blessèd Francis told him, 'After you have a psalter, you will desire and want to have a breviary; after you have a breviary, you will sit in a fancy chair, like a great prelate telling your brother, "Bring me the breviary." And speaking in this way with great intensity of spirit, he took some ashes in his hand, put them on his head, rubbing them around his head as though he were washing it, saying, "I, a breviary! I, a breviary!" He spoke this way many times, passing his hand over his head. The brother was stunned and ashamed.

Afterwards, blessèd Francis said to him, 'Brother, I was likewise tempted to have books. But, in order to know God's will about this, I took the book, where the Lord's gospels are written, and prayed to the Lord to deign to show it to me at the first opening of the book. After my prayer was ended, on the first opening of the holy gospel, this verse of the holy gospel came to me: "To you it is given to know the mystery of the kingdom of God, but to the others all things are treated in parables."'

And he said, 'There are many who willingly climb to the heights of knowledge; that person be blessèd who renounces it for the love of God.'

II,207ff>

Tuesday — *RCL Proper 17 / DEL Week 22*

A reading from 'The Assisi Compilation'.

Many months later, when blessèd Francis was at the church of Saint Mary of the Portiuncula, at a cell behind the house on the road, that brother spoke to him again about the psalter. And blessèd Francis said, 'Go and do as your Minister tells you.' When he heard this, that brother began to go back by the same road he had come.

Blessèd Francis remained on the road, and began to think over what he had said to that brother. Suddenly he yelled after him, 'Wait for me, brother, wait!' He went up to him and said, 'Come back with me and show me the place where I told you to do with the psalter what your Minister tells you.' When they returned to the spot where he had said this, blessèd Francis bent over in front of the brother and, kneeling, said to him, '*Mea culpa*, brother, *mea culpa*. Whoever wishes to be a Lesser Brother must have nothing but the tunics, a cord and short trousers the Rule allows him; and for those forced by necessity or illness, shoes.'

Whenever brothers came to him to ask advice about such things, he would give them the same answer. For this reason, he used to say, 'A person is only as learnèd as his actions show; and a Religious is only as good a preacher as his actions show;' as if to say, 'A good tree is known only by its fruit.'

II,210

Wednesday — *RCL Proper 17 / DEL Week 22*

A reading from 'The Assisi Compilation'.

Francis did not despise or disdain holy knowledge. On the contrary, he revered with great feeling those who were knowledgeable in religion. But, foreseeing the future, he knew through the Holy Spirit, and even repeated it many times to the brothers, that many brothers, under the pretext of edifying others, would abandon their vocation: that is, pure and holy simplicity, prayer and our Lady Poverty. And it will happen that, because they will afterwards believe themselves to be more imbued with devotion and enflamed with the love of God because of an understanding of the Scriptures, they will occasionally remain inwardly cold and almost empty. And so, they will be unable to return to their first vocation, especially since they have wasted the time for living according to their calling; and I fear that even what they seem to possess will be taken away from them, because they have lost their vocation. *II,207>*

Thursday — *RCL Proper 17 / DEL Week 22*

A reading from 'The Assisi Compilation'.

Blessèd Francis used to say, 'There are many brothers who, day and night, place all their energy and care in knowledge, losing their holy vocation and devout prayer. And when they have preached to others or to the people, and see or learn that some have been edified or converted to penance, they become puffed up or congratulate themselves for someone else's gain. For those whom they think they have edified or converted to penance by their words, the Lord edified and converted by the prayers of holy brothers, although they are ignorant of it. This is the will of God so that they do not take notice of it and become proud.

'These brothers of mine are my knights of the round table, the brothers who hide in deserted and remote places, to devote themselves more diligently to prayer and meditation, weeping over their sins and those of others, whose holiness is known to God, and is sometimes ignored by the brothers and people. And when their souls will be presented to the Lord by the angels, the Lord will then reveal to them the fruit and reward of their labours, that is, the many souls saved by their prayers, saying to them, "My sons, behold these souls have been saved by your prayer, and since you were faithful in little things, I will set you over many." '

II,207f

Friday — RCL Proper 17 / DEL Week 22

A reading from 'The Remembrance of the Desire of a Soul', by Thomas of Celano.

When Francis was in Rome at the home of a Cardinal, he was asked about some obscure passages, and he brought to light depths in such a way that you would think he was constantly studying the Scriptures. The Lord Cardinal said to him, 'I am not asking you as a scholar, but as a person who has the Spirit of God, and so I gladly accept the meaning of your answer, because I know it comes from God alone.'

Once, when he was sick and full of pain all over, his companion said to him, 'Father, you have always taken refuge in the Scriptures, and they always have offered you relief from pain. Please, have something from the prophets also read to you now, and maybe your spirit will rejoice in the Lord.' The saint said to him, 'It is good to read the testimonies of Scripture, and it is good to seek the Lord our God in them. But I have already taken in so much Scripture that I have more than enough for meditating and reflecting. I do not need more, my son; I know Christ, poor and crucified.'
II,316

Saturday — RCL Proper 17 / DEL Week 22

A reading from 'A Letter in Response to an Unknown Master', by Saint Bonaventure.

Hear me now on what I have to say about books and other tools. The Rule states in no uncertain terms that the brothers have the right and duty of preaching, something that, to my knowledge, is found in no other Religious Rule. Now, if they are not to preach fables but the divine Word, which they cannot know unless they read, nor read unless they have books, then it is perfectly clear that it is totally in harmony with the perfection of the Rule for them to have books, just as it is for them to preach. Furthermore, if it is not harmful to the poverty of the Order to have missals for celebrating Mass and breviaries for reciting the Hours, then it is not detrimental to have books and Bibles for preaching the divine Word. The brothers are therefore allowed to have books.

Let it not disturb you that in the beginning our brothers were simple and unlettered; rather, that very fact ought to strengthen your faith in the Order. For I confess before God that what made me love Saint Francis' way of life so much was that it is exactly like the origin and the perfection of the Church itself, which began first with simple fishermen and afterwards developed to include the most illustrious and learnèd doctors. You find the same thing in the Order of Saint Francis; in this way God reveals that it did not come about through human calculations but through Christ. For since the works of Christ do not diminish but ceaselessly grow, this undertaking was proved to be God's doing when the wise did not disdain to join the company of simple folk. They heeded the Apostle, 'If you think you are wise... you should become fools so that you may become wise.' So I beg you, dear friend, be not too fully convinced in your own mind, nor believe yourself wiser or better than all those God has called to this way of life; rather, if he has called you, do not refuse him. *VII,46,53f>*

Week of Sunday between 4 & 10 September inclusive

Sunday — *RCL Proper 18 / DEL Week 23*

A reading from 'The Testament of Saint Francis'.

After the Lord gave me some brothers, no one showed me what I had to do, but the Most High himself revealed to me that I should live according to the pattern of the holy gospel. And I had this written down simply and in a few words and the Lord Pope confirmed it for me. And those who came to receive life gave whatever they had to the poor and were content with one tunic, patched inside and out, with a cord and short trousers. We desired nothing more. We clerical brothers said the Office as other clerics did; the lay brothers said the *Our Father*; and we quite willingly remained in churches. And we were simple and subject to all.

And I worked with my hands, and I still desire to work; and I earnestly desire all brothers to give themselves to honest work. Let those who do not know how to work learn, not from desire to receive wages, but for example and to avoid idleness. And when we are not paid for our work, let us have recourse to the table of the Lord, begging alms from door to door. The Lord revealed a greeting to me that we should say: 'May the Lord give your peace.' *I,125*

See also readings for use around the feast of the Stigmata on page 363ff

Monday — *RCL Proper 18 / DEL Week 23*

A reading from 'A Mirror of the Perfection of a Lesser Brother'.

From the beginning of his conversion, blessèd Francis, with the Lord's help, like a wise builder, established himself upon solid rock, that is the greatest humility and poverty of the Son of God, calling his religion 'Lesser Brothers' because of great humility.

At the beginning of the religion, he wanted the brothers to stay in hospitals of lepers to serve them, laying the foundation of holy humility in this way. Whenever nobles and commoners came to the Order, they were told, among other things, that they had to serve the lepers humbly and stay in their houses, as it was prescribed in the first Rule.

They did not desire to have anything under heaven, except holy poverty, by which, in this world they are nourished by the Lord with bodily and spiritual food and, in the next, will attain a heavenly inheritance.

He laid the foundation both for himself and for others on the greatest humility and poverty because, although he was a great prelate in the church of God, he wanted and chose to be lowly not only in the church, but also among his brothers. In his opinion and desire, this lowliness was to be the most sublime exaltation in the sight of God and of the people.

III,290

Tuesday — *RCL Proper 18 / DEL Week 23*

A reading from 'The Remembrance of the Desire of a Soul', by Thomas of Celano.

Francis often used to go for alms by himself, both to train himself and to spare embarrassment for his brothers. But seeing that many of them were not giving due regard to their calling, he once said, 'My dearest brothers, the Son of God was more noble than we are, and yet for our sake he made himself poor in this world. For love of him we have chosen the ways of poverty. So we should not be ashamed to go for alms. The heirs of the kingdom should not at all be embarrassed by the down payment of a heavenly inheritance! I say to you that many noble and learnèd men will join our company and will consider it an honour to go begging for alms. You, who are the first fruits of such men: rejoice and be glad! Do not refuse to do what you must hand on to those holy men.'

Blessèd Francis would often say that a true Lesser Brother should not go for long periods without seeking alms. 'And the more noble my son is,' he said, 'the more eager he should be to go, because in that way merits for him are increased.'

In a certain place there was a brother who was no 'one' for begging, but was 'many' for eating. The saint observed this friend of the belly, who shared in the fruits but not in the labour, and said to him once, 'Go on your way, Brother Fly, because you want to feed on the sweat of your brothers but wish to be idle in the work of God. You are just like Brother Drone, who wants to be the first to eat the honey without doing the work of the bees.' This man of the flesh realized that his gluttony had been discovered, and he went back to the world, which he had never left.

II,296f

Wednesday — *RCL Proper 18 / DEL Week 23*

A reading from 'The Earlier Rule' of Saint Francis.

None of the brothers may be treasurers or overseers in any of those places where they are staying to serve or work among others. They may not be in charge in the houses in which they serve nor accept any office which would generate scandal or be harmful to their souls; let them, instead, be the lesser ones and be subject to all in the same house.

Let the brothers who know how to work do so and exercise that trade they have learned, provided it is not contrary to the good of their souls and can be performed honestly. For the prophet says, 'You shall eat the fruit of your labours; you are blessèd and it shall be well for you.' The Apostle says, 'Whoever does not wish to work shall not eat.' And, 'Let everyone remain in that trade and office in which he has been called.'

And for their work, they can receive whatever is necessary excepting money. And when it is necessary, they may seek alms like other poor people. And it is lawful for them to have the tools and instruments suitable for their trades.

Let all the brothers always strive to exert themselves in doing good works, for it is written, 'Always do something good that the devil may find you occupied.' And again, 'Idleness is an enemy of the soul.' Servants of God, therefore, must always apply themselves to prayer or some good work.

I,68f

Thursday — *RCL Proper 18 / DEL Week 23*

A reading from 'The Remembrance of the Desire of a Soul', by Thomas of Celano.

From the time in which Francis gave up transitory things and began to cling to the Lord, he allowed hardly a second of time to be wasted. Although he had brought into the treasury of the Lord a great abundance of merits, he remained always new, always ready for spiritual exercise. He thought it a grave offence not to be doing something good, and he considered not going forward as going backward.

Once, when he was staying in a cell near Siena, he called his companions one night while they were sleeping and said to them, 'Brothers, I prayed to the Lord that he might deign to show me when I am his servant and when I am not, for I want to be nothing except his servant. And now the gracious Lord himself in his mercy is giving me this answer: "Know that you are in truth my servant when you think, speak or do the things that are holy." And so I have called you by brothers, because I want to be shamed in front of you, if ever I am not doing any of those three.'   *II,350*

Friday — *RCL Proper 18 / DEL Week 23*

A reading from 'The Acts of the Process of Canonization' of Saint Clare.

Sister Pacifica also said Lady Clare, when she commanded her sisters to do something, did so with great fear and humility and more often than not she wished to do what she had commanded the others.

She also said that when she was so sick that she could not get up from bed, she had herself raised to sit up and be supported with some cushions behind her back. She spun thread so from her work she made corporals and altar linens for almost all the churches of the plains and hills around Assisi.

Asked how she knew these things, she replied that she saw her spinning. When the cloth was made and the sisters had sewn it, it was hand-delivered by the brothers to those churches and given to the priests who came there.

She also said the blessèd mother was humble, kind, and loving to her sisters, and had compassion for the sick. While she was healthy, she served them and washed their feet and gave them water with her own hands. Sometimes she washed the mattresses of the sick.

Asked how she knew these things, she replied she had seen her many times. *V,138f*

Saturday — *RCL Proper 18 / DEL Week 23*

A reading from 'A Letter in Response to an Unknown Master' by Saint Bonaventure.

I now come to manual labour, on which you insist a great deal, whether as a counsel or as a precept. However, to my mind, Saint Francis did not intend either to command, counsel, or admonish us to do manual labour. Rather, given the admonition of the Apostle, he lays down the manner of working for those brothers that were either too greatly or too little concerned about labour. Certain ones were so caught up with manual labour that the devotion of prayer was killed in them. Now this was dangerous, since the active life ought to serve the contemplative; therefore our holy Father gave them this formula, so that those who wished to work with their hands and knew how and were capable of it 'should do their work so that... they do not extinguish the spirit of prayer and holy devotion.' For this is the phrase that follows immediately in the text of the Rule. Notice that he does not say 'I command' or even 'I counsel' the brothers to work with their hands; nor does he say that 'the brothers who are able to labour or who know how to work, should work.' Instead, he says, 'Those brothers to whom the Lord has given the grace of working,' – which includes not only the ability but also the desire to work. Actually, he put small value on manual labour, except as a means of avoiding idleness. Although he was the most perfect observer of the Rule, I do not believe that by his own hands he ever earned so much as twelve pence or their equivalent. Instead, he greatly admonished the brothers to prayerfulness, nor did he wish that they extinguish that grace for any material gain.

Yet let not the Order displease you because of this supposed lack of manual labour, since in it you will find plenty of hard work, both in the pursuit of truth as well as the exercise of piety, humility, and all the other virtues. Besides, the brothers have the task of begging alms, cooking, taking care of the sick, washing the dishes, and attending to many other menial duties, all of which are sweeter to them than many offices of distinction. *VII,49f>*

Week of Sunday between 11 & 17 September inclusive

Sunday — *RCL Proper 19 / DEL Week 24*

A reading from 'The Deeds of Blessèd Francis and his Companions', by Ugolino of Montegiorgio.

When Saint Francis entered the town of Montefeltro, he climbed a wall in order to be more easily heard by the throng and he preached there to the multitude. When the preaching was finished, Lord Orlando said to Saint Francis, 'Brother Francis, I have an abandoned and solitary mountain in Tuscany which is called Mount La Verna. It is very suitable for those who wish to live a solitary life. If this mountain pleases you and your companions, I would very willingly give it to you for the salvation of my soul.'

Saint Francis was thoroughly inclined and desirous of finding a solitary place where he could more completely give himself to divine contemplation, so that when he heard this offer, he first gave praise to God who through his faithful people provides for his little sheep, and then he gave thanks to Lord Orlando, and said, 'My lord, when you return to your region, I will send you two of my companions. Show them this mountain and, if it seems suitable, I most willingly accept your charitable offer.' Orlando lived in a castle near Mount La Verna.

Saint Francis sent him two of his associates and he most willingly and charitably received them, and they were led to Mount La Verna. After they accepted the place there, they went to Saint Francis and told him that the place was very remote and suitable for divine contemplation. When he heard this, Saint Francis gave praise to God.   *III,453f>*

Monday — *RCL Proper 19 / DEL Week 24*

A reading from 'The Deeds of Blessèd Francis and his Companions', by Ugolino of Montegiorgio.

Francis took Brother Leo, Brother Masseo and Brother Angelo, a former knight, and together they went to La Verna. When he was climbing the mountain with his blessèd companions and was resting for a little while at the foot of an oak tree, a great number of birds flew to blessèd Francis with joy and song and a sportive flapping of their wings. Some of the birds settled on his head, some on his shoulders, some on his knees and

See also readings for use around the feast of the Stigmata on page 363ff

some on his hands. Seeing this remarkable and unusual thing, blessèd Francis said to his companions, 'I believe, my very dear brothers, that our Lord Jesus Christ is pleased that we have accepted a place on this solitary mountain where our sisters, the birds, show such pleasure at our coming.'

Then rising totally joyful in spirit, he made his way to the place where there was yet nothing but the very poor little hut made from the branches of trees. And when he saw a solitary place where, separated from the others, he could pray, he made a poor little cell on the side of the mountain, and ordered that none of his companions should come to him, nor should they allow anyone else to come except Brother Leo, because he intended to keep a forty days' fast there in honour of Saint Michael. He told Brother Leo not to come to him more than once a day with bread and water; and once at night at the time for matins; and at that time to approach him saying nothing but, 'Lord, open my lips.' And if then Francis answered from within, 'And my mouth shall declare your praise,' they would recite matins together. But if there was no immediate response, Brother Leo should leave. He ordered this because sometimes he was in such an ecstasy of spirit and so absorbed in God that he was not able to speak throughout the day or night. Brother Leo most attentively observed this precept. *III,454f*

Tuesday — *RCL Proper 19 / DEL Week 24*

A reading from 'The Major Legend of Saint Francis', by Saint Bonaventure.

Through a divine sign from heaven, Francis had learned that in opening the book of the gospels, Christ would reveal to him what God considered most acceptable in him and from him. After completing his prayer with much devotion, he took the book of the sacred gospels from the altar and had his companion, a holy man dedicated to God, open it three times in the name of the Holy Trinity. All three times, when the book was opened, the Lord's passion always met his eyes. The man filled with God understood that, just as he had imitated Christ in the actions of his life, so he should be conformed to him in the affliction and sorrow of his passion, before he would pass out of this world.

And although his body was already weakened
by the great austerity of his past life
and his continual carrying of the Lord's cross,
he was in no way terrified,

but was inspired even more vigorously
to endure martyrdom.
The unconquerable enkindling of love in him
for the good Jesus
had grown into lamps and flames of fire,
that many waters could not quench so powerful a love.

With the seraphic ardour of desires,
therefore,
he was being borne aloft into God;
and by compassionate sweetness
he was being transformed into him
who chose to be crucified
out of the excess of his love.   *II,631f*

Wednesday — *RCL Proper 19 / DEL Week 24*

*A reading from 'The Remembrance of the Desire of a Soul', by Thomas
of Celano.*

Who can express
or who can understand
how it was far from Francis to glory
except in the cross of the Lord?
To Francis alone is it given to know,
to him alone it is given to experience.
Without a doubt,
even if we were to perceive it in some sense in ourselves,
words would be unable to express such marvels,
soiled as they are by cheap and everyday things.
For this reason perhaps
it had to appear in the flesh,
since it could not be explained in words.
Therefore,
let silence speak, where word falls short,
for symbol cries out as well, where sign falls short.
This alone intimates to human ears
what is not yet entirely clear:
why that sacrament appeared in the saint.
For what is revealed by him
draws understanding and purpose from the future.
It will be true and worthy of faith,

to which nature, law and grace
will be witnesses.   *II,377*

Thursday — *RCL Proper 19 / DEL Week 24*

A reading from 'The Tree of the Crucified Life of Jesus', by Ubertino da Casale.
When Jesus appeared to Francis, his face afire and scintillating with his divinity and humanity, he poured out upon his heart and body a vigorously-flaming fire. So much so, that his heart turned to wax, melting inside him; for divine love has the power to melt, as has been said, and the power to shape, like wax flowing into the mould of a seal. Thus did Francis dissolve mentally and bodily into the engraving of the wounds of his Belovèd in the vision, and the lover was transformed into the Loved One. Fire has resilience, and while consuming earthly material, always reaches for the highest objects; characteristically it thrusts upwards. And so, the fire of divine love consuming the heart of Francis and, enkindling his flesh by burning a pattern into it, lifted him up to its own heights. Fulfilled in him then was what he used to pray would befall him:

I beg you Lord,
let the glowing and honey-sweet force of your love
draw my mind away from all things that are under heaven,
that I may die for love of the love of you,
who thought it a worthy thing to die for love of the love of me.

Therefore, those sons who have been fashioned in the likeness of their father, by the fire of his seraphic vision, must understand that their fashioning has to take place in their soul and be carried out by the glowing crucifixion of Jesus. So they will be living their lives like 'little Christs', smaller figures of Jesus, as it were, perceiving themselves in their mortal flesh transformed into Christ.   *III,190f*

Friday — *RCL Proper 19 / DEL Week 24*

A reading from 'The Major Legend of Saint Francis', by Saint Bonaventure.
Although he tried his best to hide the treasure found in the field, Francis could not prevent at least some from seeing the stigmata in his hands and feet, although he always kept his hands covered and from that time on

always wore shoes.

A number of the brothers saw them while he was still alive. Although they were men of outstanding holiness and so completely trustworthy, nevertheless to remove all doubt they confirmed under oath, touching the most sacred gospels, that this was so and that they had seen it.

But the wound in his side he so cautiously concealed that as long as he was alive no one could see it except by stealth. One brother who used zealously to take care of him induced him with a pious care to take off his tunic to shake it out. Watching closely, he saw the wound, and he even quickly touched it with three of his fingers determining the size of the wound by both sight and touch. The brother who was his vicar at that time also managed to see it by similar care. A brother who was a companion of his, a man of marvellous simplicity, when he was one day rubbing his shoulders that were weak from illness, put his hand under his hood and accidentally touched the sacred wound, causing him great pain. As a result, from that time on, he always wore underclothes made so that they would reach up to his armpits to cover the wound on his side. Also, the brothers who washed these or shook out his tunic from time to time, since they found these stained with blood, were convinced without any doubt from this evident sign of the existence of the sacred wound, which after his death, they, along with many others, contemplated and venerated with unveiled face. *II,636f>*

Saturday – *RCL Proper 19 / DEL Week 24*

A reading from 'The Considerations on the Holy Stigmata.'

Even though Francis strove to hide and conceal the mystery of the glorious Stigmata in order to avoid all occasion of worldly glory, it pleased God, who had secretly imprinted those marks, openly to manifest many miracles for his glory by the virtue of those Stigmata, especially during this journey from Alverna to Saint Mary of the Angels and later, very many in various part of the world, during the lifetime of Saint Francis and after his glorious death, in order that the hidden and marvellous power of those Stigmata, and the exceedingly great mercy and love of Christ for him to whom God had given them in a wonderful way, might be manifested to the world.

One day, Saint Francis passed through Borgo San Sepolcro. And before he came near the town, crowds from the city and the farms ran to meet him. And many of them went before him with olive branches in their hands, crying out loudly, 'Here comes the saint! Here comes the saint!'

And because of the devotion and desire that the people had to touch him, they pressed and thronged around him. But he went along with his mind raised and absorbed in contemplating God. Although he was touched or held or pulled, like someone who is unconscious, he paid no attention at all to what was being done or said around him. And he did not even notice that he was travelling through that town or district.

Now when he had passed Borgo and the crowds had gone home and he reached a leprosarium a good mile beyond Borgo, he came back to himself like someone returning from the other world, and he asked his companions, 'When will we be near Borgo?'

For his mind had been concentrating on and rapt in the splendour of heaven and he had actually not perceived the changes of time and place or the people who met him. His companions learned by experience that this happened to him several other times. *IV,1453ff>*

Week of Sunday between 18 & 24 September inclusive

Sunday — *RCL Proper 20 / DEL Week 25*

A reading from 'The Assisi Compilation'.

Two years before his death, while he was already very sick, especially from the eye disease, Francis was staying at San Damiano in a little cell made of mats.

Blessèd Francis lay there for more than fifty days, and was unable to bear the light of the sun during the day or the light of a fire at night. He stayed in the dark in the house, inside that little cell. In addition, day and night he had great pains in his eyes so that at night he could scarcely rest or sleep. This was very harmful and was a serious aggravation for his eye disease and his other illnesses.

Sometimes, he did want to rest and sleep, but there were many mice in the house and in the little cell made of mats where he was lying, in one part of the house. They were running around him and even over him, and would not let him sleep. They even disturbed him greatly at the time of prayer. They bothered him not only at night, but also during the day, even climbing up on his table when he was eating, so much so that his

See also readings for use around the feast of Saint Francis on page 369ff

companions, and he himself, considered it a temptation of the devil, which it was.

One night, as blessèd Francis was reflecting on all the troubles he was enduring, he was moved by piety for himself. 'Lord,' he said to himself, 'make haste to help me in my illnesses, so that I may be able to bear them patiently.' And suddenly he was told in spirit, 'Tell me, brother, what if, in exchange for your illnesses and troubles, someone were to give you a treasure? And it would be so great and precious that, even if the whole earth were changed to pure gold, all stones to precious stones, all water to balsam, you would still judge and hold all these things as nothing, as if they were earth, stones and water, in comparison to the great and precious treasure which was given to you. Would you not greatly rejoice?'

'Lord,' blessèd Francis answered, 'this treasure would indeed be great, worth seeking, very precious, greatly loveable and desirable.'

'Then, brother,' he was told, 'be glad and rejoice in your illnesses and troubles, because from now you are as secure as if you were already in my kingdom.' *II,184f>*

Monday – *RCL Proper 20 / DEL Week 25*

A reading from 'The Assisi Compilation'.

The next morning on rising, Francis said to his companions, 'If the emperor were to give a whole kingdom to one of his servants, should he not rejoice greatly? But, what if it were the whole empire, would he not rejoice even more?' And he said to his companions, 'I must rejoice greatly in my illnesses and troubles and be consoled in the Lord, giving thanks always to God the Father, to his only Son, our Lord Jesus Christ, and to the Holy Spirit for such a great grace and blessing. In his mercy, he has given to me, his unworthy little servant still living in the flesh, the promise of his kingdom.

Therefore for his praise, for our consolation and for the edification of our neighbour, I want to write a new *Praise of the Lord* for his creatures, which we use every day, and without which we cannot live. Through them the human race greatly offends the Creator, and every day we are ungrateful for such great graces, because we do not praise, as we should, our Creator and the Giver of all good.'

Sitting down, he began to meditate and then said,
'Most High, all-powerful, good Lord.'

He composed a melody for these words and taught it to his companions so that they could repeat it. For his spirit was then in such sweetness and consolation, that he wanted to send for Brother Pacifico, who in the world was called 'The King of Verses', and was a very courtly master of singers. He wanted to give him a few good and spiritual brothers to go through the world preaching and praising God. *II,185f*

Tuesday — *RCL Proper 20 / DEL Week 25*

'The Canticle of the Creatures', by Saint Francis.

Most High, all-powerful, good Lord,
    yours are the praises, the glory and the honour and all blessing,
to you alone, Most High, do they belong
    and no human is worthy to mention your name.
Praised be you, my Lord, with all your creatures,
    especially Sir Brother Sun,
    who is the day and through whom you give us light.
And he is beautiful and radiant with great splendour;
    and bears a likeness of you, Most High One.
Praised be you, my Lord, through Sister Moon and the stars,
    in heaven you formed them clear and precious and beautiful.
Praised be you, my Lord, through Brother Wind,
    and through the air, cloudy and serene,
            and every kind of weather,
through whom you give sustenance to your creatures.
Praised be you my Lord, through Sister Water,
    who is very useful and humble and precious and chaste.
Praised be you, my Lord, through Brother Fire,
    through whom you light the night,
    and he is beautiful and playful and robust and strong.
Praised be you, my Lord, through our Sister, Mother Earth,
    who sustains and governs us
    and who produces various fruit with coloured flowers and herbs.
I,113f

Wednesday — *RCL Proper 20 / DEL Week 25*

A reading from 'The Assisi Compilation'.

At the same time when Francis lay sick, the Bishop of the city of Assisi at the time excommunicated the Podestà [or Mayor]. In return, the man who was then Podestà was enraged, and had this proclamation announced, loud and clear, throughout the city of Assisi: no one was to sell or buy anything from the Bishop, or to draw up any legal document with him. And so they thoroughly hated each other.

Although very ill, blessèd Francis was moved by piety for them, especially since there was no one, Religious or secular, who was intervening for peace and harmony between them. He said to his companions, 'It is a great shame for you, servants of God, that the Bishop and the Podestà hate one another in this way, and that there is no one intervening for peace and harmony between them.'

And so, for that reason, Francis composed one verse for the Praises:

> Praised be by you, my Lord,
> through those who give pardon for your love,
> and bear infirmity and tribulation.
> Blessèd are those who endure in peace
> for by you, Most High, they shall be crowned.

Afterwards, Francis called one of his companions and told him, 'Go to the Podestà and, on my behalf, tell him to go to the Bishop's residence together with the city's magistrates and bring with him as many others as he can.'

And when the brother had gone, he said to two of his other companions, 'Go and sing the Canticle of Brother Sun before the Bishop, the Podestà, and the others who are with them. I trust in the Lord that he will humble their hearts and they will make peace with each other and return to their earlier friendship and love.'

When they had all gathered in the piazza inside the cloister of the Bishop's residence, the two brothers rose and one of them said, 'In his illness, blessèd Francis wrote the *Praises of the Lord* for his creatures, for his praises and the edification of his neighbour. He asks you, then, to listen to them with great devotion.' And so, they began to sing and recite to them. And immediately the Podestà stood up and, folding his arms and hands in great devotion, he listened intently, even with tears, as if to the gospel of the Lord. For he had a great faith and devotion towards blessèd Francis.

When the *Praises of the Lord* were ended, the Podestà said to everyone, 'I tell you the truth, not only do I forgive the Lord Bishop, whom I must have as my lord, but I would even forgive one who killed my brother or my son.' And so he cast himself as the Lord Bishop's feet, telling him, 'Look, I am ready to make amends to you for everything, as it pleases you, for the love of our Lord Jesus Christ and of his servant, blessèd Francis.'

Taking him by the hands, the Bishop stood up and said to him, 'Because of my office, humility is expected of me, but because I am naturally prone to anger, you must forgive me.' And so, with great kindness and love, they embraced and kissed each other.   *II,187f*

Thursday — *RCL Proper 20 / DEL Week 25*

A reading from 'The Assisi Compilation'.

Francis said that he wanted one of his brothers who knew how to preach, first to preach to the people. After the sermon, they were to sing the *Praises of the Lord* as minstrels of the Lord. After the Praises, he wanted the preacher to tell the people, 'We are minstrels of the Lord, and that is what we want as payment: that you live in true penance.'

He used to say, 'What are the servants of God if not his minstrels, who must move people's hearts and lift them up to spiritual joy?' And he said this especially to the Lesser Brothers, who had been given to the people for their salvation.

The *Praises of the Lord* that he composed, that is,
          'Most High, all-powerful, good Lord'
he called 'The Canticle of Brother Sun', who is more beautiful than all other creatures and can be most closely compared to God.

He used to say, 'At dawn, when the sun rises, everyone should praise God, who created it, because through it the eyes are lighted by day. And in the evening, when it becomes night, everyone should praise God for another creature, Brother Fire, because through it the eyes are lighted at night.'

He said, 'For we are all like blind people, and the Lord lights up our eyes through these two creatures. Because of this, we must always praise the glorious Creator for these and for his other creatures which we use every day.'

He did this and continued to do this gladly, whether he was healthy or sick. And he encouraged others to praise the Lord. Indeed, when his illness grew more serious, he himself began to say the *Praises of the Lord*, and afterwards had his companions sing it, so that, in reflecting on the praise of the Lord, he could forget the sharpness of his pains and illnesses. He did this until the day of his death.   *II,186f*

Friday – RCL Proper 20 / DEL Week 25

A reading from 'The Assisi Compilation'.

It happened that, when the season conducive to healing of the eyes arrived, blessèd Francis left Assisi, even though his eye disease was quite serious. He was wearing on his head a large capuce the brothers had made for him, with a piece of wool and linen cloth sewn to the capuce, covering his eyes. This was because he could not look at the light of day because of the great pain caused by his eye disease. His companions led him on horseback to the hermitage of Fonte Colombo, near Rieti, to consult with a doctor of Rieti who knew how to treat eye diseases.

The doctor arrived with the iron instrument used for cauterizing in eye diseases. He had a fire lit to heat the iron and, when the fire was lit, he placed the iron in it.

To comfort his spirit so it would not become afraid, blessèd Francis said to the fire, 'Brother Fire, noble and useful among all the creatures the Most High created, be courtly to me in this hour. For a long time I have loved you and I still love you for the love of that Lord who created you. I pray our Creator who made you, to temper your heat now, so that I may bear it.' And as he finished the prayer, he made the sign of the cross over the fire.

We who were with him, overcome by piety and compassion for him, all ran away, and he remained alone with the doctor.

When the cauterization was finished, we returned to him. 'You, fainthearted, of little faith,' he said to us, 'why did you run away? I tell you the truth: I felt no pain or even heat from the fire. In fact, if it is not well cooked, cook it some more!'

The doctor was greatly amazed, and noting that he did not even move, considered it a miracle. 'My brothers,' the doctor said, 'I tell you, and I speak from experience: I doubt that a strong man with a healthy body could endure such a severe burn, much less this man, who is weak and sick.'   *II,189f*

Saturday — RCL Proper 20 / DEL Week 25

A reading from 'The Assisi Compilation'.

It is not surprising that fire and other creatures sometimes showed Francis reverence because, as we who were with him saw, he loved and revered them with a great feeling of charity. He took great delight in them and his spirit was moved to so much piety and compassion towards them that he was disturbed when someone did not treat them decently. He used to speak with them with joy, inside and out, as if they could hear, understand and speak about God. And for that reason, he was often caught up in the contemplation of God.

Once, when he was sitting close to a fire, without being aware of it, his linen trousers next to the leg caught fire. He felt the heat of the fire and his companion saw that the flame was burning his trousers and ran to put out the flame. Blessèd Francis told him, 'No dearest brother, do not hurt Brother Fire.' And he did not permit him to extinguish it. So the brother ran to the brother who was his Guardian and brought him to blessèd Francis and, against his wishes, he began to put it out.

He was moved with such piety and love for it that he did not want to blow out a candle, a lamp or a fire, as is usually done when necessary. He also forbade a brother to throw away fire or smouldering wood, as is usually done, but wanted him simply to place it on the ground, out of reverence for him who created it.   *II,191*

Week of Sunday between 25 September & 1 October inclusive

Sunday — RCL Proper 21 / DEL Week 26

A reading from 'The Life of Saint Francis', by Thomas of Celano.

In the sight of God and the people of this world
the glorious father Francis had been made perfect in grace.
In all that he did he glowed brilliantly,
yet he always kept thinking
about how to undertake even more perfect deeds.
Like a soldier, well-trained in the battle camps of God,
challenging the enemy,
he wanted to stir up fresh battles.
With the Christ as leader,

See also readings for use around the feast of Saint Francis on page 369ff

he resolved 'to do great deeds',
and with weakening limbs and dying body,
he hoped for victory over the enemy in a new struggle.
True bravery knows no real limits of time,
for its hope of reward is eternal.

He burned with a great desire to return to his earlier steps towards humility; rejoicing in hope because of his boundless love, he planned to call his body back to its original servitude, although it had now reached its limit. He cut away completely the obstacle of all cares and silenced the noise of all concerns. When he had to relax this rigour because of illness, he used to say, 'Let us begin, brothers, to serve the Lord God, for up until now we have done little or nothing.'   *I,272f*

Monday — RCL *Proper 21 / DEL Week 26*

A reading from 'The Assisi Compilation'.

Once, during those days, a doctor from the city of Arezzo, named Good John, who was known and familiar to blessèd Francis, came to visit him in the Bishop's palace. Blessèd Francis asked him about his sickness, saying, 'How does my illness of dropsy seem to you, Brother John?'

For blessèd Francis did not want to address anyone called 'Good' by their name, out of reverence for the Lord, who said, 'No one is good but God alone.' Likewise, he did not want to call anyone 'father' or 'master', nor to write them in letters, out of reverence for the Lord, who said, 'Call no one on earth your father, nor be called masters.'

The doctor said to him, 'Brother, by the grace of the Lord, it will be well with you.' For he did not want to tell him that he would die in a little while.

Again blessèd Francis said to him, 'Tell me the truth. How does it look to you? Do not be afraid, for, by the grace of God, I am not a coward who fears death. With the Lord's help, by his mercy and grace, I am so united and joined with my Lord that I am equally as happy to die as I am to live.'

The doctor then told him frankly, 'According to my assessment, your illness is incurable and you will die either at the end of September or on the fourth day before the Nones of October.' Blessèd Francis, while he was lying back on his bed sick, with the greatest devotion and reverence for the Lord, stretched out his arms and hands with great joy of mind and body and said to his body and soul, 'Welcome, my Sister Death.'   *II,203f*

Tuesday — *RCL Proper 21 / DEL Week 26*

A reading from 'The Major Life of Saint Francis,' by Saint Bonaventure.

In order that his merits might increase,
for these are brought to perfection in patience,
the man of God, Francis, started to suffer from various illnesses,
so seriously that scarcely the rest of his body
remained without intense pain and suffering.
Through varied, long-lasting and continual illness
he was brought to the point
where his flesh was already all consumed,
as if only skin clung to his bones.
But when he was tortured by harsh bodily suffering,
he called his tribulations not by the name of 'pains'
but of 'Sisters'.

Once, when he was suffering more intensely than usual, a certain brother in his simplicity told him, 'Brother, pray to the Lord that he treat you more mildly, for he seems to have laid his hand on you more heavily than he should.' At these words, the holy man wailed and cried out, 'If I did not know your simplicity and sincerity, then I would from now on shrink from your company because you dared to judge God's judgements upon me as reprehensible.'

Even though he was completely worn out by his prolonged and serious illness, he threw himself on the ground, bruising his weakened bones in the hard fall. Kissing the ground, he said, I thank you, Lord God, for all these sufferings of mine; and I ask you, my Lord, if it pleases you, to increase them a hundredfold. Because it will be most acceptable to me that you do not spare me, afflicting me with suffering, since the fulfilment of your will is an overflowing consolation for me.'   *II,641*

Wednesday — *RCL Proper 21 / DEL Week 26*

A reading from 'The Remembrance of the Desire of a Soul', by Thomas of Celano.

One of the disciples of Francis, a brother of no small fame, saw the soul of the most holy father like a star ascending to heaven, having the immensity of the moon and the brightness of the sun, extending over many waters carried by a little white cloud.

Because of this, a great crowd of many peoples gathered, praising and glorifying the name of the Lord. The whole city of Assisi rushed down in a body and the whole region hurried to see the wonderful works of God, which the Lord had displayed in his servant. The sons lamented the loss of such a father and displayed their hearts' tender affection by tears and sighs.

But a new miracle turned their weeping into jubilation and their mourning into cries of joy. They saw the body of their holy father adorned with the wounds of Christ. Not the holes of the nails but the nails themselves in the middle of his hands and feet, made from his own flesh, in fact grown in the flesh itself, retaining the dark colour of iron and the right side stained red with blood. His skin, naturally dark before, now shining bright white, promised the rewards of the blessèd resurrection.

Finally, his limbs had become soft and pliable; not rigid, as usual with death, but changed to be like those of a boy. *II,388f*

Thursday — *RCL Proper 21 / DEL Week 26*

A reading from 'The Remembrance of the Desire of a Soul', by Thomas of Celano.

At that time, the Minister of the brothers of Terra di Lavoro was Brother Augustine. He was in his last hour, and had already for some time lost his speech when, in the hearing of those who were standing by, he suddenly cried out and said, 'Wait for me, father, wait! Look, I am coming with you.' The amazed brothers asked him to whom he was speaking, and he responded boldly, 'Do you not see our father Francis going to heaven?' And immediately his holy soul, released from the flesh, followed his most holy father. *II,389*

Friday — *RCL Proper 21 / DEL Week 26*

A reading from 'The Remembrance of the Desire of a Soul', by Thomas of Celano.

At the very same hour of his death, the glorious father Francis appeared to another brother of praiseworthy life, who was at that moment absorbed in prayer. He appeared to him clothed in a purple dalmatic and followed by an innumerable crowd of people. Several separated themselves from the crowd and said to that brother, 'Is this not Christ, brother?' And he replied, 'It is he.' Others asked him again, saying, 'Is this not Saint Francis?' And the brother likewise replied that it was he. For it really seemed to that brother, and to the whole crowd, as if Christ and Saint Francis were one person.

And this will not seem at all like a rash statement to those who rightly understand it, for whoever clings to God becomes one spirit with him, and that God will be all in all.

Finally, the blessèd father and the crowd arrived at a very beautiful place, watered with the clearest waters, flourishing with the beauty of flowers and full of every delightful sort of tree. There, too, was a palace of amazing size and singular beauty. The new inhabitant of heaven eagerly entered it. He found inside many brothers sitting at a splendidly-set table loaded with various delicacies and with them he delightfully began to feast.   *II,389*

Saturday — *RCL Proper 21 / DEL Week 26*

A reading from 'The Remembrance of the Desire of a Soul', by Thomas of Celano.

At that time the Bishop of Assisi had been at the church of Saint Michael because of a pilgrimage. He was returning from there and was lodging at Benevento, when the blessèd father Francis appeared to him in a vision on the night of his passing, and said to him, 'See, my father, I am leaving the world and going with Christ!' When he rose in the morning, the Bishop told his companions what he had seen and summoned a notary and had the day and hour of the passing noted. He was very saddened about this and, flowing with tears, he regretted having lost such an outstanding father. And so he returned to his own country and told it all in order, giving unending thanks to the Lord because of his gifts.   *II,390*

Week of Sunday between 2 & 8 October inclusive

Sunday — *RCL Proper 22 / DEL Week 27*

A reading from 'A Letter on the Passing of Saint Francis', attributed to Elias of Assisi.

To Gregory, his belovèd brother in Christ, the Minister of the brothers who are in France, together with all his brothers and ours, Brother Elias, a sinner, sends greetings.

Before I begin to speak, I sigh, and rightly so. My groans gush forth like water in a flood. For what I feared has overtaken me and has overtaken you. And what I dreaded has happened to me and to you. Our consoler has gone away from us and he who carried us in his arms like lambs has gone on a journey to a far-off country. He who was beloved of God and of humanity, who taught Jacob the law of life and of discipline, and gave to Israel a covenant of peace has been received into the most resplendent dwellings. We would rejoice exceedingly on his account, yet for our own part we must mourn, since in his absence darkness surrounds us and the shadow of death covers us. It is a loss for all, yet it is a trial singularly my own, for he has left me in the midst of darkness, surrounded by many anxieties and pressed down by countless afflictions. For this reason, I implore you, mourn with me, brothers, for I am in great sorrow and, with you, in pain. For we are orphans without a father and bereaved of the light of our eyes.

In truth, in very truth, the presence of our brother and father Francis was a light, not only for us who were near, but even to those who were far from us in calling and in life. He was a light shed by the true light to give light to those who were in darkness and sitting in the shadow of death, to guide our feet into the way of peace. He did this because the true Daystar from on high shone upon his heart and enkindled his will with the fire of his love. By preaching the kingdom of God and turning the hearts of fathers to their children and the rebellious to the wisdom of the just, he prepared for the Lord a new people in the world. His name reached distant coasts and all lands were in awe at his marvellous deeds.

II,489

Monday — *RCL Proper 22 / DEL Week 27*

A reading from 'A Letter on the Passing of Saint Francis,' attributed to Elias of Assisi.

For this reason, sons and brothers, do not mourn beyond measure. God, the father of orphans, will give us comfort by his holy consolation. And if you weep, brothers, weep for yourselves and not for our brother and father, Francis. For 'in the midst of life, we are caught in death,' while he has passed from death to life. Rejoice, for, like another Jacob, he blessed all his sons before he was taken from us and forgave them all the faults which any one of us might have committed, or even thought of committing, against him.

And now, after telling you these things, I announce to you a great joy and a great miracle. Such a sign that has never been heard of from the dawn of time except in the Son of God, who is Christ the Lord.

Not long before his death, our brother and father appeared crucified, bearing in his body the five wounds which are truly the marks of Christ. His hands and feet had, as it were, the openings of the nails and were pierced front and back, revealing the scars and showing the nails' blackness. His side, moreover, seemed opened by a lance and often emitted blood.

As long as his spirit lived in the body, there was no beauty in him for his appearance was that of a man despised. No part of his body was without great sufferings. By reason of the contraction of his sinews, his limbs were stiff, much like those of a dead man. But after his death, his appearance was one of great beauty gleaming with a dazzling whiteness and giving joy to all who looked upon him. His limbs, which had been rigid, became marvellously soft and pliable, so that they would be turned this way and that, like those of a young child. *II,489f*

Tuesday — *RCL Proper 22 / DEL Week 27*

A reading from 'A Letter on the Passing of Saint Francis', attributed to Elias of Assisi.

My brothers, bless the God of heaven and praise him before all, for he has shown his mercy to us. Hold fast the memory of our father and brother, Francis, to the praise and glory of him who made him so great among people and gave him glory in the sight of angels. Pray for him, as he begged us, and pray to him that God may make us share with him in his holy grace. Amen.

On the fourth day before the nones of October, the Lord's Day, at the first hour of the preceding night, our father and brother went to Christ. I am sure, dearest brothers, that when this letter reaches you, you will follow the footprints of the people of Israel as they mourned the loss of their great leaders, Moses and Aaron. Let us, by all means, give way to tears, for we are deprived of so great a father.

Indeed, it is in keeping with our love for him that we rejoice with Francis. Still, it is right to mourn him! It belongs to us to rejoice with Francis, for he has not died but gone to the fair in heaven, 'taking with him a bag of money and will not return until the full moon'.

At the same time, it is right for us to weep for Francis. He who came and went among us, as did Aaron, who brought forth from his storehouse both the new and the old and comforted us in all our afflictions, has been taken from our midst. Now we are like orphans without a father. Yet, because it is written, 'The poor depend on you and you are the helper of orphans,' all of you, dearest brothers, must earnestly pray that, though this earthen jar has been broken in the valley of Adam's children, the Most High Potter will deign to repair and restore another of similar honour, who will rule over the multitude of our race and go before us into battle like a true Maccabee.

And, because it is not useless to pray for the dead, pray to the Lord for his soul. Let each priest say three masses, each cleric the Psalter, and the lay brothers five Our Fathers. Let the clerics also recite in common the vigil office. Amen.

Brother Elias, Sinner.   *II,490f*

Wednesday — *RCL Proper 22 / DEL Week 27*

A reading from 'The Evening Sermon on Saint Francis', preached at Paris on 4 October 1262, by Saint Bonaventure.

We admire the heavens because of their vast extent. They contain all things. Saint Francis can be likened to this feature of the heavens because of his all-embracing love which went out to everyone. We read in the Book of Sirach, 'I alone have compassed the circuit of the heaven.' This can be said of the love that is in God and in us, for it also has compassed the heavens which contain everything. Yet only the righteous dwell in heaven. Love embraces all that love commands, but such love is found only in the virtuous. It was through love that Christ humbled himself and underwent death. The Book of Sirach tells us, 'Look upon the rainbow and praise him who made it.' What is this rainbow except the cross of Christ? Therefore, the sign of Christ's cross had to be found on this man of heavenly virtue, Saint Francis, whose love was boundless. He had love without limit for everyone. Love spends itself for sinners without counting the cost. Saint Francis was not content with preaching God's word only to the Christian faithful who listen with glad hearts and accept it willingly. He even went to the Saracens to proclaim the gospel in the hope that he might be put to death for his faith in Christ, and so become a martyr.

How is it that we, wretched as we are, have such cold hearts that we are not prepared to endure anything for our Lord's sake? Our hearts neither burn nor glow with love. Ardent love is a quality of the heart and the stronger this love burns in a person's heart, the more heroic and virtuous are his deeds. Do you desire to imprint Christ crucified on your heart? Do you long to be transformed into him to the point where your heart is aflame with love? Just as iron when heated to the point where it becomes molten can take the imprint of any mark or sign, so a heart burning fervently with love of Christ crucified can receive the imprint of the crucified Lord himself or his cross. Such a loving heart is carried over to the crucified Lord or transformed into him. This is what happened with Saint Francis. *II,726f*

Thursday — *RCL Proper 22 / DEL Week 27*

A reading from 'The Sermon on the Feast of the Transferal of the Body of Saint Francis', preached at Paris, 25 May 1267, by Saint Bonaventure.

I began with the text, 'Friend, go up higher.' These are Christ's words inviting to the wedding feast those guests found to be humble whom the Lord exalts and desires to exalt. Immediately before these words, the Lord advises, 'When you are invited, go and sit in the lowest place.' Saint Francis, having been invited to Christ's wedding feast, sat in the lowest place. That is to say, he clothed himself in a shabby habit and he founded the Order of Lesser Brothers. He did not qualify the word 'Lesser' in any way, but simply and unconditionally called his Order the Order of Lesser Brothers. The Lord said to the humble guest, the one who had taken a lower place, 'Friend, go up higher.' Notice the Lord calls the humble his friends, and this text may be taken as addressed to the holy confessor Francis, who so humbled himself that he wanted to be a lesser brother and sit in the lowest place. To this man who made himself humble and lowly for Christ's sake, the Lord says, 'Friend, go up higher,' raising, as it were, 'the poor from the dust.'

Jesus calls Saint Francis his 'friend' for a number of special reasons. First, due to his truly humble spirit in all that was committed to him, he was a *faithful* friend of the Lord. Second, because of his utter purity of heart in everything he pledged himself to do, he was a *congenial* friend of the Lord. Third, on account of the serenity of his contemplative soul, he was an *intimate* friend of the Lord. And fourth, because the marks of Christ's cross were imprinted on his body, he became, as Christ's friend, 'conformed to his likeness'. The word, *Friend*, therefore, is addressed to

Saint Francis because he was a faithful, congenial and intimate friend of the Lord, conformed to him by the marks of the stigmata on his body.

His glory has been made great on earth. The Lord honoured shepherds, prophets and lawgivers. He gave his love to fishermen and made them princes. God loved all these and finally, after them, he set his love on merchants. He greatly loved Saint Francis who was a merchant. He made him a true merchant which Saint Francis became when he found the pearl of heavenly glory. He teaches us also to purchase the pearl.

Let us ask the Lord to give us in this life the grace to buy that pearl so that, together with Saint Francis, we may obtain the reward of the heavenly kingdom. May he grant us this, who lives and reigns for ever and ever. Amen.   *II,738f,746>*

Friday — *RCL Proper 22 / DEL Week 27*

A reading from 'The Morning Sermon on Saint Francis', preached at Paris, 4 October, 1267, by Saint Bonaventure.

I am afraid that if I preach with too much restraint, God will be angry with me. On the other hand, if I set myself to speak at great length on the glories of Saint Francis, I fear that some may think that, in praising him, I am really seeking praise for myself. It is difficult for me to speak on this matter. My aim, however, is to describe to you a holy and perfect man, so that each of you may strive to imitate him. And in doing this, I wish to put before you the example of Saint Francis, adhering all the while to the truth. At the beginning, let us pray to the Lord that he will grant me to say and you to hear what is to his praise and glory and for our salvation.

We began with the text from Isaiah, 'Behold my servant ...' The meaning of these words refers primarily to our Lord Jesus Christ. However, what is true of the head may be applied to the members on account of their likeness and closeness to the head. Thus, these words may fittingly be understood of any holy and perfect person. But they highlight in a pre-eminent way the unique and perfect holiness of Saint Francis with regard to its root, its loftiness and its radiance.

The root of perfect holiness lies in deep humility, its loftiness in well-tried virtue, and its radiance in consummate love. Endowed with deep humility we are sustained by God; by well-tried virtue, we are made pleasing to him; and in consummate love we are taken up to God and brought closer to our neighbour. Consequently, in this text, Saint Francis is commended for his deep humility, for which he was sustained by God, as its opening words say, 'Behold my servant whom I uphold.' Then he is commended for his well-tried virtue which made him pleasing to God, as the text continues, 'my chosen, in whom my soul delights.' Third, he is commended for his consummate love whereby he passed over into God and opened his heart to his neighbour, as the text concludes, 'I have put my spirit upon him ...'

Who, then, is such a perfect saint? Listen well. It is the person endowed with deep humility, well-tried virtue, and consummate love. The root of holiness begins in humility, develops through well-tried virtue, and is crowned in consummate love. Humility moves God to sustain us, well-tried virtue makes us pleasing to him, but consummate love brings us to be totally rapt in God and to share what we have with others.

II,748f

Saturday — *RCL Proper 22 / DEL Week 27*

A reading from 'The Lauds', by Jacopone da Todi.

This is the mission of love, to make two one;
it unites Francis with the suffering Christ.
It was Christ in his heart that taught him the way
and that love shone forth in his robe streaked with colour.

The burning love of Christ, whose depths are lost to sight,
enfolded Francis, softened his heart like wax,
and there pressed its seal, leaving the marks
of the One to whom he was united.

I have no words for this dark mystery;
how can I understand or explain
the super-abundance of riches,
the disproportionate love of a heart on fire?

Who can measure the intensity of that fire?
We only know that the body could not contain it
and it burst out through the five wounds,
that all might see that it dwelt therein.

No saint ever bore such signs upon his body —
sacred mystery, revealed by God!
It is best to pass over this in silence;

let only those who have experienced it speak.

Wondrous stigmata, manifestation of the holy,
you give witness to the awesome presence behind the awesome sign.
All will be clear at the end, when the last joust is over,
in the presence of those who follow the cross!

O my arid soul, dry of tears, run – take the bait;
drink of these waters and never turn away
until you are drunk with love.
Oh, that we might die at this sacred spring!   *IX,189*

Week of Sunday between 9 & 15 October inclusive

Sunday — *RCL Proper 23 / DEL Week 28*

A reading from 'The Major Legend of Saint Francis', by Saint Bonaventure.

Humility,
the guardian and embellishment of all the virtues,
had filled Francis, the man of God, with abundance.
In his own opinion
he was nothing but a sinner,
though in truth he was a mirror and the splendour
of every kind of holiness.
As he had learned from Christ,
he strove to build himself upon this
like a wise architect laying a foundation.
He used to say that it was for this reason
that the Son of God came down
from the height of his Father's bosom
to our lowly estate
so that our Lord and Teacher might teach humility
in both example and in word.

Therefore, as Christ's disciple, he strove to regard himself as worthless in his own eyes and those of others, recalling what had been said by his supreme Teacher: 'what is highly esteemed among mortals is an abomination before God.' He used to make this statement frequently: 'What a person is before God, that he is and no more.' Therefore, judging that it was foolish to be elated by worldly favours, he rejoiced in insults and was saddened by praise. If nothing else, he would rather hear himself blamed than praised, knowing that the former would lead to change his life, while the latter would push him to a fall. And so frequently when people extolled the merits of his holiness, he commanded one of the brothers to impress upon his ears words that were, on the contrary, insulting. When the brother, though unwilling, called him a boor and a mercenary, unskilled and useless, he would reply, exhilarated in mind and face, 'May the Lord bless you, my belovèd son, for it is you who are really telling the very truth and what the son of Pietro Bernardone needs to hear.'

II,569f

Monday — *RCL Proper 23 / DEL Week 28*

A reading from 'The Admonitions' of Saint Francis.

'Blessèd are the peacemakers, for they will be called the children of God.'

Servants of God cannot know how much patience and humility they have within themselves as long as they are content. When the time comes, however, when those who should make them content do the opposite, they have as much patience and humility as they have at that time and no more.

Those people are truly peacemakers who, regardless of what they suffer in this world, preserve peace of spirit and body out of love of our Lord Jesus Christ.

Blessèd are those servants who no more exalt themselves over the good the Lord says or does through them than over what the Lord says or does through another. They sin who wish to receive more from their neighbour than what they wish to give of themselves to the Lord God.

Blessèd are those servants who do not consider themselves any better when they are praised and exalted by people than when they are considered worthless, simple and looked down upon, for what we are before God, that we are and no more.

I,133ff>

Tuesday — *RCL Proper 23 / DEL Week 28*

A reading from 'The Remembrance of the Desire of a Soul', by Thomas of Celano.

Francis, the man of God, not only showed himself humble to the great but also to his peers and to the lowly, more willing to be admonished and corrected than to admonish others. For example, one day he was riding a donkey, since he was too weak and sickly to walk, and he passed through the field of a peasant who was working there. The peasant ran to him and asked anxiously if he were Brother Francis. When the man of God humbly answered that he was, the peasant said, 'Try hard to be as good as everyone says you are, because many people put their trust in you. So I am warning you: never be different what people expect!' When the man of God, Francis, heard this, he got down from the donkey on to the ground and, prostrate before the peasant, humbly kissed his feet, thanking him for being so kind to admonish him.   *II,339*

Wednesday — *RCL Proper 23 / DEL Week 28*

A reading from 'The Remembrance of the Desire of a Soul', by Thomas of Celano.

When Saint Francis came to Imola, a city of the Romagna, he presented himself to the Bishop of that region and asked him for permission to preach. But the Bishop said, 'Brother, I preach to my people and that is enough.' Saint Francis bowed his head and humbly went outside, but less than an hour later he came back in. 'What do you want now, brother?' the Bishop asked. Blessèd Francis replied, 'My lord, if a father throws his son out by one door, he should come back in by another!' The Bishop, overcome by humility, embraced him with a smile, saying, 'From now on, you and your brothers have my general permission to preach in my diocese. Holy humility earned it!'   *II,342*

Thursday — *RCL Proper 23 / DEL Week 28*

A reading from 'The Legend of Saint Clare'.

This woman,
the cornerstone and foundation of her Order,
from the very beginning
sought to place the building of all virtues

on the foundation of holy humility.

For she promised holy obedience to blessèd Francis and never deviated from her promise. Three years after her conversion, declining the name and office of Abbess, she wished in her humility to be placed under others rather than above them and, among the servants of Christ, to serve more willingly than to be served.

Compelled by blessèd Francis, however,
she accepted the government of the Ladies,
out of which
fear, not arrogance,
was brought forth from her heart,
and freedom did not increase,
as did service.

What is more,
the higher she was perceived in this type of prelacy,
the more worthless she became in her own judgement,
the more ready to serve,
the more unworthy she considered herself of veneration by others.

She never shirked any familial chores, to such an extent that she very often washed the hands of the sisters, assisted those who were seated at table, and waited on those who were eating. Rarely would she give an order, instead she would do things spontaneously, preferring rather to do things herself than to order her sisters. She herself washed the mattresses of the sick; she herself, with that noble spirit of hers, cleansed them, not running away from their filth nor shrinking from their stench. She frequently and reverently washed the feet of the serving sisters who returned from outside and, after washing them, kissed them. Once when she was washing the feet of one of these servants, while bending to kiss them, that sister, not tolerating such humility, withdrew her foot and, with it, struck the lady on her mouth. Yet she calmly took the foot of the sister again and, on its sole, placed a firm kiss. *V,266f*

Friday — *RCL Proper 23 / DEL Week 28*

A reading from 'The Little Flowers of Saint Francis'.

Once Saint Francis was staying in the place of the Portiuncula with Brother Masseo of Marignano, a man of great holiness, discernment and grace in speaking of God, for which Saint Francis loved him very much. One day, Saint Francis was returning from the woods and from prayer and, when he was at the edge of the woods, that same Brother Masseo, wanting to test how humble he was, went up to him and, as if joking, said, 'Why after you, why after you?' Saint Francis responded, 'What do you mean?' Brother Masseo said, 'I am saying why does the whole world come after you, and everyone seems to desire to see you and hear you? You are not a handsome man in body, you are not someone of great learning, you are not noble; so why does the whole world come after you?'

Hearing this, Saint Francis was overjoyed in spirit and, turning his face to heaven, stood for a long time with his mind lifted up into God. Then returning to himself, he knelt down and gave praise and thanks to God. Then, with great fervour of spirit, he turned to Brother Masseo and said, 'Do you want to know why the whole world comes after me? I have this from those eyes of the Most High God, which gaze in every place on the good and on the guilty. Since those most holy eyes have not seen among sinners anyone more vile, nor more incompetent, nor a greater sinner than me; to perform that marvellous work, which he intends to do, he has not found a more vile creature on the earth, and therefore he has chosen me to confound the nobility and the greatness and the strength and the beauty and the wisdom of the world, so that it may be known that every virtue and every good is from him and not from the creature, and no person may boast in his sight. But whoever boasts must boast in the Lord, to whom is every honour and glory for ever.' Brother Masseo was shocked at such a humble response, said with such fervour, and knew certainly that Saint Francis was truly grounded in humility.   *III,583*

Saturday — *RCL Proper 23 / DEL Week 28*

A reading from 'The Little Flowers of Saint Francis'.

Saint Francis wanted to make Brother Masseo humble, so that he would not lift himself up in vainglory because of the many gifts and graces God gave him, but by virtue of humility with these to grow from virtue to virtue. Once when he was staying in a solitary place with those truly holy first companions of his, among whom was the same Brother Masseo, he said one day to Brother Masseo, in front of all the companions, 'O Brother Masseo, all these companions of yours have the grace of contemplation and prayer; but you have the gift of preaching the word of

God to content the people. So I want you to have charge of the door and alms and cooking, so that these brothers may pursue contemplation. And when the other brothers eat, you will eat outside the door of the place, so that those who come to the place, before they start knocking, can be satisfied by some good words of God from you, so there will be no need, then, for anyone besides you to go outside. And do this in merit of holy obedience.' Brother Masseo pulled back his capuce and bowed his head and humbly accepted and carried out this obedience for many days, taking charge of the door, alms and cooking.

The companions, as men enlightened by God, began to feel great remorse in their hearts over this, considering that Brother Masseo was a man of great perfection like them and even more, and the whole burden of the place was placed on him and not on them. For this reason all of them, moved by one will, went to ask the holy father that he be pleased to distribute those duties among them, since their consciences could not bear that Brother Masseo carry so many burdens. Hearing this, Saint Francis accepted their advice and agreed with their will. He called Brother Masseo and said to him, 'Brother Masseo, your companions want to do part of the jobs I gave to you, so I want these jobs to be divided.' Brother Masseo said, with great humility and patience, 'Father, whatever you assign me, all or part, I will consider it all God's doing.' Then Saint Francis, seeing the humility of Brother Masseo and the charity of the others, preached to them a wonderful and great sermon about most holy humility, teaching them that the greater the gifts and graces God gives us, the more we must be humble, because without humility no virtue is acceptable to God. When he had finished preaching, he distributed the jobs with very great charity.   *III,585f*

Week of Sunday between 16 & 22 October inclusive

Sunday — *RCL Proper 24 / DEL Week 29*

A reading from 'The Remembrance of the Desire of a Soul', by Thomas of Celano.

The power of love
had made Francis
a brother to other creatures;
no wonder the charity of Christ
made him even more a brother
to those marked with the image of the Creator.

He would say that nothing should be placed ahead of the salvation of souls and would often demonstrate this with the fact that the only-begotten Son of God saw fit to hang on the cross for the sake of souls. From this arose his effort in prayer, his frequent travel in preaching and his extraordinary behaviour in giving example.

He would not consider himself a friend of Christ unless he loved the souls which Christ loved. For him this was the principal cause for revering the doctors of theology: they are the helpers of Christ, who carry out with Christ this office. With all the unbounded affection of the depths of his heart, he embraced the brothers themselves as fellow members in the household of the same faith, united by a share in an eternal inheritance.   *II,358*

Monday — *RCL Proper 24 / DEL Week 29*

A reading from 'The Admonitions' of Saint Francis.

The Lord says, 'Love your enemies, do good to those who hate you and pray for those who persecute and slander you.'

For they truly love their enemies who are not hurt by an injury done to them, but because of love of God, are stung by the sin of their soul. Let them show them love by their deeds.

Blessèd are they who support their neighbours in their weakness as they would want to be supported were they in a similar situation.

Blessèd are the servants who return every good to the Lord God, because those who hold onto something for themselves 'hide the money of their Lord God' within themselves, and what they think they have will be taken away from them.

Blessèd are the servants who love their brother or sister as much when they are sick and cannot repay them, as when they are well and can repay them.

Blessèd are the servants who love and respect their brother or sister as much when they are far away from them as when they are with them, and who would not say anything behind their back that they would not say with charity in their presence. *I,132ff>*

Tuesday — *RCL Proper 24 / DEL Week 29*

A reading from 'The Remembrance of the Desire of a Soul', by Thomas of Celano.

Great was the compassion of Francis towards the sick, and great his concern for their needs. If lay people's piety sent him tonics he would give them to the others who were sick, even though he had greater need than them. He had sympathy for all who were ill and, when he could not alleviate their pain, he offered words of compassion. He would eat on fast days so that the weak would not be ashamed of eating, and he was not embarrassed to go through the city's public places to find some meat for a sick brother.

However, he also advised the sick to be patient when things were lacking and not stir up a scandal if everything was not done to their satisfaction. Because of this, he had these words written in one of the Rules: 'I beg all my sick brothers that, in their illness, they do not become angry or upset at God or the brothers. They should not anxiously seek medicine, or desire too eagerly to free the flesh, that is soon to die and is an enemy of the soul. Let them give thanks for all things and let them desire, however, to be as God wills them to be. For God teaches with the rod of punishment and sicknesses those whom he has destined for eternal life; as he himself has said, "Those I love, I correct and chastise." '

II,359f

Wednesday — *RCL Proper 24 / DEL Week 29*

A reading from 'The Assisi Compilation'.

Once when blessèd Francis was at Rivo Torto, a certain brother, a spiritual man, an elder in religion, was staying there. He was very sick and weak. Considering him, blessèd Francis was moved to piety towards him. The brothers in those days, sick and healthy, with cheerfulness and patience, took poverty for abundance. They did not take medicines in their illnesses, but more willingly did what was contrary to the body. Blessèd Francis said to himself, 'If that brother would eat some ripe grapes early in the morning, I believe it would help him.'

One day, therefore, he secretly got up early in the morning and called that brother and took him into the vineyard which is near that same church. He chose a vine that had grapes that were good and ready for eating. Sitting down with that brother next to the vine, he began to eat some grapes so that the brother would not be ashamed to eat alone and, while they were eating them, that brother praised the Lord God. As long as he lived, he always recalled among the brothers, with great devotion and flowing tears, the mercy the holy father had done to him.   *II,152*

Thursday — *RCL Proper 24 / DEL Week 29*

A reading from 'The Earlier Rule' of Saint Francis.

Let all the brothers be careful not to slander or engage in disputes; let them strive, instead, to keep silence whenever God gives them the grace. Let them not quarrel among themselves or with others but strive to respond humbly, saying, 'I am a useless servant.' Let them not become angry because 'whoever is angry with his brother is liable to judgement; whoever says to his brother "fool" will be liable to fiery Gehenna.'

Let them love one another, as the Lord says, 'This is my commandment, that you love one another as I have loved you.' Let them express the love they have for one another by their deeds, as the Apostle says, 'Let us not love in word or speech, but in deed and in truth.'

Let them revile no one. Let them not grumble or detract from others, for it is written, 'Gossips and detractors are detestable to God.' Let them be modest by showing graciousness towards everyone. Let them not judge or condemn. As the Lord says, let them not consider the least sins of others; instead, let them reflect more upon their own sins in the bitterness of their soul. Let them struggle to enter through the narrow gate, for the Lord says, 'The gate is narrow and the road that leads to life constricted; those who find it are few.'   *I,72*

Friday — *RCL Proper 24 / DEL Week 29*

A reading from 'The Assisi Compilation'.

Once, when he was at Colle[strada] in the county of Perugia, Saint Francis met a poor man whom he had known before in the world. He asked him, 'Brother, how are you doing?' The man malevolently began to heap curses on his lord, who had taken away everything he had. 'Thanks to my liege-lord, may the Almighty God curse him, I am very badly off!'

Blessèd Francis felt more pity for the man's soul, rooted in mortal hatred, than for his body. He said to him, 'Brother, forgive your lord for the love of God, so you may set your soul free, and it may be that he will return to you what he has taken. Otherwise, you will lose not only your property but also your soul.' He replied, 'I cannot entirely forgive him unless he first gives back what he took.' Blessèd Francis had a mantle on his back, and said to him, 'Here, I will give you this cloak, and beg you to forgive your lord for the love of the Lord God.' The man's mood sweetened and, moved by this kindness, he took the gift and forgave the wrongs.   *II,140*

Saturday — *RCL Proper 24 / DEL Week 29*

A reading from 'The Remembrance of the Desire of a Soul', by Thomas of Celano.

Saint Francis usually passed the whole day in an isolated cell, returning to the brothers only when pressed by necessity to take some food. He did not leave it for dinner at the assigned time because his hunger for contemplation was even more consuming, and often completely over-powered him.

Now it happened once that two brothers, with a way of life worthy of God, came to the place at Greccio from far away. The only reason was to see the saint and to receive his blessing, which they had long desired. When they arrived, they did not find him, for he had already left the common area for a cell. They were greatly saddened. Since an uncertain outcome demanded a long stay, they left completely discouraged, believing their failure was caused by their faults.

Blessèd Francis' companions accompanied them, comforting them in their discouragement. But when they had walked about a stone's throw away from the place, the saint suddenly called after them and said to one of his companions, 'Tell my brothers who came here to look back towards me.' And when those brothers turned their faces to him, he made the sign of the cross over them and affectionately blessed them. They became so joyful at receiving both their wish and even a miracle that they returned home praising and blessing the Lord. *II,277f*

Week of Sunday between 23 & 29 October inclusive

Sunday — *RCL Proper 25 / DEL Week 30*

A reading from 'The Life of Saint Francis', by Thomas of Celano.

Whenever he used to say 'Your name, O holy Lord', Francis was moved in a way beyond human understanding. He was so wholly taken up in joy, filled with pure delight, that he truly seemed a new person of another age.

For this reason, he used to gather up any piece of writing, whether divine or human, wherever he found it: on the road, in the house, on the floor. He would reverently pick it up and put in in a sacred or decent place because the name of the Lord, or something pertaining to it, might be written there.

Once a brother asked why he so carefully gathered bits of writing, even writings of pagans where the name of the Lord does not appear. He replied, 'My son, I do this because they have the letters which make the glorious name of the Lord God. And the good that is found there does not belong to the pagans nor to any human being, but to God alone 'to whom belongs every good thing.' *I,251f*

Monday — *RCL Proper 25 / DEL Week 30*

A reading from 'The Assisi Compilation'.

Blessèd Francis had this as his highest and main goal: he was always careful to have and preserve in himself spiritual joy internally and externally, even though from the beginning of his conversion until the day of his death he greatly afflicted his body. He used to say that if a servant of God always strives to have and preserve joy internally and externally which proceeds from purity of heart, the devils can do him no harm. They would say, 'Since the servant of God has joy both in tribulation and in prosperity, we do not know where to find an entrance to enter him and do him harm.'

One day, he reproved one of his companions who looked sad and long-faced. He told him, 'Why are you sad and sorrowful over your offences? It is a matter between you and God. Pray to him, that by his mercy he may grant you the joy of his salvation. Try to be joyful always around me and others, because it is not fitting that a servant of God appear before his brother or others with a sad and glum face.

'I know that the devils envy me because of the gifts which the Lord has granted me in his mercy. Because they cannot harm me through myself, they try to hurt me through my companions. If they cannot do harm either through me or my companions, they withdraw in great confusion. Indeed, whenever I feel tempted and depressed and I look at the joy of my companion, because of that joy I turn away from the temptation and depression and towards inner joy.'   *II,229f*

Tuesday — *RCL Proper 25 / DEL Week 30*

A reading from 'A Letter of Saint Francis'.

Brother Leonard related that one day at Saint Mary of the Angels, blessèd Francis called Brother Leo and said, 'Brother Leo, write.' He responded, 'Look, I am ready!' 'Write', he said, 'what true joy is.

'A messenger arrives and says that all the Masters of [the university of] Paris have entered the Order. Write, this is not true joy! Or, that all the prelates, archbishops and bishops beyond the mountains, as well as the King of France and the King of England [have entered the Order]. Write, this is not true joy! Again, that my brothers have gone to the non-believers and converted all of them to the faith; again, that I have so much grace from God that I heal the sick and perform many miracles. I tell you, true joy does not consist in any of these things.'

'Then what is true joy?'

'I return from Perugia and arrive here in the dead of night. It is winter time, muddy, and so cold that icicles have formed on the edges of my habit and keep striking my legs and blood flows from such wounds. Freezing, covered with mud and ice, I come to the gate and, after I have knocked and called for some time, a brother comes and asks, "Who are you?" "Brother Francis," I answer. "Go away!" he says, "this is not a decent hour to be wandering about! You may not come in!" When I insist, he replies, "Go away! You are simple and stupid! Do not come back to us again! There are many of us here like you: we do not need you!" I stand again at the door and say, "For the love of God, take me in tonight!" And he replies, "I will not! Go to the Crosier's place and ask there."

'I tell you this: if I had patience and did not become upset, true joy, as well as true virtue and the salvation of my soul, would consist in this.'

I,166f

Wednesday — *RCL Proper 25 / DEL Week 30*

A reading from 'The Remembrance of the Desire of a Soul', by Thomas of Celano.

The holy man Francis insisted that spiritual joy was an infallible remedy against a thousand snares and tricks of the enemy. He used to say, 'The devil is most delighted when he can steal the joy of spirit from a servant of God. He carries dust which he tries to throw into the tiniest openings of the conscience, to dirty a clear mind and a clean life. But if spiritual joy fills the heart, the serpent casts its poison in vain. The devils cannot harm a servant of Christ when they see him filled with holy cheerfulness. But when the spirit is teary-eyed, feeling abandoned and sad, it will easily be swallowed up in sorrow, or else be carried away towards empty enjoyment.' The saint therefore always strove to keep a joyful heart, to preserve the anointing of the Spirit and the oil of gladness.

He avoided very carefully the dangerous disease of *acedia* [or depression], so that when he felt even a little of it slipping into his heart, he quickly rushed to prayer. For he used to say, 'When a servant of God gets disturbed about something, as often happens, he must get up at once to pray and remain before the Most High Father until he gives back to him the joy of salvation. But, if he delays, staying in sadness, that Babylonian sickness will grow and, unless scrubbed with tears, it will produce in the heart permanent rust.'

II,329f

Thursday — *RCL Proper 25 / DEL Week 30*

A reading from 'The Assisi Compilation'.

Once when blessèd Francis was in Rieti because of the disease of his eyes, he was staying for a few days in a room of Teobaldo Saraceno. One day he said to one of his companions, who while in the world knew how to play a lute, 'Brother, the children of this world do not understand divine things. Contrary to the will of God, they use instruments such as lutes, the ten-stringed harps, and other instruments, for the sake of vanity and sin, which in times past were used by holy people to praise God and offer consolation to souls. Therefore, I would like you to obtain secretly from some upright person, a lute on which you could play for me a decent song and, with it, we will say the words and praises of the Lord, especially because my body is tormented with disease and pain. So I wish by this means to change that pain of my body to joy and consolation of spirit.'

For, during his illness, blessèd Francis composed some *Praises of the Lord* which he had his companions recite sometimes for the praise of God, the consolation of the spirit and also for the edification of his neighbour.

'Father,' the brother answered him, 'I would be embarrassed to obtain one, especially because the people of this city know that I played the lute when I was in the world. I fear they will suspect me of being tempted to play the lute again.'

Blessèd Francis told him, 'Then, brother, let it go.'

The following night, around midnight, blessèd Francis was keeping vigil. And behold, around the house where he was staying he heard the sound of a lute playing a melody more beautiful and delightful than he had ever heard in his life. The one playing it would go some distance away so that he could barely be heard, and then returned, but was always playing. And he did this for over an hour.

Blessèd Francis, considering that it was the work of God and not of any human being, was overjoyed, and with an exultant heart with deep feeling he praised the Lord who was so kind as to console him with such a great consolation.

When he arose in the morning, he said to his companion, 'My brother, I asked you for something and you did not grant it. But the Lord, who consoles his friends in their sufferings, was kind enough to console me last night.'

He then told him everything that had happened. *II,168f*

Friday — *RCL Proper 25 / DEL Week 30*

A reading from a sermon by Saint Bonaventure.

One of the brothers was once living with the blessèd Francis outside a castle near Siena, that is to say at Montepulciano. He said that while they were there, they had nothing to eat but some dry bread. So they went and sat outside the church and ate the dry bread and drank some water. Then they went into the church and Francis began to be filled with great exaltation. Thus he remained for a long time, until his companion began to be weary. Afterwards, the brother asked him how he had felt, and the blessèd Francis replied that since his conversion he had never known such joy.   *IV,1872*

Saturday — *RCL Proper 25 / DEL Week 30*

A reading from 'The Assisi Compilation'.

When blessèd Francis lay gravely ill in the palace of the Bishop of Assisi, in the days after he returned from Bagnara, the people of Assisi, fearing that the saint would die during the night without them knowing about it, and that the brothers would secretly take his body away and place it in another city, placed a vigilant guard each night around the palace walls.

Blessèd Francis, although he was gravely ill, to comfort his soul and ward off discouragement in his severe and serious infirmities, often asked his companions during the day to sing the *Praises of the Lord* which he had composed a long time before in his illness. He likewise had the *Praises* sung during the night for the edification of their guards, who kept watch at night outside the palace because of him.

When Brother Elias reflected that blessèd Francis was so comforting himself and rejoicing in the Lord in such illness, one day he said to him, 'Dearest brother, I am greatly consoled and edified by all the joy which you show for yourself and your companions in such affliction and infirmity. Although the people of this city venerate you as a saint in life and in death, nevertheless, because they firmly believe that you are near death due to your serious and incurable sickness, upon hearing praises of this sort being sung, they can think and say to themselves, "How can he show such joy when he is so near death? He should be thinking about death." '

'Do you remember,' blessèd Francis said to him, 'when you saw the vision at Foligno and told me that it told you that I would live for only two years? Before you saw that vision, through the grace of the Holy Spirit, who suggests every good in the heart, and places it on the lips of the faithful, day and night I often considered my end. But from the time you saw that vision, each day I have been even more zealous reflecting on the day of my death.'

He continued with great intensity of spirit, 'Allow me to rejoice in the Lord, Brother, and to sing his praises in my infirmities because, by the grace of the Holy Spirit, I am so closely united and joined with my Lord that, through his mercy, I can well rejoice in the Most High himself.'
                                                                  II,203

Week of Sunday between 30 October & 5 November inclusive

All Saints' Sunday — Fourth Sunday Before Advent

Sunday — *RCL Proper 26 / DEL Week 31*

A reading from 'A Mirror of the Perfection of a Lesser Brother'.

The most blessèd Father Francis, having in a certain way transformed the brothers into saints by the ardour of his love and the fervent zeal which he had for their perfection, often used to ponder within himself about the qualities and virtues which should abound in a good Lesser Brother.

And he used to say that a Lesser Brother is one who would possess the life and qualities of the following holy brothers: namely, the faith and love of poverty which Brother Bernard most perfectly had; the simplicity and purity of Brother Leo, who was truly a man of most holy purity; the courtly bearing of Brother Angelo, who was the first soldier to enter the Order and was endowed with every courtesy and kindness; the friendly manner and common sense of Brother Masseo, together with his attractive and gracious eloquence; the mind raised up in contemplation which Brother Giles had even to the highest perfection; the virtuous and constant prayer of Brother Rufino who, whatever he was doing, even sleeping, always prayed without ceasing and whose mind was always intent on the Lord; the patience of Brother Juniper, who achieved the perfect state of patience because he always kept in mind the perfect truth of his low estate and the ardent desire to imitate Christ through the way of the cross; the bodily and spiritual strength of Brother John of Lauds, who at that time in his robust body surpassed everyone; the charity of Brother Roger, whose life and conduct were spent in ardent love; the solicitude of Brother Lucidus, who had the greatest care and concern and did not want to remain in any place for a month, and when he enjoyed staying in some place, would immediately leave, saying, 'We do not have a dwelling here on earth, but in heaven.'   *III,333*

Monday — *RCL Proper 26 / DEL Week 31*

A reading from 'The Little Flowers of Saint Francis'.

Sir Saint Francis, the most devout servant of the Crucified, had become almost blind and saw little because of severe penance and constant weeping. Once, he left the place where he was and went to a place where

Brother Bernard was, to speak with him about divine things. On reaching the place, he found that he was in prayer in the woods, completely lifted up and joined with God. So Saint Francis went into the woods and called him: 'Come', he said, 'and talk to this blind man.' And Brother Bernard did not reply at all, since he was a man of great contemplation and had his mind suspended and lifted up to God. But he had a singular grace in speaking of God, as Francis had experienced more than once; and it was for this reason that he desired to speak with him. After a pause, he called him a second and a third time in the same way. And each time, Brother Bernard did not hear and did not reply and did not come to him. So Saint Francis left, a little discouraged, surprised and unhappy within himself that Brother Bernard, called three times, did not come to him.

Leaving with this thought, Saint Francis, when he had gone a little way, said to his companion, 'Wait here for me.' And he went away to a solitary place and, throwing himself down in prayer, prayed to God to reveal to him why Brother Bernard did not reply to him. And while he was there, a voice from God came to him that said this: 'O poor little man, what are you upset about? Should a person leave God for a creature? When you called him, Brother Bernard was joined to me. And therefore he could not come to you, nor respond to you. So do not be surprised if he could not answer you. He was so much outside himself that he did not hear anything you said.' As Saint Francis received this answer from God, he immediately returned to Brother Bernard in a great hurry, to accuse himself humbly of the thought that he had against him.

III,570

Tuesday — *RCL Proper 26 / DEL Week 31*

A reading from 'The Lesser Annals', by Luke Wadding.

Once when Saint Francis was about to eat with Brother Leo, he was greatly delighted to hear a nightingale sing. So he suggested to his companion that they should also sing praise to God alternately with the bird. While Leo was pleading that he was no singer, Francis lifted up his voice and, phrase by phrase, sand his duet with the nightingale. Thus they continued from Vespers to Lauds, until the Saint had to admit himself beaten by the bird.

Thereupon the nightingale flew onto his hand, where he praised it to the skies and fed it. Then he gave it his blessing and it flew away.

IV,1881f

A reading from A Bolognan manuscript.

A certain noble countess once sent some fishes to the blessèd Francis by the hand of two of her servants. While these men were on their way, one of them was thinking in his heart, 'If I manage to see the blessèd Francis and to speak to him, then I shall know that I am saved. If I fail, then I shall know that I am lost.' Having arrived at the place where the friars were living, they were most graciously received by Brother Angelo, who was then in charge of the friary. After having had something to eat, the young man who had entertained this strange thought in his heart asked whether he might speak to Brother Francis. 'My dearest brother,' replied Brother Angelo, 'we have strict commands from Brother Francis not to allow anyone who is not one of the brothers to go near him, except in great necessity. Otherwise, his prayers will be interrupted. So you see, it is impossible for you to see him now.' When the poor boy heard this, he was terribly upset and, throwing himself on the ground, burst into tears. At this, Brother Angelo did his best to comfort him, asking him why he was so miserable and what was in his heart. After a long time, the young man opened his heart to Brother Angelo and told him all that had happened.

Then Brother Angelo took him by the hand and led him to the place where the blessèd Francis was. When Francis saw them, he cried out in great excitement to Brother Angelo, 'What is all this, Brother Angelo?'; to which Brother Angelo replied, 'Dear Father, be patient, for it is really essential that this young man should speak to you.' And Francis said, 'All right, but only if it is really necessary.' Then Brother Angelo explained to the blessèd Francis all that this young man had been thinking.

Then the saint rose up and went out of the place where he had been sitting and, running to the boy, embraced him and, taking off his own girdle, bound it about him from head to foot. Then, having comforted him, he said, 'My dear little son, take care that you never allow such a thought to enter again into your heart, for be assured that such a temptation is both serious and dangerous.' And having received Saint Francis' blessing, the young man went home so overjoyed that he could never express what he felt. *IV,1866f*

Thursday — *RCL Proper 26 / DEL Week 31*

A reading from 'The Little Flowers of Saint Francis'.

The first companions of Saint Francis strove with all their strength to be poor in earthly things and rich in virtues, by which one arrives at true riches, heavenly and eternal.

It happened that one day when they were gathered together to speak about God, one of them gave this example: 'There was someone who was a great friend of God, and he had great grace in active humility that he thought himself the greatest of sinners. This humility sanctified him and confirmed him in grace, and made him grow constantly in virtues and the gifts of God, and never allowed him to fall into sin.' As Brother Masseo heard such wonderful things about humility and realized that this was a treasure of eternal life, he began to be so inflamed with love and desire for this virtue of humility that, raising his face to heaven in great fervour, he made a vow and a very firm promise never to be happy in this world until he felt this virtue perfectly in his soul. And from then on he remained almost constantly enclosed in a cell, mortifying himself with fasting, vigils, prayers and loud weeping before God, to receive from him this virtue, without which he believed himself worthy of hell, and with which that friend of God was so gifted, as he had heard.

As Brother Masseo remained many days with this desire, he happened one day to go into the woods and, in fervour of spirit, walked through the woods pouring out tears, sighs and cries, asking God for this divine virtue with fervent desire. And since God willingly hears the prayers of the humble and contrite, as Brother Masseo remained in this state, a voice came from heaven and called him twice, 'Brother Masseo! Brother Masseo!' Knowing in spirit that it was the voice of Christ, he replied, 'My Lord!' And Christ said to him, 'And what do you want to give to have this grace you ask?' Brother Masseo responded, 'Lord, I want to give the eyes in my head.' And Christ said to him, 'And I want you to have the grace and the eyes too.' At these words, the voice disappeared; and Brother Masseo remained full of such grace of that desired virtue of humility and of the light of God that from then on he was always jubilant.

III,622f

Friday — RCL Proper 26 / DEL Week 31

A reading from 'The Little Flowers of Saint Francis'.

Brother Rufino was so absorbed in God through constant contemplation that he became as if unaware and mute. He very rarely spoke and, besides, he did not have the grace, the urge, or ability to preach. Nevertheless, Saint Francis once ordered him to go to Assisi and preach to the people whatever God should inspire him. At this, Brother Rufino responded, 'Reverend Father, I beg you to excuse me and not send me because, as you know, I do not have the grace of preaching, and I am simple and uneducated.' Then Saint Francis said, 'Because you did not obey promptly, I command you under holy obedience that in just your breeches, naked as you were born, get to Assisi, and go into a church naked as you are, and preach to the people.' At this command, the same Brother Rufino stripped himself and went to Assisi, and went into a church. After making his reverence to the altar, he climbed into the pulpit and began to preach. Children and adults began to laugh at such a thing and they were saying, 'Look, these men are doing so much penance that they are going crazy, out of their minds!'

In the meantime, as Saint Francis reflected on the prompt obedience of Brother Rufino, who was one of the great gentlemen of Assisi, and on the harsh command that he had given him, he began to rebuke himself, saying, 'Where did you get such presumption, son of Pietro Bernardone, you vile little man, to command Brother Rufino, one of the great gentlemen of Assisi, to go and preach naked to the people like a madman? By God, you will experience yourself what you command of others!' In fervour of spirit, he quickly stripped himself naked in the same way and went to Assisi, taking Brother Leo with him, who carried his habit and that of Brother Rufino. When the Assisians saw Saint Francis in that same state, they mocked him, thinking that he and Brother Rufino had gone mad from too much penance. Saint Francis went into the church where Brother Rufino was preaching in these words, 'My dear people, flee from the world and abandon sin; give back what belongs to others, if you want to avoid hell; observe the commandments of God, loving God and your neighbour, if you want to go to heaven; do penance, if you want to possess the kingdom of heaven.' And then Saint Francis climbed into the pulpit naked and began to preach so wonderfully about despising the world, about holy penance, voluntary poverty, the desire for the heavenly kingdom, about the nakedness and shame of the passion of our Lord Jesus Christ, that all who were at the sermon, men and women in great numbers, began to weep loudly, with amazing devotion and compunction of heart; and not only there, but through all of Assisi there was such weeping that day over the passion of our Lord Jesus Christ that there was never anything like it.

With the people edified in this way and consoled by the action of Saint Francis and Brother Rufino, Saint Francis re-clothed Brother Rufino himself and, thus re-clothed, they returned to the place of the Portiuncula, praising and glorifying God.   *III,620f*

Saturday — *RCL Proper 26 / DEL Week 31*

A reading from 'The Remembrance of the Desire of a Soul', by Thomas of Celano.

Once, when Saint Francis was passing by a village near Assisi, a certain John, a very simple man, was ploughing in the field. He ran to him saying, 'I want you to make me a brother; for a long time now I have wanted to serve God.' The saint rejoiced, noticing the man's simplicity, and responded to his intention, 'Brother, if you want to be our companion, give to the poor if you have anything and, once rid of your property, I will receive you.' He immediately unyoked the oxen and offered one to Saint Francis, saying, 'Let us give this ox to the poor! I am sure I deserve to get this much as my share of my father's things.' The saint smiled, but he heartily approved his sense of simplicity. Now, when the parents and younger brothers heard of this, they hurried over in tears, grieving more over losing the ox than the man. The saint said to them, 'Calm down! Here, I will give you back the ox and only take away the brother.' And so he took the man with him and, dressed in the clothing of the Order, he made him his special companion because of his gift of simplicity.

Whenever Saint Francis stayed in some place to meditate, simple John would immediately repeat and copy whatever gestures or movements the saint made. If he spat, John would spit too; if he coughed, he would cough as well, sighing or sobbing along with him. If the saint lifted up his hands to heaven, John would raise his too, and he watched him intently as a model, turning himself into a copy of all his actions. The saint noticed this, and once asked him why he did those things. He replied, 'I promised to do everything that you do. It is dangerous for me to leave anything out.' The saint delighted in this pure simplicity, but gently told him not to do this anymore. Shortly after this, the simple man departed to the Lord in this same purity. The saint often proposed his life as worth imitating, merrily calling him not Brother John but Saint John. *II,368f*

Week of Sunday between 6 & 12 November inclusive

Third Sunday Before Advent

Sunday — *RCL Proper 27 / DEL Week 32*

A reading from 'The Major Legend of Saint Francis', by Saint Bonaventure.

Not long after [Francis and Bernard had found their vocation in the gospels], five other men were called by the same Spirit, and the number of Francis' sons reached six. The third among them was the holy father Giles, a man indeed filled with God and worthy of his celebrated reputation. Although he was a simple and unlearnèd man, he later became famous for his practice of heroic virtue, as God's servant had prophesied, and was raised to the height of exalted contemplation. For through the passage of time, he was continually intent on elevations of the soul; and he was so often rapt into God in ecstasy, as I myself have observed as an eyewitness, that he seemed to live among people more like an angel than a human being. *II,544*

Monday — *RCL Proper 27 / DEL Week 32*

A reading from 'A Mirror of the Perfection of a Lesser Brother'.

At the beginning of the religion, when blessèd Francis was staying at Rivo Torto with only two brothers whom he had at that time, the third brother, a man named Giles, came to him from the world to receive his life. When he had stayed there for a few days, still wearing his secular clothes, a poor man happened to come to the place asking alms of blessèd Francis. Turning to Giles, blessèd Francis said to him, 'Give the poor brother your cloak.' Immediately, with great joy, he took it off his back and gave it to the poor man. It then seemed to him that, at that moment, the Lord immediately had infused new grace into his heart because he had given the poor man his mantle with joy. So he was

received by blessèd Francis and constantly progressed in virtue to a very
great state of perfection. *III,284f*

Tuesday — *RCL Proper 27 / DEL Week 32*

A reading from 'The Life of Brother Giles'.

After a time, by permission of Saint Francis, Brother Giles went once to
visit the church of Saint James the great, in Galicia; and during the whole
journey only once did he take something to eat, on account of the great
famine which then afflicted that country. For once, as he went along
asking alms and finding no one to give him any charity, it chanced that in
the evening he halted by a threshing floor, where there were still some
unthreshed beans; these he gathered up and made them his supper.
There he slept that night, because he willingly sojourned in places solitary
and remote from human habitation, that he might the better give himself
to vigil and prayer. And he was so much refreshed by God in this
supper that he could not have thought it possible to be so well-fed even
if he had eaten of a whole range of dishes.

As he went further on his way, he met a beggar on the road, who asked
him for alms for the love of God. And Brother Giles in his charity, having nothing but the habit he wore, cut the hood away from his old cloak
and gave it to the poor man for the love of God; and thus for twenty days
he journeyed on without a hood. As he returned through Lombardy, a
man called to him, to whom he went readily enough, thinking that he
wanted to give him some alms; but as he stretched out his hand, the other
placed in it a couple of dice, inviting him to play. And Brother Giles,
replying humbly, said, 'God forgive you, my son,' and went on his way.
In this way he went through the world, receiving much contempt and
taking it all peacefully. *XII,266f*

Wednesday — *RCL Proper 27 / DEL Week 32*

A reading from 'The Life of Brother Giles'.

Brother Giles went, with the permission of Saint Francis, to visit the Holy
Sepulchre of Christ, and got as far as the port of Brindisi where he was
detained several days because there was no ship ready. So, wishing to live
by his own toil, he got hold of a bucket, filled it with water, and went
about the town crying, 'Who wants water?' And by his toil he earned his
bread and what was necessary for the life of his body for himself and his

companion; and afterwards he crossed the sea and visited the Holy Sepulchre and the other holy places with great devotion.

On his way back he was detained in the city of Ancona for several days; and because he was accustomed to live by the labour of his hands, he made baskets of rushes and sold them, not for money but for bread for himself and his companion. For the same hire he also carried the dead to the cemetery. When this failed him he returned to the table of Jesus Christ, begging alms from door to door; and thus, with much toil and poverty, he went back to Saint Mary of the Angels.   *XII,268>*

Thursday — *RCL Proper 27 / DEL Week 32*

A reading from 'The Sayings of Brother Giles'.

Once Brother Giles asked a friar, 'What do these great professors say contemplation is?' The friar said, 'I do not know.' So he said, 'Do you want to hear what it is seems to me to be?' And the friar replied, 'Tell me.' Brother Giles asserted, 'Contemplation has seven stages: Fire, perfume, trance, contemplation, zest, equipoise, and glory.

'By fire I mean a sort of light which dawns so as to light up the spirit. Next comes the perfume of supernatural scent, which gives off a kind of marvellous aroma, which is recorded in the Canticle of Canticles: "Your name spoken is a spreading perfume; that is why the maidens love you." Next comes trance: the spirit, delighted by the perfume, is enraptured and withdrawn from the physical senses. Next comes contemplation, because the spirit at this stage is almost disembodied and it can perceive God with wonderful precision. Next comes zest, which is that keen sweetness tasted by a soul in contemplation. A psalm mentions it: "Taste and see how good the Lord is: happy the one who takes refuge in him." Equipoise comes when the spirit, savouring the supernatural sweetness, relaxes over it. And finally glory appears, because the spirit finds itself in such great peace that it wields peace enthusiastically and vibrates with immense joy. A psalm sings: "I shall be completely satisfied when your glory is revealed."

'The Bible teaches many works of mercy, like clothing the naked, feeding the hungry, and so on. Yet it is of prayer that the Lord says, "Such are the worshippers the Father demands" *(Jn 4:24)*. Good actions dress the soul in a certain splendour, but prayer is a many-splendoured thing.

Friars who live holy lives are like wolves. Only pressing necessity can make wolves prowl, and they never loiter in populated areas.' *XL,83f,81*

Friday — *RCL Proper 27 / DEL Week 32*

A reading from 'The Deeds of Blessèd Francis and his Companions'.

Once, during the lifetime of Brother Giles there was a great Master of the Order of Preachers who for many years endured the greatest doubt about the virginity of the Mother of Jesus Christ. For it seemed to him that it was impossible to be both mother and virgin. Yet, as truly a man full of faith, he grieved over such a doubt as this, and he wished some inspired man would free him from it. Hearing that Brother Giles was an illustrious man, he went to him.

The holy Brother Giles, knowing in spirit that he was coming, what his purpose was, and the battle he was enduring, went out to meet him. Before he reached the friar preacher, he struck the ground with his staff which he carried in his hand, and said, 'O Friar Preacher, a virgin before the birth!' And immediately a very beautiful lily sprang up where Giles struck the ground with his staff. Striking the ground a second time, he said, 'O Friar Preacher, a virgin during the birth!' And another lily sprang up. Striking the ground a third time, he said, 'O Friar Preacher, a virgin after the birth!' And immediately a third lily sprang up. After this, Giles fled.

That friar preacher was entirely freed from the temptation, and from then on he always had a great devotion towards the holy Brother Giles.

III,564

Saturday — *RCL Proper 27 / DEL Week 32*

A reading from 'Franciscan Sayings', by Bartholomew of Pisa.

When Brother Giles once came to Assisi, the friars took him round their new home, showing him the splendid buildings which they had put up, and apparently taking great pride in them. But when Brother Giles had carefully looked at them all, he said to the brethren, 'You know, brethren, there's only one thing you're short of now, and that's wives!' The brothers were deeply shocked at this; so Brother Giles said to them, 'My brothers, you know well enough that it is just as illegal for you to give up poverty as to give up chastity. After throwing poverty overboard it is easy enough to throw chastity as well.'

IV,1843

Week of Sunday between 13 & 19 November inclusive

Second Sunday Before Advent

Sunday — *RCL Proper 28 / DEL Week 33*

A reading from 'The Life of Brother Juniper'.

One of the first companions of Saint Francis was a certain Brother Juniper, a man of profound humility, of great fervour and charity. Once, at Saint Mary of the Angels, Brother Juniper went to visit a sick brother, and with great compassion asked him, 'Can I do you any service?' The patient replied, 'It would be a great comfort to me if you could get me a pig's foot to eat.' Immediately Brother Juniper said, 'Leave it to me, you shall have it at once.' So off he went and snatched a knife from the kitchen, and ran in fervour of spirit to the wood where a number of pigs were feeding, and having thrown himself upon one of them cut off its foot and fled. He returned, washed, dressed and cooked the foot and took it to the invalid, who ate it eagerly to the great consolation and joy of Brother Juniper, while he in high spirits, to amuse the sick man, recounted his assault on the pig.

In the meantime the keeper of the pigs, who had seen him cutting off the foot, went and told the whole affair in detail with great indignation to his master, who, when he had heard it, came to the house of the brothers, calling them hypocrites, thieves, liars, rascals and good-for-nothings, and saying, 'Why did you cut off my pig's foot?' But Saint Francis, thought it over and said to himself, 'Can Brother Juniper really have done this?' And he had Brother Juniper called to him secretly, and asked him, 'Did you cut off the foot of a pig in the wood?' And Brother Juniper, answered him joyfully, 'It is true, dear Father, I did.' To this Saint Francis angrily replied, 'O Brother Juniper, why have you caused such a great scandal? I command you by holy obedience to run after that man, throw yourself at his feet, and tell him your fault, for you have certainly gone too far this time.'

Brother Juniper was astonished at these words, and amazed that anyone would take offence at such an act of charity, because it seemed to him that temporal goods were nothing at all, except in so far as they were charitably shared with one's neighbour. Nevertheless he ran off, overtook the man, who had by no means recovered his equanimity but was still angry beyond measure, and told him how and why he had cut off the foot of the pig. But he said it all with such fervour and joy as if he had done the man a great favour for which he ought to be greatly rewarded.

The man, beside himself with fury, started calling Brother Juniper a fool, a madman and a robber; but Brother Juniper could not work out why he was being abused, and taking no notice of such words began to tell his story all over again, saying he had only done it out of charity, and suggesting the man should do the same with all his pigs. Seeing Brother Juniper speak with such simplicity and humility, eventually the man came to himself and acknowledged the fault of his speaking and acting so violently towards the brothers. And so he went and had the pig killed and cooked and brought it with much devotion and many tears to Saint Mary of the Angels where he gave it to the brothers in compensation for the abuse he had given them.

Then Saint Francis, considering the simplicity and patience under adversity of the holy Brother Juniper said to his companions and the others who were present, 'Would to God, my brothers, that I had a whole forest of such Junipers!'   *XII,237ff>*

Monday — *RCL Proper 28 / DEL Week 33*

A reading from 'The Life of Brother Juniper'.

Brother Juniper had such pity and compassion for the poor that, whenever he saw anyone badly clothed, he immediately took off his tunic and the hood from his head and gave it to them. Because of this the Guardian forbade him under obedience to give away the whole of his tunic or any part of his habit to anyone. A few days later he met a poor man half-naked, who asked Brother Juniper for alms for the love of God. The brother, with much compassion, replied, 'I have nothing I could give you except my tunic, and I am bound under obedience by my superior not to give that to anyone, or even a part of my habit; but if you pull it off my back, I will not do anything to stop you.'

His words did not fall on deaf ears. Straightaway the beggar pulled his tunic over his head and went his way, leaving Brother Juniper naked. When he returned home they asked him where his tunic was, to which he replied, 'A good man pulled it off my back and went away with it.' As this virtue of compassion grew within him he was no longer content with giving away his tunic, but gave also the cloaks of the others, and the books and ornaments of the church, and all that he could lay his hands on to the poor. For this reason the brothers left nothing open or lying about, because Brother Juniper gave everything away for the love of God and to his praise.   *XII,247f*

Tuesday — *RCL Proper 28 / DEL Week 33*

A reading from 'The Life of Brother Juniper'.

Brother Juniper was one day at Assisi deeply meditating before the altar of the convent. It was near the time of the Nativity of our Lord, and the altar was very richly decked and adorned. The sacristan asked Brother Juniper to remain and watch by it, while he went away to get something to eat. And as he continued in devout meditation, a poor woman came and begged alms for the love of God. Brother Juniper said, 'Wait a moment, and I will see whether I can get you something from the ornaments of the altar.' On the altar there was a fringe of gold, richly worked, with little silver bells of great value. Brother Juniper said, 'These bells are not needed,' and he took a knife and cut them all off, and gave them to the poor woman.

The sacristan had not eaten more than three or four mouthfuls before he began to think again about Brother Juniper's ways and to worry what might have become of the ornaments of the altar which he had left in his charge. So he quickly got up from the table and rushed back to the church. When he got there he saw the fringe of the altar cut up and all the bells gone, at which he was greatly angered and scandalized. But Brother Juniper, seeing his distress, said, 'Do not worry about those bells, I gave them to a poor woman who was in great need of them. Here they were of no use whatsoever.' Hearing this, the sacristan in much distress immediately ran through the church and all over the city, looking everywhere to see if he could find them again; but he neither found them nor anyone who had seen anything of them. Therefore, returning to the convent in a rage, he took up the fringe and carried it to the Minister General, who was then at Assisi, and said, 'Father General, I ask for justice against Brother Juniper who has ruined my fringe, the best there was in the sacristy; look at how he has cut it to pieces, and torn off all the silver bells, and says that he has given them away to a poor woman.' The Minister answered, 'Brother Juniper has not done this, but your own stupidity; for you ought to know by now what he gets up to. I am only surprised that he has not given away the whole thing. All the same, I will correct him severely for this whole affair.' And calling all the brothers together in chapter, he summoned Brother Juniper, and in the presence of all the community rebuked him severely on account of the silver bells.

XII,248ff>

Wednesday — *RCL Proper 28 / DEL Week 33*

A reading from 'The Life of Brother Juniper'.

Once, calling all the brothers together in chapter, the Minister General summoned Brother Juniper, and in the presence of all the community rebuked him severely on account of something that he had done, and was so angry that he raised his voice until he became quite hoarse.

Brother Juniper was not concerned about his words, because he delighted in reproaches, but instead began to think of a remedy for the hoarseness of the Father General. Having received his reproof, he went off to the city, and ordered a porridge to be made of flour and butter. When a good part of the night was past he returned, lit a candle and went with his porridge to the cell of the Minister, and knocked. The Minister opened the door and, seeing him there, with the lighted candle and the porridge in his hand, asked softly, 'What is this?' Brother Juniper replied, 'My Father, when you reproved me today for my faults, I noticed that your voice became hoarse – I think that it must have been through excess of fatigue; and therefore I considered how to find a remedy, and had this porridge made for you; therefore go ahead and eat it, for I assure you it will soften your chest and your throat.' The Minister answered him, 'What hour is this to come and disturb people!' And Brother Juniper said, 'Look, it is made on purpose for you. Go on, eat it, for it will do you a great deal of good.' But the Minister, angry at the lateness of the hour and his importunity, told him to go away, saying that at such an hour he had no desire to eat, and calling him names such as rascal and a good-for-nothing. Brother Juniper therefore, seeing that neither requests nor coaxing would move him, said, 'My Father, since you will not eat, do this much for me: hold the candle, and I will eat it.' Then the Minister, being a pious and devout man and perceiving the simplicity and piety of Brother Juniper, and that all this was done by him out of pure devotion, said to him, 'Well, look, since you insist, you and I will eat it together.' And together they ate the porridge with a fervent charity each for the other; and they were refreshed much more by each other's devotion than they were by the bodily nourishment.   *XII,250f>*

Thursday — *RCL Proper 28 / DEL Week 33*

A reading from 'The Life of Brother Juniper'.

As Brother Juniper was once going to Rome, where the fame of his sanctity had already widely spread, many of the people of Rome, through their great devotion for him, went out to meet him. Seeing so many people coming, Brother Juniper planned in his mind how to turn their reverence into emptiness and absurdity. There were two children by the wayside who were playing at see-saw, having placed one piece of wood across another, and each of them holding on by one end they went up and down. Brother Juniper therefore helped one of the children off the plank, and got on it himself, and so began to see-saw up and down with the other child. In the meantime the people came up and were amazed to see Brother Juniper acting like this. Nevertheless with great devotion they greeted him, and waited until he might finish his game of see-saw, to accompany him with all honour to the convent. Brother Juniper, however, took little notice of all their salutations, reverence and waiting on him, but remained much absorbed in his balancing. After waiting like this for a long time, some began to be annoyed and to say, 'How stupid this is!' Others, knowing his ways, only conceived a greater devotion for him; but all the same they all departed, and left Brother Juniper to his see-saw. When they were all gone, Brother Juniper got down, quite consoled because he had seen that many thought him to be a fool. So he went on his way and entered Rome in all meekness and humility, and so arrived at the convent of the Lesser Brothers.   *XII,254f*

Friday — *RCL Proper 28 / DEL Week 33*

A reading from 'The Life of Brother Juniper'.

When Brother Juniper was once staying in a very small house belonging to the brothers, it happened that for some reason all the brothers were obliged to go out, and only Brother Juniper remained in the house. Therefore the Guardian said, 'Brother Juniper, all of us are going out; so see that, when we come home, you have cooked some small refreshment for the brothers on their return.' And Brother Juniper replied very willingly, 'Leave it to me!'

When all the others had gone, Brother Juniper said to himself, 'What a waste of time this is, making a brother stay in the kitchen and keeping him away from his prayers! Even though I have only been made cook this once, I will cook so much food that there will be enough for all the brothers and more, for a whole fortnight.' So off he went off to the farm, and brought several large earthenware pots for cooking, and gathered fresh and dried meat, poultry, eggs and herbs, as well as plenty of firewood. Lighting his fire, he put everything on to boil – birds in their feathers, and eggs in their shells, and all the other things in the same way.

When the brothers returned home, one of them, who was well aware of Brother Juniper's simplicity, went straight to the kitchen, and found many huge pots on a raging fire. Sitting himself down, he looked on with astonishment, saying nothing but watching with what care Brother Juniper attended to his cooking. After watching him for some time to his great amusement, the other brother went out of the kitchen, found the rest, and said to them, 'I think Brother Juniper is cooking for a wedding.' The brothers thought he was joking, but Brother Juniper presently lifted his pots from the fire and rang the bell for the meal. As they went in to dinner, he entered the refectory with all his dishes, his face crimsoned with fatigue and the heat of the fire, and said to them all, 'Eat well, and then let us all go to prayer, and nobody need think of cooking any more for a while, for I have cooked enough dinner today to last for a fortnight.' And he placed his stew, of which there was not a pig in all the Roman province famished enough to have eaten it all, on the table before the brothers. But Brother Juniper praised up his cooking, to give them an appetite, and seeing the brothers ate nothing, he said, 'Now poultry like this is excellent food for the brain, and such a stew as this will strength-en your bodies, it is so good.' And the brothers remained lost in devout astonishment at Brother Juniper's piety and simplicity.

But the Guardian, annoyed at such stupidity and so much waste of good food, reproved him with great severity. Then Brother Juniper all at once threw himself on the ground on his knees before the Guardian, and acknowledged his fault against him and against all the brothers, saying, 'I am the worst of men, always wasting the good things of God and of the Order.' And sorrowfully he went away, and would not appear before any of the brothers all that day. But when he was gone, the Guardian said, 'Well-belovèd brothers, I wish that every day this brother of ours could spoil as many good things as today if we had them, as an example to us all; for out of his great simplicity and charity he has done all this.'

XII,255ff>

Saturday — *RCL Proper 28 / DEL Week 33*

A reading from 'The Life of Brother Juniper'.

While Brother Juniper was staying once in the valley of Spoleto, he heard of a great solemnity then going on at Assisi, at which a great number of people were assisting with much devotion, and he decided that he wanted to assist at it also. So he stripped himself of all but his breeches, and thus he went his way, passing through Spoleto and right through the middle of the city, and finally arrived at the convent. The brothers, much put out and scandalized at his appearance, rebuked him sharply, calling him foolish and imbecile and reproaching him with bringing confusion on the whole Order of Saint Francis, and wanted to chain him up as a madman. And the Minister General also, who was then at the convent, called him up before all the brothers, and in the presence of the whole community gave him a stern and severe reproof. After many words of vigorous indignation, he said to him, 'The nature of your fault is such, and so great, that I do not know what penance to impose on you.' Then Brother Juniper replied, as one who delighted in his own confusion, 'My Father, I will tell you: let me, for penance, return to the place which I left to attend this feast in exactly the same way that I came.'   *XII,258f*

Week of Sunday between 20 & 26 November inclusive
Sunday Next Before Advent

Sunday — Christ the King — *RCL Proper 29 / DEL Week 34*

Note that this reading is apposite to the feast of Christ the King: should that feast be celebrated on another date, this reading should be transferred to it and another (unused) reading used in its stead.

A reading from 'The Little Flowers of Saint Francis'.

Among the other wise and holy brothers and sons of Saint Francis, those whom Solomon says are the 'glory of a father', there was in our times in the Province of the March, Brother John of Fermo who, because of the long time he stayed in the holy place of La Verna, and there passed from this life, was also called Brother John of La Verna, because he was a man of outstanding life and great holiness.

One day, when Brother John was walking through the woods, afflicted and troubled as he was, he was tired and sat down next to a beech tree; and he stayed there with his face all wet with tears looking towards heaven. Suddenly Jesus Christ appeared near him on the path by which Brother John had come, but Christ did not say anything. Brother John saw him and, recognizing clearly that he was Christ, immediately threw himself at his feet and, with uncontrolled weeping, humbly begged him, 'Help me, my Lord, because without you, my most sweet Saviour, I remain in darkness and grief; without you, Son of the Most High God, I am in confusion and shame; without you, I am deprived of all good and blinded, because you are the light of souls; without you I am lost and damned, because you, Jesus Christ, are the true life of souls and the life of lives; without you I am sterile and dried up, because you are the fountain of every gift and every grace; without you I am completely desolate, because you are Jesus, our redemption, love and desire, the bread that restores and the wine that gladdens the choirs of angels and the hearts of all the saints. Enlighten me, O most gracious Master and most kind Shepherd, because, though unworthy, I am your little sheep.'

But since the desire of holy men, that God delays in granting, inflames them to greater love and merit, the blessèd Christ departed without granting it and without saying anything to him, and went away by that same path. Then Brother John jumped up and ran after him and once again threw himself at his feet, and with holy insistence held him back and with devout tears begged him, saying, 'O most sweet Jesus Christ, have mercy on me in my tribulation. Hear me, through the abundance of your mercy and the truth of your salvation, and give me the joy of your face and your merciful glance, because the whole earth is filled with your mercy.' And Christ departed again and said nothing to him, nor did he give him any consolation; and acted like a mother to a child when she wants him to desire the breast, and makes him come after her crying, so that he will then take it more willingly.

So Brother John with even greater fervour and desire followed Christ, and when he reached him, the blessèd Christ turned to him and looked at him with a happy and kind expression and, opening his most holy and merciful arms, embraced him most sweetly; and as those arms were opened Brother John saw shining rays of light coming from the sacred breast of the Saviour, which illuminated all the wood and his whole self, body and soul.' *III,649ff>*

Monday — RCL Proper 29 / DEL Week 34

A reading from 'The Little Flowers of Saint Francis'.

Brother John of La Verna, since he had perfectly denied every worldly and temporal delight and consolation, and had placed all his delight and all his hope in God, was granted by the divine goodness wonderful consolations and revelations, especially on the solemnities of Christ. Therefore once, when the solemnity of the Nativity of Christ was approaching, he confidently awaited consolations from God in the sweet humanity of Jesus. And the Holy Spirit put into his spirit such great and abundant love and fervour of Christ's charity, by which he had humbled himself to take our humanity, that it really seemed to him that his soul was snatched from his body and was burning like a furnace. Unable to bear that burning, he suffered and melted completely and cried out in a loud voice, because through the force of the Holy Spirit and the great heat of love, he could not restrain himself from crying out. In that same moment of boundless heat there came with it such a strong and certain hope of salvation that he would not believe for anything in the world that if he died then he would have to pass through purgatory. And this love lasted for a good six months: he did not have that excessive heat constantly; rather it came to him at certain hours of the day.

And during this time he later received wonderful visitations and consolations from God; and he was enraptured many times, as seen by that brother who first wrote these things. Among other times, one night he was so raised and rapt in God that he saw in him, the Creator, all created things, heavenly and earthly, and all their perfection and ranks and distinct orders. And he then knew clearly how each created thing appeared to its Creator, and how God is above and inside and outside and beside all created things. Then he knew one God in three Persons, and three Persons in one God, and the infinite charity that made the Son become incarnate by obedience to the Father. And finally in that vision he knew that there was no other way by which the soul may go to God and have eternal life except through the blessèd Christ, who is the way, the truth and the life of the soul.   *III,655*

Tuesday — RCL Proper 29 / DEL Week 34

A reading from 'The Little Flowers of Saint Francis'.

To that same Brother John the following wonderful event occurred at Mogliano, according to what is recounted by the brothers who were present there. On the first night after the octave of Saint Lawrence, and within the octave of the Assumption of our Lady, after he had said matins in church with the other brothers, the anointing of divine grace came over him, and he went into the garden to contemplate the Passion of Christ and to prepare with all his devotion to celebrate the Mass, which it was his turn to sing that morning. And while contemplating the words for the consecration of the body of Christ, that is, *Hoc est corpus meum*, and considering the infinite charity of Christ, by which he willed not only to purchase us with his precious blood, but also to leave his most worthy body and blood as the food of souls, the love of the sweet Jesus began to grow within him with so much fervour and sweetness that his soul could no longer endure so much sweetness, so he cried out loudly, as if drunk in spirit, repeating to himself *Hoc est corpus meum* and, in saying these words, he seemed to see the blessèd Christ with the Virgin Mary and a multitude of angels. And in saying this he was enlightened by the Holy Spirit about all the deep and high mysteries of that most high Sacrament.

When dawn came, he entered the church and went to the altar to vest and began Mass. And as he went on, the further he proceeded, the more the love of Christ and that fervour of devotion grew, and with it he was given an inexpressible feeling of God, one that he himself did not and could not express in words. Finally reaching the act of consecration, after saying half of the words over the host, that is *Hoc est enim*, there was no way he could go further, and he just kept repeating those same words, that is, *Hoc est enim*. At this, as he stood there in this anxiety without going further, the Guardian and the other brothers and also many lay people who were in church to hear Mass came up to the altar and were amazed to see and consider the actions of Brother John, and many of them were crying from devotion. Finally, after a long time, that is when God pleased, Brother John said *corpus meum* in a loud voice; and immediately the form of the bread disappeared, and in the host appeared the blessèd Jesus Christ incarnate and glorified, and he was rapt out of himself; and with his soul suspended from bodily feeling, his body fell backward and, if he had not been held by the Guardian, who was behind him, he would have fallen flat on the ground. At this the brothers and the lay people who were in church, men and women, ran to him, and he was carried into the sacristy as if dead, since his body was cold like a dead body, and his fingers were so contracted that they could hardly be straightened or moved. He lay like this, half-dead or rather enraptured until terce, and it was summer.   *III,656f>*

Wednesday — *RCL Proper 29 / DEL Week 34*

A reading from 'The Deeds of Blessèd Francis and his Companions'.

When Brother Pietro and Brother Conrad of Offida were staying together in the family at the place of Forano in the Custody of Ancona, Brother Conrad went into the woods to meditate on the things of God. Brother Pietro followed him secretly to see what would happen to him. Brother Conrad began to pray very devoutly and tearfully to the most Blessèd Virgin that she would obtain this grace for him from her Son: that he would be able to experience some of that sweetness which the holy Simeon felt on the day of the Purification when he held Christ, the blessèd Saviour in his arms.

That most merciful Lady heard his plea and suddenly there was the Queen of glory with her blessèd Son in such a bright light, which not only put the darkness to flight, but also outshone every other light. Approaching Brother Conrad she placed in his arms that child more beautiful than any other son. Brother Conrad received him most devoutly, pressed his lips to his, and embraced him breast to breast, and he melted completely in those embraces and kisses of charity. Brother Pietro, however, saw all this in the clear light and from it also experienced a wonderful consolation. He remained hidden in the woods. The Blessèd Virgin Mary departed with her Son, and brother Pietro hurriedly retraced his steps. When Brother Conrad returned, all merry and rejoicing he was called by Brother Pietro, 'O heavenly brother you have had a great consolation today!' Brother Conrad said, 'What do you mean brother Pietro, what do you know about what I have?' Brother Pietro replied, ' I know very well that the most Blessèd Virgin and her blessèd Son visited you.' Hearing this, Brother Conrad, because he was truly humble, wanted it to be a secret and asked him not to tell anyone. For there was such love between these two that they seemed to have one heart and one soul.

III,528

Thursday — *RCL Proper 29 / DEL Week 34*

A reading from 'The Little Flowers of Saint Francis'.

Near the beginning of the Order, while Saint Francis was alive, a young man of Assisi came to the Order, and he was called Brother Simon, and God adorned him and gifted him with so much grace and so much contemplation and elevation of spirit that his whole life was a mirror of holiness, as I heard from those who were with him for a long time. He rarely was seen outside the cell and, if he was with the brothers sometimes, he always spoke of God. He had never learned grammar and nevertheless he spoke of God and the love of Christ so deeply and highly that his words seemed supernatural.

Once through his devout speaking a young man from San Severino was converted, one who was a very vain and worldly young man in society, noble in blood and very delicate in body. And Brother Simon, when receiving the young man into the Order, kept his secular clothes with him, as the young man stayed with Brother Simon to be informed about the Rule's observance. Because of this the demon, striving to prevent every good thing, put into him such a strong impulse and such a burning temptation of the flesh that the young man could not resist it by any means. For this reason he went to Brother Simon and said to him, 'Give me back the clothes that I wore in the world, because I cannot resist the temptation of the flesh any longer.' And Brother Simon, having great compassion for him, said to him, 'My son, sit down here with me for a little while.' And he began to speak to him of God, in such a way that the whole temptation left him; and then after a while, as the temptation returned, and he kept asking for his clothes, Brother Simon would drive it away by speaking of God.

Having done this several times, finally one night that temptation attacked him more strongly than usual, and he could not resist it for anything in the world. He went to Brother Simon demanding absolutely to have his secular clothes, because he could by no means stay there any more. Then Brother Simon, as he usually did, had him sit down beside him and, as he was speaking to him of God, the young man leaned his head onto Brother Simon's breast out of melancholy and sadness. Then Brother Simon, because of the great compassion he had towards him, raised his eyes to heaven and, praying to God devoutly for him, was enraptured and heard by God; then he returned to himself, and the young man felt himself completely freed from that temptation, as if he had never felt it. Rather, the heat of the temptation changed into the heat of the Holy Spirit, because he was near burning coal, that is, near Brother Simon, and he became all inflamed with love of God and neighbour.

III,633ff>

Friday — *RCL Proper 29 / DEL Week 34*

A reading from 'The Remembrance of the Desire of a Soul', by Thomas of Celano.

Blessèd Francis was greatly consoled by God's visitations which reassured him that the foundations of the religion would always remain unshaken. He was also promised that the number of those being lost would undoubtedly be replaced by those being chosen. Once he was disturbed by some bad examples. In his disturbance he turned to prayer and received a scolding from the Lord, 'Why are you so upset, little man? Have I set you up as shepherd over my religion so that you can forget that I am its main protector? I have entrusted this to you, a simple man, so that the things that I work in you for others to imitate may be followed by those who want to follow. I have called; I will preserve, and I will pasture; and I will raise up others to make up for the fall of some, so that, even if they have not been born, I will have them born! So do not be upset, but work out your salvation, for even if the religion should come to number only three, by my gift it will still remain forever unshaken.'

From that time on blessèd Francis used to say that the virtue of a single holy person overwhelms a great crowd of the imperfect, just as the deepest darkness disappears at a single ray of light.   *II,349*

Saturday — *RCL Proper 29 / DEL Week 34*

A reading from a medieval Franciscan manuscript.

Once when Brother Leo and the Blessèd Francis were talking to one another on the mountain of La Verna, the Saint pointed to a certain stone and said, 'O Brother Leo, little sheep, wash that stone with water.' Then, when Brother Leo had done this, he said, 'Wash it with wine.' When he had done that the Saint said, 'Wash it with oil.' This also Brother Leo did; and then Francis said, 'Wash it with balsam.' 'And how,' said Brother Leo, 'am I to find any balsam here?' Then Saint Francis said to him, 'Know, O little sheep of God, that that is the stone on which the Lord once sat when he appeared before me; and that is why I told you to wash

it four times. For God then promised me four things for the Order –
first, that whoever loves the brethren and the Order with all their heart
shall, with God's blessing, make a good end; secondly, that everyone who
unjustly persecutes the Order shall be soundly punished; thirdly, that no
brother who is evil or who continues in wickedness shall survive for long
without being either dismissed or put to shame; and fourthly, that our
Order shall last to the end of the world.'   *IV,1904*

January

1 January — Naming & Circumcision of Jesus

See page 29.

7 January — Angela of Foligno, Tertiary, 1309

While still a wife and mother Angela, with the help of her confessor, began to dedicate her life to prayer and works of charity. On the death of her husband and children, she entered the Franciscan Third Order and developed a vivid mystical prayer life. She continued to serve the poor and sick of Foligno and acted as beggar for their needs. With her confessor she wrote her Book of Visions and Instructions.

A Reading from 'The Book of the Blessèd Angela of Foligno'.

Once, when I was standing in the church and at the moment when people kneel down at the elevation of the body of Christ, words such as these were addressed to me by the Blessèd Virgin: 'My daughter, so sweet to my Son.' She spoke very humbly and in such a way that I experienced a new feeling in my soul, one of utmost sweetness. And she said, 'My daughter, sweet to my Son and to me. My Son has already come unto you and you have received his blessing.' By this she was making me understand that her Son was at that moment already on the altar, and it was as if she was telling me something new and it filled my soul with such great joy that I cannot find words for it, nor do I believe that there is anyone who could express it properly. This joy was so great that I was even amazed afterward that I could in any way stand on my feet while I was experiencing it.

And the Blessèd Virgin also told me, 'Now that you have received the blessing of my Son, it is fitting that I, too, come to you and give you my blessing so that just as you received the blessing of the Son you also receive the blessing of his mother. Receive then my blessing. May it be yours from both my Son and myself. Work with all your might at loving, for you are much loved, and you are called upon to attain something infinite.' And then my soul experienced a joy such as never before.

When these words were coming to an end, at the moment when the body of Christ was elevated by the priest, I genuflected and adored him and the same joy increased. *X,157f*

16 January — First Franciscan Martyrs 1220

A reading from the Chronicle of Jordan of Giano.

In the year 1219 in the tenth year of his conversion, Brother Francis in a Chapter held at Saint Mary of the Angels, sent brothers to France, Germany, Hungary, Spain, and the other Provinces of Italy into which the Brethren had not yet penetrated. Those who went to Germany did not know the language, and when asked if they wanted shelter or food or other things of the sort, they replied 'Ja' and in this way received a good welcome. However when they were asked if they were heretics they replied 'Ja'. Whereupon some of them were beaten, some imprisoned, and others stripped and led naked to the local court. Then the brethren perceived they could win no fruit in Germany and returned to Italy.

Of those who went to Spain five went on to Morocco in 1220, these were, Berardus, Peter, Otto, Accursius, and Adjutus. These five after preaching in public against Mahomet were crowned with martyrdom.

Now when the life and history of these martyr brothers had been brought to Blessèd Francis, he heard himself praised and saw the assembled brothers glorying in their brothers' martyrdom. Whereupon, as he held himself in utmost scorn and condemned praise and glorying, he put aside the history and forbade it to be read, saying, 'Let each glory in their own suffering and not in that of another.'

Thus that first sending forth came to nought, perhaps the time was not opportune, since 'there is a time and opportunity for every business.'

XIV,132f>

20 January — Thanksgiving for the Society of the Divine Compassion

The first Franciscan community in the Church of England since the Reformation, the Society of the Divine Compassion, was founded on the 20 January 1894, when James Adderley, Henry Chappel and Ernest Hardy made their vows for one year. That day the Society moved to Plaistow, East London and faithfully ministered there until its own dissolution in 1952.

A reading from 'A Franciscan Revival', printed by the SDC in 1908.

The Society of the Divine Compassion is a community of priests, deacons, and communicant laymen, banded together in a common life of poverty, chastity, and obedience for the glory of our Lord and Saviour Jesus Christ and the benefit of his Holy Catholic Church, to worship him and to work for him and for all, especially the poor and suffering, in imitation of the Divine Master, seeking the help of one another in thus obeying him.

The life of the SDC is a humble effort to imitate the Incarnate Life of our divine Lord. It has its parish work, where it lives a neighbourly life, going out to the more active work of the ministry of preaching and missions; its workshops among the people, where it repairs clocks and watches, works its printing presses. It seeks to live a poor life, sharing the privation and discomfort of ordinary poor people. All work is held to be equally sacred. All are held in equal respect.

The Community does not by its rule or its spirit sever itself from all connection with the outside world; still, a 'Religious vocation' if it is real must be an attraction to a life, not a work. Really the truest vocation would best be described as a supernatural attraction to the cross. The work is rather for the life than the life for the work; the work may always change, the life will be that which changes not, that which the world can neither give nor take away – the soul's secret response to its secret call as it learns in Poverty to depend on, in Obedience to obey, in Charity to unite itself with, the one all-satisfying rest and peace, the blessèdness of the love of God.   *XXIX,1f>*

February

2 February — Presentation of Christ in the Temple (Candlemass)

See page 59.

6 February — Peter Baptist, Paul Miki & Companions, Martyrs of Japan, 1597

After many years of mission work in the Philippines, Peter Baptist and five other friars left for Japan in the year 1593. They converted many to Christianity, built churches and a hospital, but were eventually arrested by the authorities. Taken to Nagasaki, Peter Baptist and his companions, together with three members of the Society of Jesus and fifteen Franciscan Tertiaries, were executed by crucifixion on 5 February 1597.

A reading from the letters of Saint Peter Baptist of 4 January and 2 February, 1597.

Of the friars here, six were arrested and kept in prison for several days.

With them were three Japanese of the Society of Jesus – one of them professed – and also other Christian faithful. There are twenty of us all together. We are now travelling in this rather cold month of the winter. They are conducting us with cavalry and a strong guard. On some days more than two hundred men were assigned to keep us under guard. In spite of this we have great consolation, and we continue to rejoice in the Lord because according to the sentence pronounced against us we are to be crucified for having preached the law of God contrary to the king's command. The rest were condemned because they are Christians.

Those who wish to die for Christ now have a golden opportunity. I think that the faithful of this region would have been greatly consoled if Religious of our Order had been here, but they may rest assured that as long as this king rules, men in our habit will not live long in Japan because he will quickly send them to eternal life. May he get us there.

The sentence pronounced against us was written on a sign and carried before us. The sign read that we were condemned to death because we preached the law of Nauan (i.e. the law of Christ) contrary to the command of Taycosama, and would be crucified when we reached Nagasaki. For this we were very happy and consoled in the Lord since we had forfeited our lives to preach his law.

For the love of God let your charity commend us to God that the sacrifice of our lives may be acceptable in his sight. From what I have heard here, I think we will be crucified this coming Friday, because it was on a Friday that they cut off a part of each one's ear at Miyako, an event we accepted as a gift from God. We all ask you, then, with great fervour to pray for us for the love of God.

Dearest brothers, help us with your prayers that our death may be acceptable to the majesty of God in heaven where, God willing, we hope to go. We will remember you. We have not forgotten your love here. I have loved you and still love you with all my heart. I wish you the peace and love of our Lord Jesus Christ. Farewell, dearest brothers, because there is no longer any time to speak to you. Till we meet in heaven. Remember me.   *XIII,25ff*

6 February — Founding of the Community of Saint Clare, Freeland, 1950

After six years training in the contemplative life alongside the sisters of the convents at Wantage near Oxford, and Tymawr in Wales, the Community of Saint Clare found its own home at Freeland, Oxford, where the first 'Poor Clare'sisters were professed in the Church of England on 6 February 1950. The community continued to grow with the dedication of a new chapel in 1961, and the acquisition of the Old Parsonage as a retreat house. Printing work began in the late 1960s. After Vatican II, contacts with Roman Catholic Poor Clares were increasingly friendly and the community was invited to take part in the meetings of the Association of Saint Clare from its beginning. One result was that the community which had been known as the Community of Saint Clare from its beginning was asked to adopt the initials OSC – Order of Saint Clare – as an indication that they are one community in that part of the Franciscan family.

A reading from a letter by one the founding sisters of the Community of Saint Clare.

Algy, Charles, and Lothian [all First Order SSF friars] were the early influences on the community. It was all Algy's idea but, without the wisdom and pastoral care of the other two, I do not think we would still be here. Algy's understanding of women was limited, though his inspiration was boundless, and this inspiration was balanced by as much understanding of other communities of Clares as was then available to him.

It was not the climate for much contact between communities and Mother Annie Louise of Wantage with whom he conferred was not a

Franciscan. So it was left to the early sisters to find their own way (with Algy's entire approval). This was probably a very good thing as it saved us from some of the hazards of being dominated by a male priest founder! However, until his death, Algy's influence was profound – he was the director of each individual sister and Charles and Lothian were very much assistants. But then the other two, and later David and Michael, shared the direction of the spiritual life of us all and without them, and the brothers and sisters who succeeded them, our own differing ideas and ideals would probably have torn us apart.

They all shared the view that it was, after all, we who were called to live this life and they could not tell us how it should be. This was why, for our first several years, no contact was permitted between the Clares and the [other] Friars, or, for that matter, between the Clares and other communities. We were to be an enclosed community and, until our essential foundations were firmly established, we needed some protection from other, even Franciscan, influences. This was sometimes misunderstood by the Brothers – and it was difficult for us to accept – but time proved its real wisdom and from it grew our present closeness as a real part of the Franciscan family. *XXXV*

7 February — Colette, Poor Clare, Founder of the Colettine Reform, 1447

Colette was born in Corbie, France, in 1381. When she was 21 years old she began following the Rule of the Franciscan Third Order, living a life devoted to prayer as an anchoress in a small room attached to a church. After four years she left her cell and, with the encouragement of the Pope, became a Poor Clare, establishing many monasteries following a strict observance of the Rule of Saint Clare. Her reform movement is still thriving today.

A reading from 'The Testament of Saint Colette'.

My dearly belovèd sisters, learn to esteem your holy vocation, its high dignity and its great perfection; for ignorance of this is very hurtful but a just appreciation very salutary. Bear in mind that you have found the true path through God's inspiration and loving call; for our dear Saviour has said that none can come to him except the Father draw them by his inspiration.

Recall to mind, then, dearly belovèd sisters that you have been called by the grace of God to the practice of perfect obedience and that you ought always and in all things to obey save in sin, since the Lord Jesus became obedient even to death. If we be submissive to God he will show himself condescending to us. Rid yourselves, then, of all self-will.

After this renunciation of ourselves, our Lord wills that we should carry the cross of our vow of poverty. O holy poverty, emblem of our redemption, precious jewel, and secure pledge of the Kingdom of Heaven! The cross of holy poverty, which we must never lay aside, consists in the observance of perpetual fast, in bearing cold and going barefoot, in lying on hard beds and being content with rough and scanty fare and in being assiduous in spiritual and corporal works.

Recall, also, that you ought to imitate the spotless lamb, Jesus Christ, a virgin and Son of the Virgin, by purity of heart and body unto death. By your vow of angelic chastity you become the faithful spouses of Jesus, and merit the honour of the angels, as being the true spouses of their Lord and King.

How salutary is strict enclosure! How happy is the lot of those who have to guard it and allow none to enter save the messengers of the true King! O right worthy and sublime virtue!

Let us hold fast, then, by the promise we have made, and if through human frailty we be found wanting in any thing let us hasten to purge ourselves by holy penance. Set your minds on holy living and on a happy death.

May the Father in his mercy and the Son by his passion and the Holy Spirit the fountain of peace and of sweetness and of love fill you with all consolations. Amen.   *XXXVIII,App >*

15 February — George Potter, Friar, 1960

'Father Potter of Peckham' as he was known, was an Anglican parish priest in a poor area of South East London just after the First World War. Great were the needs of the area and his enthusiasm drew together men willing to work for the people. The vision was Franciscan and the Brotherhood of the Holy Cross was formed. Considerable work was done with homeless boys and homes were set up. The work carried on during the Second War although bombed out of one property. Father Potter was closely involved with the amalgamation of communities to form the Society of Saint Francis and although he himself did not join, not long after his death the remaining BHC brothers became part of SSF.

A reading from the 'Brotherhood of the Holy Cross Quarterly'.

We still get many applications from men who want to join us. We always welcome such for a short visit, so that we can get to know one another. I just want to say that we cannot offer a home to men who merely want a quiet peaceful life or for such as seem to have made a mess of everything else. We want men who have some talents to give in the service of Christ and the poor. At the moment we want a builder and a carpenter, and some teachers and a cook. Some men who visit us really need a nursery. Others come laden with Office Books almost as large as the Post Office Directory and they seem shocked when I give them Mrs Beeton's Cookery Book instead.

We want men with a love of souls, and we can only offer little comfort and plenty of hard work, but if they can take a share in the great adventure, I can assure them that they will find a happiness that surpasses everything.

The aim of the Brotherhood was, and still is, to emulate the example of our Blessèd Master in humble service, shown as it was in his washing the feet of his disciples. The stained towel of the Upper Room is symbolic of that love which is expressed by humble, loving service to others.

When we meet our Blessèd Master at the end, I feel that the fact that we have been regular members of the 'Guild of St. Anti-macassar' for many years will not be of prime importance. He will be mainly interested in our endeavours to bring others to the knowledge of his love.

We shall not want to do this until we get that personal link with him, and as we strengthen that link we shall come to realize that as we depend on him, so he depends on us. We can never be the fullest use to him until others see that we have that peace and love, faith and joy that they wish they possessed, and we can get that only by a deeper personal devotion to our Blessèd Master. *XXXII>*

24 February — Vocation of Francis, 1208

In the stages that make up the conversion of Francis, some events stand out. One of these is his response to the gospel read on an apostles' feast day. This is held to be Saint Matthias day (celebrated in the Church on this date at that time) and, from the response Francis made, it is seen to be the moment when his vocation took on the form that would later characterize the Franciscan movement.

A reading from 'The Major Legend of Saint Francis', by Saint Bonaventure.

While her servant Francis
was living in the church of the Virgin Mother of God,
he prayed to her
who had conceived and brought to birth the Word,

full of grace and truth,
imploring her with continual sighs
to become his advocate.
Through the merits of the Mother of Mercy,
he conceived and brought to birth
the spirit of the truth of the gospel.

One day when he was devoutly hearing a mass of the Apostles, the gospel was read in which Christ sends out his disciples to preach and gives them the gospel form of life, that they may not keep gold or silver or money in their belts, nor have a wallet for their journey, nor may they have two tunics, nor shoes, nor staff. Hearing, understanding, and committing this to memory, this friend of apostolic poverty was then overwhelmed with an indescribable joy. 'This is what I want;' he said, 'this is what I desire with all my heart.'

Immediately, he took off the shoes from his feet, put down his staff, denounced his wallet and money, and satisfied with one tunic, threw away his leather belt and put on a piece of rope for a belt. He directed all his heart's desire to carry out what he had heard and to conform in every way to the rule of right living given to the apostles.   *II,542*

25 February — Rosina Mary Rice & the Founding of the Community of Saint Francis, 1905

Rosina Eleanor Rice had originally made her religious profession in the Church of England as a Sister of Bethany in 1884 and worked with the sisters in the parish of Our Most Holy Redeemer, Clerkenwell, in London. As time went on, she found having a much better standard of living than those she was called to serve became unendurable. In January 1905, with permission, she left to live a life of greater poverty. Together with a small group of sisters, Mother Rosina Mary formed a community that would follow the Rule of Saint Clare in all but enclosure, first in Hull, and then at Dalston in East London. Dr Winnington Ingram, Bishop of London, gave his approval and by tradition the Community of Saint Francis came into being on 25 February 1905. In 1911 Mother Rosina joined the Roman Catholic community of the Franciscan Missionary Sisters of the Sacred Heart at Peekskill in New York, USA.

A reading from 'Corn of Wheat', by Elizabeth CSF.

Mother Elizabeth and the other sisters had heard earlier in 1946 from Sister Mary Claudia in New York that Mother Rosina Mary (now Sister Mary Magdalene) was very ill and near the end of her life. She died on 9 April and was buried in the cemetery at Mount St. Francis, Peekskill, the place which had been her home for thirty-five years. Sister Mary Claudia wrote, 'All her life, at least the part I know of, passed before my mind. The struggle of 1910 – the yielding – the acceptance of God's will – the days of sorrow for the separation from loved ones left behind in her belovèd England – but above all the unshakeable faith and deep-rooted conviction that the step she had taken was right, and the deep humility and unflagging determination to follow wherever her soul was led, be the path rough and stony (these places were not lacking) or lit up with the Smile of God. Nothing could deter her – and now she rests – her aching body struggling for the last time, her heart so full of love and tenderness. Thoughtful of those who are tending her, her only anxiety is less she may disturb them too much. Her life will not be written except in the hearts and memories of those who have been so privileged as to come close to her. She will not be canonised officially – but I am sure in the eyes of God and the whole heavenly court, Sister stands judged one of the chosen ones of God – precious in his All-holy sight.'   *XX,67*

March

2 March — Agnes of Prague, Poor Clare, 1282

Agnes, daughter of a King of Bohemia and a Queen of Hungary seemed destined for courtly life. The death of one suitor (when she was only three years old!) and her jilting by another years later led her father to refuse further offers and allowed Agnes to continue with charitable works. Meeting friars and learning of Clare she founded a hospice and built a convent which she lived in for the next fifty four years. The letters of Clare to Agnes are almost the only personal writings of Clare to survive and cover the last twenty years of her life.

A reading from 'The Second Letter of Saint Clare to Blessèd Agnes of Prague'.

To the daughter of the King of kings, the servant of the Lord of lords, the most worthy Spouse of Jesus Christ, and, therefore, the most noble Queen, Lady Agnes: Clare, the useless and unworthy servant of the Poor Ladies: greetings and a life always of the highest poverty.

I give thanks to the Giver of grace from whom, we believe, every good and perfect gift proceeds, because he has adorned you with such splendours of virtue and illuminated you with such marks of perfection, that, since you have become such a diligent imitator of the Father of all perfection, you might be made perfect and his eyes do not see anything imperfect in you.

This is that perfection with which the King himself will take you to himself in the heavenly bridal chamber where he is seated in glory on a starry throne, because you have despised the splendour of an earthly kingdom and considered of little value the offers of an imperial marriage. Instead, as someone zealous for the holiest poverty, in a spirit of great humility and the most ardent charity, you have held fast to the footprints of him to whom you have merited to be joined as a Spouse.

But since I know that you are adorned with many virtues, I will spare my words and not weary you with needless speech, even though nothing seems superfluous to you if you can draw some consolation from it. But because one thing is necessary, I bear witness to that one thing and encourage you, for love of him to whom you have offered yourself as a holy and pleasing sacrifice, that you always be mindful of your resolution like another Rachel always seeing your beginning.

What you hold, may you always hold.
What you do, may you always do and never abandon.
But with swift pace, light step,
   unswerving feet,
   so that even your steps stir up no dust,
may you go forward
   securely, joyfully, and swiftly,
   on the path of prudent happiness,
not believing anything,
   not agreeing with anything
   that would dissuade you from this resolution
   or that would place a stumbling block for you on the way,
so that you may offer your vows to the Most High
   in the pursuit of that perfection
      to which the Spirit of the Lord has called you.   *V,40f*

7 March — Helen Elizabeth Christmas, A Founder of the Community of Saint Francis, 1950

When six sisters left the young, Anglican Community of Saint Francis in 1910 to join the Roman Catholic Society of the Atonement in the USA, only three sisters remained and Helen Elizabeth the only one in life profession. She was appointed Mother and guided the little community for many years. A nurse by training and an able administrator, she oversaw the growth at Dalston in the East end of London, and the extension of the ministry of the community into care of the old and incurably sick.

A reading from 'Corn of Wheat', by Elizabeth CSF.

Helen Elizabeth Christmas was by all accounts a formidable woman. A nurse who had worked under her at Guy's hospital, and who later assisted the community in their nursing home, recalled how in the hospital her reputation as a stickler for discipline evoked the whispered warning as she approached, 'Psst, here comes Christmas!' The Lord added indomitable courage to her strong character. She was superlative in her offering; nothing could ever be enough for God, and she looked for no less in her companions. She was to write later, 'The Franciscan life being rather a new idea [in the Church of England], novices coming found it was not only the simple happy life we profess to live, but a hard one; and that sanctification, consisting as it does as much in the use of a dust pan and brush as in the swinging of a censer, was not quite what they had bargained for in their testing. Many went home again.

'Those aspiring to this life should not just venture as an experiment – coming with the idea of "seeing how I like it". That was not what the first followers of Saint Francis did, but at the outset made a very generous surrender of themselves to God, burning their boats with full trust in him, come what may in the future. Those who are able to do this will find it a delightful adventure, though the Cross will also be there.'

She died on 7 March, 1950 at the age of 77. One of the patients, among the first to come in 1919, wrote of her: 'She came into my life at a dark and difficult period and I found her always a light and inspiration. After the Home was rebuilt, and with the aid of her devoted group of Sisters, indeed a faithful few, the true Franciscan spirit and courage of the Reverend Mother seemed to shine at its highest in the renewed effort to knit up the broken threads and carry forward the good work over again; her sublime faith in all she undertook that all would go well; her words of comfort to us on special occasions; her keen sense of humour over the funny little everyday happenings in the Home and elsewhere; her love of music and her beautiful voice, both speaking and singing; all these and many other memories will be the echoes in our daily lives.' *XX,21f,69>*

7 March — Joseph Crookston, Friar, Founder of the (Episcopal Church) Order of Saint Francis, 1979

Joseph was a priest in the Episcopal Church in the USA and felt the call to Franciscan Religious life. A Third Order had already been founded in 1917 and interest was growing in possible First and Second Orders. The First Order, called The Order of Saint Francis, formally began on Holy Cross Day in 1919 and slowly established itself. Parish ministry, retreat work and support of the marginalized were the chief ministries. In 1967, the OSF united with the Society of Saint Francis, becoming the American Province of the SSF.

A reading from 'A Pastoral Letter for New Year 1966', by Father Joseph.

We are committed to the belief that we need redemption, that each of us is a sinner who by God's grace is transformable, and that each of us who is using at least ordinary diligence is being transformed into Christlikeness. Each of us finds it hard to realize that the faults we condemn in others are almost certain to be our own faults to which we are blind. We delude ourselves by hating in others what we should first of all hate in ourselves. Much of our censure of others prevents us from giving ourselves to the self-transformation to which God's love is calling us, so that God can love Christlikeness in us. Let us not confuse our aspirations with our attainments. We must use what irritates us in others to find fault within ourselves and, as we dearly love ourselves, so to love and excuse those whose faults are clear to ourselves. This is one of the secrets of holiness.

It is the duty of anyone who exercises any superiorship to help the others along in the path of transformation. Doubtless each superior does this imperfectly. When we fault our superiors as being bad or worse than we are, we may be right in our judgement, but this judgement of them is in no way helpful to us for growth in the patience and humility and charity of Christ. We are stupid indeed to refuse the grace which awaits if we make proper use of a superior's fault-finding.

Further, no matter how belittled a rebuke may make us feel, we do God and ourselves much wrong if we lose a sense of our own dignity. Each of us needs to boast: 'I am a creature so loved by God that he gave his Son to die for my redemption and transformation, and I will now take pride in this chance to become more Christlike.' *XXI*

25 March — Annunciation of our Lord
to the Blessèd Virgin Mary

A reading from the 'Salutation of the Blessèd Virgin Mary' and the antiphon 'Holy Virgin Mary', by Saint Francis.

Hail, O Lady
Holy Queen,
Mary, holy Mother of God,
who are the Virgin made Church,
chosen by the most Holy Father in heaven
whom he consecrated with his most holy belovèd Son
and with the Holy Spirit the Paraclete,
in whom there was and is
all fullness of grace and every good.

Hail, his Palace!
Hail, his Tabernacle!
Hail, his Dwelling!
Hail, his Robe!
Hail, his Servant!
Hail, his Mother!

And hail all you holy virtues
which are poured into the hearts of the faithful
through grace and enlightenment of the Holy Spirit,
that from being unbelievers,
you may make them faithful to God.

Holy Virgin Mary,
among the women born into the world,
there is no one like you.
Daughter and servant
of the Most High and supreme King
and of the Father in heaven,
Mother of our most holy Lord Jesus Christ,
Spouse of the Holy Spirit;
pray for us
with Saint Michael the Archangel,
all the powers of heaven
and all the saints,
at the side of your most holy belovèd Son,
our Lord and Teacher.   *I,163,141*

28 March — William Sirr, Friar, Monk, Solitary, 1937

Father William lived and died a member of a Franciscan community, The Society of the Divine Compassion, but was given permission to try to found an enclosed Order for men. He established the monastery of Saint Mary at the Cross, Glasshampton in Worcestershire. A man of great prayer, his spiritual and pastoral advice benefited many. Sadly, William of Glasshampton was never able to found an Order, and towards the end of his life he was able to say, 'We must not mind being a failure – Our Lord died on the cross a failure.' His gifts of prayer, courage, kindness and the ability to trust in God's purposes continue to be an influence and attract all manner of souls to the monastery, now in the care of the Society of Saint Francis.

A reading from 'Watchman, What of the Night', by Father William.

There can be no doubt of the pressing need there is of men who will deliberately go apart and be with God and, moreover, be willing to stay there. They must be men wholly surrendered and determined with dauntless courage to stand faithfully at the ramparts of God through much tedious toil and many painful vicissitudes, to triumph gloriously over impatience and broken efforts, and to endure right on to the end, whatever the cost may be. 'I give myself to prayer.' This is the way prescribed by God. It is in this direction such men of God have always gone. They are 'the Lord's remembrancers' *(Isa 62.6)*.

It would be wrong to leave the impression that this experience of struggle and effort and pain is the only experience that accompanies such abandonment to the call for love of God to a life of prayer. It is necessary to emphasize the cost we must be prepared to pay for the pearl of great price, just as we would warn any child of what it will cost him in the shape of years of monotonous toil before he can hope to become proficient in any secular calling. The higher the aim is, the greater and longer assuredly must be the perseverance in endurance, before we can expect to attain our end and reach our goal. This is the toil of the journey to God, this is the labour that leads to heaven. Do not therefore fly in dismay from the way of salvation. His Majesty loves exceedingly courageous souls. *XXII*

31 March — Andrew Ernest Hardy, Friar, 1946

Father Andrew SDC was a founding brother of the Society of Divine Compassion. He was the first priest to be ordained in a Religious habit in the Church of England since the Reformation. Most of his ministry was in the East End of London and he was an able poet, playwright, painter, preacher and pastor.

A reading from a letter of Father Andrew SDC.

Father Henry and I had a retreat by ourselves in a remote country village near Ely in a time of deep snow. We kept ten days in silence, except for our Sunday ministries, and we heard each other's confessions; we came up to London and were professed in the Church of Saint Pancras by the Bishop of St Albans, going on now for forty years ago – thirty-seven or thirty-eight years – I never can remember dates or distances of time.

As I kneel here now I thank God for every bit of it, the pain as well as the peace, for I know that it has all been God's care for my soul and his patient way of shaping my life. The failures have all been on my side, the patience has all been on God's side and, all the while, whatever has happened, God's grace has been given to me to make me a better man. If one looks at the end of life as being a result of happiness, then it is hard to see much purpose or principle in life; but if one looks at the end of life as being a result of sanctity and final perfection, and if one believes in God's directing and shepherding love the whole time, then one can find all sorts of marks that God's providence has been over one's life and that, if one had been spared a pain, one would have lost a gain of grace and virtue that came to one through it.

I do not know where this letter will find you. I hope you are getting to the condition when you are really careless where you are, because if our abiding place is the presence of God and our peace is in our surrender to his will, then as a matter of fact the place we are in is not dependent upon the place we live in. We have learned to know, then, something of the everywhere of eternity, something of the here and now of the presence of God. *XXIV,99f*

April

3 April — Benedict the Black, Friar, 1589

Benedict's parents were slaves brought from Africa to work on an estate in Messina, Sicily. Freed at the age of 18, Benedict continued to work as a farmer, but later joined a group of hermits near Palermo. When the Pope ordered all hermits to join an established Order, Benedict became a Friar Minor of the Observance at Palermo, and was given the job of cook, later to become Novice Master and then Guardian. His holiness and kindness were renowned, and many came to him for spiritual guidance. Benedict has been taken as a patron saint by African-Americans.

A reading from 'The Life of Saint Francis', by Thomas of Celano.

Blessèd Francis once said to the brothers with joy, 'Be strong, dear brothers, and rejoice in the Lord. Do not be sad, because you seem so few, and do not let my simplicity or yours discourage you. The Lord has shown me that God will make us grow into a great multitude, and will spread us to the ends of the earth. I must also tell you what I saw about your future, though it would please me more to remain silent, if charity did not compel me to tell you. I saw a great multitude of people coming to us, wishing to live with us in the habit of a holy way of life and in the rule of blessèd religion. Listen! The sound of them is still in my ears, their coming and going according to the command of holy obedience. I seemed to see highways filled with this multitude gathering in this region from nearly every nation. The French are coming, Spaniards are hurrying, Germans and the English are running, and a huge crowd speaking other languages is rapidly approaching.'

When the brothers heard this, they were filled with wholesome joy, either because of the grace which the Lord God had conferred on his holy one, or because they eagerly thirsted for the profit of their neighbours, whom they wanted to increase in number daily in order to be saved. *1,205f*

10 April — William of Ockham, Friar, Philosopher, Teacher of the Faith, 1347

William was born in Ockham (probably modern-day Woking) in Surrey. After becoming a friar he studied and taught theology at the University of Oxford. In 1324 he was summoned to Avignon by Pope John XXII to defend himself against a charge of teaching dangerous doctrine. He was never condemned, but was later excommunicated after getting involved in the debate over Franciscan poverty. William was eventually reconciled with the Church, and is recognised as one of the most influential philosopher-theologians of the fourteenth century.

A reading from 'A Letter in Response to an Unknown Master', by Saint Bonaventure.

One thing remains, my dear friend: that we say something about brothers who take up the study of philosophy, so that here as in other things we might also be in agreement. Let me say that if curiosity displeases you, it displeases me too; indeed, it displeases all good friars, just as it does God and his angels. I am not defending those who childishly waste their time over useless writings but detest them just as you do. One thing I advise both of us, however: that our zeal be enlightened, so that we despise no more than we should, nor things that should not be despised. Perhaps curiosity should be numbered among the petty and venial sins. For people can hardly reap the grain without the chaff and the divine Word without the human. These are separated by the fire of compunction and devotion, which winnows the grain of truth from the chaff of mere verbiage. And perhaps some who seem curious are actually being studious. For if someone were to study the opinions of heretics so that by avoiding their teachings he might better understand the truth, such a person would not be curious, nor a heretic, but a Catholic. And so, if the writings of the philosophers are sometimes of much value in understanding truth and refuting errors, we are not departing from the purity of faith if we at times study them, especially since there are many questions of faith which cannot be settled without recourse to them. Just as the children of Israel carried off the vessels of Egypt, so also the doctors of theology should make their own the teachings of philosophy. You therefore should not be surprised if those who enter the Order with little education acquire much knowledge within it.   *VII,52f>*

16 April — Commemoration of the Taking of Vows by Francis, 1208

This event can be dated, as Bernard's distribution of all his worldly goods took place eight days before Giles joined the brothers on Saint George's Day in 1208. The centrality of the gospel is emphasized and the Order is founded with the first three Brothers, Francis, Bernard of Quintavalle and Peter.

A reading from 'The Anonymous of Perugia'.

Two men from Assisi, inspired by divine grace, humbly approached Francis. One of these was Brother Bernard, and the other, Brother Peter. They told Francis simply, 'We wish to live with you from now on and do what you are doing. Tell us, therefore, what we should do with our possessions.' Overjoyed at their coming and their resolve, he answered them kindly, 'Let us go and seek counsel from the Lord.'

So they went to one of the city's churches. Upon entering it, they fell on their knees and humbly prayed, 'Lord, God, Father of glory, we beg you in your mercy, show us what we are to do.' After finishing the prayer they asked the priest who was there, 'Sir, would you show us the gospel of our Lord Jesus Christ.'

And, since before this happened none of them knew how to read very well, when the priest opened up the book, they immediately found the passage: 'If you wish to be perfect, go, sell everything you possess and give to the poor, and you will have a treasure in heaven.'

Opening up the book a second time, they discovered: 'Whoever wishes to come after me ...'

When they opened up the book for the third time, they came upon: 'Take nothing for your journey ...'

When they heard this, they were filled with great joy and exclaimed: 'This is what we want, this is what we were seeking.' And blessèd Francis said: 'This will be our Rule.' Then he told both of them: 'Go, and may you fulfil the Lord's counsel as you heard it.' *II,37f*

16 April — Founding of the Poor Clares of Reparation & Adoration, 1924

Sister Mary Christine PCR made her profession in perpetual vows on 16 April 1924 and became the community's first Mother. It is considered their foundation date although several sisters had been living together for some while preparing for that day.

Until its demise, this community had been the only Poor Clare nuns in the Episcopal Church in the USA. They had been nurtured by their close contact with the Order of Saint Francis and eventually had their convent alongside that of the brothers on Long Island. Never very many in number they faithfully maintained the life of prayer until the death of the last sister in January 2000.

A reading from the Funeral Oration for Sister Mary Christine PCR.

A Religious is one who makes a special gift to God in ways that are not required. One who says to God, 'I believe that you have offered me a vocation to self-sacrifice which is an invitation to give myself to you in special ways; and because you do not require it of me under pain of sin, but only hold it before me as an opportunity to express my love for you, I choose to do it as a free-will offering.' Our Lord in his human nature made such a gift of himself to God, and we know that it was consummated through much pain and suffering and temptation. The servant is not above his master. It is so with us. The Religious no matter how much joy she finds in her vocation, has chosen for herself the Way of Calvary.

Often we think that we should give ourselves to God by one swift triumphant act of dedication, when we are invested with the habit, or when we profess our vows, and that from then on we should be in a fixed state of joyful consecration. But it was not so with our Lord and it is not so with us. The oblation of oneself in the Religious state is an act of continuous giving, of persevering mortification of self. Often the flesh rebels and the spirit quails. 'If it be possible let this cup pass from me.' All of us Religious have these moments. Our sister had them. Once, I remember, in a time of illness and interior trial she was very sad, and I offered to try to procure her a dispensation because of her bodily infirmities, and she rejected the suggestion as if it were from Satan himself. She lived and she died as one who had given herself to God in the consecration of the three vows. She persevered to the end. She paid the debt of self-sacrifice which she had assumed by her profession. Therefore, she is not without honour. *XXXIV,44>*

21 April — Conrad of Parzham, Friar, 1894

Conrad spent most of his life as the porter at the Capuchin Friary in Altoetting, Bavaria. His duties were to answer the door to the many pilgrims who came to visit the nearby shrine to Mary, to receive their gifts and give alms to the poor. He was known for his great patience and prayerfulness, speaking little, but guiding others to God by his presence.

A reading from the letters of Saint Conrad of Parzham.

Let us always endeavour to lead a truly interior life hidden in God. It is such a beautiful experience to converse with the good Lord. If we are truly recollected, nothing can stand in our way, even in the midst of the work our vocation requires of us. We will come to love silence, because whoever talks much will never arrive at a truly interior life.

My way of life consists above all in loving and suffering while contemplating, adoring, and admiring the love of God for us poor creatures. I will unite myself to the love of my God at all times until the end. I am continually united with his love, and nothing stands in my way. While carrying out my many duties I am often so intimately united with him that I talk with him as confidently as a child with his father. I tell him all my concerns, my wishes, whatever bothers me, and I beg him to give me his grace with the greatest confidence, even after committing some imperfections. Then I beg him with all humility to pardon me because I want to become a good son. I want to love him with all my heart.

Let us give ourselves over completely to our dear and good heavenly Father. Let us always love him, and our hearts will be enlarged. There must be no standing still. Our love must become a flame which destroys within us all that does not unite us intimately with him.

I must close now. I could go on and on. Love has no limits. I would have to write much more but I do not have the time. The bell is ringing to call me once more to praise God.　　　　　*XXXIX,180f>*

23 April — Giles of Assisi, Friar, 1262

Giles was one of the first followers of Saint Francis. After going on pilgrimages to the shrine of Saint James at Compostela and to the Holy Land, he settled in Monte Ripido near Perugia, dedicating himself to a contemplative life. Many came to him for counsel and remembered the wit and wisdom of his words. He was one of the longest lived of the early companions of Saint Francis, maintaining to the end a commitment to the radical poverty of the early friars.

A reading from 'The Golden Sayings of Brother Giles'.

Brother Giles once said, 'It is a remarkably good habit for someone to be their own conqueror. If you know how to triumph over yourself, you know how to vanquish your enemies and how to win through to a life of perfection.

'It is a towering virtue for someone to let themselves be bossed about by everyone. That kind of person becomes ruler of the world.'

A Religious once complained in the presence of Brother Giles about an annoying command. Holy Brother Giles said to him, 'See here, my friend, the more you gripe, the more you burden yourself, while the deeper you bow your head in reverence and lowliness towards obedience, the sweeter and lighter it will be. You do not want to be ill treated in this world, but you want to be honoured in the next? That proverb rings true: if the cost you now refuse, you cannot have the thing you choose. Do not be astonished if your neighbour sometimes turns on you. Even Martha, holy though she was, tried to set the Lord against her own sister. Martha was indeed wrong in complaining about Mary because, although Mary seemed to have lost the use of speech, sight, hearing, taste and movement, yet she did more work than Martha. Try to be soft-spoken and virtuous. Fight your vices. Bear annoyance and shame patiently. Nothing matters but victory over self. It is a small thing to direct souls to God if you have not first won the war against yourself.'   *XL,62f*

24 April — Fidelis Roy of Sigmaringen, Friar, Martyr, 1622

Before entering the Capuchin Friars at the age of thirty-five, Fidelis practiced law in Alsace, where his labours on behalf of the poor earned him the name 'advocate of the poor'. After serving several terms as Guardian, he was commissioned by the recently established Congregation for the Propagation of the Faith to work for the return of the Swiss Canton of Graubunden to Roman Catholicism. While preaching at Seewis he was dragged from the pulpit and beaten to death.

A reading from 'The Spiritual Exercises of Saint Fidelis of Sigmaringen'.

'O Lord, what have I that I can call my own? What have I that I have not received from you? But if everything has been given to me, how can I glory in anything? One who takes for himself the glory of your goodness is a thief and a robber, like the devil who attempted to steal your glory. What reason have I, dust and ashes, to be proud? Eternal God and Father of the humble, when I am tempted to vainglory, give me humility, the parent of all virtues, so that, enlightened by true self-knowledge, I, a vile worm and mere ashes, may blush with shame and despise myself in the sight of your majesty.

'For your sake alone, I will bear all things and willingly submit myself to everyone. Rather than thinking highly of myself, I will consider myself worthless and abject, and desire that all others hold me in like regard.'

XVI,41

28 April — Luchesio & Buonadonna, Tertiaries, 1260

Luchesio and Buonadonna were a married couple living as merchants in the town of Poggibonzi. After meeting Saint Francis around the year 1213, they decided to devote themselves to a life of penance and works of charity, but without joining celibate Religious communities. Thus they were among the first members of the Third Order established by Francis. They both died on 28 April, 1260.

A reading from 'The Major Legend of Saint Francis', by Saint Bonaventure.

Under the guidance of heavenly grace,
the shepherd Francis led
the little flock of twelve brothers
to Saint Mary of the Portiuncula,
that where the Order of Lesser Brothers had had its beginning
by the merits of the mother of God,
it might also begin to grow with her assistance.
There, also,
having become a herald of the gospel,
he went about the cities and towns
proclaiming the kingdom of God
not in words taught by human wisdom,
but in the power of the Spirit.
To those who saw him,
he seemed to be a person of another age as,
with his mind and face always intent on heaven,
he tried to draw them all on high.
As a result,
the vineyard of Christ began
to produce buds with the sweet smell of the Lord
and, when it had produced
flowers of sweetness, of honour, and of respectability,
to bring forth abundant fruit.

For set on fire by the fervour of his preaching, a great number of people bound themselves by new laws of penance according to the rule which they received from the man of God. Christ's servant decided to name this way of life the Order of the Brothers of Penance. As the road of penance is common to all who are striving towards heaven, so this way of life admits clerics and lay, virgins and married of both sexes. How meritorious it is before God is clear from the numerous miracles performed by some of its members. *II,553*

May

9 May — Catherine of Bologna,
Poor Clare, Artist, 1463

Catherine became a Franciscan tertiary at the age of fourteen and, three years later, joined a group of Religious women at Ferrara in Italy who eventually became a community of Poor Clares. Together, the sisters gained a great reputation for holiness and austerity. Catherine was then appointed abbess at a new monastery founded in Florence. Her creative work included the painting of miniatures and illumination of manuscripts, as well as writing a book on the spiritual life for novices.

A reading from 'The Seven Spiritual Weapons', by Saint Catherine of Bologna.

In the name of the eternal Father and of his only begotten Son Christ Jesus, the splendour of the Father's glory, for love of whom, with jubilation of heart, I cry, saying to his refined servants and spouses:
> Let every lover who loves the Lord
> come to the dance singing of love.
> Let her come dancing all afire,
> desiring only him who created her
> and separated her from the dangerous worldly state.

Whoever from deep within her noble and zealous heart wishes to take up the cross, let her first take up the arms necessary for such battles. First is diligence; second, distrust of self; third, confidence in God; fourth, memory of his passion; fifth, memory of one's own death; sixth, memory of the glory of God; seventh and last, the authority of Holy Scripture as it gives the example of Christ Jesus in the desert.

The seventh weapon is the memory of Holy Scripture which we must carry in our hearts and from which, as from a most devoted mother, we must take counsel in all the things we have to do. With this weapon, our Saviour Christ Jesus conquered and confounded the devil in the desert.

And be on guard that you are not deceived by the mere appearance of good, for the devil sometimes appears in the appearance of Christ or the Virgin Mary or in the shape of an angel or a saint. Therefore, in every apparition that might occur, take up the weapon of Scripture which shows how the mother of Christ comported herself when the angel Gabriel appeared to her. She said to him, 'What is this greeting?' Follow her example in every appearance and feeling, and you will want to test much better whether it is a good or a wicked spirit before you listen to him.

Now, belovèd sisters, I have written these things principally for all my dear novices who are newly entered onto the field of the spiritual battle and for those who must succeed them in the future. God alone can give understanding and strength against his enemies. *XXIII,31f,41f,82*

12 May — Leopold Mandich of Herceg Novi, Friar, 1942

Bogdan John Mandich was born on this day into a noble and rich Bosnian family which, due to the political struggles of the time, found itself impoverished. He joined the Capuchins at sixteen but with the fond hope of returning to Bosnia and working for the unity of the church there. It never happened. Instead, due to his poor health and his tiny stature, he was assigned to work in the confessional in Padua. He remained in Padua until his death on 30 July, 1942.

A reading from the Capuchin Sacramentary.

Leopold transformed the confessional into an experience of human dignity, a personal encounter of compassion, respect and understanding. There every penitent experienced the mercy of God and the kindness of a priest. Leopold once remarked, 'Some say that I am too good. But if you come and kneel before me, is not this sufficient proof that you want to have God's pardon? God's mercy is beyond all expectation.'

When accused of leniency in assigning penances, Leopold would respond, 'If the Lord wants to accuse me of showing too much leniency towards sinners, I will tell him that it was he who gave me this example, and I have not died for the salvation of souls, as he did.'

Leopold would often remark, 'Be at peace; place everything on my shoulders. I will take care of it.' He once explained, 'I give my penitents only small penances because I do the rest myself.' At night times he would spend hours in prayer, explaining, 'I must do penance for my penitents.' *XVII*

15 May — Pachomius, Founder of Christian Community Monasticism, 346

Pachomius was born of pagan parents in Upper Egypt, and as a young man was conscripted into the imperial army. After his discharge he became the disciple of a Christian hermit, and then in about 320 founded a monastery at Tabennisi near the Nile. Gifted with the ability to inspire by the personal charisma of his leadership, and to organise the details of community life, he is honoured as the founder of cenobitic (communal) monasticism.

A reading from 'The Life of Pachomius'.

Pachomius heard of an old hermit called Abba Palamon. He was a great monk who lived a little way from the village. Pachomius left his house and vegetable garden and the palm trees in the charge of an old man, for the poor, and went to visit Palamon. He knocked on the door. The old man looked out through the window and said to him roughly, 'Who is it? Why are you knocking?' 'Father, if you please, I want to be a monk with you.' 'No, you are not able. It is hard to be a monk. Many have come and have left.' 'Try me, Father, and you will know.' 'It is necessary first to try yourself before you can begin. My rule, which I learnt from my fathers, is hard. I eat nothing until sunset all through the summer. In winter I eat only every second or third day. I take bread and salt without oil and without wine. I keep watch until midnight, often all night, to pray and to meditate on the words of God. I also work with my hands weaving palm leaves or reeds and whatever I earn I give to the poor.' Pachomius answered him enthusiastically, 'All that I will do. I have confidence, with the help of God and of your prayers.' Palamon opened the door to him and he went in. After three months he received the habit of the monks.

The two lived together a life of sacrifice and of prayer. Together they worked making bags and mats. They did not work for themselves but for the poor. During the night watch, when they felt that they wanted to sleep they went out to carry baskets of sand from place to place and the effort kept them awake. In all things, Pachomius was obedient and his patience grew, and Palamon was glad.

One day Pachomius went into the desert for a distance of some two kilometres. He came to an abandoned village at the side of the Nile. It was Tabennisi. There he began to pray for a long while. Then he heard a voice which said to him, 'Pachomius, remain here. Build a monastery. Young monks will come to you.' On his return he told Palamon the story. Palamon began to weep because Pachomius, who had been with the old man seven years, was going to leave him. 'I believe, he said, that word comes from God. His will be done.' They returned to Tabennisi together and built a cell for Pachomius.

A month later Palamon fell ill. The brothers sent word to Pachomius. Pachomius went back from Tabennisi to take care of him. He remained there until the Lord came to visit Palamon. Pachomius buried him, then he returned to Tabennisi.   *XXVI,5f,9f>*

16 May — Margaret of Cortona, Penitent, Tertiary, 1297

Margaret was born to a family of farmers in Laviano, Tuscany in 1247. Her mother died when she was a young girl, and she had a very unhappy relationship with her stepmother. After moving away from home she lived with a knight called Arsenio for nine years, with whom she had a son, though they were never married. One day she discovered Arsenio murdered, and was shocked into a life of penance. After moving to Cortona Margaret joined the Franciscan Third Order and lived a life of asceticism and prayer, as well as establishing a hospital and founding a congregation of Tertiary sisters.

A reading from 'The Revelations of Saint Margaret of Cortona'.

About three o'clock in the afternoon, when she was spiritually present at that terrifying moment when Jesus bowed his head and committed his soul to his Father, Margaret's head sank upon her chest, and she seemed really dead. She remained in this condition until vespers, in the presence of the Religious and the weeping crowd of the faithful.

At the hour of vespers she arose, looking radiant and as though she had risen from the dead with Christ! She lifted her eyes joyfully to heaven and thanked God for such a marvellous grace. Then, coming out of her ecstasy, like another Mary Magdalene she still sought for her Saviour, asking those whom she met for him. Going home, she shut her door, and without taking any food she began to weep and cry out:

'O my Love! O sweet Jesus, who has hidden you from my love? My only good, where have you fled? O Jesus, my joy, where shall I seek you? I cannot live without you – do not conceal yourself from me any longer, you who are the delight of my life, you who sweetly refresh my burning heart!'

She continued thus to sigh and weep until Monday, when our Lord appeared to her and talked with her and consoled her: 'Formerly you used to read the account of my Passion out loud, and you would give way to your tears and pain. Now, out of fear of those who criticise and who rashly attribute your suffering and tears to pride, you are forcing yourself to remain completely silent. Take care not to remain silent about my Passion on account of the empty talk of worldly persons.

'Since you desire to please only me, your Creator and Redeemer, why should you not read the narrative of my Passion with those sobs and groans that bring you grace and forgiveness?'

Margaret yielded to this divine warning, and henceforth she wept aloud and in public over Christ's Passion, crying out as she contemplated each of his tortures: 'O my Lord, it was the power of your love that drove you to this!' *XVIII,24f*

17 May — Paschal Baylon, Friar, 1592

Paschal Baylon was a shepherd before joining the Friars Minor in Spain in 1564. He served the community in various positions and wrote several treatises. He had a special devotion to Jesus in the Blessèd Sacrament. In 1897 he was declared 'Patron of all Eucharistic Congresses and Societies of the Blessèd Sacrament'.

A reading from the writings of Paschal Baylon.

Seek God above all things. It is right for you to seek God before and above everything else, because the majesty of God wishes you to receive what you ask for. This will also make you more ready to serve God and will enable you to love him more perfectly.

Let all your prayers be motivated by this intention and when you pray, do so out of love, in season and out of season. Detach your heart from things of this world and consider that there is nothing else in this world except you and God alone. Never, not even for a brief moment, turn your heart from God. Let your thinking be simple and lowly; always, without wearying, focus your attention on what is above you, and let the love of God be like oil poured over everything.

Whenever you receive some gift from the Lord, offer yourself to him entirely with joy and gladness. Humble and despise yourself; renounce your own will so that you can devote yourself body and soul to his service. Make frequent, even countless, acts of thanksgiving, rejoicing in God's power and goodness. He grants you favours and blessings for which you now render him thanks. Rejoice and exult that you have been enriched with graces and blessings. Place little value on the good or advantage to yourself in order to serve God more faithfully. *XIII,102*

18 May — Felix Porri of Cantalice, Friar, 1587

Felix was born in 1515 and joined the Capuchin Friars in 1543. For forty years he exercised the office of questor in Rome, where he was renowned for his wonderful simplicity, innocence and charity. He died there in 1587, and in 1712 became the first Capuchin Friar to be canonised.

A reading from the Capuchin Sacramentary.

Felix normally spoke little outside the friary. Even within the friary, what he had to say was more often than not an exhortation to others to give a good example. His style was frank and direct. He might tell someone, 'I want to correct you.' He often reminded Capuchin preachers, 'Preach in order to convert people, not to make a name for yourselves.' At times he would quote Brother Giles' quip, 'Bo,bo,bo, assai dico e poco fo!' ('Tsk, tsk, tsk, a lot of talk, but no action!'). To Cardinal Julius Santori, the Capuchin Cardinal Protector, Felix once said, 'My lord Cardinal, you were designated to protect us, not to interfere with matters that pertain to the superiors of the Order.' He advised Sixtus V, 'When you become Pope, be Pope for the glory of God and the good of the church. Otherwise, it would be better for you to remain a simple friar.' The same Pope would occasionally encounter Felix questing and would ask for a piece of bread. One day, Felix gave him a piece of stale black bread and remarked to the Franciscan Pope, 'Excuse me, holy Father, but you are still a friar.' *XVII*

20 May — Bernardine of Siena, Friar, 1444

A few years after joining the Observant friars in 1402, Bernardine began a spectacular career as a popular preacher, travelling all over Italy. He is best remembered for his propagation of devotion to the Holy Name of Jesus. He rose to high office in the Observants and many joined because of his reputation. Not long before he died he resigned office so as to return to his favourite task of preaching.

A reading from the sermons of Bernardine of Siena.

The name of Jesus is the crowning glory of preachers. It is due to him that their preaching and its reception are blessed with extraordinary enlightenment. How else in the world could the fervent light of faith be kindled so suddenly if not by the name of Jesus? Is it not by the light of this name that God is said to have called us into his own glorious light? To the enlightened who see light in that light, Saint Paul says: 'You were once all darkness, now you are all light in the Lord; walk then as children of the light'. It is not a name to be hidden, it is to be proclaimed for its light to shine. An unclean heart and a sordid mouth are no fit way to speak this name. The preacher should be a choice vessel, holding and proffering this name.

Paul carried the name of Jesus everywhere, in his preaching, his letters, his miracles, his example. He praised the name of Jesus continuously; its praise was always on his lips.

Therefore, the Church, the spouse of Christ, enlightened by his witness, rejoices in the words of the prophet: 'Lord you have instructed me from my youth and I shall proclaim your wonders for ever'. And we are exhorted: 'Sing to the Lord and bless his name, tell from day to day of his salvation', that is of Jesus our Saviour.   *XIII,71f*

24 May — Dedication of the Basilica of Saint Francis

A reading from the Major Legend of the life of Saint Francis by Saint Bonaventure.

In the year one thousand, two hundred and thirty, when the brothers had assembled to celebrate a general chapter at Assisi, the body of Francis, dedicated to God, was translated on the eighth of the calends of June to the basilica constructed in his honour.

> While that sacred treasure was being carried,
> marked with the seal of the Most High King,
> he whose likeness he bore
> deigned to perform many miracles,
> so that through his saving fragrance
> the faithful in their love
> might be drawn to run after Christ.
> It is truly fitting
> that the blessèd bones of one who,
> through the grace of contemplation,
> was pleasing to God, belovèd by him in life,
> and borne by him into paradise
> like Enoch,
> and of one who,
> through the zeal of love,
> was snatched up into heaven in a fiery chariot
> like Elijah,

that these blessèd bones,
already blossoming among those heavenly flowers
of the garden of an eternal spring,
should flower again
with a wonderful permeating fragrance
from their place of rest.

Just as that blessèd man
had shone in his life with marvellous signs of virtue,
so from the day of his passing until the present,
in different parts of the world,
he shines with outstanding examples of miracles
through the divine power that glorifies him.
Remedies for all sicknesses, necessities and dangers
are conferred
through his merits
on the blind and the deaf,
the mute and the crippled,
the paralytic and the dropsical,
the possessed and the leper,
the shipwrecked and the captive.
But also many dead are miraculously brought back to life
through him.
Thus the magnificence
of the power of the Most High
doing wonders for his saint
shines forth to the faithful.
To him be honour and glory
for endless ages of ages.
Amen.   *II,648*

31 May — Visit of the Blessèd Virgin Mary to Elizabeth

A reading from 'Five Feasts of the Child Jesus', by Saint Bonaventure.

What is happening here? It is nothing other than the heavenly Father impregnating the soul, as it were, and making it fruitful by a divine seed. The power of the Most High comes upon the soul and overshadows it with a heavenly coolness, which tempers the desires of the flesh and gives help and strength to the eyes and to the spirit.

It is a joyous conception which leads to such contempt of the world and to such longing for heavenly works and the things of God. No matter how fleetingly up to this point, even in the midst of distress, the things of the Spirit have been tasted, the things of the flesh lose their savour.

Now, with Mary, the soul begins to climb the hill country because, after this conception, earthly things lose their attraction, and the soul longs for heavenly and eternal things. The soul begins to flee the company of those with minds set on earthly things and desires the friendship of those with hearts set on heavenly things. It begins to take care of Elizabeth, that is, to look to those who are enlightened by divine wisdom and ardently inflamed by love.

The faithful soul should consider well how pure, holy and devout was the conversation of the two saints, how godly and salutary their counsel, how admirable their holiness, and all they achieved to their mutual benefit, as they inspired one another by word and example towards greater virtue.

If you recognize that you have conceived God's most dear Son by a sacred resolve to strive for perfection, then like a woman in labour, hasten with desire and longing towards a happy delivery.   *VIII,140f>*

June

13 June — Antony of Padua, Friar, Teacher of the Faith, 1231

Antony was inspired to move from the Augustinians to the Franciscans by the first Franciscan Martyrs in 1220. He became a vigorous preacher and missioner and because of his theological knowledge began the process of education of the early friars. He died in Padua aged only thirty six.

A reading from 'The Deeds of Blessèd Francis and his Companions'.

Saint Antony of Padua, that admirable vessel of the Holy Spirit, was one of the chosen disciples of blessèd Francis. While he was preaching before the Pope and cardinals in a Council where there were Greeks and Latins, French, Germans, Slavs, English, and many others of diverse tongues and languages, Saint Francis called him his bishop. Filled with the breath of the Holy Spirit, inflamed by the tongue of an apostle, and pouring out the honey-sweet word of God, he held them suspended in great admiration and devotion because all those of such diverse languages gathered at the Council heard him sharply and clearly and understood him distinctly. It seemed that the ancient miracle of the apostles had been renewed as they said in amazement: 'Is he not a Spaniard? How do we all hear him in our own native language, Greeks and Latins, French and Germans, Slavs and English, Lombards and foreigners?'

The Pope, amazed at the profound things set before them from the Holy Scriptures by Saint Antony, said, 'He is truly "the Ark of the Covenant" and "the repository of Holy Scripture." '

Such were the knights that Saint Francis, our leader, had, capable of feeding not only the flock of Christ but even the Vicar of Christ and his venerable college with the rich food of the Holy Spirit, supplying them with heavenly weapons against the snares of the enemy.   *III,519*

24 June — Birth of John the Baptist

A reading from 'The Remembrance of the Desire of a Soul', by Thomas of Celano.

'Francis'
was the name of this servant and friend of the Most High.
Divine Providence gave him this name,
unique and unusual,

that the fame of his ministry should spread even more rapidly
throughout the whole world.
He was named John by his mother
when, being born again through water and the Holy Spirit
he was changed from a child of wrath
into a child of grace.

This woman was a friend of all complete integrity,
with some of the virtue of Saint Elizabeth,
of whom we read in Scripture,
she was privileged to resemble and act,
both in the name she gave her son
and in her prophetic spirit.
For when her neighbours were admiring
Francis' greatness of spirit and integrity of conduct
she asked them,
as if prompted by divine premonition,
'What do you think this son of mine will become?
You will see
that he shall merit to become a son of God!'

The name John,
refers to the mission which he received;
the name Francis
to the spread of his fame which quickly reached everywhere,
once his turning to God was complete.
Thus, he used to keep the feast of John the Baptist
more solemnly than the feasts of all other saints,
because the dignity of this name
marked him with a trace of mystical power.

John prophesied enclosed within the hidden confines
of his mother's womb.
Francis,
still unaware of God's guidance
foretold things to come.   *II,241ff>*

30 June — Ramon Llull, Tertiary, Mystic, 1316

Ramon, a native of Majorca, had a number of claims to fame. He was one of the first great mystics of Iberia, a Christian apologist, a linguist and a founder of language schools for mission. He was also a missionary and a writer of many tracts and books. His long life ended returning from a mission to the Muslims in Tunis at the age of eighty-five.

A reading from 'The Book of the Lover and the Belovèd', by Ramon Llull.

The lover was walking in a foreign land, where he thought he would find his belovèd, when he was attacked on the road by two lions. The lover feared death, for he wanted to live in order to serve his belovèd. He sent his memory to his belovèd, so that love would be with him during his passing, and help him withstand death. While the lover was remembering his belovèd, the lions came up to him humbly and licked the tears from his weeping eyes, and kissed his hands and feet. And the lover continued in peace in search of his belovèd.

The lover wandered over mountains and valleys, but could find no place to escape from the prison in which love held captive his body, his thoughts, and all his desires and joys. While the lover was wandering in this troubled way, he came upon a hermit asleep near a lovely spring. The lover awakened the hermit, and asked him if he had seen his belovèd in his dreams. The hermit answered that his thoughts were held captive in love's prison equally whether he was awake or asleep. The lover was very pleased to have found a fellow-prisoner, and they both wept, for the belovèd had such few lovers. *XV,203f*

July

1 July — Junipero Serra, Friar, 1784

Miguel Jose Serra was born on the island of Mallorca off the coast of Spain in 1713. At the age of sixteen, he left his farming parents and became a friar, taking the name Junipero. Feeling called to the missions of New Spain, he travelled to Mexico, and then on to California, founding many missions in the present day United States of America.

A reading from 'A Book of Exemplary Stories'.

Brother John, a man of great holiness who was the special companion and confessor of Brother Giles until the latter's death, used to recount this story. He heard it from Brother Giles himself, who was the fourth brother to enter the Order. Brother Giles said, 'When there were only seven of us brothers in the Order – no more than that – the blessèd father Francis gathered us together one day at Saint Mary of the Portiuncula in the woods that used to come right up to the place. And there, celebrating the first council meeting or holding the first chapter, as it were, he spoke thus: "I know, my dearest brothers, that the Lord has called us not only for our own salvation. Therefore, I want us to scatter among the nations, going about the world spreading the word of God and giving an example of virtue."

'We humbly responded, "We are lay brothers. What can we do for the salvation of the world?" He answered, "Go forth, secure of the help of God. And you have written on our hearts these two assurances that the Lord himself gave us: 'Cast your care upon the Lord and he will sustain you!' " He said this to remove any hesitancy we might have, since he was sending us without any provision into unknown regions. And he also quoted that saying from the gospel: "Do not worry about what you are to eat or what you are to say. It will not be you that are speaking, but the Spirit of your Father speaking in you." And this he said in answer to those of us who said, "We are illiterate", wanting by these words to comfort and strengthen our hearts to be confident that our God the Most High would make up for our defects, when we act in a spirit of compassion and hope in him.'   *III,799f*

10 July — Veronica Giuliani, Poor Clare, 1727

When Veronica's mother, Benedetta, was dying she called her five daughters to her bedside and entrusted each of them to one of the five wounds of Jesus. Veronica was given the wound in his side, and always maintained a devotion to the Sacred Heart of Jesus. At the age of seventeen, she joined the Capuchin Poor Clares, serving in many roles but particularly as novice mistress and then abbess. When Veronica was thirty-seven, she received the stigmata, the wounds of Jesus, in her own body.

A reading from the Diary of Saint Veronica Giuliani.

For several days now I am experiencing a certain disposition in my heart which I do not understand, so I will merely describe the effects it produces in me. The first is a keen awareness of my faults and a deep sorrow for them, a burning desire for the conversion of souls for whom I would offer my blood and life, a great trust in God's mercy and in the kindness and love of the Blessèd Virgin Mary.

The second effect is this: though I feel myself abandoned and submerged in a sea of temptations, as soon as I experience this hidden sense I seem to be completely at ease, filled with great peace and firmly supported by the will of God.

Then there is a third effect: when I am interiorly disturbed by vexations from the devil and turn myself exteriorly to other things, going to and fro in the performance of my duties, this hidden operation causes me to perform everything without close attention on my part. The result is I find the work completed but I do not know how. This is my experience, especially in important matters as in the reception of the sacraments, in prayer, and in our spiritual colloquies. I feel myself afflicted with such loathing, so spiritless, devoid of feeling that it seems impossible to go on living such a life. And in this condition, going to a confessor seems a waste of time. Nevertheless, I scarcely become aware of this working in my heart when I find myself so changed, strengthened, and encouraged that even in great aridity, adversity, and insensibility every task, however difficult, becomes easy. All for the glory of God! *XIII,122f*

11 July — Benedict of Nursia, Father of Western Monasticism, c.550

Born in Nursia, not far from Assisi, around the year 480, Benedict was sent to Rome to study. Shocked by the corruption in society, he withdrew to live as a hermit at Subiaco. He quickly attracted disciples and established a series of small monasteries in the neighbourhood. In middle age, Benedict moved south with a small group of monks and set up a monastery at Monte Cassino, where he spent the rest of his life. His Rule for Monks shows him to be saturated in the Scriptures, passionately in love with God, extremely understanding of the human frailty of his monks and wise in leading them to achieve their potential as children of God; he was humorous, kindly, just and demanding.

A reading from 'A Rule for Monks' by Saint Benedict.

Just as there is a wicked zeal of bitterness which separates from God and leads to hell, so there is a good zeal which separates from evil and leads to God and eternal life. This, then, is the good zeal which those who follow the monastic way must foster with fervent love: 'They should each try to be the first to show respect to the other' *(Romans 12.10)*, supporting with the greatest patience one another's weaknesses of body or character, and earnestly competing in obedience to one another. None are to pursue what they judge best for themselves, but instead what they judge better for someone else.

Amongst themselves they show the pure love of brothers: to God, loving fear, to their abbot, unfeigned and humble love. Let them prefer nothing whatever to Christ, and may he bring us all together to eternal life. *XXV*

15 July — Bonaventure, Friar, Bishop, Teacher of the Faith, 1274

Bonaventure was called from the post of the friars' Master of Theology at the University of Paris in 1257 to become their Minister General. It was at a crucial period in their history and it is not without some basis that he has been called 'the second Founder of the Order'. Bonaventure's writings are many and as well as the 'Major Legend', the life of Saint Francis, his mystical works are still valued today.

A reading from 'The Soul's Ascent to God', by Saint Bonaventure.

It seems amazing when it has been shown that God is so close to our souls that so few should be aware of the First Principle within themselves. Yet the reason is close at hand: for the human mind, distracted by cares, does not enter into itself through memory; clouded by sense images, it does not turn back to itself through intelligence; allured away by concupiscence, it does not turn back to itself through desire for inner sweetness and spiritual joy. Thus lying totally in these things of sense, it cannot re-enter into itself as into the image of God.

When one has fallen down, he must lie there unless someone lend a helping hand for him to rise. So our soul could not rise completely from these things of sense to see itself and the Eternal Truth in itself unless Truth, assuming human nature in Christ, had become a ladder, restoring the first ladder that had been broken in Adam. Therefore, no matter how enlightened one may be by the light of natural and acquired knowledge, he cannot enter into himself to delight within himself in the Lord unless Christ be his mediator, who says, 'I am the door. If anyone enters through me, he will be saved; and he will go in and out and will find pastures.' But we do not draw near to this door unless we believe in him, hope in him and love him. Therefore, if we wish to enter again into the Truth as into paradise, we must enter through faith in, hope in and love of Jesus Christ, the mediator between God and humanity, who is like the tree of life in the middle of paradise.   *VI,87*

21 July — Lawrence Russo of Brindisi, Friar, 1619

Lawrence entered the Capuchin Friars in 1575 and went on to teach theology to the brothers and was also involved in many works of the Order. He became Vicar General and also ambassador for the Duke of Bavaria and the Pope. He was a renowned preacher and travelled throughout Europe and many of his writings were explanations of the Catholic faith.

A reading from a Homily of Saint Lawrence of Brindisi.

It is well known how difficult it is for the soul to dispel the yearning for worldly honours, status, titles, riches, pleasure and all those other temporal benefits which human nature considers so desirable. The reason this is so is that we fear shame, contempt, affront, poverty and anything else that smites carnal sensibility. Therefore, the world is truly a huge and formidable giant.

Before the arrival of David, Goliath terrified the entire Israelite army. David was only a humble youth of lowly birth, a shepherd unskilled in the art of war, but he was fortified with divine valour. Descending into the arena, he engaged the giant in single combat, vanquished him, brought him to the ground and killed him. In the same way, Francis vanquished and triumphed over the world.

Saint John says that 'all that is in the world is lust of the flesh, lust of the eyes, and the pride of life.' Francis overcame all these vices: the first by chastity and bodily penance; the second by voluntary poverty, desiring neither to have nor possess anything in this world; and the third by constant effort to humble himself and subject himself to every creature. To combat these three vices Francis established his Order, founding it on the three vows: most humble obedience and subjection, highest and most austere poverty and mendicancy, and purest and most shining chastity. His purpose in instituting this very demanding and severe form of life was to subdue the flesh and subjugate the spirit.   *XVI,70*

27 July — Mary Magdalene of Martinengo, Poor Clare, 1737

Mary Magdalene Martinengo was born at Brescia in Northern Italy in 1687. At the age of eighteen, she joined the Poor Clares of Santa Maria della Neve in her home town. She served her community as novice mistress, portress and superior, and was known for her humility and cheerful obedience. Many came to her for encouragement and advice, benefiting from her gifts of spiritual discernment and counsel.

A reading from the treatise 'On Humility', by Blessèd Mary Magdalene Martinengo.

God is essentially holy, holiness itself, and it seems to me that he takes particular delight in it and wishes to be praised more for it than for any other of his attributes. We see this in the highest spirits as they sing without end: holy, holy, holy, and adore God's holiness in profound silence. And as they soar to greater heights of love, they cover their faces and declare that they are at a complete loss to fathom, to love, and to praise God's holiness, although they never cease to proclaim it.

The humble soul partaking of God's holiness acts in like manner. First it fixes its gaze on the sacred humanity of Jesus Christ, the God-man, in which it beholds the sum of the most eminent holiness. It then impresses this image on its mind and determines to imitate it. And as it carries out this determination, it conforms itself to Jesus Christ. With this divine model before its gaze and written in its heart, the humble soul gradually becomes holy, and day after day contemplates new holiness with a clearer and sharper focus and with greater determination to imitate it. Then abandoning self and putting aside image and impression, the humble soul makes its way to God unencumbered, and he embraces it and makes it holy with his own holiness.

God himself wants us to acquire a high degree of holiness. He made his desire known in saying, 'You shall be holy because I am holy'; and before his passion Jesus raised his eyes and hands to his Father and prayed, 'Holy Father, sanctify them in truth.' Rise up, then, my soul and be immersed in this sea of holiness and never leave it so that you may be made holy by God's own holiness.   *XIII,172f*

August

If 2 August is being kept as the Feast of Dedication, the reading is on page 139. Otherwise, either of the following readings may be used.

2 August — Mary of the Angels

A reading from 'A Mirror of the Perfection of a Lesser Brother'.

Although blessèd Francis knew the kingdom of heaven
was established in every corner of the earth,
and believed that divine grace could be given
to God's chosen ones in every place,
he nevertheless knew from his own experience
that the place of Saint Mary of the Portiuncula
was especially full of grace
and was filled with visits of heavenly spirits.
So he often told the brothers:
'See to it, my sons, that you never abandon this place.
If you are thrown out of one door,
go back through another,
for this is truly a holy place,
and the dwelling place of Christ and his Virgin Mother.
Here
the Most High increased our numbers,
when we were only a few;
here
he enlightened the souls of his poor ones
with the light of his wisdom;

here
he kindled our wills with the fire of his love;
here
all who pray wholeheartedly will receive what they ask
while offenders will be severely punished.
Therefore, my sons, hold this place,
truly the dwelling place of God,
with all reverence
and as most worthy of all honour,
particularly dear to him and to his Mother.
In this place
in cries of joy and praise
with your whole heart
here praise God the Father
and his Son, the Lord Jesus Christ,
in the unity of the Holy Spirit.   *III,329ff*

2 August — Portiuncula Indulgence

*This famous plenary indulgence is offered to all repentant pilgrims who go to
the little chapel of Saint Mary of the Angels on 2 August. No evidence of it
being granted appears in any early source or any Papal document before the
latter half of the thirteenth century. As more pilgrims streamed to the chapel
the brothers began to collect evidence for the Indulgence, which has been val-
idated and expanded by the Papacy, the latest pronouncement being in 1921.*

**A reading of the Evidence for the Portiuncula Indulgence, given by Lord
James Coppoli in 1277.**

Lord James Coppoli of Perugia told me, Brother Angelo, Minister of the
brothers, in the presence of other brothers, that he once asked brother
Leo, the companion of Saint Francis, whether the indulgence, which is
attached to the Portiuncula, was true or not. He answered in the affir-
mative, and then related what the blessèd Francis had himself told him:
namely, that he had petitioned the Pope to attach an indulgence to the
Church of the Portiuncula on the anniversary of its consecration. And
the Pope asked for how long he wanted this remission to be. For one
year? For three years? At length they had got as far as seven years, but
still Francis was not satisfied. Then the Pope said to him, 'Well, for how
long then?' And Francis replied, 'Holy Father, if it please your Holiness,
my wish is that, because of the great benefits which God has distributed

there and will yet distribute, all those who come there truly contrite and having confessed their sins may receive the remission of all their sins, so that no further punishment is attached to them.' The Pope replied, 'I grant it; let it be so.'

When the cardinals became aware of this, they told the Pope that he should revoke it, because it would be to the prejudice of the Holy Land Indulgence. But the Pope said, 'I certainly shall not revoke it now that I have promised it.' They replied, 'Put as much limit on it as you can.' And then the Pope said it was valid for only the length of one natural day each year.

When blessèd Francis left the Pope he heard a voice saying to him, 'Francis, know that, just as this indulgence has been given on earth, so has it been ratified in heaven.' Then Saint Francis said to brother Leo, 'Keep this secret to yourself and do not divulge it until the time of your death is near, because this is not yet the time for it. This indulgence will be hidden for a time, but the Lord will bring it to light and it will be made manifest.'   *III,809*

4 August — Jean-Baptiste Vianney, Curé d'Ars, Spiritual Guide, Tertiary, 1859

Jean-Baptiste Marie Vianney was born in Dardilly near Lyons in 1786 of parents who were farmers and devout Catholics. He spent much of his childhood working as a shepherd and had little formal education. After being drafted into and deserting from Napoleon's army, he began studying for the priesthood and was ordained in 1815 despite his poor academic record. He spent most of his life as the parish priest of the remote village of Ars-en-Dombes. From there his reputation for asceticism, spiritual counsel and the miraculous effects of his intercession spread throughout France and brought a constant stream of penitents to his door. He has now been named patron of all diocesan priests.

A reading from the catechetical instructions of Jean-Baptiste Vianney.

My children, reflect that a Christian's treasure is not on earth but in heaven. Therefore our thoughts should turn to where our treasure is. Ours is a noble task: that of prayer and love. To pray and to love, that constitutes the greatest possible happiness for us in this life.

Prayer is nothing less than union with God. When the heart is pure and united with God it is consoled and filled with sweetness; it is transfigured by a wonderful light. In this intimate union with God it is as if two pieces of wax were moulded together; they can no longer be separated. This union of God with us, insignificant creatures that we are, is a truly wonderful thing, a happiness beyond our comprehension.

We had deserved to be left abandoned, unable to pray; but in his goodness, God has permitted us to speak with him. Our prayer is an incense that is delightful to God.

My children, I know your hearts are small, but prayer will enlarge them and make them capable of loving God. Prayer is a foretaste of heaven, an overflowing of heaven. It never leaves us without sweetness; it is like honey, running down into the soul and sweetening everything with which it comes into contact. When we pray truly, difficulties melt like snow in the sunshine.

Prayer makes time pass quickly, and is so pleasant that one loses all sense of time. When I was a parish priest of Bresse, it happened once that virtually all my colleagues were ill, and as a result I had to make long journeys during which I used to pray to God; and I can assure you, the time did not seem long to me. Indeed, there are those who completely lose themselves in prayer, like fish in water, because they are absorbed in God. There is no division in their hearts. How I love such noble souls!

As for ourselves, how often do we come casually into church without the slightest idea of why we have come or what we need to ask God for. And yet when we call on a neighbour we suddenly have no difficulty in remembering why we have called. It was as if we are saying to God, 'Sorry, I can only spare a couple of words now because I need to get on.' And yet, it is my belief that, if we were to speak to God out of a living faith and a pure heart, we should receive all we ask.   *XXXVI,263f*

6 August — Transfiguration of Our Lord

A reading from 'The Tree of Life', by Saint Bonaventure.

To strengthen the human spirit with hope of eternal reward, Jesus took Peter, James and John up a high mountain by themselves. He revealed to them the mystery of the Trinity and foretold that he would be rejected in his passion. He showed the glory of his future resurrection in his transfiguration. The Law and the Prophets gave testimony to him in the apparition of Moses and Elijah, The Father and the Holy Spirit in the voice and the cloud.

So the soul devoted to Christ
strengthened in truth and borne to the summit of virtue,
can faithfully say with Peter:

Lord it is good for us to be here,
in the serene joy of contemplating you.
When heavenly repose and ecstasy are given to the soul,
it will hear the secret words
which no mortal is permitted to speak.   *VI,135*

8 August — Dominic, Friar,
Founder of the Order of Preachers, 1221

For some years, Dominic led an uneventful life as the prior of a group of Augustinian Canons. Then he began to train both men and women in communities which, by their poverty, prayer and preaching, would be a witness against the heteradox Albigensians, otherwise known as the Cathars. This new movement of Dominics became the foundation of the Friar preachers. A good organizer, his Order was soon approved by the Papacy and it grew rapidly and became a tool in the struggle for orthodoxy. He met Francis and, although their spiritual charisms differed, they greatly respected each other. From the beginning, the Order of Preachers was based on learning and sound teaching, which has defined the Dominicans through the centuries.

A reading from 'The Assisi Compilation'.

The Lord of Ostia, who was later to become the Supreme Pontiff, was greatly edified by the words of Francis and Dominic and gave unbounded thanks to God. And as they left that place, blessèd Dominic asked Saint Francis to be kind enough to give him the cord he had tied around him. Francis was slow to do this, refusing out of humility what the other was requesting out of charity. At last the happy devotion of the petitioner won out, and he devoutly put on the gift under his inner tunic. Finally they clasped hands and commended themselves to each other with great sweetness. And so one saint said to the other, 'Brother Francis, I wish your Order and mine might become one, so we could share the same form of life in the Church.'

At last when they had parted from each other, Saint Dominic said to many bystanders, 'In truth I tell you, the other Religious should follow this holy man Francis, as his holiness is so perfect.'   *II,148f*

Readings for the Feast of Saint Clare

The next seven days of readings form a whole, covering the period prior to and after the death of Saint Clare.

8 August

A reading from 'The Legend of Saint Clare'.

It is not surprising that the rigour of her life, observed for a long period of time, subjected Clare to sicknesses, consumed her strength, and enervated the vigour of her body. Therefore the very devoted children of the holy mother suffered with her and lamented with their tears those 'deaths' which she willingly endured each day. Finally, blessèd Francis and the Bishop of Assisi prohibited the holy Clare to continue that deadly fast of three days, directing her to let no day pass without taking at least an ounce and a half of bread.

While serious affliction of the body
usually generates that of the spirit,
it shone far differently
in Clare.
For she maintained
a festive and joyful appearance
in every one of her mortifications
so that
she either seemed not to feel
her corporal afflictions
or
to laugh at them.

From this
it is clearly given
to our understanding
that
the holy joy
with which she was flooded within
overflowed without
because the love of the heart
lightens
the scourges of the body.   *V,272*

9 August

A reading from 'The Versified Legend of Saint Clare'.

For forty years this virgin ran in the stadium of poverty
   seeking to reach the prize of life, in the hope of which,
   taking a rough path, she freely submits to many trials.
When she was close to death because of her ailment's severity,
   Christ resolved to defer her passing,
   so that his Roman Protector could solemnly conduct her funeral
   and add fitting honours to those rites.
While the Supreme Pontiff was pausing in Lyons,
   the mother was greatly weakened by her serious illness
   and her children's hearts were afflicted with bitter sorrows.
And behold, a short while after her decline, the whole Curia arrived in
Perugia.
   After he learned that she was seriously ill,
   that Bishop to whom the title of the venerable see of Ostia was given
   hastened to see the ailing woman.
By his office and his holy sensitivity, this man had been a father,
   a zealous disciple, and a dear friend to her.
   He gives her the bread of Christ's life giving body
   and strengthens her remaining daughters with his sweet word.
With her tears, the resolute virgin entrusts to him her sisters
   and the other company of her sisters, and asked, above all,
   that a document of the Apostolic See would confirm
   for them the title to a life in poverty.
He promises and fulfils the request that Clare begs.   *V,221f>*

10 August

A reading from 'The Versified Legend of Saint Clare'.

When Clare asked that all her sins be forgiven by him,
   the Pope replied, 'Would that I needed such forgiveness.'
   After he had absolved her, the most high father blessed her.
When everyone had left, because the virgin had received
   the sacred food of Christ from the Minister's hands,
   with her eyes lifted up and her hands folded towards the Lord,
   the crying mother spoke to her disciples:
'My little children, praise God, whose kindness

granted me these gifts in his goodness.'
The daughters of the dying mother surrounded her bed.
  Their eyes shed tears, the recesses of their hearts
  bring forth sighs, and a bitter calamity afflicts their hearts.
The mournful departure itself brings them to tears.
  Neither hunger itself nor lack of sleep relieves their sorrow.
  Not night's rest, not the delight of a daily repast,
  their tears are their drink, and grief their food.
Mourning brings down the night
and day follows with an intensity of sorrow.   *V, 224*

11 August

A reading from 'The Versified Legend of Saint Clare'.

Who could narrate these things without crying
  or who could suppress tears from welling up, when a sad event
  causes sorrow and tears and nothing else to flow?
Death brings tears, but life's continuance brings joy.
The most holy virgin silently turns to herself and says to her soul:
  'Proceed, go forth safely. Your fortunate Guide is at hand.
  Your very Creator, who brought you forth from nothing,
  made you holy, and holds you as your Guardian,
  and loves you always as a mother loves her children.'
When one of the sisters asked to whom she was speaking,
  she says, 'I am saying this to my blessèd soul.'
  The heavenly company was not far from her.
Turning to a certain sister, the mother says, 'Do you see,
  the King of heaven whom I see?'
  The hand of the Most High falls upon her.
Then she has a vision, turns her eyes to the door
  and sees a band of virgins dressed in white
  carrying golden garlands on the crown of their heads.
One more brilliant than the others walks among them,
  carrying a brilliant diadem.
Proceeding to the bed upon which the spouse lay,
  the more brilliant one bent over her
  and gave her a sweet embrace.
Then the virgins offer a shimmering cloak
  which covers Clare's body,

and with everyone eagerly assisting
the bridal chamber is prepared for her.
And Death becomes the entrance to life and the gate of heaven.
V,226>

12 August

A reading from 'The Versified Legend of Saint Clare'.

News of the virgin's passing immediately moved all citizens,
so many came there at the same time and the gathering
became so great that the land seemed deserted.
The people proclaim her blessèd, revere her as a saint,
and their tears are mixed among their praises.
The following morning the Bishop of the Roman See
hastened to Clare's funeral with an entourage of friars.
The citizens joined them. When the time had come
for the funeral rites which were carried out as usual,
the friars began the mother's tearful funeral.
The Pope declared that it would be better to sing
the Office of the Virgins. But that outstanding Bishop
of the renowned see of Ostia, replied that a matter of such importance
would be better treated more maturely,
[for she had not yet been declared a saint].
Thus the Solemn Mass was followed.
Because they did not consider that so holy, so noble and so precious
a pledge would be safe or deserving so far from the citizens,
Clare's splendid body was carried amid the hymns, praises,
the jubilation of the crowd, and the blast of the trumpets
to the church named for Saint George.
It was there that the sacred remains of Francis were at first placed,
so that the father who was a leader of the living and a way to life
might prepare the very place and tomb for the deceased.   *V,228f>*

13 August

A reading from 'The Bull of Canonization of Saint Clare'.

Alexander, Bishop, servant of the servants of God, to all our venerable
brothers, the archbishops and bishops established throughout the kingdom of France: health and apostolic blessing.

Clare,
shines brilliantly:
brilliant by her bright merits,
by the brilliance of her great glory in heaven,
and by the brilliance of her sublime miracles on earth.

Clare,
her strict and lofty way of Religious life radiates here on earth,
while the magnitude of her eternal rewards glows from above
and her virtue dawns upon all mortal beings with magnificent signs.

Clare,
endowed here below with the privilege of the highest poverty,
repaid on high by priceless abundance of treasure
and shown full devotion and great honour by all.

O Clare,
endowed with so many brilliant titles!
Bright even before your conversion,
brighter in your manner of living,
brighter still in your enclosed way of life,
and brightest in splendour after the course of your mortal life!

In this Clare
a clear mirror of example has been given to this world;
by this Clare
the sweet lily of virginity is offered among the heavenly delights;
through this Clare
remarkable remedies are felt here on earth.

She gave light in life;
she is radiant in death.

She was brilliant on earth,
she is resplendent in heaven!   *V,238>*

14 August

A reading from 'The Bull of Canonization of Saint Clare'.

Therefore, because it is fitting that the universal Church venerate Clare
on earth whom the Lord exalted in heaven; because her sanctity of life
and miracles are very evident from a thorough and careful investigation,

a distinct examination and a solemn discussion – even though, both near and far, her deeds were known widely before this.

By the common advice and assent of our brothers and all the prelates who were then at the Holy See, and relying firmly upon the divine omnipotence, We, by the authority of the blessèd Apostles, Peter and Paul, and our own, have directed she be inscribed in the catalogue of the holy Virgins.

Therefore, We admonish and earnestly exhort all of you, commanding through the apostolic letters addressed to you, that you devoutly and solemnly celebrate the feast of this same virgin on the twelfth of August and that you have it venerably celebrated by your subjects, so you may merit to have a pious and diligent helper before God.

And that a multitude of people may come together more eagerly and in greater numbers to venerate her tomb, and that her feast day may be honoured with greater numbers, We, relying on the mercy of the All-Powerful God and on the authority of his apostles Peter and Paul, grant an indulgence of one year and forty days from the punishment due to their sins to all who are truly contrite and have confessed their sins, and humbly seeking her aid go each year with reverence to the tomb on the feast of this same virgin or during its octave.

Given at Anagni, the twenty sixth day of September, 1255, in the first year of our pontificate.   *V,245>*

14 August — Maximilian Kolbe, Friar, Martyr, 1941

Born of devout parents, Maximilian Mary Kolbe joined the Conventual Friars and, after studying in Rome and ordination, he taught in a seminary. He founded a magazine for the propagation of the Christian faith, which grew rapidly. After a period in Japan he was recalled to be the Guardian of a large community in Niepokalanow in Poland. At the outbreak of war he dispersed the friars and turned the friary into a refugee camp for Poles and Jews. Publishing work continued and it was for this that he was arrested and interned in Auschwitz. He volunteered to take the place of a prisoner who had been randomly picked to die, knowing that it would mean his own death. He supported the others in the group in their dying and was himself put to death on this day in 1941.

A reading from the letters of Saint Maximilian Kolbe.

Dear brother, see the greatness of human dignity conferred by God's mercy. By obedience we surmount, so to speak, the limits imposed on us by our own weakness; we are made conformable to God's will which in his infinite wisdom and prudence guides us to act correctly. As a matter of fact by clinging to God's will – and no creature can resist it – we surpass everything in power.

This is the way of wisdom and prudence, this is the only way we can render the greatest glory to God. If there were another and more suitable way Christ surely would have shown it to us by his own words and example. But sacred scripture described his long sojourn in Nazareth in these words: 'He was subject to them', and painted the picture of the rest of his life for us in the colours of obedience, thus showing that he had come to earth to do the will of his Father.

Therefore, let us love our most loving Father in heaven with the greatest love and let our obedience be the proof of our perfect love which we put into practice especially when we are asked to give up our own will. There is no more authoritative book to teach us to grow in God's love than the book of Jesus crucified. *XIII,267f*

15 August — Blessèd Virgin Mary

A reading from 'The Major Legend of Saint Francis', by Saint Bonaventure.

Francis embraced the mother of the Lord Jesus
with an inexpressible love
since she made the Lord of Majesty a brother to us
and, through her,
we have obtained mercy.

In her, after Christ, he put all his trust and made her the advocate of him and his brothers and, in her honour, he used to fast with great devotion from the Feast of the Apostles Peter and Paul to the Feast of the Assumption.

He was joined in a bond of inseparable love
to the angels
who burn with a marvellous fire
to pass over into God
and to inflame the souls of the elect.

Out of devotion he used to spend the forty days after the Feast of the Assumption of the glorious Virgin in fasting and continual prayer.

II,598

25 August — Louis Capet, Christian Monarch, Patron of the Third Order, 1270

Louis IX's long reign as King of France was noted for its cultural achievements and almsgiving and the care of the sick and the poor were promoted. Friars were guests at his table. Unfortunately his crusading expeditions were not successful and he died of typhus during the crusade of 1270.

A reading from the 'Deeds of Blessèd Francis and his Companions'.

Saint Louis, King of France, decided to make a pilgrimage to shrines for seven years. He had heard the truthful rumours of Brother Giles' amazing holiness, and in his heart decided by all means to visit him. Therefore, on his pilgrimage he turned towards Perugia where he heard Brother Giles was staying. Arriving like a poor, unknown pilgrim, at the brothers' door, escorted by a few companions, he urgently asked for Brother Giles, without revealing his identity. Brother Giles was told that a pilgrim was asking for him. In spirit Brother Giles immediately knew that this was the King of France. As if intoxicated he left his cell and ran quickly to the door. There they both rushed together in amazing embraces and fell to their knees in devout kisses, as if they had known each other before and were the oldest of friends. After showing these signs of charitable love, neither said a word to each other, and observing complete silence they departed from each other.

The other brothers were grieved that they had not spoken and Giles said to them, 'Dearest brothers, do not be surprised if we did not say anything to each other, because as soon as we embraced, the light of divine wisdom revealed his heart to me, and my heart to him. If we had wished to describe by using the sounds of the voice things which we felt inside, that very speaking would have caused desolation rather than consolation to both of us. Therefore you should know that the king departed wonderfully consoled.' *III,517*

September

7 September — Douglas Downes, Friar, Co-Founder of the Society of Saint Francis, 1957

Brother Douglas SSF was an Anglican priest who developed a profound concern for the poor during his ministries in London, India and as a chaplain in the First World War. In 1922, he was led to re-found a young Franciscan community in Dorset, England and, as a friar, became an inspiring witness in his commitment to wayfarers and other disadvantaged groups. This work, combined with his humility and holiness, made a major contribution to the charism of the Society of Saint of Francis.

A reading from a sermon preached before the University of Cambridge on 25 October 1942, by Brother Douglas SSF.

'When I sent you forth without purse, and scrip, and shoes, lacked ye anything?' They said, 'Nothing.' *(Lk 22.35)*

It must have been a tremendous help and encouragement to the faith of the Apostles that they were able to answer in this way. They had gone out on the roads of Palestine lacking practically everything that that an Eastern traveller would naturally require, and they found in a wonderful way God had supplied all their needs; so that they were able to declare triumphantly that they had lacked nothing. Saint Luke tells us how the seventy returned with joy saying, 'Lord even the devils are subject to us through your name.'

In the same way Saint Francis and his first followers tramped the roads of Italy in utter dependence on God; and we know how wonderfully the power of God was released through their lives. It is part of the Rule of our Brotherhood of Saint Francis that we should go from time to time 'on the roads' and share our lives with the tramps in the casual wards and common lodging houses.

I do not wish to exaggerate, but I feel that I can truly say that holy poverty has been the gateway into a fellowship of a kind that could not have been discovered in any other way. Far outweighing all the discomforts, all the disagreeableness and disappointments we have sometimes had to bear, has been the joy of wonderful fellowship and friendship with many of the poor. We have found that poverty has overcome the barriers due to difference of birth, education and manner of life in a way that we would never have deemed possible.

Some of our wisest thinkers are wondering today how democracy will work in the post-war world – unless a new spirit of unselfishness is born in every individual and every class, unless in our economic life the motive of private profit is somehow transformed into the motive of public service....and we ask is there any hope of eradicating the selfishness ingrained in the very structure of our social order? Can we exorcise this acquisitive instinct that is so rampant, and awaken that higher instinct of joy in loving service which we might have seen predominant if only Christ had been accepted as the Lord of our life?

It may be that the fate of our civilisation will depend on whether there are enough Christian leaders among the younger generation who will give up at least part of their life to win people for Our Lord in this way.

XXX,62f

8 September — Birth of the Blessèd Virgin Mary

A reading from 'The Book of the Gentile and the three Wise Men', by Ramon Llull.

The Christian said, 'The Son of God was born with human nature, so that in human nature there would be born greater virtue of justice and humility.'

The Gentile asked, 'Tell me, this woman you mention who gave birth to the Son of God, of what King was she a daughter? Or what sort of nobility can a woman have so that God would want to take on human nature in her and be born from her?'

The Christian replied, 'It is true that our Lady was of the house of David, who was a noble and most honourable king, yet the father of our Lady Saint Mary was not a king nor was her mother a queen; they were instead humble folk. And our Lady was a woman poor in earthly possessions, but in virtues she was richer and nobler than any other creature, with the exception of her Son. In fact, this woman was so poor that when she gave birth to the Saviour of the world, she had no house in which to do so, and she gave birth in a stable. All this was to show the great humility of the Son of God. For if the Son of God had wanted to be born of a queen, as ruler of all kingdoms of the world, he could easily have done so; but it would not have shown humility against pride and justice against injustice.'

XV,136f

10 September — Agnellus of Pisa,
& the Coming of the Friars to Canterbury, 1224

A reading from 'The Chronicle of Thomas of Ecclestone'.

In the year of our Lord 1224, in the time of the Lord Pope Honorius, in the same year, as that in which he confirmed the Rule of the blessèd Francis, the Friars Minor first arrived in England, at Dover, being four clerks and five laymen.

The clerks were these: first, Brother Agnellus of Pisa, in orders a deacon, in age about thirty, who at the last General Chapter had been designated by blessèd Francis as Minister Provincial for England; he had been Custodian at Paris, and had borne himself there so discreetly as to win the highest favour among the brethren and layfolk alike by reason of his renowned holiness.

The second was Brother Richard of Ingworth, an Englishman by birth, a priest and preacher, and more elderly; he was the first member of the Order who preached publicly north of the Alps. The third was Brother Richard of Devon, also an Englishman by birth, in orders an acolyte, in age a youth; he left us many examples of long-suffering and obedience. The fourth was Brother William of Ashby, still a novice, wearing the hood of a probationer, like these others English by birth, youthful in age, and in his standing.

Now the laymen were these: first, Brother Henry of Treviso, then Brother Lawrence of Beauvais, Brother William of Florence, Brother Melioratus, and Brother James.

These nine were conveyed across to England in loving wise by the monks of Fecamp, and by them courteously sustained in their need. When they reached Canterbury, they abode for two days at the Priory of the Holy Trinity. Thence without delay four of them went on to London. The other five betook themselves to a priests' hostel, where they remained until they had found a place for themselves. For, shortly after, a small room under a schoolhouse was granted them, where by day they sat uninterruptedly as though shut in. But when the scholars had returned home at evening, they came into the schoolhouse in which they had sat and there made them a fire and sat beside it. And sometimes they set on the fire a little pot containing dregs of beer, when it was time to drink at the evening collation, and they put a saucer in the pot and drank in turn, and one by one they spoke some word of edification. And one who was their associate in this unfeigned simplicity and holy poverty, and merited to be a partaker thereof, bore witness that their drink was sometimes so thick that, when the saucers had to be heated, they poured water upon it, and thus drank it with joy. *XIV,6ff >*

14 September — Holy Cross Day

A reading from 'The Considerations on the Holy Stigmata'.

The day before the Feast of the Cross in September, while Saint Francis was praying secretly in his cell, an angel appeared to him and said on God's behalf, 'I encourage you and urge you to prepare and dispose yourself humbly to receive with all patience what God wills to do in you.'

Saint Francis answered, 'I am prepared to endure patiently whatever my Lord wants to do to me.'

And after he said this, the angel departed.

The next day came, that is, the Feast of the Cross. And Saint Francis, sometime before dawn, began to pray outside the entrance of his cell, turning his face towards the east. And he prayed in this way, 'My Lord Jesus Christ, I pray you to grant me two graces before I die; the first is that during my life I may feel in my soul and in my body, as much as possible, that pain which you, dear Jesus, sustained in the hour of your most bitter Passion. The second is that I may feel in my heart, as much as possible, that excessive love with which you, O Son of God, were inflamed in willingly enduring such suffering for us sinners.'

And remaining for a long time in that prayer, he understood that God would grant it to him, and that it would soon be conceded to him to feel those things as much as is possible for a mere creature. *IV,1448*

15 September — Mary at the Cross

A reading from 'The Deeds of Blessèd Francis and his Companions'.

Brother Pietro and Brother Conrad bound each other to an agreement that whatever consolation the mercy of God should grant to one of them should be revealed to the other in the charity of God.

After agreeing to this pact, one day Brother Pietro was devoutly meditating on the passion of Christ, and how his most blessèd Mother and John, his most belovèd disciple, remained co-crucified with him, and how our blessèd father Francis stood crucified before the Crucified. And he had a devout curiosity to know which of them grieved more: the Mother who gave birth to him; the belovèd disciple, who slept on his breast; or the most devoted Francis, who was crucified with the Crucified.

While he remained in this holy and devout meditation with many tears, suddenly the Blessèd Virgin Mary, Mother of God, appeared to him, and Blessèd John the Evangelist and our Blessèd Father Francis, dressed in the brilliant robes of blessèd glory. As they stood before Brother Pietro who was shaking with fear, Blessèd John comforted him, saying, 'Do not fear, dearest brother in the Lord, because we have come to console you and to solve your doubt. You should know that, even though his Mother and I grieved more than anyone over the Passion of Christ, after us Blessèd Francis grieved more than everyone, and for this reason you see him in such glory.' *III,555*

Readings for the Stigmata of Saint Francis

The following three readings form a whole, covering the events of the Stigmata.

16 September

A reading from 'The Major Legend of Saint Francis', by Saint Bonaventure.

It was the custom for the angelic man Francis
never to rest from the good,
rather, like the heavenly spirits on Jacob's ladder,
he either ascended into God
or descended to his neighbour.
For he had so prudently learned
to divide the time given to him for merit,
that he spent some of it working for his neighbour's benefit
and dedicated the rest
to the tranquil excesses of contemplation.
Therefore,
when he emptied himself
according to the demands of time and places
to gain the salvation of another,
leaving the restlessness of the crowds,
he would seek the secrets of solitude and a place of quiet,
where freeing himself more freely for the Lord,
he would shake off the dust that might have clung to him
from the time spent with the crowds.

Therefore,
two years before he returned his spirit to heaven,
after a variety of many labours,
he was led by the divine providence
to a high place apart called Mount La Verna.
When according to his usual custom
he had begun to fast there for forty days
in honour of Saint Michael the Archangel,
he experienced more abundantly than usual
an overflow of the sweetness of heavenly contemplation,
was on fire with an ever intense flame of heavenly desires,
and began to be aware more fully of the gifts of heavenly grace.
He was carried into the heights,

not as a curious searcher of the supreme majesty
crushed by its glory,
but as a faithful and prudent servant,
exploring God's good pleasure,
to which, with the greatest ardour, he desires
to conform himself in every way.   *II,630*

17 September

A reading from 'The Major Legend of Saint Francis', by Saint Bonaventure.

On a certain morning about the feast of the Exaltation of the Cross, while Francis was praying on the mountainside, he saw a Seraph having six wings, fiery as well as brilliant, descend from the grandeur of heaven. And when in swift flight, it had arrived at a spot in the air near the man of God, there appeared between the wings the likeness of a man crucified, with his hands and feet extended in the form of a cross and fastened to a cross.

He marvelled exceedingly
at the sight of so unfathomable a vision,
knowing that the weakness of Christ's passion
was in no way compatible
with the immortality of the seraphic spirit.
Eventually he understood from this,
through the Lord revealing it,
that Divine Providence had shown him a vision of this sort so that
the friend of Christ might learn in advance
that he was to be totally transformed
into the likeness of Christ crucified,
not by the martyrdom of his flesh,
but by the enkindling of his soul.
As the vision was disappearing,
it left in his heart a marvellous fire
and imprinted in his flesh a likeness of signs
no less marvellous.

For immediately the marks of nails began to appear in his hands and feet just as he had seen a little before in the figure of the man crucified. His hands and feet seemed to be pierced through the centre by nails, with the heads of the nails appearing on the inner side of the hands and the upper side of the feet and their points on the opposite sides. The heads of the nails in his hands and his feet were round and black; their points were oblong and bent as if driven back with a hammer, and they emerged from the flesh and stuck out beyond it. Also his right side, as if pierced with a lance, was marked with a red wound from which his sacred blood often flowed, moistening his tunic and underwear.   *II,632f*

18 September

A reading from 'The Major Legend of Saint Francis', by Saint Bonaventure.

As Christ's servant realized that he could not conceal from his intimate companions the stigmata that had been so visibly imprinted on his flesh, he feared to make public the Lord's sacrament and was thrown into an agony of doubt whether to tell what he had seen or be silent about it. He called some of the brothers and, speaking in general terms, presented his doubt to them and sought their advice. One of the brothers, Illuminato, by name and by grace, understanding that Francis had seen something marvellous that made him seem completely dazed, said to the holy man, 'Brother, you should realize that at times divine sacraments are revealed to you not for yourself alone but also for others. You have every reason to fear that if you hide what you have received for the profit of many, you will be blamed for burying that talent.' Although the holy man used to say on occasions: 'My secret is for myself', he was moved by Illuminato's words. Then, with much fear, he recounted the vision in detail, adding that the one who had appeared to him had told him some things which he would never disclose to any person as long as he lived. We should believe, then, that those utterances of that sacred Seraph marvellously appearing to him on the cross were so secret that people are not permitted to speak of them.

After true love of Christ
transformed the lover into his image,
when the forty days were over that he spent in solitude
as he had desired,
and the feast of Saint Michael the Archangel
had also arrived,
the angelic man Francis
came down from the mountain,
bearing with him

the likeness of the Crucified,
depicted not on tablets of stone or on panels of wood
carved by hand,
but engraved on parts of his flesh
by the finger of the living God.
And because it is good to keep hidden
the sacrament of the King,
the man aware of the royal secret
would then hide from mortals those sacred signs.
Since it is for God to reveal what he does for his own great glory,
the Lord himself,
who had secretly imprinted those marks,
openly revealed some miracles through them
so that the hidden and marvellous power of the stigmata
would display a brilliance of signs.   *II,633f*

18 September — Joseph of Cupertino, Friar, 1663

After a short time with the Capuchins, Joseph became a Conventual friar and was ordained in 1628. He was known for his humility, patience and obedience, and his commitment to a life of prayer. The renown of his spiritual gifts, and the frequent occurrence of levitation during prayer made him the focus of much attention. He was investigated by the Inquisition, but exonerated.

A reading from the thoughts and sayings of Saint Joseph of Cupertino.

The three most important things for a Religious are: to love God with all one's heart, to praise him continually, to be a light to others by one's good example. No one intent on living a spiritual or Religious life can ever reach perfection without the love of God. Those who have love are rich even though they may be unaware of their riches, and those who do not have love are indeed very unfortunate. As the sun by its rays adorns the leaves and branches of plants with colours and keeps each vigorous in its proper species, so the grace of God by its illumination adorns us with virtues, enkindles in us the fire of love, makes us beautiful in God's sight and brings our nature to perfection without inflicting any injury.

Clearly, what God wants above all is our will which we received as a free gift from God in creation and possess as though our own. When we train ourselves to acts of virtue it is with the help of grace from God from whom all good things come that we do this. The will is what we have as our unique possession. God is therefore most pleased if we renounce our own will and place ourselves completely in God's hand.

As a fruit tree bears most fruit when it is carefully tended, so we proceeding along the way of God must always grow and advance in virtue so that we can bear the choicest fruits of sanctity, give an example of virtue to draw others and lead them safely to the way of the Lord. To bear sufferings and misfortunes patiently for the love of God must be considered a special grace which God grants to those who love him.

Consider the birds of the air; they come down to the ground to get food but swiftly fly back into the air. Similarly the servants of God must stay on the earth only as long as is necessary and soar up quickly again to heaven in spirit to praise and glorify God. Note too how careful birds are not to land in muddy places and how they avoid tumbling into the dirt. In like manner we must not involve ourselves in things that defile the soul but soar again in spirit to glorify the Most High God by our holy deeds. *XIII,90f>*

23 September — Pio Forgione, Friar, Mystic, 1968

Francesco Forgione joined the Capuchin friars in 1903 at Benevento in Italy and took the name Pio. He moved to San Giovanni Rotondo in 1916 and remained there except for brief interludes for the rest of his life. In 1918, as he prayed before the crucifix in the choir of the old church, he received the gift of the stigmata, the wounds of Christ, which remained with him until his death nearly fifty years later.

A reading from the letters of Padre Pio.

Always be careful, especially in prayer. To succeed better, remember that grace and the taste of prayer are not drawn from earth but heaven. It is necessary that we use the greatest care and every effort to dispose ourselves, but always humbly and calmly. Even if we should use all our strength, we are not the ones who pray and draw grace by our own efforts. It is necessary that we hold our hearts open to heaven and wait for the heavenly dew to descend. Do not forget this, my daughter. How many courtiers come and go in the presence of the king, unable to speak to him or hear him. They are only seen by him. In this way, we show ourselves as the king's true servants. This is the way to be in the presence of God, just by declaring with our will that we want to be his servants. This is a holy and excellent way, pure and perfect. You may laugh, but I am speaking seriously.

We put ourselves in the presence of God to speak to him and to hear his voice by means of his internal inspiration and illumination. Usually this gives us great pleasure, because it is a significant grace for us to speak to so great a Lord; when he replies, thousands of perfumes descend on the soul and cause great joy.

If you can speak to our Lord, praise him, listen to him. If you cannot speak because you are uncouth, do not be unhappy. Shut yourself up in a room, and similar to a courtier, pay him homage. He who sees you will be pleased with your patience. He will prefer your silence.

On some other occasion he will prefer to console you. Then he will take you by the hand, speak to you, and walk a hundred times with you along the paths of his garden of prayer. Even if that never happens, which is really impossible, because the Father cannot bear to see his creatures in perpetual turmoil, be content all the same. Our obligation is to follow him. Consider it a great honour and grace that he should take us into his presence. *XIX,150f*

29 September — Michael & All Angels

A reading from 'The Remembrance of the Desire of a Soul', by Thomas of Celano.

Saint Francis venerated the angels with the greatest affection, for they are with us in battle, and walk with us in the midst of the shadow of death. He said that such companions should be revered everywhere, and invoked as protectors. He taught that their gaze should not be offended, and no one should presume to do in their sight what he would not do in the sight of others. And since in choir one sings the psalms in the presence of the angels, he wanted all who were able to gather in the oratory and sing psalms wisely.

He often said the Blessèd Michael should be especially honoured because his duty is presenting souls to God. In honour of Saint Michael he would fast with great devotion for forty days between the Feast of the Assumption and Saint Michael's feast day. For he used to say, 'Each person should offer God some special praise or gift in honour of such a great prince.' *II,373f*

Readings for the Feast of Saint Francis

The readings for the next nine days form a whole, being the period prior to and after the death of Francis.

28 September

A reading from 'The first Life of Saint Francis', by Thomas of Celano.

When Francis saw his final day drawing near,
as shown to him two years earlier by divine revelation,
he called to him the brothers he chose.
He blessed each one as it was given to him from above,
just as Jacob of old, the patriarch, blessed his sons.
He was like another Moses
about to ascend the mountain
that the Lord had shown him,
when imparting blessings on the children of Israel.
When brother Elias sat down on his left side with the other brothers around him, the blessèd father crossed his arms and placed his right hand on Elias' head. He had lost the sight of his bodily eyes, so he asked, 'Over whom am I holding my right hand?' 'Over brother Elias,' they replied. 'And this is what I wish to do,' he said, 'I bless you, my son, in all and through all, and just as the most High has increased my brothers and sons in your hands, so too, upon you and in you, I bless them all. May the king of all bless you in heaven and on earth. I bless you as I can, and more than I can, and what I cannot do may the One who can do all things do in you. May God remember your work and your labours, and may a place be reserved for you among the rewards of the just. May you receive every blessing you desire and may your every worthy request be fulfilled.'

'Goodbye, all my sons. Live in the fear of God and remain in him always, for a great test will come upon you and tribulation is drawing near! Happy are those who will persevere in what they have begun: many will be separated from them by the scandals that are to come. But now I am hurrying to the Lord and I am confident that I am going to my God whom I have served in my spirit.'

He was staying then in the palace of the Bishop of Assisi, and he asked the brothers to carry him quickly to the place of Saint Mary of the Portiuncula. For he wanted to give back his soul to God in that place where he first came to know perfectly the way of truth.   *1,276f*

29 September

A reading from the 'Assisi Compilation'.

Francis, realising that he was getting sicker by the day, had himself carried on a litter to the church of Saint Mary of the Portiuncula, since he could no longer ride horseback because of his severe illness. When those who were carrying him passed by the hospital along the road, he asked them to place the litter on the ground. Since he could hardly see because of the serious and prolonged eye-disease, he had the litter turned so that he would face the city of Assisi. Raising himself up slightly on the litter, he blessed the city of Assisi. 'Lord,' he said, 'just as I believe that at an earlier time this city was the abode of the wicked and evil, with a bad reputation throughout all this region; so now I realise that because of your abundant mercy and in your own time, you have shown an abundance of mercies to it. Now it has become the abode of those who acknowledge you, give glory to your name, offer the fragrance of good life, doctrine, and good reputation to the whole Christian people. I ask you, therefore, Lord Jesus Christ, Father of mercies, not to consider our ingratitude. May it always be mindful of the abundant mercies which you have shown to it, that it always be an abode for those who acknowledge you, and glorify your name blessèd and glorious throughout the ages. Amen.'

After saying these things, he was carried to Saint Mary of the Portiuncula. *II,120*

30 September

A reading from the 'Assisi Compilation'.

One of the brothers said to blessèd Francis, 'Father, you should know the truth: unless the Lord sends his own remedy from heaven to your body, your sickness is incurable and, as the doctors have already said, you do not have long to live. I told you this to comfort your spirit, that you may always rejoice in the Lord, inside and out; especially so that your brothers and others who come to visit you may find you rejoicing in the Lord, since they know and believe that you will die soon. Thus, as they see this and, after your death, others hear about it, your death, like your life and manner of living, may be held in remembrance by all.'

Although racked with sickness, blessèd Francis praised God with great fervour of spirit and joy of body and soul, and told him, 'If I am to die soon, call Brother Angelo and Brother Leo that they may sing to me about Sister Death.'

Those brothers came to him and, with many tears, sang the Canticle of Brother Sun and the other creatures of the Lord, which the saint himself had composed in his illness for the praise of the Lord and the consolation of his own soul and that of others. Before the last stanza he added one about Sister Death:

'Praised be you, my Lord, through our Sister Bodily Death
from whom no one living can escape.
Woe to those who die in mortal sin.
Blessèd are those whom death will find in your most holy will,
for the second death shall do them no harm.'   *II,120f*

October

1 October

A reading from the 'Assisi Compilation'.

Francis wrote to Lady Jacoba, a holy widow devoted to God, but before the letter was sent she arrived and she said, 'While I was praying, a voice within me said "Go, visit your father, blessèd Francis, without delay, and hurry, because if you delay long you will not find him alive. Moreover take cloth for his tunic, as well as the ingredients for making that particular confection that he likes. Take with you also a great quantity of wax and incense." '

The lady made that confection the holy father wanted to eat. He ate only a little of it, however, since he was near death, and daily his body was becoming weaker on account of his illness.

She also had many candles made which would burn around his holy body after his death. From the cloth she had brought for his tunic, the brothers made him the tunic in which he was buried. He himself ordered the brothers to sew pieces of sackcloth on the outside of it as a sign and example of most holy humility and poverty. It happened, as it pleased God, that during the same week that Lady Jacoba arrived, blessèd Francis passed to the Lord.   *II,122f>*

2 October

A reading from 'The Remembrance of the Desire of a Soul', by Thomas of Celano.

As he was wasted by that grave illness which ended all his sufferings, Francis had himself placed naked on the naked ground, so that in that final hour, when the Enemy could still rage, he might wrestle naked with the naked. The fearless man awaited triumph and, with hands joined, held the crown of justice. Placed on the ground and stripped of his sackcloth garment, he lifted up his face to heaven as usual, and, totally intent upon that glory, he covered the wound on his right side with his left hand, so no one would see it. Then he said to his brothers, 'I have done what is mine; may Christ teach you what is yours!'

Seeing this his sons wept streams of tears, drawing sighs from deep within, overwhelmed with sorrow and compassion.

Meanwhile, as their sobs somewhat subsided, his Guardian, who by divine inspiration better understood the saint's wish, quickly got up, took the tunic, underwear and sackcloth hood, and said to the father, 'I command you under holy obedience to acknowledge that I am lending you this tunic, underwear and hood. And so that you know that they in no way belong to you, I take away all your authority to give them to anyone.' The saint rejoiced, and his heart leaped for joy seeing that he had kept faith until the end with Lady Poverty. For he had done all this out of zeal for poverty, not wanting to have at the end even a habit of his own, but one borrowed from another.

> After this the saint raised his hands to heaven
> and glorified his Christ;
> free now from all things, he was going to him free.   *II,386*

3 October

A reading from 'The Remembrance of the Desire of a Soul', by Thomas of Celano.

As the brothers shed bitter tears and wept inconsolably, the holy father had bread brought to him. Francis blessed and broke it, and gave each of them a piece to eat.

He also ordered a book of the Gospels to be brought and asked that the Gospel according to Saint John to be read to him starting from that place which begins, 'Before the feast of the Passover'. He was remembering that most sacred Supper, the last one the Lord celebrated with his disciples. In reverent memory of this, to show his brothers how much he loved them, he did all of this.

The time that remained to him before his passing he spent in praise of God, teaching his belovèd companions how to praise Christ with him. As best he could, he broke out into this psalm: 'With my voice I cried to the Lord, With my voice I beseeched the Lord.' He also invited all creatures to the praise of God, and exhorted them to love, by some words which he had composed earlier. Even death itself, terrible and hateful to everyone, he exhorted to praise, and going to meet her joyfully, invited her to be his guest, saying, 'Welcome, my Sister Death!' And to the doctor he said, 'Be bold, brother Doctor, foretell death is near; for to me she will be the gate of Life!' But to the brothers he said, 'When you see I have come to my end put me out naked on the ground as you saw me naked before, and once I am dead, allow me to lie there for as long as it takes to walk a leisurely mile.'

(Note to the reader: Francis died after Vespers on 3 October, which in the calendar made his date of death 4 October. So the following short reading may be added to the above or used on its own later in the day).

That evening before nightfall, after vespers, when blessèd Francis passed to the Lord, many birds called larks flew low above the roof of the house where blessèd Francis lay, wheeling in a circle and singing.

The hour came.
All the mysteries of Christ
were fulfilled in him,
and he happily took flight to God.

One of his disciples, a brother of no small fame, saw the soul of the most holy father like a star ascending to heaven, having the immensity of the moon and the brightness of the sun, extending over many waters carried by a little white cloud.   *II,387f & II,129*

4 October

A reading from 'The Life of Saint Francis', by Thomas of Celano.

Francis' brothers and sons had assembled with the whole multitude of people from the neighbouring cities, rejoicing to take part in such solemn rites. They spent that entire night of the holy father's death in the praises of God. The sweet sound of jubilation and the brightness of the lights made it seem that angels were keeping vigil.

When day was breaking, the multitude of the city of Assisi gathered with all the clergy. They lifted his sacred body from the place where he had died and carried it with great honour to the city, singing hymns and praises with trumpets blaring. They all took branches of olive and other trees and solemnly followed the funeral procession, bringing even more candles as they sang songs of praise in loud voices.

With the sons carrying their father and the flock flowing the shepherd who was hastening to the Shepherd of them all, he arrived at the place where he first planted the Order of the Poor Ladies. They laid him out in the church of San Damiano, home to those daughters he gained for the Lord. The small window was opened, the one used by those servants of Christ to receive the sacrament of the Lord's Body. The coffin was also opened: in it lay hidden the treasure of supercelestial powers; in it he who had carried many was now carried by a few.

The Lady Clare!
Clearly a woman of true brilliance and holiness,
the first mother of all the others,
the first plant of that holy Order:
she comes with her daughters
to see the father
who would never again
speak to them or return to them,
as he was quickly going away.
They looked upon him,
groaning and weeping with great anguish of heart.   *I,284f*

5 October

A reading from 'The Major Legend of Saint Francis', by Saint Bonaventure.

Finally reaching the city of Assisi with great rejoicing, with all reverence they placed the precious treasure they were carrying [the body of Saint Francis] in the church of Saint George.
There, as a boy, he learned his letters,
there, he later preached for the first time,
and there, finally, he received his first place of rest.

Immediately,

the holy man began
to reflect the light radiating from the face of God
and glitter with many great miracles.
Thus the sublimity of his holiness
which, while he was still in the flesh,
had been familiar to the world as a guide for conduct
through examples of perfect righteousness,
was approved from heaven
where he is now reigning with Christ
as a confirmation of faith
through miracles performed by the divine power.

In different parts of the world,
his glorious miracles
and the abundant benefits obtained through him,
inflamed many to devotion to Christ
and incited then to reverence for his saint.
These wonderful things
which God was working
through his servant Francis
– acclaimed by word of mouth
and testified to by facts –
came to the ears
of the Supreme Pontiff, Gregory IX.   *II,647f*

6 October

A reading from 'The Major Legend of Saint Francis', by Saint Bonaventure.

That shepherd of the church, Gregory IX, was fully convinced of Francis' remarkable holiness: not only from hearing of the miracles after his death, but also from his own experience during his life. Having seen with his own eyes and touched with his own hands, he had no doubt that Francis was glorified in heaven by the Lord. In order to act in conformity with Christ, whose vicar he was, after prayerful consideration he decided to glorify him on earth by proclaiming him worthy of all veneration.

In order to certify to the whole world the glorification of this most holy man, he had the known miracles recorded and attested to by appropriate witness. These he submitted to the examination of those cardinals who seemed less favourable to his cause. This material was examined carefully and approved by all. He decreed, with the unanimous advice and assent of his brothers and of all the prelates who were then in the curia, that he should be canonized. He came personally to the city of Assisi in the one thousand, two hundred and twenty-eighth year of the Incarnation of the Lord, on the seventeenth day of the calends of August, and enrolled the blessèd father in the catalogue of the saints, in a great and solemn ceremony.   *II,648*

22 October — Peter of Alcantara, Friar, Reformer, 1562

Peter of Alcantara was a friar dedicated to the reform of the church. He joined the discalced (barefoot) Friars Minor in 1515 and was soon given positions of responsibility in the community, first as the superior of a new house and then as Minister Provincial. He slept and ate little, but was tireless in preaching on parish missions. In 1554 he received permission to form a group of friars who would follow the Rule of Saint Francis with greater rigour, later known as the Alcantarines. For some years he offered spiritual direction to Saint Teresa of Jesus, encouraging her in the reform of the Carmelite Order.

A reading from a letter of Saint Peter of Alcantara to Saint Teresa of Avila.

If any wish to follow Christ's counsel concerning greater perfection let them follow it, because it was not given more for men than for women, and Christ himself will grant success as he has to many others who have followed him.

But when we see that there is some want in the monasteries of poor women let us reflect that this comes about because they bear poverty reluctantly, not as the counsel of the Lord. Neither do I praise poverty for poverty's sake; I praise only that poverty which we patiently endure for the love of our crucified Redeemer and I consider this far more desirable than the poverty we undertake for the love of poverty itself; for if I thought or believed otherwise I would not seem to be firmly grounded in faith.

But in all these matters I place my confidence in Christ and firmly believe his counsels to be the best because they are divine. And even if God's counsels impose no obligation binding under sin, nevertheless one's obligation to be perfect in imitation of him is a more important matter than that they leave a person without blame. I say that they do impose an obligation because they urge one on to perfection and in this way make a person holier and more pleasing to God. Moreover I consider the poor in spirit blessèd, as the Lord himself says, that is, those voluntarily poor in spirit as I myself have experienced although I put more faith in God than in my own experience.

May the Lord grant you, Mother Prioress, such an abundance of light that you may be able to understand this truth and put it into practice. Do not believe those who from a lack of light or from disbelief affirm the contrary because they have never tasted how sweet God is. Instead believe those who serve him and love him and for love of him renounce all things of the world that are not necessary. *XIII,154f>*

23 October — John of Capistrano, Friar, 1456

John studied law at the University of Perugia and was later appointed governor of that city. After a time in prison during a civil war he became an Observant Franciscan friar. Together with James of the March he studied theology under Bernardine of Siena, and went on to become a highly successful preacher throughout Europe, drawing many into the Order. He died in Austria in 1456.

A reading from the treatise 'Mirror of the Clergy', by Saint John of Capistrano.

Those who are called to the table of the Lord must glow with the brightness that comes from the good example of a praiseworthy and blameless life. They must completely remove from their lives the filth and uncleanness of vice. Their upright lives must make them like the salt of the earth for themselves and for the rest of humanity. The brightness of their wisdom must make them like the light of the world that brings light to others. They must learn from their eminent teacher, Jesus Christ, what he declared not only to his apostles and disciples, but also to all the priests and clerics who were to succeed them, when he said, 'You are the salt of the earth. But what if salt goes flat? How can you restore its flavour? Then it is good for nothing but to be thrown out and trampled underfoot.'

It is indeed a double task that worthy priests perform, that is to say, it is both exterior and interior, both temporal and spiritual, and, finally, both a passing task and an eternal one. Therefore, just as the sun rises over the world in God's heaven, so clerics must let their light shine before others so that they may see their good deeds and give praise to their heavenly Father.

You are the light of the world. Now a light does not illumine itself, but instead it diffuses its rays and shines all around upon everything that comes into its view. So it must be with the glowing lives of upright and holy clerics. By the brightness of their holiness they must bring light and serenity to all who gaze upon them. They have been placed here to care for others. Their own lives should be an example to others, showing how they must live in the house of the Lord.   *XIII,159ff>*

30 October — Dedication of Consecrated Churches of the Order

See page 139.

November

1 November — All Saints' Day

A reading from 'The Little Flowers of Saint Francis'.

At the time when Brother James of Fallerone, a man of great holiness, was seriously ill in the place at Mogliano, in the Custody of Fermo, Brother John of La Verna, who was then staying in the place at Massa, hearing of his illness, because he loved him as his dear father, began praying for him, asking God devoutly in mental prayer to restore the health of his body, if that were best for his soul. And while he was praying devoutly, he was rapt into ecstasy and he saw in the air above his cell, which was in the woods, a great army of angels and saints, with such splendour that the whole area around him was illuminated. And among these angels he saw this sick brother for whom he was praying, standing in bright and shining white clothing. He also saw among them the blessèd father Saint Francis adorned with the sacred Stigmata of Christ and great glory. He also saw there and recognised the holy Brother Lucido and Brother Matteo the elder of Monte Rubbiano, and other brothers whom he had never seen or known in this life. And as Brother John was looking with great delight at that blessèd troop of saints, it was revealed to him with certainty the salvation of the soul of that sick brother, and that he would die from that illness, but not immediately, and that he would go to Paradise, though it was better for him to purify himself a little in Purgatory. The same Brother John had great joy at that revelation, over the salvation of the soul, which felt nothing of the death of the body, and with great sweetness of spirit he called out to him within himself, 'Brother Giacomo, my sweet father! Brother Giacomo my sweet brother! Brother Giacomo, most faithful servant and friend of God! Brother Giacomo, companion of the angels and member of the blessèd!' And in this certainty and joy he returned to himself, and he immediately departed from the place and went to visit the same Brother Giacomo at Mogliano.

And finding him so gravely ill that he could hardly speak, he announced to him the death of the body and the salvation and glory of the soul, according to the certainty he had received by divine revelation. Brother James received him with happiness in his spirit and on his face, with great joy and a cheerful laugh, thanking him for the good news he brought to him, and commending himself to him with devotion. After these things were said and the hour of his passing neared, Brother James began to say devoutly this verse of the Psalm: 'In peace in eternal life I will fall asleep and rest;' and after saying this verse, with a cheerful, joyous expression he passed from this life. *III,653f>*

2 November — All Souls' Day

A reading from 'The little Flowers of Saint Francis'.

Once, while Brother John of La Verna was saying Mass, on the day after All Saints' Day, for all the souls of the dead, as the church required, he offered that most high Sacrament (which because of its efficacy, the souls of the dead desire above all the other good things which can be done for them) with such charity and feeling of compassion that he seemed as if completely melted by the sweetness of pity and fraternal charity. Therefore, in that Mass as he devoutly raised the Body of Christ and offered it to God the Father, he prayed that for love of his blessèd Son Jesus Christ, who was hung on the Cross to redeem souls, he should be pleased to free from the sufferings of Purgatory the souls of the dead, created and redeemed by him. Then he immediately saw an almost infinite number of souls leave Purgatory, like innumerable sparks of fire from a lighted furnace, and he saw them rise into heaven through the merits of the Passion of Christ, who is offered daily for the living and the dead in that most sacred host, worthy of adoration for ever. *III,652*

8 November — John Duns Scotus, Friar, Teacher of the Faith, 1308

John Duns Scotus came from Scotland, being born near the town of Berwick, and joined the Friars Minor at Dumfries. He studied at Oxford and Paris and became one of the leading theologians of his day. He defended the doctrine of the Immaculate Conception of Mary and the essential free will of humanity. He died while teaching at the Franciscan school in Cologne.

A reading from 'A Letter in Response to an Unknown Master', by Saint Bonaventure.

What shall I say about those who take the professor's chair, since the Rule declares that 'those who are illiterate should not be eager to learn?' Also, the gospel says that we should not be called 'master'. I maintain that the Rule does not forbid study to the literate, for though Francis was not very well educated as a youth, he later advanced in learning in the Order, not only by praying but also by reading. And that you might appreciate how much the study of Holy Scripture delighted him, let me tell you what I myself heard from a brother who is still living. Once a New Testament came into Francis' hands, and since so many brothers could not all use it at once, he pulled the leaves apart and distributed the pages among them. Thus each one could study and not be a hindrance to the others. Moreover, the clerics he received into the Order he held in the greatest reverence, and at his death he ordered the brothers to venerate the teachers of Sacred Scripture as those from whom they received the words of life.

Therefore, I say that the gospel teaches us that all the ambition and pretentiousness associated with this title of 'master' must be condemned and in no way sought after, but that the duty or office must indeed be assumed. For who are better fit to teach the gospel than those who profess and observe it? Does not the gospel itself say: 'Whoever keeps these commandments and teaches them will be called great in the kingdom of heaven?' I therefore condemn, as you do, any ostentation associated with the office of master, but I commend the office itself. Yes, I condemn the pretentious brother and maintain that he is entirely unworthy of the teaching office; but I praise the studious one, since I believe that the authority to teach the gospel of Christ belongs to him more than anyone else. *VII,50ff>*

15 November — Mary of the Passion, Founder of the Franciscan Missionaries of Mary, 1904

Born in 1839, Helene de Chappotin de Neuville was known to be both a realist and a mystic. Always attentive to the promptings of the Spirit, she gave herself entirely to the service of life. Saint Francis became the epitome of her ideals and on founding the Franciscan Missionaries of Mary in 1877 she took the name Mary of the Passion. She burned with the same desire as he did to love and have others love Divine Love in their turn. Her call was to live the gospel at the service of the Universal Mission – beyond every frontier, 'even the most dangerous and distant', and to witness to true bonds of universal fraternity and solidarity, interdependence and communion among all.

A reading from the 'Spiritual Notes' of Mary of the Passion.

Love, be my only good, just as you were all to my father Saint Francis. How much I beg God to be my all.

I had a clear view during prayer and again during the day, that the lack of stability is one of the difficulties which cause holiness to elude the soul. She loves herself and because of this, she cannot remain steadfast in God; she constantly needs to be stirring and seeking self-satisfaction. Happy the soul who is poor and who knows how to remain quiet and uncomplaining on life's cross.

Love seemed to me to be infinite beauty and truth; the Son is the fire of this love and the Holy Spirit, if you wish, the light of this fire, but I cannot adequately express it. To love this love is something so beautiful. We who are so finite become in a sense infinite as a result of the destruction of self-love, because God-love, his oneness, his light, shine in our souls and are reflected there. The less there is of self, the more God is there. Dear Saint Francis came close to me, he seemed present there. If you knew how I loved him and how he loved me, how I hoped to be the child of this father and of his dear lady.

At adoration I was absorbed by the memory of the morning's meditation. I was consumed with love for Jesus and Saint Francis, I could have remained there for hours. *XXVII*

18 November — Elizabeth of Hungary, Philanthropist, Patron of the Third Order, 1231

Elizabeth was the daughter of King Andrew II of Hungary, and married Prince Louis of Thuringia. She dedicated herself to works of mercy, having a large hospital built, caring for lepers and feeding the hungry, as well as raising her four children. She died in 1231 at the age of twenty-four, and was canonised four years later. She is also a patron of Catholic Charities.

A reading from a letter of Conrad of Marburg, Saint Elizabeth's spiritual director.

Elizabeth's holiness began to come to its full flower. All her life she had been the comfort of the poor: now she became the helper of the starving. Outside one of her castles she built a hospice and gathered in it sick, diseased and crippled men and women. Besides, anyone who came asking for alms received unstinted gifts from her charity. She did the same wherever her husband's jurisdiction ran, pouring out all the resources she had in all parts of his territories, until in the end she sold even her jewels and her sumptuous dresses.

She went twice a day to see the sick, in the early morning and at nightfall, and it was those with the foulest diseases she made her personal care. She fed them herself, made and cleaned their pallets, carried them in her arms and nursed them in whatever way they needed. Her husband, of happy memory, gave a completely ungrudging consent to all she did. When he died she felt she should now attempt the heights of perfection. She came to me and begged me with tears to let her beg her way from door to door.

On the Good Friday of that year, after the altars had been stripped, she knelt in front of the altar of the chapel she had given to the Friars Minor and laid her hands on it. Then in their presence she renounced her own will, her earthly estate and all that our Saviour counsels us in the gospel to put aside. *XXXVII,200*

19 November — Agnes of Assisi, Poor Clare, 1253

Agnes was the sister of Clare and her first follower. Together they established the community at San Damiano, against the will of their family. Later a group of Benedictine nuns asked to become a community of their Order, and Agnes was sent to be their Abbess. She went on to establish other monasteries in northern Italy, returning to Assisi when Clare was dying. She herself followed Clare in death three months later.

A reading from 'The Letter of Agnes of Assisi to her sister Clare'.

To her venerable mother and the woman beloved in Christ beyond all others, to the Lady Clare and her whole community, Agnes, the lowly and least of Christ's servants, humbly presents herself with all obedience and devotion with best wishes for her and them for whatever is sweet and precious in the eyes of the Most High King.

The lot of all has been so established that one can never remain in the same state or condition. When someone thinks that she is doing well, it is then that she is plunged into adversity. Therefore, you should know, Mother, that my soul and body suffer great distress and immense sadness, that I am burdened and tormented beyond measure and am almost incapable of speaking, because I have been physically separated from you and my other sisters with whom I had hoped to live and die in this world. This distress has a beginning, but it knows no end. It never seems to diminish; it always gets worse. It came to me recently, but it tends to ease off very little. It is always with me and never wants to leave me. I believed that our life and death would be one, just as our manner of life in heaven would be one, and that we who have one and the same flesh and blood would be buried in the same grave. But I see that I have been deceived. I have been restrained; I have been abandoned; I have been afflicted on every side.

On the one hand there is no one of all my dear ones to console me; but on the other hand I am very much consoled and you can congratulate me for this: I have found great harmony and no factions here, which is beyond belief. Everyone has received me with great happiness and joy, and has very devoutly promised me obedience and reverence. They all commend themselves to God, to you and to your community, and I commend myself and them to you in all things and in every way, that you may have a solicitous concern for me and for them as you have for your own sisters and daughters. Know that I and the sisters wish to observe inviolate for all the days of our lives your admonitions and precepts. I beseech you to ask Brother Elias to visit me more often to console me in the Lord.   *V,109f>*

23 November — Algy Robertson, Friar, Co-Founder of the Society of Saint Francis, 1955

An Anglican priest, Algy Robertson first pursued his Franciscan vocation in a multi-racial community in India. However, poor health necessitated his return to Britain in 1930, where he became instrumental in the union of various Franciscan groups into the Society of Saint Francis. He was a sought-after spiritual director, and noted for the power of his preaching and as a missioner. Alongside his organizational skills, his theology of sacramental friendship provided a strong foundation of the charism of the Franciscan community which was his greatest contribution.

A reading from a letter to the Third Order of the Society of Saint Francis, Lent 1943, from Father Algy SSF.

In Saint Francis we see the ascetic. He is very stern with himself: he strips himself. He embraces poverty, he will permit no self-indulgence whatever. Many of the modern sentimental admirers of the Poverello think of his gentle compassion, which is indeed a glorious trait in his character, but they miss the other things. His life is marked by a deeply-costly renunciation. We would desire a revival of the Franciscan spirit today. What shall we say are the motives lying behind the renunciation of Saint Francis? Partly, indeed, the motive must have been a desire on the part of this most sensitive, loving and generous man to make himself poor in order to live alongside the poor. His tender heart was hurt by the privilege and inequalities which were produced by the possession of wealth. He longed to help the poor 'down and outs', so he went among them, himself voluntarily made poor and 'down and out'. He wanted to serve the lepers so he and his followers went to live among them in their squalid hovels outside Assisi.

More than that, Francis knew that to become poor is to become dependent. We are only in a true relationship with God our Father when we recognize our insufficiency; when our pride is broken down; when we are truly humble – and look up to our Father in clinging dependence. But we will know nothing of Saint Francis' vision if we have not seen something of the need in our own souls for this dependence. Yet we have not said everything. It is in the Crucified that Francis finds the mainspring of this dependence. After all, it was while he was kneeling before the crucifix that he heard the divine voice speak to him, and on the mountain top it was the marks of the Crucified that he received in his body to seal him as the Lord's own. *XXXI*

24 November — All Departed Franciscans

A reading from 'The little Flowers of Saint Francis'.

Once, a certain brother, thinking over his sins, gave himself to doing such penance that continually for fifteen years, except for the common Lent which he made with the other brothers, always fasted three days a week on bread and water, always going barefoot and wearing only one tunic; and he never slept after Matins.

During this time, Saint Francis passed from this miserable life. And that brother, having continued such penance for many years, one night after Matins, was overcome with such a temptation to sleep that he could in no way resist sleep and keep awake as he usually did. Finally, unable to resist sleep or to pray, he went to bed to sleep. As soon as he put down his head, he was caught up and led in spirit to the place where an angel had flown.

When he arrived at the door of the palace where the angel was, the porter asked him, 'Who are you, and who have you come to see?' The brother replied, 'I am a Lesser Brother.' The porter said, 'Wait, because I want to bring Saint Francis here to see if he knows you.' As he went to get Saint Francis, the brother began to look at the marvellous walls of this palace, and those walls appeared to be so shining and clear that he clearly saw the choirs of saints and what was done there. While he was standing there, he was dumbfounded by what he saw: Saint Francis was coming with Brother Bernard and Brother Giles, and behind Saint Francis such a multitude of men and women saints who had followed him in life that it seemed innumerable. As Saint Francis reached him, he said to the porter, 'Let him enter, because he is one of my brothers.'

And as soon as he entered there, he felt so much consolation and so much sweetness that he forgot all the troubles he had, as if they had never existed. Then Saint Francis led him inside, pointing out many wonderful things to him, and then he said to him, 'My son, you must return to the world and remain there for seven days, in which you must carefully prepare yourself, because after seven days I will come for you, and then you will come with me to this place of the blessèd.' And Saint Francis was covered with a wonderful mantle, decorated with the most beautiful stars; and his five stigmata were like five beautiful stars of such brightness that they lit up the whole palace with their rays. And Brother Bernard had on his head a crown of the most beautiful stars, and Brother Giles was adorned by a marvellous light. And he met many other holy brothers among them, whom he had not seen in the world. Then, given permission by Saint Francis, he returned, although unwillingly to the world.

As he awoke and returned to himself, the brothers were ringing for prime, so he had not been in that state except from matins to prime, although it seemed to him to have been there many years. As he recounted this vision in detail to his Guardian, within seven days he began to have a fever and, on the eighth day, Saint Francis came for him, according to his promise, with a great multitude of glorious saints and brought his soul to the kingdom of the blessèd, to eternal life.   *III611ff>*

26 November — Leonard of Port Maurice, Friar, 1751

Leonard joined the Friars Minor in 1697, but soon contracted tuberculosis and was close to death. He vowed that if he recovered, he would dedicate his life to missions, which he did, preaching missions and retreats throughout Italy for the next forty years. He promoted the Stations of the Cross and reverence for the Holy Name of Jesus. He also helped to establish many ritiros (houses of recollection). In 1923, he was named patron of those who preach parish missions.

A reading from the writings of Saint Leonard of Port Maurice.

'With desolation is the land made desolate because there are none that consider in their heart.' Behold the source of all our woes: no one considers what should be carefully examined; from this flows the manifold disarray in our actions. First of all, no attention is paid to the last things; God's blessings and all that the Son of God endured for us in his bitter passion are consigned to oblivion; the obligations and duties of each one's state in life are negligently discharged; no precaution is taken against the dangers that beset our life from all sides. Since the world then is filled with iniquity Jeremiah rightfully complains when he says, 'All the land is desolate with desolation.'

Is there a remedy for these evils? Indeed there is! I should like to explain on bended knees to all prelates, pastors, priests and other ministers of God that this remedy is at hand, at least in great part: the devout exercise of the Way of the Cross. If by their zeal and care this devotion spreads through individual parishes and churches it will indeed be a powerful protection against the surging tide of vice and fill all with the greatest blessings of virtue who engage in loving reflection on the sufferings and love of Jesus Christ.

What salutary insights will the continued meditation on the bitter passion of the Son of God stir up in the soul! Daily experience has taught me that by this devout form of prayer people's lives are quickly changed for the better. For the Way of the Cross is the antidote for vice, the cleansing of unbridled desires and an effective incentive to virtue and holiness of life. Indeed, if we set the excruciating sufferings of the Son of God portrayed in so many vivid pictures before the eyes of the soul we can hardly refrain from abhorring the defilements of our own life because of the abundant light that fills our souls. Nay, I should rather say we will be urged on to repay such great love with our own love, or at least to bear willingly the misfortunes that from time to time in every walk of life fall to our lot.   *XIII,196f*

28 November — James of the March, Friar, 1476

James was born in central Italy, studied law at Perugia, and continued with studies in theology after joining the Friars Minor. He was a very popular preacher and travelled throughout Europe, helping to spread devotion to the Holy Name of Jesus. He also worked to help those in debt, establishing non-profit credit organisations. With John of Capistrano, Albert of Sarteano and Bernardine of Siena he was one of the 'four pillars' of the Observant Franciscans.

A reading from a sermon of Saint James of the March.

'Some seed fell on good soil, grew up and yielded grain a hundredfold.' This refers to the hearts of the faithful made fertile by the abundant grace of the Holy Spirit, where the word of God sows contrition for sins, the violet of humility, the rose of charity, the lily of chastity, fear and love of God, a desire for things eternal, disparagement of the goods of earth, the beauty of all virtues.

Belovèd and most holy word of God! You enlighten the hearts of the faithful, you satisfy the hungry, console the afflicted; you make the souls of all productive of good and cause all virtues to blossom; you snatch souls from the devil's jaw; you make the wretched holy, and people of earth citizens of heaven.

When is the Holy Spirit received? During the preaching of the word of God. When do you deplore sins? When have you forgiven an injury? During the preaching of God's word. When have you put aside ill will? During the preaching of the word of God. When do you acquire patience and when have you found a soul that was lost? During the preaching of God's word. When have you come to know God? During the preaching of God's word. What keeps people in the faith? The preaching of God's word. What did Christ command his apostles to do? To preach. What plants grace and virtues in souls? Preaching the word of God, because it is not you who speak.

O most holy preaching more precious than any treasure! Blessèd are they who listen to you because you are a great light illuminating the whole world. *XIII,204f>*

29 November — All Franciscan Saints

A reading from 'The Little Flowers of Saint Francis'.

A young man, very noble and refined, came to the Order of Saint Francis. After a few days, at the instigation of the demon, he began to feel such disgust for the habit which he was wearing that it seemed to him that he was wearing a filthy rag. He loathed the sleeves and hated the capuce; and he thought its length and roughness were an unbearable burden. His distaste for the religion also increased and he finally decided to give up the habit and return to the world.

He had already taken up the custom, as his master had taught him, that whenever he passed in front of the altar of the convent, in which the Body of Christ was reserved, to kneel with great reverence, pull back his capuce, and to bow with his arms crossed. It happened that on the night when he was to depart and leave the Order he had to pass in front of the altar of the friary. As he passed, according to his custom, he knelt down and made his reverence. Immediately he was caught up in spirit, and a marvellous vision was shown to him by God. For he saw in front of him, an almost infinite multitude as in a procession, two by two, clothed in very beautiful robes of precious cloth. Their faces and hands shone like the sun, and they walked along with the singing and music of angels. When the young man saw this, he was amazed and did not know what that procession meant. Nevertheless, when the whole procession had passed by, he ran towards the ones at the end and, with great fear, asked them, 'Dear friends, I beg you, please tell me who are these marvellous people forming this venerable procession?' They replied, 'Son, realise that we are all Lesser Brothers who have now come from the glory of paradise. These robes of beautiful cloth which we wear were given to us by God in exchange for the harsh tunics which we patiently wore in the religion. The glorious brightness which you see in us was given to us by God for the humility and patience, holy poverty and obedience and chastity which we observed to the end.' When these words ended, the

youth returned to himself and, comforted by this vision, he drove away from himself every temptation. He acknowledged his fault before the Guardian and the brothers, and from then on he longed for the harshness of penance and of clothing, and he finished his life within the Order in great holiness.
III,600f>

December

8 December — Conception of the Blessèd Virgin Mary

A reading from the works of John Duns Scotus.

Concerning the mother of Jesus and the salvation which was hers;
  a salvation which preceded her birth,
  absolute and perfect
  and for the rest of humanity now only in process.
We are all grateful to our Lord Jesus Christ
  for Mary's salvation
  which in a certain sense is more than ours
  because it went down to the very roots.

When Christ is the subject I would rather make the mistake of ascribing too much praise to him rather than too little! And when it does not contradict the authority of the Church and Scripture then it is safer to assert that which conforms to the honour of the Virgin Mary – that she was never tainted by original sin.
  God wills to love.
  God wills to be loved.
  God wills to have co-lovers of himself.
  The perfect mediator has to effect a perfect mediation
    in respect of the person in whose favour he mediates
    and in the perfection of his function as mediator.
  Mary was the one above all
for whom he became mediator.
  Therefore Christ achieved
    the most perfect mediation and redemption
    in his own function as mediator and redeemer
    in regard to Mary.
    XXVIII

15 December — Mary Frances Schervier, Tertiary, 1876

Mary Frances Schervier became a Third Order Franciscan in 1844, and the following year she and four companions established a Religious community. Their work was to care for the poor, particularly in hospitals and homes for the agèd. The community became known as the 'Franciscan Sisters of the Poor', and spread beyond France to the rest of Europe, the USA and throughout the world.

A reading from a letter of Blessèd Mary Frances to the Sisters of the Congregation.

In his farewell discourse, the Lord told his belovèd disciples that all people would recognise them as his disciples, if they would love one another, and that the sign of their love for him would consist in their faithful keeping of his commandments. Our Lord then added, 'You are my friends if you do what I command you. The command I give you is this, that you love one another.' In these present times let us take to heart especially this particular teaching of our divine Lord, let us apply it to ourselves and endeavour to put it into practice.

If we do this faithfully and zealously, we will experience the truth of the words of our father Saint Francis, who says that love lightens all difficulties and sweetens all bitterness. We will likewise partake of the blessing which Saint Francis promised to all his children, both present and future, after having admonished them to love one another even as he had loved them and continues to love them.

And now that we know the will of our divine Lord, expressed so faithfully in the exhortation of our holy father Francis, there remains but one thing, that we fulfil the same and confidently wait 'to be blessed with the eternal blessing of our Lord Jesus Christ' and of our seraphic father Francis. *XIII,29f*

24 December — Jacopone da Todi, Friar, Poet, 1306

Jacopone was born in the 1230s, became a successful lawyer and married the beautiful and noble Vanna di Bernardino di Guidone. She was tragically killed when, at a party, the balcony on which she and others were dancing collapsed. Driven nearly out of his mind by grief Jacopone became a homeless penitent eventually ending up as a Friar Minor. His support for the Franciscan Spirituals and their rigorous interpretation of the Rule led to his imprisonment by Pope Boniface VIII. He died three years after his release, on Christmas Eve, at a monastery of Poor Clares.

(Note to reader: if this reading is used on 24 December, the reading for Christmas Eve in the Temporale should be transferred to Christmas Day or one of the days of Christmastide).

A reading from 'The Lauds', by Jacopone da Todi.

I know well, O highest wisdom,
that if I am mad, it is your doing –
this dates from the day I surrendered myself to Love,
laid aside my old self and put on you
and was drawn – I know not how – to new life.
How can my heart ever endure your love in its fullness?
If there is fault in my immoderate love it is yours,
not mine: it was you who led the way, Love.

You did not defend yourself against that Love
that made you come down from heaven to earth;
Love, in treading this earth
you humbled and humiliated yourself,
demanding neither dwelling place nor possessions,
taking on such poverty so that we might be enriched!
In your life and in your death you revealed
the infinite love that burned in your heart.

'Love, Love, the world cries out,
'Love, Love,' shouts all of creation.
Love, Love, so inexhaustible are you
that those who clasp you close desire you all the more!
Love, Love, perfect circle, those who enter into you
with their whole heart love you forever. For you are warp and woof
of the robe of those who love you, filling them with such delight
that they call out again and again, 'Love!'   *IX>,262ff*

Bibliography & Reference

The system of reference is simple: all books and other material used as sources have been allocated a roman numeral from one to forty, or rather I to XL. This is shown in the left column below. That roman number is attached to the end of each day's reading, together with the page number in the source book on which it can be found. The abbreviation *f* or *ff* after the page reference implies that the text continues on the following page or pages in the source book.

Thus the reference at the end of the reading on Advent Sunday of *II,68f* tells the reader that 'The Legend of the Three Companions' can be found in the second volume of *Francis of Assisi - Early Documents, The Founder*, and the particular text (and therefore context) can be found on pages 68 and 69.

Occasionally, the symbol > is used in the reference to indicate a minor abbreviation of the text to make the length of the passage chosen suitable for a daily reading, without losing the integrity of the original text. Other minor changes to the text have been made to comply with British-English orthography.

I   **Francis of Assisi - Early Documents, Volume I, The Saint**
Editors: Regis J Armstrong OFM Cap,
     J A Wayne Hellmann OFM Conv,
     William J Short OFM
New City Press, New York, London, Manila; 1999

II   **Francis of Assisi - Early Documents, Volume II, The Founder**
Editors: Regis J Armstrong OFM Cap,
     J A Wayne Hellmann OFM Conv,
     William J Short OFM
New City Press, New York, London, Manila; 2000

III   **Francis of Assisi - Early Documents, Volume III, The Prophet**
Editors: Regis J Armstrong OFM Cap,
     J A Wayne Hellmann OFM Conv,
     William J Short OFM
New City Press, New York, London, Manila; 2001

IV   **St Francis of Assisi - Omnibus of Sources**
Edited by Marion A Habig OFM
Franciscan Press, Quincy, 1972, 1991& SPCK, London, 1973

V   **Clare of Assisi - Early Documents**
Edited by Regis J Armstrong OFM Cap
Franciscan Institute Publications, St Bonaventure University, New York, 1993

VI	Bonaventure – 'The Soul's Journey into God', 'The Tree of Life', 'The Life of Saint Francis' – *in the 'Classics of Western Spirituality' Series* Translated by Ewert Cousins *Paulist Press, Mahwah, New Jersey, 1978*
VII	Works of Saint Bonaventure – Volume V: *Saint Bonaventure's Writings Concerning The Franciscan Order* Translated by Dominic Monti OFM *Franciscan Institute Publications, St Bonaventure University, New York, 1994*
VIII	Bonaventure – Mystic of God's Word Translated by Timothy J Johnson *New City Press, New York, London, Manila; 1999*
IX	Jacopone da Todi – The Lauds – *in the 'Classics of Western Spirituality' Series* Translated by Serge & Elizabeth Hughes *SPCK, London, 1982*
X	Angela of Foligno – Complete Works – *in the 'Classics of Western Spirituality' Series* Translated by Paul Lachance OFM *Paulist Press, Mahwah, New Jersey, 1993*
XI	Franciscan Readings – English Version of *Vitam Alere* Edited by Marion A Habig OFM *Franciscan Herald Press, Chicago, 1979*
XII	The Little Flowers of Saint Francis of Assisi Revised by Thomas Okey *London, Hollis and Carter, no date*
XIII	Proper Offices of Franciscan Saints and Blessèds in the Liturgy of the Hours English Speaking Conference, OFM 1975 *Franciscan Liturgical Projects, Washington DC, 1975*
XIV	The Coming of the Friars Minor to England & Germany – *Chronicles of Thomas of Eccleston & Jordan of Giano* Translated by G Salter, from critical edition of Little & Boehmer *Dent & Son, London, 1926*

XV   **Doctor Illuminatus – Ramon Llull Reader**
Edited & Translated by Anthony Bonner
with a new translation of *The Book of the Lover and the Beloved*
by Eve Bonner
Princeton University Press, Princeton, 1993

XVI   **A Poor Man's Legacy –** *An Anthology of Franciscan Poverty*
Edited by Cyprian Lynch OFM
Franciscan Pathways 1988
Franciscan Institute, Saint Bonaventure's, New York, 1988

XVII   **The Capuchin Sacramentary**
text by Patrick McSherry OFM Cap
North America Capuchin Conference,
Capuchin Province of Saint Joseph, Detroit, 1995

XVIII   **The Revelations of Margaret of Cortona,**
The Franciscan Magdalene
Anga-Marie Hiral OFM
Franciscan Institute Press 1952

XIX   **Padre Pio – The Wonder Worker**
Edited by Brother Francis Mary Kalvelage FI
Franciscan Friars of the Immaculate Conception,
New Bedford MA, USA, 1999

XX   **Corn of Wheat –**
Life and History of the Community of Saint Francis
Mother Elizabeth CSF
Becket Publications, Oxford, 1981

XXI   **A Pastoral Letter from Father Joseph OSF**
for the New Year, 1966
Published in The Little Chronicle, *1966*
The Archives, Little Portion Friary, Mt. Sinai, New York

XXII   **Watchman, What of the Night?**
Father William SDC
Mowbrays & Co Ltd, London & Oxford, 1935

XXIII   **The Seven Spiritual Weapons, by Catherine of Bologna**
Translated by Hugh Feiss & Daniela Re
Peregrina Translation Series 25
Peregrina Publishing Co. Ontario Canada 1998

XXIV   **Life and Letters of Father Andrew SDC**
Compiled by Kathleen Burne
Mowbray & Co Ltd, London & Oxford, 1948

XXV   Rule of St Benedict
Local translation, in use at OSB, Burford Priory, Oxford

XXVI   The Life & Teaching of Pachomius
in 'The Wellsprings of Faith' Series
Brother Anthony Marrett-Crosby OSB,
Sister Mary Dominique OC, Dame Mary Groves, OSB
Gracewing/Fowler Wright Books, Leominster, 1998

XXVII   He speaks to me in the heart of his church
– the spiritual notes of Mother Mary of the Passion
Edited by A Sister FMM
FMM Grottaferrata, Rome, 1971

XXVIII   Blessed John Duns Scotus
Edited by Herbert Schneider OFM, translated by Roland Walls
Friends of Duns Scotus at Nunraw Abbey, Haddington, no date

XXIX   A Franciscan Revival
Society of the Divine Compassion
SDC Press, Plaistow, London, 1908

XXX   A Sermon preached to the University of Cambridge
by Br Douglas SSF, 25 October 1942
Cambridge Review, 1942

XXXI   A letter to the Third Order of the Society of Saint Francis
from Father Algy SSF
Lent, 1943
Hilfield Friary Archives

XXXII   Brotherhood of the Holy Cross Quarterly, Vol 11, No 10
& More Father Potter of Peckham
Father Potter BHC
Hodder & Stoughton, London, 1958

XXXIV   Poor Clares & Related Communities in the Episcopal Church
Brother Justus SSF
The Archives, Little Portion Friary, Mt. Sinai, New York

XXXV   Letter from a Founding Sister
of the Community of Saint Clare
Hilfield Friary Archives

XXXVI   Celebrating the Saints
Compiled & Edited by Robert Atwell
Canterbury Press Norwich, 1998

XXXVII	Treasury of the Catholic Church – *Two Thousand Years of Spiritual Writing* Compiled by Teresa de Bertodano *Darton Longman & Todd, London, 1999*
XXXVIII	The Rule of Saint Clare & Constitutions of the Poor Clare Nuns of the Reform of Saint Colette *Private printing, Dublin, 1932*
XXXIX	The Capuchin Way, *Lives of Capuchins*, Volume I, part 2 Father Costanzo Cargoni OFM Cap *North American Capuchin Conference, 1996*
XL	Golden Words – Sayings of Brother Giles Translated by Ivo Sullivan OFM *Franciscan Herald Press, Chicago, 1966*

Index

Feasts of our Lord

Annunciation, 25 Mar   318
Ascension, *Thursday of Easter 6*   127
Baptism, *Sunday after Epiphany*   41
Christmas, 25 Dec   23
Good Friday   95
Easter   97
Epiphany, 6 Jan   35
Holy Cross Day, 14 Sep   361
Maundy Thursday   95
Naming & Circumcision, 1 Jan   29
Presentation (Candlemass), 2 Feb   59
Transfiguration, 6 Aug   348

Feasts of the Blessed Virgin Mary

Blessèd Virgin Mary, 15 Aug   356
Blessèd Virgin Mary, Birth of the, 8 Sep   359
Blessèd Virgin Mary, Conception of the, 8 Dec   389
Blessèd Virgin Mary, Visit to Elizabeth, 31 May   336
Mary at the Cross, 15 Sep   361
Mary of the Angels, 2 Aug   345

Feasts of Francis & Clare

Clare of Assisi, Founder of the Minoresses, 11 Aug   350ff
Francis of Assisi, Friar, Founder of the Friars Minor, 4 Oct   369ff
Francis, Commemoration of the taking of vows by , 16 Apr   322
Francis, Dedication of the Basilica of, 24 May   334
Francis, Stigmata of, 17 Sep   363ff
Francis, Vocation of, 24 Feb   312
Portiuncula Indulgence, 2 Aug   346

Feasts of Holy Men & Women

Agnellus of Pisa, & the Coming of the Friars to Canterbury, 10 Sep   360
Agnes of Assisi, Poor Clare, 19 Nov   382
Agnes of Prague, Poor Clare, 2 Mar   314
Algy Robertson, Friar, Co-Founder of the Society of St Francis, 23 Nov   384
All Departed Franciscans, Commemoration of, 24 Nov   385
All Franciscan Saints, 29 Nov   388
All Saints' Day, 1 Nov   378
All Souls' Day, 2 Nov   379
Andrew Ernest Hardy, Friar, 31 Mar   320
Angela of Foligno, Tertiary, 7 Jan   305
Antony of Padua, Friar, Teacher of the Faith, 13 Jun   337
Benedict of Nursia, Father of Western Monasticism, 11 Jul   342
Benedict the Black, Friar, 3 Apr   321
Berard & Companions, First Franciscan Martyrs, 16 Jan   306
Bernardine of Siena, Friar, 20 May   333
Bonaventure, Friar, Bishop, Teacher of the Faith, 15 Jul   342

Catherine of Bologna, Poor Clare, Artist, *9 May*   328
Colette, Poor Clare, Founder of the Colettine Reform, *7 Feb*   310
Conrad of Parzham, Friar, *21 Apr*   324
Dominic, Friar, Founder of the Order of Preachers, *8 Aug*   349
Douglas Downes, Friar, Co-Founder of SSF, *7 Sep*   358
Elizabeth of Hungary, Philanthropist, Patron of the Third Order, *18 Nov*   382
Felix Porri of Cantalice, Friar, *18 May*   333
Fidelis of Sigmaringen, Friar, Martyr, *24 Apr*   326
George Potter, Friar, *15 Feb*   311
Giles of Assisi, Friar, *23 Apr*   325
Helen Elizabeth Christmas, a Founder of CSF, *7 Mar*   316
Jacopone da Todi, Friar, Spiritual, Poet, *24 Dec*   390
James of the March, Friar, *28 Nov*   387
Japan, Martyrs of, *6 Feb*   308
Jean-Baptiste Vianney, Curé d'Ars, Spiritual Guide, Tertiary, *4 Aug*   347
John the Baptist, Birth of, *24 Jun*   337
John of Capistrano, Friar, *23 Oct*   377
John Duns Scotus, Friar, Teacher of the Faith, *8 Nov*   380
Joseph Crookston, Friar, Founder of the Order of St Francis, *7 Mar*   317
Joseph of Cupertino, Friar, *18 Sep*   366
Junipero Serra, Friar, *1 Jul*   340
Lawrence Russo of Brindisi, Friar, Teacher of the Faith, *21 Jul*   343
Leonard of Port Maurice, Friar, *26 Nov*   386
Leopold Mandich of Herceg Novi, Friar, *12 May*   329
Louis Capet, Christian Monarch, Patron of the Third Order, *25 Aug*   357
Luchesio & Buonadonna, First Tertiaries, *28 Apr*   327
Margaret of Cortona, Penitent, Tertiary, *16 May*   331
Mary Frances Schervier, Tertiary, *15 Dec*   390
Mary Magdalene of Martinengo, Poor Clare, *27 Jul*   344
Mary of the Passion, Founder of FMM, *15 Nov*   381
Maximilian Kolbe, Friar, Martyr, *14 Aug*   355
Pachomius, Founder of Christian Community Monasticism, *15 May*   330
Paschal Baylon, Friar, *17 May*   332
Peter of Alcantara, Friar, Reformer, *22 Oct*   376
Pio Forgione, Friar, Mystic, *23 Sep*   367
Ramon Llull, Tertiary, Mystic, *30 Jun*   339
Rosina Mary Rice & the Founding of CSF, *25 Feb*   313
Veronica Giuliani, Poor Clare, *10 Jul*   341
William of Ockham, Friar, Philosopher, Teacher of the Faith, *10 Apr*   321
William Sirr, Friar, Monk, Solitary, *28 Mar*   319

Other Commemorations
Community of St Clare, Freeland, Founding of the, *6 Feb*   309
Dedication of All Franciscan Churches, *2 Aug or 30 Oct*   139
Michael & All Angels, *29 Sep*   368
Poor Clares of Reparation & Adoration, Founding of the, *16 Apr*   323
Society of the Divine Compassion, Thanksgiving for the, *20 Jan*   306